The Cambridge Companion to D. H. Lawrence contains fourteen chapters by leading international scholars. They provide a series of new perspectives on one of the most important and controversial writers of the twentieth century. These specially commissioned essays offer diverse and stimulating readings of Lawrence's major novels, short stories, poetry and plays, and place Lawrence's writing in a variety of literary, cultural and political contexts, such as modernism, sexual and ethnic identity, and psychoanalysis. The concluding chapter addresses the vexed history of Lawrence's critical reception throughout the twentieth century. The volume, which will be of interest to scholars and students alike, features a detailed chronology and a comprehensive guide to further reading.

CAMBRIDGE COMPANIONS TO LITERATURE

CAMBRIDGE COMPANIONS TO CULTURE

THE CAMBRIDGE
COMPANION TO
D. H. LAWRENCE

EDITED BY
ANNE FERNIHOUGH

PUBLISHED BY THE PRESS SYNDICATE OF THE UNIVERSITY OF CAMBRIDGE
The Pitt Building, Trumpington Street, Cambridge, United Kingdom

CAMBRIDGE UNIVERSITY PRESS
The Edinburgh Building, Cambridge CB2 2RU, UK
40 West 20th Street, New York, NY 10011-4211, USA
10 Stamford Road, Oakleigh, VIC 3166, Australia
Ruiz de Alarcón 13, 28014 Madrid, Spain
Dock House, The Waterfront, Cape Town 8001, South Africa

http://www.cambridge.org

First published 2001

Printed in the United Kingdom at the University Press, Cambridge

Typeface Monotype Sabon 10/13pt   *System* QuarkXpress® [SE]

A catalogue record for this book is available from the British Library

Library of Congress Cataloguing in Publication data

The Cambridge Companion to D. H. Lawrence / edited by Anne Fernihough.
        p.   cm. – (Cambridge companions to literature)
        Includes bibliographical references.
    ISBN 0 521 62339 1 (hardback) – ISBN 0 521 62617 X (paperback)
1. Lawrence, D. H. (David Herbert), 1885–1930 – Handbooks, manuals, etc.   I. Title:
Companion to D. H. Lawrence.   II. Fernihough, Anne.   III. Series.

PR6023.A93 Z595 2001
823′.912–dc21   00-063001

ISBN 0 521 62339 1 hardback
ISBN 0 521 62617 X paperback

CONTENTS

Contents

CHRIS BALDICK is Professor of English at Goldsmiths College, University of London, and author of *In Frankenstein's Shadow* (1987), *Criticism and Literary Theory 1890 to the Present* (1996) and other works of literary history. His next book will be *The Oxford English Literary History Volume X: 1910–1940*.

FIONA BECKET is Lecturer in English Literature at the University of Leeds. She is the author of *D. H. Lawrence: The Thinker as Poet* (1997), and of articles on Lawrence, and is currently working on a critical guide to Lawrence. She has recently co-edited a volume of essays on aspects of contemporary Irish Studies called *Ireland in Proximity: History, Gender, Space* (1999).

MICHAEL BELL is Professor of English and Comparative Literary Studies at the University of Warwick. He writes mainly on fiction from Cervantes onwards and on the relations between philosophy and literature. His books include *Primitivism* (1972), *The Sentiment of Reality: Truth of Feeling in the European Novel* (1983), *F. R. Leavis* (1988), *D. H. Lawrence: Language and Being* (1992), *Gabriel García Márquez: Solitude and Solidarity* (1993), *Literature, Modernism and Myth* (1997) and *Sentimentalism, Ethics and the Culture of Feeling* (2000).

CON CORONEOS is Lecturer in English at St John's College, Cambridge. He has published a number of articles on modernism, and his book *Space, Conrad, Modernity* is forthcoming from Oxford University Press. He is currently working on a dictionary of modernism and on a study of theories of laughter with particular reference to Georges Bataille.

PAUL EGGERT is Director of the Australian Scholarly Editions Centre at the Australian Defence Academy, University of New South Wales in Canberra, and associate professor in its School of English. He has edited two titles in the *Cambridge Works of D. H. Lawrence* and co-edited, with

John Worthen, *Lawrence and Comedy* (1996). He works on editorial theory and is currently preparing editions of Conrad's *Under Western Eyes* and the Australian classic, *Robbery Under Arms* by Rolf Boldrewood.

ANNE FERNIHOUGH is Fellow, Lecturer and Director of Studies in English at Girton College, Cambridge. She is the author of *D. H. Lawrence: Aesthetics and Ideology* (1993) and of the introduction to the New Penguin edition of *The Rainbow* (1995) as well as numerous articles on nineteenth- and twentieth-century literature. She recently edited Katherine Mansfield's *In a German Pension* for Penguin (1999), and is currently working on a study of modernism in a range of social and political contexts.

SANDRA M. GILBERT is Professor of English at the University of California, Davis. The author of *Acts of Attention: The Poems of D. H. Lawrence* (1972; revised edition 1990), she is also co-author, with Susan Gubar, of *The Madwoman in the Attic: The Woman Writer and the Nineteenth-Century Literary Imagination* (1979) and a three-volume sequel, *No Man's Land: The Place of the Woman Writer in the Twentieth Century* (1987, 1988, 1994). In addition, among other works she has published five collections of verse, most recently *Ghost Volcano* (1995) and *Kissing the Bread: New and Selected Poems* (2000), and a memoir, *Wrongful Death* (1995).

MARK KINKEAD-WEEKES, Emeritus Professor of English at the University of Kent at Canterbury, has written eleven articles on Lawrence and was the editor of *Twentieth-Century Interpretations of 'The Rainbow'* (1971) and the scholarly Cambridge edition of that novel (1989). He is also the author (1996) of Volume II of the Cambridge biography of D. H. Lawrence: *Triumph to Exile (1912–1922)*. He has written books on Richardson (*Samuel Richardson: Dramatic Novelist*, 1973) and Golding (*William Golding: A Critical Study*, 1961, enlarged edition, 1984), and many articles on English, American, African and Caribbean literature.

DREW MILNE is the Judith E. Wilson Lecturer in Drama and Poetry in the Faculty of English, University of Cambridge, and Fellow in English at Trinity Hall. He was the editor of the journal *Parataxis: Modernism and Modern Writing*, and co-edited *Marxist Literary Theory: A Reader* (1996) with Terry Eagleton. Forthcoming studies include work on Marxism, philosophy and modern theatre. His published books of poetry include *Sheet Mettle* (1994), *Bench Marks* (1998) and *familiars* (1999).

PAUL POPLAWSKI is Senior Lecturer in English at Trinity College Carmarthen in Wales. His books on Lawrence include *D. H. Lawrence: A*

Reference Companion (1996) and he has just completed work on the third edition of *A Bibliography of D. H. Lawrence* by the late Warren Roberts (forthcoming). He has also published a book on Jane Austen and is currently editing an *Encyclopedia of Literary Modernism* for Greenwood Press.

RICK RYLANCE is Professor of Modern English Literature and Dean of the School of Arts and Letters at Anglia Polytechnic University, Cambridge, and a Fellow of the Royal Society of Arts. He has published widely on nineteenth- and twentieth-century literary and intellectual history. His work on Lawrence includes *Sons and Lovers: A New Casebook* (1996). His most recent book is *Psychological Theory and British Culture 1850–70* (2000), and he is presently writing *The Oxford English Literary History Volume XI: 1930–1970*.

MORAG SHIACH is Professor of Cultural History in the School of English and Drama at Queen Mary and Westfield College, University of London. She is the author of *Discourse on Popular Culture* (1989) and *Hélène Cixous: A Politics of Writing* (1991), and has edited *Feminism and Cultural Studies* (1999). She is currently completing a book on labour and selfhood in the modernist period.

HUGH STEVENS lectures in the Department of English and Related Literature at the University of York. He is the author of *Henry James and Sexuality* (1998) and has co-edited, with Caroline Howlett, a volume of essays entitled *Modernist Sexualities* (2000). He is currently working on a book on Lawrence, sex and ethnicity.

HELEN SWORD, Associate Professor of English at Indiana University, is the author of *Engendering Inspiration: Visionary Strategies in Rilke, Lawrence, and H.D.* (1995) and has published numerous articles on twentieth-century literature. Her current research project, *Ghostwriting Modernism* (forthcoming from Cornell University Press), traces intersections between modernist writing and the tropes of popular spiritualism.

TRUDI TATE is a Visiting Professor at the Goethe University, Frankfurt, and a member of Clare Hall, Cambridge. She is editor of *Women, Men and the Great War: An Anthology of Stories* (1995), co-editor with Suzanne Raitt of *Women's Fiction and the Great War* (1997), and author of *Modernism, History and the First World War* (1998). She is currently working on a cultural history of the Crimean War.

MARIANNA TORGOVNICK, Professor of English at Duke University, is the author of five books, including two studies of primitivism: *Gone*

Primitive: Savage Intellects, Modern Lives (1990) and *Primitive Passions: Men, Women, and the Quest for Ecstasy* (1997). As Marianna De Marco Torgovnick, she won an American Book Award for *Crossing Ocean Parkway* (1994), a book of memoir and cultural criticism. She is currently writing a book about the continuing effects of the Second World War in our time.

JOHN WORTHEN is Professor of D. H. Lawrence Studies at the University of Nottingham. His many publications on Lawrence include the first volume of the Cambridge biography, *The Early Years: 1885–1912* (1991). He has recently completed collaborative editions (with Lindeth Vasey and Hans-Wilhelm Schwarze) of the 1916 version of *Women in Love* and of Lawrence's *Plays*; he is currently working on Lawrence's *Prefaces, Introductions and Reviews*, and (with Lindeth Vasey and Ezra Greenspan) on *Studies in Classic American Literature*. All these volumes will appear in the Cambridge Edition of the Works and Letters of D. H. Lawrence.

ACKNOWLEDGEMENTS

First and foremost I would like to thank all the contributors for their hard work and enthusiasm. I am especially grateful to John Worthen who gave me the opportunity to edit this volume. Michael Bell, Michael Black, Howard Mills and Hugh Stevens made helpful suggestions in the early stages, and Morag Shiach agreed to write a chapter at very short notice when one contributor had to pull out. I thank the computer officers at Girton College, Simon Bellow and Andrew Leader, for their patience with my seemingly endless technical hitches, and the staff at Cambridge University Press, especially Josie Dixon, Ray Ryan and Robert Whitelock, for seeing the book through. I am indebted to the Mistress and Fellows of Girton College and to my colleagues, Juliet Dusinberre and James Simpson, for all their encouragement. Gwyneth Fernihough, Jane Wood and Tony Wood have been an invaluable source of help and support. Above all, thank you to Rupert Wood, without whom this and much else would have been impossible.

1885   David Herbert Richards Lawrence born in Eastwood, Nottinghamshire, the fourth child of a collier, Arthur John Lawrence, and Lydia, *née* Beardsall.

1891–98   Attends Beauvale Board School.

1898–1901   Attends Nottingham High School, having won a County Council scholarship.

1901   Works briefly as a clerk at a surgical appliances factory in Nottingham, then becomes seriously ill with pneumonia.

1902   Starts friendship with Jessie Chambers of Haggs Farm, Underwood.

1902–5   Works as a pupil-teacher at the British School, Eastwood. Placed in the first division of the first class in the King's Scholarship exam in December 1904.

1905–6   Works as uncertificated teacher at the British School. Writes his first poems and starts his first novel, 'Laetitia' (later *The White Peacock*, 1911).

1906–8   Studies for teacher's certificate at Nottingham University College, qualifying in 1908. In 1907 wins *Nottinghamshire Guardian* Christmas short-story competition with 'A Prelude', submitted under name of Jessie Chambers.

1908–11   Works as elementary teacher at Davidson Road School, Croydon.

1909   Ford Madox Hueffer (later Ford) starts to publish DHL's poems and stories in the *English Review* and recommends *The White Peacock* to Heinemann. DHL writes *A Collier's Friday Night* and first version of 'Odour of Chrysanthemums'.

1910   Writes 'The Saga of Siegmund' (later *The Trespasser*, 1912), based on the experiences of Helen Corke, a friend and fellow teacher in Croydon. Writes the first version of *The Widowing of Mrs. Holroyd* (1914). Starts to write 'Paul Morel' (later *Sons and Lovers*, 1913). DHL's mother dies in December. Becomes engaged to Louie Burrows.

1911 A severe attack of pneumonia forces DHL to give up teaching. 'The Saga of Siegmund' accepted by Duckworth; DHL revises it as *The Trespasser*.

1912 Breaks off engagement to Louie. Returns to Eastwood and meets Frieda (*née* von Richthofen), the wife of Ernest Weekley, Professor at University College, Nottingham. Travels in Germany and Italy with Frieda. Frieda gives up her husband and children for DHL. DHL writes the final version of *Sons and Lovers* in Gargagno, Italy.

1913 *Love Poems* published. Writing includes *The Daughter-in-Law* (1965), 200 pages of 'The Insurrection of Miss Houghton' (abandoned), and 'The Sisters' (later to split into *The Rainbow*, 1915, and *Women in Love*, 1920). Also writes the first versions of 'The Prussian Officer' and 'The Thorn in the Flesh' (1914). *Sons and Lovers* published in May, establishing Lawrence's literary reputation. DHL and Frieda spend the summer in England and befriend Katherine Mansfield and John Middleton Murry. They return to Italy in September.

1914 Rewrites 'The Sisters' (now called 'The Wedding Ring') and arranges for Methuen to publish it. Returns to England and marries Frieda in July. Outbreak of war confines them to England. Writes *Study of Thomas Hardy* and starts *The Rainbow*. Friendships with Ottoline Morel, Cynthia Asquith, Bertrand Russell and E. M. Forster.

1915 Finishes *The Rainbow*. Quarrels with Russell. *The Rainbow* published in September, suppressed in October, prosecuted and banned for obscenity in November. DHL and Frieda move to Cornwall.

1916 Writes *Women in Love*. Publishes *Twilight in Italy* and *Amores*.

1917 *Women in Love* rejected by publishers. Begins *Studies in Classic American Literature* (1923) and publishes *Look! We Have Come Through!* DHL and Frieda evicted from Cornwall on suspicion of spying. Starts *Aaron's Rod* (1922).

1918 Publishes *New Poems*. Writes *Touch and Go* (1920) and the first version of 'The Fox' (1920).

1919 Falls seriously ill with flu. Travels in Italy with Frieda, settling in Capri.

1920 Writes *Psychoanalysis and the Unconscious* (1921). Settles in Taormina, Sicily. Writes *The Lost Girl* (1920), *Mr Noon* (1984) and many of the poems in *Birds, Beasts and Flowers* (1923). *Women in Love* published.

1921   Visits Sardinia and writes *Sea and Sardinia* (1921). Finishes *Aaron's Rod* and writes *Fantasia of the Unconscious* (1922).

1922   Stays in Ceylon, then travels to Australia. Writes *Kangaroo* (1923). Settles in Taos, New Mexico, moving to the Del Monte Ranch in December. Rewrites *Studies in Classic American Literature*.

1923   Spends summer in Chapala, Mexico, and writes 'Quetzalcoatl', the first version of *The Plumed Serpent* (1926). Quarrels with Frieda who returns to Europe. Travels in USA and Mexico, rewriting Mollie Skinner's *The House of Ellis* as *The Boy in the Bush* (1924). Returns to England in December.

1924   DHL and Frieda return to New Mexico in March accompanied by Dorothy Brett. During summer on the Kiowa Ranch, DHL writes *St. Mawr* (1925), *The Woman Who Rode Away* (1925) and 'The Princess' (1925). In August suffers a bronchial haemorrhage. His father dies in September. In October, moves to Oaxaca, Mexico, starts *The Plumed Serpent* and writes most of *Mornings in Mexico* (1927).

1925   Finishes *The Plumed Serpent*. Nearly dies of typhoid and pneumonia in February. Diagnosed with tuberculosis in March. Returns to Europe in September, spending a month in England, then settling in Italy.

1926   Writes *The Virgin and the Gipsy* (1930). Visits England for the last time in late summer. Returning to Italy, writes the first version of *Lady Chatterley's Lover*. Befriends Aldous and Maria Huxley. Starts to paint.

1927   Finishes second version of *Lady Chatterley's Lover*. Writes *Sketches of Etruscan Places* (1932) and the first part of *The Escaped Cock* (1928). Starts final version of *Lady Chatterley's Lover* (1928).

1928   Finishes *Lady Chatterley's Lover* and arranges for its publication in Florence. Writes the second part of *The Escaped Cock* (1929). Travels with Frieda to Switzerland, then settles in the south of France. Writes many of the poems in *Pansies* (1929).

1929   Unexpurgated typescripts of *Pansies* seized by police; exhibition of paintings in London raided by police. Writes *Nettles* (1930), *Apocalypse* (1931) and *Last Poems* (1932).

1930   Admitted to Ad Astra Sanatorium in Vence at start of February;

discharges himself on 1 March; dies at Villa Robermond, Vence, on 2 March.

1935   Frieda sends Angelo Ravagli (whom she later marries) from the Kiowa Ranch to Vence to have DHL exhumed and cremated. His ashes are brought back to the ranch.

1956   Frieda dies and is buried at the ranch.

ABBREVIATIONS

Letters of Lawrence

The following seven volumes make up *The Letters of D. H. Lawrence*, all published by Cambridge University Press.

(i.)   Volume I, ed. James T. Boulton (1979)
(ii.)   Volume II, ed. George T. Zytaruk and James T. Boulton (1982)
(iii.) Volume III, ed. James T. Boulton and Andrew Robertson (1984)
(iv.)   Volume IV, ed. Warren Roberts, James T. Boulton and Elizabeth Mansfield (1987)
(v.)   Volume V, ed. James T. Boulton and Lindeth Vasey (1989)
(vi.)   Volume VI, ed. James T. Boulton and Margaret H. Boulton, with Gerald M. Lacy (1991)
(vii.) Volume VII, ed. Keith Sagar and James T. Boulton (1993)

Works of Lawrence

A   *Apocalypse and the Writings on Revelation*, ed. Mara Kalnins; with an introduction and notes by Mara Kalnins (London: Penguin, 1995)
AR   *Aaron's Rod*, ed. Mara Kalnins; with an introduction and notes by Steven Vine (London: Penguin, 1995)
EmyE   *England, My England and Other Stories*, ed. Bruce Steele; with an introduction and notes by Michael Bell (London: Penguin, 1995)
F&P   *Fantasia of the Unconscious and Psychoanalysis and the Unconscious* (Harmondsworth: Penguin, 1971; repr. 1986)
Fox   *The Fox, The Captain's Doll, The Ladybird*, ed. Dieter Mehl; with an introduction and notes by David Ellis (London: Penguin, 1994)
Hardy   *Study of Thomas Hardy and Other Essays*, ed. Bruce Steele (Cambridge: Cambridge University Press, 1985)

K	*Kangaroo*, ed. Bruce Steele; with an introduction and notes by Macdonald Daly (London: Penguin, 1997)
LCL	*Lady Chatterley's Lover*, ed. Michael Squires; with an introduction and notes by Michael Squires (London: Penguin, 1994)
MEH	*Movements in European History*, ed. Philip Crumpton (Cambridge: Cambridge University Press, 1989)
MM	*Mornings in Mexico* (Harmondsworth: Penguin, 1986)
P	*Phoenix: The Posthumous Papers of D. H. Lawrence*, ed. Edward D. McDonald (London: Heinemann, 1936)
PII	*Phoenix II: Uncollected, Unpublished and Other Prose Works by D. H. Lawrence*, ed. Warren Roberts and Harry T. Moore (London: Heinemann, 1968)
Plays	*The Plays of D. H. Lawrence*, ed. Hans Schwarze and John Worthen (Cambridge: Cambridge University Press, 1999)
PO	*The Prussian Officer and Other Stories*, ed. John Worthen; with an introduction and notes by Brian Finney (London: Penguin, 1995)
Poems	*The Complete Poems of D. H. Lawrence*, ed. Vivian de Sola Pinto and Warren Roberts (Harmondsworth: Penguin, 1977; repr. 1994)
PS	*The Plumed Serpent*, ed. L. D. Clark; with an introduction and notes by L. D. Clark and Virginia Crosswhite Hyde (London: Penguin, 1995)
Q	*Quetzalcoatl: The Early Version of The Plumed Serpent*, ed. Louis L. Martz (Redding Ridge, CT: Black Swan Books, 1995)
R	*The Rainbow*, ed. Mark Kinkead-Weekes; with an introduction and notes by Anne Fernihough (London: Penguin, 1995)
RDP	*Reflections on the Death of a Porcupine and Other Essays*, ed. Michael Herbert (Cambridge: Cambridge University Press, 1988)
SCAL	*Studies in Classic American Literature* (Harmondsworth: Penguin, 1971; repr. 1990)
SEP	*Sketches of Etruscan Places and Other Italian Essays*, ed. Simonetta de Filippis; with an introduction and notes by Simonetta de Filippis (London: Penguin, 1999)
SL	*Sons and Lovers*, ed. Helen Baron and Carl Baron; with an introduction and notes by Helen Baron and Carl Baron (London: Penguin, 1994)
SM	*St. Mawr and Other Stories*, ed. Brian Finney; with an introduction and notes by Charles Rossman (London: Penguin, 1997)
Symbolic	*The Symbolic Meaning: The Uncollected Versions of Studies in Classic American Literature*, ed. Armin Arnold (London: T. J. Winterson, 1962)

T	*The Trespasser*, ed. Elizabeth Mansfield; with an introduction and notes by John Turner (London: Penguin, 1994)
TI	*Twilight in Italy and Other Essays*, ed. Paul Eggert; with an introduction and notes by Stefania Michelucci (London: Penguin, 1997)
WL	*Women in Love*, ed. David Farmer, Lindeth Vasey and John Worthen; with an introduction and notes by Mark Kinkead-Weekes (London: Penguin, 1995)
WP	*The White Peacock*, ed. Andrew Robertson; with an introduction and notes by Michael Black (London: Penguin, 1995)
WWRA	*The Woman Who Rode Away and Other Stories*, ed. Dieter Mehl and Christa Jansohn; with an introduction and notes by N. H. Reeve (London: Penguin, 1996)

The Cambridge Biography of Lawrence

EY	John Worthen, *D. H. Lawrence: The Early Years 1885–1912* (Cambridge: Cambridge University Press, 1991)
TE	Mark Kinkead-Weekes, *D. H. Lawrence: Triumph to Exile 1912–1922* (Cambridge: Cambridge University Press, 1996)
DG	David Ellis, *D. H. Lawrence: Dying Game 1922–1930* (Cambridge: Cambridge University Press, 1998)

ANNE FERNIHOUGH

Introduction

This volume opens and ends with puzzlement: at the start of chapter 1, Rick Rylance reflects on the puzzlement of Lawrence's earliest reviewers as they struggled to ascertain the literary and social provenance of his work: was 'D. H. Lawrence' a man or a woman, what was his or her social background, and to what literary tradition did these strange fictions belong? Chris Baldick closes the last chapter with puzzlement as to what the readers of the new century will make of a writer whose reputation, both literary and personal, has undergone extraordinary vicissitudes, fluctuating more wildly than that of any other twentieth-century British author. There seems to be hardly anyone else who has generated such extreme reactions in his readers, from people at one end of the spectrum who have tried to 'become' Lawrence to people who have felt contaminated by reading him. That reading and writing about Lawrence can be a bewildering and often problematic enterprise is a fact that all the contributors to this book touch on in different ways. For Rick Rylance, Lawrence's early work disturbs and unsettles its readers because it is itself wrestling with the 'chronically disturbed' relations between mind and body in an age where materialist scientific theories have denied any divine agency in the natural world. For Marianna Torgovnick in chapter 2, Lawrence pushes his critics into starkly polarised positions: either they ritualistically rehearse his views or they reject him out of hand. The problem, she argues, is how to negotiate between these extremes. For Hugh Stevens in chapter 3, attempts to interpret a work like *Women in Love* in political terms can all too easily 'lead to a banality which is absolutely at odds with the novel's power'. And so the problems posed by Lawrence's work proliferate from chapter to chapter.

Lawrence's prose is intellectually and emotionally demanding. Its uneven-ness, its tendency to repetition and excess, its sometimes outrageous flouting of aesthetic norms, its sudden moments of bathos, are notorious. For Marianna Torgovnick, Lawrence's predicament is that of someone who is radically out of sync with his culture, 'wanting what he cannot yet name, working with ideas and vocabulary drawn from systems of thought funda-mentally at odds with his desires', and this may partly account for the inter-pretative and aesthetic difficulties he poses.[1] Another factor may be Lawrence's socially and culturally deracinated existence. A miner's son whose mother harboured middle-class aspirations, he later married a German aristocrat with whom he went on to live an itinerant, at times poverty-stricken, life across four continents. He never really *belonged* to any specific social class, nor indeed to any literary or artistic group. In Virginia Woolf's words, he was 'not a member . . . of a settled and satisfied society', and this, for Woolf, explained the sense of restlessness in *Sons and Lovers*, a novel 'full of stir and unrest and desire for something withheld'.[2]

But perhaps the most immediate explanation for the instability of Lawrence's fictions lies in the voracious and eclectic reading which was a staple of Lawrence's life, no matter where he happened to be. Ford Madox Hueffer, the influential editor of the *English Review* who encouraged Lawrence early in his career, was deeply impressed by the breadth of Lawrence's reading, observing that he 'moved among the high things of culture with a tranquil assurance'.[3] But Lawrence did not restrict himself to the classics, or indeed to literary material. His reading took in, amongst other subjects, evolutionary theory, philosophy, sociology, anthropology, psychoanalytical theory, religion and ethics. John Worthen, describing the self-educative programme that Lawrence embarked upon with his girlfriend Jessie Chambers in the period between school and college, explains how Lawrence was no passive reader, but took '*possession* of the thoughts of others . . . turn[ing] them into what he wanted' (*EY*, 122). Perhaps this rapid absorption of such a range of conflicting discourses explains the charges of 'formlessness' or unevenness as a writer that dogged Lawrence throughout his career. He was piqued by Hueffer's complaint that 'The Saga of Siegmund' (an early version of *The Trespasser*) had 'no construction or form' (i. 339), and Hueffer's criticism of the 'Saga' as a 'hybrid' work seemed to point to the blurring of generic boundaries which is so characteristic of Lawrence's writing.[4] In chapter 6 of this volume, Con Coroneos and Trudi Tate emphasise this feature of the short stories, and for Michael Bell in chapter 10, *Lady Chatterley's Lover* reads in parts like 'a mixture of fable and lay sermon' (191).

One of the most striking ways in which Lawrence criticism has changed over the past few years is that there is apparently no longer any need to try to smooth these difficulties away as there once might have been. On the con-trary, as the chapters here demonstrate, critics today seem to thrive on the sense of disjunction and disorientation produced by Lawrence's writing. An early reviewer of some of the tales noted their preoccupation with what he called 'the queer dark corners' of life, and today, when 'queer' has become a literary critical term in its own right, that early reviewer's observation takes on a new resonance.[5] Eve Sedgwick's tracing of the etymology of the term is illuminating: 'The word "queer" itself means *across* – it comes from the Indo-European root – *twerkw*, which also yields the German *quer* (transverse), Latin *torquere* (to twist), English *athwart*.'[6] Whilst Sedgwick's own work is primarily concerned with gender, she is also, like Lawrence, interested in those components of human identity which, in her words, 'can't be subsumed under gender and sexuality at all: the ways that race, ethnicity, postcolonial nationality criss-cross with these *and other* identity-constituting, identity-fracturing discourses'.[7] Several of the chapters in this volume spring to mind here. Hugh Stevens's chapter, for example, focuses on the densely tangled tropes of race, eros and death in *Women in Love*, while Mark Kinkead-Weekes shows how issues of gender in the 1924 novellas (especially 'The Woman Who Rode Away' and 'The Princess') are inextricable from questions of colonial identity. Interestingly, Con Coroneos and Trudi Tate use the same metaphor as Sedgwick, that of crossing a line, to describe the unsettling quality of Lawrence's short story 'Smile', where 'a line [is] crossed from laughter to death' (106). On a multiplicity of levels, Lawrence's writing does exactly that: it crosses lines, between linguistic and social registers, between literary genres and traditions, between whole discourses and disciplines. It is this refusal to respect lines or boundaries which, more than anything else, accounts for both the bafflement and the fascination of many of Lawrence's readers, and for the difficulty of doing critical justice to his works.

It is perhaps small wonder, then, that Lawrence's position on the literary map has, at times, seemed far less secure than that of, say, Joyce or Woolf. But it is worth noting that this has only really been true within academic circles. In the broader cultural sphere, Lawrence has retained his popularity. The numerous lists of 'best books of the century' or 'greatest works of art of the century' have frequently included one or more of Lawrence's best-known novels, and, at the time of writing this introduction, BBC Radio 4 is embarking on a celebration of his work.[8] He has, moreover, enjoyed a genuinely international reputation, his influence stretching far beyond the Anglophone world. He has been seen as the champion of freedom and individualism in countries with oppressive government regimes, such as China. Different countries have privileged different parts of the Lawrence canon, some countries, such as Poland and India, favouring the poetry over the prose.[9] In his own lifetime, though, Lawrence's literary success was all too brief, promise mutating into notoriety almost overnight with the banning of *The Rainbow* in 1915, when Lawrence was just thirty years old. What he would have made of his posthumous canonisation one can only imagine. He was canonised in both senses of the term: the 1950s witnessed his installation, at the hands of F. R. Leavis and others, into the 'canon' of English literature as he began to appear with increasing frequency in school and university curricula. Then, in the wake of the famous *Lady Chatterley* trial of 1960, he was canonised in a different sense, becoming, as Chris Baldick terms it in chapter 14, 'one of the patron saints of the 1960s', not just the most prized of modern British writers, but also a cultural icon for a whole generation. For Lawrence's life was championed as much as his writing. As Baldick shows, he became a working-class hero, seen to be injecting new life into a desiccated social system, a stance with which many identified in the freer social climate of the 1960s.

This was all set to change, at least in Britain and America, with the appearance of Kate Millett's ground-breaking and hard-hitting work *Sexual Politics* (1970), which knocked Lawrence off the pedestal he had been occupying as a sexual and moral example in the 1960s. Millett's reading of *Lady Chatterley's Lover* made Lawrence into the subtle conveyor of a masculine message through a feminine consciousness.[10] Elsewhere in the world, though, Lawrence's popularity showed no signs of waning. The critical response in a country such as Korea, for example, which started in 1926, has continued to escalate unabated. As recently as 1998, there were thirty academics teaching in South Korean universities with Ph.D.s on Lawrence – probably a greater number than in any other country with the possible exception of the USA.[11]

When one considers the successive waves of critical and theoretical practice that have shaped academia since Lawrence's death, some sense can be made of his tumultuous afterlife. His popularity was at its height when various forms of Anglo-American New Criticism were dominating literary study, with their post-Romantic emphasis on organic form, on the importance of an intuitive response to literature, and on the inadequacies of paraphrase or logical explication. Cleanth Brooks, for example, had warned against 'the heresy of paraphrase', a phrase suggesting that literary texts were sacred life forms that should not be tampered with.[12] This chimed in with Lawrence's own frequently voiced hatred of rational analysis, and with his use of organicist imagery in his own literary and cultural criticism. Today it might be argued that the generic hybridity and the unevenness of much of Lawrence's writing make it radically incompatible with this notion of organic form. Yet it seems as true now as it did back then that Lawrence's writing *is* particularly difficult to paraphrase, even if this is no longer to do with some quasi-religious notion of the ineffability of art. Paradoxically, although the New Critical movement evolved as a pedagogic tool to meet the needs of teachers of literature as an academic subject, its post-Romantic overtones were, in essence, anti-academic. The same could be said of F. R. Leavis's work. Leavis's own marginal, and embattled, position within the academy, together with his championing of Lawrence, reinforced the notion that Lawrence and academia, like oil and water, do not mix. In this way, the academic study of Lawrence became a curiously self-defeating enterprise, reduced to the tautological replication of Lawrence's own terminology and the ritualistic rehearsing of his prophecies. As Linda Williams explains, Lawrence criticism became 'a question of showing that criticism was a "real", personally felt, and above all "vital" response activated through one's very life . . . The heady amalgam of life and work turned Lawrence into an Example to us all.'[13] Just as the boundaries between Lawrence's life and his work had seemed so permeable, so the boundaries between the *reader's* life and Lawrence's work also seemed to dissolve. The arrival of Kate Millett's *Sexual Politics* on the critical scene was shocking not just because it demonised what had previously been sanctified (Lawrence's view of sexual relations), but because its own plain-speaking, no-nonsense idiom was not afraid to demystify Lawrence's post-Romantic rhetoric, and to commit the 'heresy' of paraphrasing it. For many, this has remained the stumbling block of Millett's approach.

What Millett had in common with earlier critics was that there was still very little attention being paid to the linguistic complexities of Lawrence's work. The metaphors governing Lawrence criticism, medical metaphors (of sickness and health), legal metaphors (of trial, accusation, defence) and Biblical metaphors (of the prophet in the wilderness), had always been, and continued to be, very author-centric. Lawrence himself had set this trend, differing from contemporaries such as Joyce, Woolf, Eliot and Pound in that (as Michael Bell points out in chapter 10) he did not self-consciously privilege the linguistic medium in which he worked. His savage mockery of 'critical twiddle-twaddle about style, and form, all this pseudo-scientific classifying and analysing of books' seemed to foreclose on the possibility of formal analysis of his works.[14] Nor, as Paul Eggert stresses, did he go along with the impersonality theories present in the modernist period, so that there was a strong sense of authorial presence in much of his writing. Perhaps this was why the most precarious period for Lawrence, in Britain at least, came with the impact of French post-structuralist theory on literary criticism in the late 1970s and 1980s. Lawrence could appear to be naively logocentric, relying on the 'metaphysics of presence' which Derridean critics were at pains to deconstruct. Paradoxically, though, as John Worthen so clearly demonstrates in his analysis of a passage from *Sons and Lovers*, authorial presence is by no means easy to pin down in Lawrence's fictions.

The 1990s saw a largescale drift towards a more interdisciplinary notion of cultural studies and away from a narrowly literary approach. Hence Lawrence's very hybridity, which had always made him difficult to pigeon-hole, gave him a newfound legitimacy as an object of study. Lawrence was nothing if not a cultural critic himself. In a single, five-page essay ostensibly on the novel, Lawrence can quite typically be found discussing, in and amongst a range of classical and popular novels, such diverse topics as Van Gogh's painting, ancient Assyrian and Egyptian art, philosophy, science, religion and sexual relations.[15] Today's cultural critics share this eclectic approach to reading and writing. Further, the opening up of feminism into a broader-based and more flexible concept of gender studies has transformed Lawrence criticism, together with the increasing interest from the 1990s onwards in issues of race, ethnicity and nationality. In all these areas, critics are finding, perhaps against their expectation, that Lawrence's work is a rich vein to be tapped.

The impact of new kinds of historicism on literary research has made us realise more clearly than before how many of Lawrence's excesses were the excesses of his own rapidly metamorphosing and politically unstable culture. With all his idiosyncrasies, he *was* very much a product of his time, tirelessly alert to the cultural trends of his day and voracious in his absorption of new ideas. Morag Shiach shows in her chapter, for example, how Lawrence's interest in a psycho-biological model of subjectivity was by no means eccentric. He was, she stresses, drawing on the social and medical models of psychic life and psychic health available in his time: theories of traumatic neurasthenia, hysteria, depression. Despite his itinerant life, then, and despite his resistance to official cultural 'movements', Lawrence was not working in a cultural vacuum. What *was* distinctive about Lawrence was perhaps less the particular views he expressed in his letters and essays than the unashamed, even naive, openness with which he articulated them, not to mention his inconsistency. For if Lawrence's reputation has see-sawed dramatically, it has been no more erratic than his own views on the many issues, cultural, social and political, that he addressed in the vast number of letters, essays and reviews he wrote in his short lifetime. Between 1979 and 1993, the Cambridge edition of the complete letters was published. Stretching to seven volumes in all, this vast body of material enables us to see even more clearly than before just how restless and unsettled Lawrence's opinions were. To take gender relations as just one example, Lawrence wrote to a fellow writer, Edward Garnett, in 1912, 'It seems to me queer you prefer to present men chiefly – as if you cared for women not so much for what they were in themselves as for what the men saw in them. So that after all in your work women seem not to have an existence, save they are the projections of the men . . . No, I *don't* think you have a high opinion of women' (i. 470). Yet it was the same Lawrence who wrote to Katherine Mansfield in 1918, 'I do think a woman must yield some sort of precedence to a man, and he must take this precedence. I do think men must go ahead absolutely in front of their women, without turning round for permission or approval from their women' (iii. 302). Perhaps this breathtaking inconsistency was part of what T. S. Eliot had in mind when he complained that Lawrence had 'an incapacity for what we ordinarily call thinking', but such a comment arguably betrays a failure to come to terms with Lawrence's particular intellectual mode.[16] It is 'rhetorical' in the true sense of the word: it seeks to persuade at the moment of writing, or, as Paul Eggert puts it in chapter 9, Lawrence 'must have known in some part of himself that there were brackets around his truth-claims; but he could not write as if there were' (171). His disclaimer in a letter of 1913, 'Don't ever mind what I say. I am a great bosher and full of fancies that interest me' (i. 503), is telling in this respect. The availability, too, through the Cambridge edition, of the different versions of particular texts, supports Eggert's argument about the 'provisionality' of Lawrence's writing. These texts suggest contingency, 'change and variation, response to accident', rather than organic growth to some predestined goal of literary perfection. The development of computer-generated hypertext, enabling students to view successive states of a text simultaneously, will doubtless reinforce this point. But if each of these constantly shifting stages is taken in isolation, one could be forgiven for taking it as a final statement.

Those who have never read very much Lawrence are quick to condemn him as an extremist, isolating one phase of his work, one single text, or even one single letter, as representative of the whole oeuvre. So they present him as the priest of a cult of the phallus, or as the puritanical proselytiser of monogamous marriage, or perhaps as the proto-fascistic promoter of leadership. To read a substantial amount of Lawrence's work soon puts paid to these parodic versions of him, even if at times Lawrence is his own best parodist. Whilst is true that much of his writing, especially in the discursive as opposed to fictional mode, is as insistent as it is inconsistent, it is also true that reading Lawrence is a more complex process than his reputation as an extremist would suggest. Three aspects of his writing which contribute to this complexity are emphasised by the contributors to this volume: his use of multiple consciousnesses (Rylance and Worthen); his refusal to comply with the dualistic codes he sets up (Stevens and Baldick); and the 'provisionality' of his assertions (Eggert).

Given his brief lifetime (he died at the age of forty-four), Lawrence's literary output was quite astounding, both in terms of quantity and in terms of generic diversity. A volume of this kind could never be comprehensive; it could never represent every important text within Lawrence's oeuvre, nor every important issue within Lawrence criticism. So, for example, some of the 1920s novels and some of the travel writings are not represented. An attempt has been made to address as wide a range of works as possible without sacrificing detailed attention to particular texts, and to focus on those topics most likely to be of interest and relevance to today's students. In Part I, the focus is primarily on particular texts or groups of texts within the Lawrence canon; in Part II, the emphasis is on contexts and critical issues. But in practice, of course, the division is by no means clearcut, nor is it desirable that it should be.

In chapter 1, Rick Rylance contextualises the early works in terms of the conflicting evolutionary theories circulating in Lawrence's time. He shows how Lawrence was someone working at the limits of the available literary, social and scientific paradigms. He analyses Lawrence's use of free indirect discourse, a narrative method which produces a sense of a multi-aspected, disjunctive reality: there is no overarching narrator's voice to provide a synthesised, comprehensive view. This technique also enables Lawrence to create the complex social fabric of a work like *Sons and Lovers*, in which 'identity is formed interpersonally'. In chapter 2, Marianna Torgovnick reads *The Rainbow* against the available models for writing about sex in Lawrence's own time, both literary models and those supplied by the relatively new 'science' of sexology. She argues that, whilst Lawrence's treatment of sex in *The Rainbow* is more direct and less aestheticised than that of his modernist contemporaries, it is nonetheless the antithesis of pornography, which is premissed on the replicability or interchangeability of its sexual episodes. Equally, it is the antithesis of the typologising of sexual behaviour to be found in the works of sexologists such as Havelock Ellis. Ultimately, for Torgovnick, Lawrence is distinguished by his attempt to *narrate* sex, to embed it in a narrative continuum and to integrate it into the texture of a wider experience. In chapter 3 on 'The Prussian Officer' and *Women in Love*, Hugh Stevens links the subjection and power struggle central to the relationships in these works to the global power struggles of the First World War and 'the fundamental act of subjection which Lawrence sees as central to the modern crisis of Europe – our subjection to the nation state'. Stevens connects Lawrence's own wartime experiences, including the banning of *The Rainbow* and his medical examinations at the hands of the military authorities, to a crisis in his sense of Englishness, and to his mapping of an idealised, transgressive sexuality onto other races and nations.

Mark Kinkead-Weekes opens chapter 4 with Doris Lessing's definition of racism as an 'atrophy of the imagination' and takes this as the starting-point for a post-colonial analysis of some of Lawrence's 1920s writing. Through detailed biographical contextualisation, he charts Lawrence's oscillating responses to racial and colonial issues, his imaginative successes and failures.

'Quetzalcoatl', for example, the early version of *The Plumed Serpent*, emerges as a more exploratory and less assertive novel than the more stridently ideological but better-known later version. Morag Shiach in chapter 5 reads *Lady Chatterley's Lover* not for what it has to say about sex, but, more unusually, for what it has to say about work. She delineates the unstable relations between industrial labour and selfhood in this novel, and shows how creative forms of self-realisation are set off against empty and degenerate forms of subjectivity. She concludes that, in a novel in which, as in so many of Lawrence's works, history and myth are so subtly imbricated, more integrated forms of labour can only be imagined, not realised.

In chapters 6 and 7, on the tales and poems respectively, the emphasis is less on contexts and more on the formal properties of the works themselves. In both these chapters, there is an emphasis on genres *within* genres. Just as, for Con Coroneos and Trudi Tate, the short stories encompass 'sketches and novellas, naturalistic tales, fables, apologues, satires and ghost stories', so Helen Sword shows how the poetry is by turns imagist, confessionalist, nature poetry, satire, mysticism. The contributors stress how, in both the short story and poetic genres, Lawrence eludes easy classification. In both these chapters, too, there is an emphasis on 'darkness' (what Woolf famously called 'the dark places of psychology'[17]), whether of sexual panic, loss of control, unnerving laughter in the tales, or the erotic violence lurking in some of the poems. In chapter 8 on Lawrence as dramatist, John Worthen explains how a particular cultural and economic climate, together with the lack of personal support Lawrence received at crucial stages, prevented him from developing his full potential in this genre. Lawrence's versions of the dramatic and the comic 'were left to find alternative routes through his writing'. Worthen then analyses a passage from *Sons and Lovers*, tracing the subtle shifts of narrative point of view in order to show how Lawrence's talent, even within the novel genre, and even when no one is actually speaking, is 'essentially dramatic'.

Paul Eggert opens Part II with the critical issue of biography, a particularly resonant one where Lawrence is concerned. As noted above, Lawrence never went along with the theories of aesthetic autonomy promoted in his lifetime by T. S. Eliot and others, so that critics have found it oddly difficult or inappropriate to try to separate 'the man who suffers and the mind which creates'. Eggert's overview of the recent three-volume Cambridge biography of Lawrence shows afresh how the life and the writing fed each other, and how the life can be brought to bear on the writing in critically meaningful ways. Lawrence's love of role-play from an early age, for example, can be linked to the *provisionality* of his writing mentioned above, and to the 'risk-taking polarizations and extremes' which typify much of his work. For

Michael Bell in chapter 10, the cultural context is that of literary modern-ism, Lawrence's relation to which has always been a matter of debate. Bell argues that Lawrence was neither straightforwardly modernist nor anti-modernist, but engaged in a parallel project. Whilst he shared many of the concerns of his modernist contemporaries, concerns such as time and myth for example, his approach was less programmatic and self-conscious than theirs. Rather than rejecting his Romantic heritage as Eliot and Pound did, Lawrence sought to transform it from within, and in his emphasis on the cen-trality of feeling, he can be seen as the 'repressed conscience' of modernism.

In chapter 11, Drew Milne addresses the difficult task of reading Lawrence *politically*, arguing that Lawrence's politics have too often been conflated with sexual politics. He shows how Kate Millett, for example, turns sexual politics into the master narrative in Lawrence's works. Focusing on *St. Mawr*, Milne argues that Lawrence's novels dramatise a rejection of politics. But equally importantly, they reject the attempted sexual solutions to the political problems posed. Such solutions, or moments of sexual transcen-dence, are shown within the terms of Lawrence's novels to be merely illu-sory; they do not provide the ground for genuine political resistance to existing social structures. In this sense, Milne suggests, there is a more self-critical dimension to Lawrence's fictions than has perhaps been recognised. In chapter 12, Fiona Becket explores the intersections between Lawrence's writing and psychoanalysis, tracing Lawrence's struggle to retrieve the 'unconscious' from Freud and to develop his own, alternative genealogy of consciousness. She examines Lawrence's idiosyncratic language of the body in his essays on the unconscious. For Becket, this language of solar plexuses and lumbar ganglions is a deliberate attempt on Lawrence's part to close the gap between the literal and the metaphorical in discussions of the uncon-scious. The determined misogyny of *Fantasia* is contextualised in terms of Lawrence's own illnesses and his troubled marriage at the time of writing. Becket also highlights crucial differences between Lawrence and Freud: where Freud, for example, seeks to normalise his 'sick' patients and reinte-grate them into society, Lawrence sees society itself as 'sick'.

Aptly enough at the start of a new millennium, Sandra Gilbert's focus is on Lawrence and apocalypse. She analyses the visions of sociocultural apoc-alypse, of the transfiguration of an exhausted culture, to be found in some of the late poetry, and is fascinated by the ways in which such apocalyptic moments are gendered and sexualised. She describes Lawrence as 'the ulti-mate pre-postmodernist' in his repudiation of the 'hopeless, horizonless aes-thetic' which we would now associate with postmodernism and suggests that 'we are bemused, even bewitched, by the ways *he doesn't* fit into our current systems of thought'. In the final chapter, Chris Baldick addresses the turbulent history of Lawrence's critical and cultural afterlife, tracing its phoenix-like 'cycles of immolation and revival'. He shows how the polarisation of Lawrence critics set in as soon as Lawrence died, as did the medical and Biblical metaphors that dominated these critical controversies including the *Lady Chatterley* trial. Baldick argues that these polarised views failed to come to terms with the self-contradictoriness of Lawrence's work, and that only with the rediscovery of this principle did Lawrence critics 'come of age'. He concludes by speculating as to the possible directions of future work on Lawrence.

As Baldick's chapter shows all too clearly, Lawrence, more than most writers, comes with cultural baggage. But for a new, less encumbered, twenty-first-century generation of students, the idolatry and the demonising which have burdened Lawrence criticism in the past are not within living memory. Both responses suggested a reluctance to historicise Lawrence, a desire to make him into an arbiter and a spokesperson for *our* culture, for *our* relationships, standing or falling in those terms. Certainly, at times it does feel as if Lawrence is reading us rather than the other way round. Many of the cultural trends he attacked so vociferously have continued into our own time. The technology-driven, virtual culture we now inhabit, for instance, is the culture Lawrence dreaded. What he would have made of relationships conducted via the internet, one can all too easily imagine. Shortly before his death he was complaining that 'We don't *want* to look at flesh and blood people – we want to watch their shadows on a screen. We don't *want* to hear their actual voices: only transmitted through a machine.'[18] But if Lawrence seems, at such times, to stand outside his own point in history, to bridge the gap between his own culture and ours, at other times he makes us feel that gap acutely. Some aspects of the culture he inhabited are profoundly alien to us. To use Rebecca West's phrase, we don't always feel, after reading him, that we have 'stayed in safety'.[19] This brings us back to the problem of the polarised responses, of identification or alienation, that Lawrence evokes in his readers. But why, in the end, would we only wish to read those writers who replicate ourselves? Interest in Lawrence at both academic and popular levels is still strong, suggesting that we don't always choose to 'stay in safety'.

NOTES

1 *Gone Primitive: Savage Intellects, Modern Lives* (Chicago: Chicago University Press, 1990), p. 172.
2 'Notes on D. H. Lawrence', in *Collected Essays*, 4 vols. (London: Hogarth Press, 1966), I. 352–55 (pp. 355, 354).
3 Cited in *D. H. Lawrence: A Composite Biography*, ed. Edward Nehls, 3 vols. (Madison: University of Wisconsin Press, 1957–59), I. 116.

4 See also i. 492 ('They want me to have form . . . and I won't').

5 Gerald Gould, *New Statesman*, 26 December 1914, p. 298.

6 Eve Kosofsky Sedgwick, *Tendencies* (London: Routledge, 1993), p. xii.

7 Ibid., p. 9.

8 BBC Radio 4, between 12 September and 11 October 1999. On 20 July 1998 the *New York Times* published a list of the titles, in order of merit, of the 100 best books of the century, a list drawn up by the editorial board of the New York Modern Library, a branch of Random House. Three of Lawrence's books were on the list, *Sons and Lovers* (no. 9), *The Rainbow* (no. 48) and *Women in Love* (no. 49). On 15 October 1999, the *Bookseller* published a 'list of lists', distilled from numerous other 'best of the century' lists. This was a list of books 'that have influenced human thought and action in the twentieth century'. *Sons and Lovers* and *Lady Chatterley's Lover* were both included.

9 See *The Reception of D. H. Lawrence Around the World*, ed. Takeo Iida (Fukuoka, Japan: Kyushu University Press, 1999), p. xi.

10 *Sexual Politics* (1970; London: Virago, 1977), p. 239.

11 Jungmai Kim, 'The Reception of D. H. Lawrence in Korea', in *The Reception of D. H. Lawrence Around the World*, pp. 255–69.

12 Cleanth Brooks, *The Well Wrought Urn* (New York: Harcourt, Brace & Co., 1947), pp. 192–214.

13 Linda Ruth Williams, *D. H. Lawrence* (Plymouth: Northcote House in association with the British Council, 1997), p. 3.

14 'John Galsworthy', in *Hardy*, 207–20 (p. 209).

15 'Morality and the Novel', in *Hardy*, 171–76.

16 T. S. Eliot, *After Strange Gods: A Primer in Modern Heresy* (New York: Harcourt, Brace & Co., 1934), p. 63.

17 Virginia Woolf, 'Modern Fiction', in *The Essays of Virginia Woolf*, ed. Andrew McNeillie (London: Hogarth Press, 1986–), IV (1994), 157–65 (p. 162).

18 'Men Must Work and Women as Well', in *PII*, 582–91 (p. 590).

19 Rebecca West, 'Elegy [D. H. Lawrence]', in *Rebecca West; A Celebration* (Penguin: Harmondsworth, 1978), pp. 383–95 (p. 383).

I
TEXTS

I

RICK RYLANCE

Ideas, histories, generations and beliefs: the early novels to *Sons and Lovers*

The puzzle of the early work: *The White Peacock*

What gave Lawrence's work its distinctive character in the second decade of the twentieth century? Reviewers of the first three novels appeared perplexed. There was confusion about the author's social milieu and gender, and irritation that provincial fiction should be so learned in literary and intellectual allusion.[1] His characters moved unpredictably between 'public-houses and dinner parties' and had deplorable grooming rituals: 'among their habits is a trick of messing and caressing and stroking each other's hair or arms'. [2] This zoological sneer loped after Lawrence throughout his career. Behind it lurked worries about evolutionary descent from the apes and, more worrying still, the possibility of degenerate reversion. But amid fretfulness about his carelessness with social and literary form, and his shocking lack of sexual reticence (a charge that began with *The Trespasser* in 1912), the central issue was bewilderment about his meaning. Few denied his talent; fewer still had a collected sense of where it led:

> what does our author really mean by these pictures of wasted lives and ill-matched marriages? Is he a new prophet of the old fallacy of 'returning to Nature'? It sometimes looks like it, and yet the apologue which explains the title of *The White Peacock* does not suggest this as a moral, for surely the game-keeper who reverted violently 'to Nature' after freeing himself from his unnatural wife, 'the white peacock', did not make much of his experiment.[3]

This attempt to restore a troubling text to a recognisable message is clearly mistaken, but the misanthropic gamekeeper, Annable, *is* puzzling. He appears suddenly in the middle of the novel and fascinates the narrator, Cyril Beardsall, who likes his physique and outlaw style. The sexual and social ambivalence of such figures is often remarked. There is a homoerotic shimmer around Annable and, like Mellors in *Lady Chatterley's Lover*, he is better born and educated than he appears. The Cambridge-educated son of a 'big cattle dealer', his father's bankruptcy cut short his degree and, he tells Cyril, he became a curate before marrying into the gentry. His marriage foundered on differences of rank and culture as his wife was enthralled by 'souly' poets and painters. Annable became a piece of 'rough': 'I was her animal – son animal – son bœuf. I put up with that for above a year. Then I got some servant's clothes and went' (*WP*, 151). His story captures something of the challenge of Lawrence's early work: hard to 'place' or explain, unconventional, rebarbative and dissident, it sets an interpretative problem. For Annable's life reverses stories articulating ideals of social integration, romantic harmony and cultural pride. A narrative about a worthy unfortunate and his lady-rescuer is given a sarcastic twist, as is a tale about artistic guardianship by the wealthy. And Annable's lost religious faith produces not soul-agony, but aggressive nihilism.

Annable reveals his life to Cyril among the gothic ruins of a derelict church. Symbolic of lost faith, the church takes its place with other ruins in a decrepit social order whose image would be fixed as a waste land by T. S. Eliot's famous poem eleven years later. In *The White Peacock* there is the run-down estate, the economically disintegrating farm, the 'degraded hall' of Colwick Park, the London slums and the dilapidated shell of the Crystal Palace.[4] The novel struggles with change from the outset, 'musing in old age' (1) on a world beginning to appear unrecognisable. Violet Hunt, in the left-wing *Daily Chronicle,* noted that 'there appears to be no "county" at all, no great families, no squires, hardly even a parson'.[5] There is, however, plenty of infrastructural alteration: the agricultural depression, slum life in Nottingham, 'outcast London', emigration. The volatility is reflected in George's impulsive career in farming, business and politics. Meanwhile, mining capital is entrenched nationally, instead of locally, by the Tempest family, and Leslie moves smoothly into his role as a Tory MP. The social façade of this life – fake pastoral picnics, charity tennis parties 'for the Missionaries, or the unemployed, or something' (18), the company of 'advanced' artists – feebly compensates for Lettie's decline into stoic gloom.

Amidst structural upheaval, Annable's opinions are as uncomfortable as his alien name alongside Cyril, George and Leslie.

> He was a man of one idea: – that all civilisation was the painted fungus of rottenness. He hated any sign of culture. I won his respect one afternoon when he found me trespassing in the woods because I was watching some maggots at work in a dead rabbit. That led us to a discussion of life. He was a thorough materialist – he scorned religion and all mysticism . . . When he thought, he reflected on the decay of mankind – the decline of the human race into folly and weakness and rottenness. 'Be a good animal, true to your animal instinct' was his motto. (146–47)

The ex-parson is now an extreme materialist, but the passage disconcerts for other reasons. It is difficult, for instance, to evaluate the irony loaded into the third and fourth sentences. They begin and end positively – 'I won his respect . . . That led us to a discussion of life' – but are punctuated by maggots munching on a rabbit. The target of the irony is, however, uncertain. Is it Annable's nihilism? Is it Cyril himself, unalert to his own strange absorption in a carcass? Meanings are simply tangled in effects.

Techniques like this are common in Lawrence and were a source of early readers' confusions. But they are also a major source of that intricate valency of attitude, and open responsiveness to complex lives, which Lawrence treasured in the novel as a modern form. Asked about Annable by a shocked Jessie Chambers (his then girlfriend), his intentions were clear: '"He *has* to be there. Don't you see why? He makes a sort of balance. Otherwise it's too much one thing, too much *me*."'[6] The reply indicates Lawrence's need to polarise his thinking, juxtaposing wavering Cyril against dogmatic game-keeper, refinement against brutality, gentility against poverty, youth against sour maturity.[7] But the unsynthesised dialectic, like the indefinite irony, is without resolution. The deliberate uncertainty embedded in style and structure matches uncertainties about historical and intellectual development in both the author and his characters. For Jessie Chambers, Annable 'seemed to be a focus for all Lawrence's despair over the materialistic view of life he felt compelled to accept for lack of an alternative'.[8] This is a key statement because it establishes the intellectual orbit of the early work. But the issue is not as straightforward as Chambers implies.

Lawrence and nineteenth-century evolutionary argument

For Lawrence's generation the word 'materialism' meant the denial of divine agency in the natural world. Natural processes, materialists believed, occurred as a result of the material properties of nature rather than by supernatural design or intervention.[9] Throughout the nineteenth century, therefore, materialism was a derogatory label fixed by Christians on developments in biology, the bio-medical sciences, psychology and other areas. One result was the familiar schism between science and religion emphasised in the debate on evolutionary theory. This emphasis is, in a sense, misleading because such developments affected sciences other than biology (such as physics and physiology), and because the theory of evolution itself had several very different strands within it which, in Lawrence's lifetime, were not yet ordered by the 'synthesis' of Darwinism and Mendelian genetics.[10] Nonetheless, evolution was perceived to drive a wedge between truth and orthodoxy, humanity and the cosmos. It also altered perceptions of humanity's physical embodiment. For Lawrence's generation, the relations of mind to body, and human to animal, were chronically disturbed, as reflected in the anxieties of his reviewers.

Jessie Chambers recalled Lawrence's encounter with materialistic ideas as traumatic:

> It came in full blast with T. H. Huxley's *Man's Place in Nature*, Darwin's *Origin of Species*, and Haeckel's *Riddle of the Universe*. This rationalistic teaching impressed Lawrence deeply. He came upon it at a time of spiritual fog, when the lights of orthodox religion and morality were proving wholly inadequate, perplexed as he was by his own personal dilemma. My feeling was that he tried to fill up a spiritual vacuum by swallowing materialism at a gulp. But it did not carry him very far. He would tell me with vehemence that nature is red in tooth and claw, with the implication that 'nature' included human nature. Yet . . . his dominant feeling seemed to be a sense of hopelessness.[11]

The recollection is generically familiar with its Tennysonian motifs ('nature . . . red in tooth and claw', 'spiritual fog') and crude choice between 'materialism' and 'orthodox religion' which produces 'hopelessness'. It illustrates the proximity of Lawrence's generation to the great Victorian thinkers (Huxley, for example, had died only in 1895).[12] In *Sons and Lovers*, Paul Morel's development beyond Christianity is gradually and carefully noted. He proceeds through sceptical questioning, mockery and agnosticism ('at the Renan *Vie de Jésus* stage') to an exposed, quasi-existentialist position at the close.[13] The novel is interested in the psychological eddies and scuffles of this development – Paul enjoys tormenting Miriam with his unbelief for instance – but there is no strong sense that the loss of religious belief is, in itself, desolating. Paul's eventual crisis has metaphysical components, but they are not a main cause.

The same was true for Lawrence. Like many, he was eager to find a way to negotiate between materialism and spirituality.[14] He was enthusiastic about William James's book *Pragmatism* in 1907 which, while favouring secular science, tried to respect spiritual needs. In 1909, he wrote to his old botany lecturer, the Unitarian Ernest Smith, that life 'seems to me barbarous, recklessly wasteful and destructive, often hideous and dreadful . . . but on the whole beautiful' (i. 147). This more balanced awareness needs to be read against Jessie Chambers's account because it reflects real, if complex, developments. Unitarian Christianity, with its conviction that matter and spirit were indivisible, helped scientists like Smith out of the impasse, and Lawrence noted Unitarianism's appeal for 'advanced' opinion in *Sons and*

Lovers (p. 301). The problem with some commentary on Lawrence's encounter with evolutionary and materialistic ideas is that it is captured by an 'either-for-it-or-against-it' paradigm. But Lawrence tried to think through available options and refused the revolving door of that classic Victorian stalemate. The characteristically angular, zigzag pattern of his intellectual development negotiated between opposed ideas, and the unsettled forms of his fictions respond to this. The early novels present disorderly stories or effects partly because he explores the limits of models of coherent explanation, beginning with Christianity and moving to evolutionary materialism.

Lawrence grappled with these issues during the composition of *The White Peacock*. His letter of 3 December 1907 to the Congregationalist minister in Eastwood, the Revd Robert Reid, is a formal announcement of doubt. Lawrence writes that he cannot reconcile faith with evidence of God's apparent tolerance of suffering in the slums of Nottingham and London (i. 40). But the case is not only moral or political. Lawrence uses evolutionary terminology to avoid the 'catastrophe' narrative presented later by Jessie Chambers. He describes his position as 'undergoing modification' and conducts an imaginary argument in which Reid suggests that faith is 'belief in a hypothesis that cannot be proved'. Lawrence replies:

> But sir, there must at least be harmony of facts before a hypothesis can be framed. Cosmic harmony there is – a Cosmic God I can therefore believe in. But where is the human harmony, where the balance, the order, the 'indestructibility of matter' in humanity? And where is the *personal, human* God? Men – some – seem to be born and ruthlessly destroyed; the bacteria are created and nurtured on Man, to his horrible suffering. Oh, for a God-idea I must have harmony – unity of design. Such design there may be for the race – but for the individual, the often wretched individual? (i. 41)

The letter develops Lawrence's already powerful wish for exploration through imagined scenes and polarised opinion. His theatrical (but not insincere) response – 'But, sir, there must . . .' – is spoken in character, taking the tone of the great Victorian debates on materialism, and making use of language familiar from scientific discourse, specifically relating to established precepts like the 'indestructibility of matter', and the form of scientific propositions (consistency in the data sustains the validity of hypotheses, for example). Lawrence also makes what was, by that time, a fairly common separation of the human from the cosmological.

By 1900 most advanced opinion agreed that disparate spheres of knowledge (for example cosmology and ethics) need not bind one another to common explanation. There was agreement about this among liberal churchmen and scientific thinkers alike, not least because it keeps opponents apart in their separate domains. But the argument has other advantages. When the materialist Huxley took this position in 'Evolution and Ethics', his influential Romanes lecture in 1893, he illustrated how human values could be extracted from materialistic determinism. Huxley saw ethics in a dependent, but not determined, relation to nature. The strife of the natural world, obeying the mechanisms of survival, was undeniably brutal. But it did not follow that humanity should imitate such ethically inert behaviour. On the contrary, our ability to intervene ethically not only defines our humanity, it gives an evolutionary advantage because ethical behaviour emphasises co-operation rather than predation.[15] Such a position is not without difficulties (the origins and forms of these ethical standards remain unexplained, for instance), but it opens a different line of thinking, one which avoids the ethical void imagined by Jessie Chambers.

Typically, however, Lawrence did not follow this road straightforwardly. The letter to Reid accepts this bifocal thinking, but reverses the evaluations. For Huxley, the natural order is traumatic, the ethical order auspicious. For Lawrence, there may be 'Cosmic harmony', but humanity is caught in chronic confusion and suffering. This partly explains the apparently incoherent disintegration of the human order expressed in the early fiction. His concern is with the chasm that opens between the human and the natural orders, between individual and group, and between experience and the perception of value. Writing to Reid, he calls these 'the great human discrepancies' (i. 41), and it is this aching sense of discrepancy which gives the early novels their characteristic plangency.

'Art and the Individual: A Paper for Socialists' delivered at the Eastwood Debating Society three months later in March 1908 continues the discussion. Characteristically, in the polarising habit of Lawrence's thinking, it puts the opposite case. It argues that aesthetic culture is as important to socialism as the elimination of want. This is argued from an evolutionary perspective. Lawrence claims that evolutionary processes are not traumatic; in fact, they generate an aesthetically and spiritually inspiring sense of fittingness:

> Unconsciously, I think, we appreciate some of the harmony of this mutual adaptability, and that is how aesthetics come to be allied to religion, for they are a recognition . . . of the great underlying purpose which is made visible in this instance, and which it is, perhaps, the artist's duty to seek. This universal Purpose is the germ of the God-Idea. It may be as the plant develops from the germ, it is twisted and clipped into some fantastic Jehovah shape, but –: [the paragraph deliberately breaks off][16]

Evolution reveals a harmony 'twisted and clipped' into distorted shape by religious orthodoxy, but religious feeling is not derided. In fact it harmonises with naturalistic understanding. Lawrence sees art and human culture playing a profound role in evolution because they foster the apprehension of the orderly growth which lies beneath a chaotic, apparently disorderly surface.

Lawrence's sources for this spiritually meaningful form of evolutionary development are a hybrid lot, not all fully absorbed.[17] But it is not a Darwinian vision. Darwinian evolution occurs through chance mutation and the random production of better-adapted forms. There is neither rule, order nor purpose in it. Instead, Lawrence draws upon an alternative theory which had considerable currency at the end of the nineteenth century (though it is now discounted), that associated with the French biologist Jean-Baptiste Lamarck. Lamarck believed that 'acquired characteristics' could be transmitted from generation to generation. This means that characteristics acquired by parents are passed to their offspring. These might be strong arms, or dextrous fingers, or advantageous mental attitudes. Successor generations may develop these 'acquired characteristics' or allow them to decline, but either way the important point is that humans, to some degree, can intervene in the evolutionary sequence which can, therefore, become purposive, orderly and unalienated.

It is not known whether Lawrence read Lamarck, but he found similar ideas in Schopenhauer's essay 'The Metaphysics of [Sexual] Love' (1818) which he read enthusiastically in 1906–07.[18] Schopenhauer took it for granted that '[i]n the child the qualities transmitted by both parents continue to live, fused and united into one being'.[19] Schopenhauer's essay often interests Lawrence scholars because of its unusually strong statement of the role of the sex-drive in human affairs, but it also offers a way of thinking about the relationship between generations:

> What is decided by [the sex drive] is nothing less than the *composition of the next generation* . . . the being, the *existentia*, of these future persons is absolutely conditioned by our sexual impulse in general, so is their nature, their *essentia*, by the individual selection in the satisfaction of the impulse, i.e. by sexual love; and by this it is in every respect irrevocably fixed.[20]

Schopenhauer's sexual-reproductive determinism eventually alienated Lawrence, but his ideas do release an important theme, that '[t]he collected *love affairs* of the present generation, taken together, are accordingly the human race's serious *meditatio compositionis futurae, e qua iterum pendent innumerae generationes* [meditation on the composition of the future generation on which in turn innumerable generations depend]'.[21]

Love choices: *The Trespasser*

The idea that a generation's love choices not only tell their own story but predict the historical sequence gave Lawrence important subject matter, though, like many, he was uncertain how to evaluate its implications. In *Sons and Lovers* it is said of Mrs Morel that 'She still had her high moral sense, inherited from generations of Puritans. It was now a religious instinct' (25). The implication is that sub-cultural habits can become a quasi-biological force (an 'instinct'). In *The Trespasser*, Siegmund's passion for Helena is similarly described: 'The changes in him were deeper, like alteration in his tissue. His new buds came slowly, and were of a fresh type' (93). The emphasis on histological change (tissue alteration), and the use of botanical and biological vocabulary (buds of a fresh type), is very striking.

Equally important, however, is the fact that, in the dramatic action, these ideas are under enquiry. Mrs Morel's Puritan 'instinct' suggests cultural and trans-generational continuity, but it brings her into violent collision with her husband and, in the novel, she is the last of the line. In *The Trespasser*, Siegmund's deep-tissue change is, in fact, illusory. Half a page later Lawrence adds: 'Siegmund looked at her and continued smiling. His happiness was budded firm and secure' (93). The retrospective irony – the relationship is, in fact, radically insecure and Siegmund commits suicide – is a product of an unsignalled use of free indirect speech which now allocates the apparent objectivity of the botanical metaphor to Siegmund's consciousness, withdrawing its authority.

Lawrence tests models of coherent development, predictable growth and secure values. He tests them against a vision of splintering *incoherence* which emphasises lack of continuity, the lonely, often deluded abandonment of individuals, and the evacuation of received values. The action of *The White Peacock*, like that of *The Trespasser*, takes place largely within a single generation whose personnel become dispersed. *Sons and Lovers* examines two generations with similar themes of scattering and disconnection. *The Rainbow* (the next completed novel) covers three. It is as if each book looks further down the family tree to test what slow pattern might be found. In the first three novels, the chaotic record of the love choices, and the shortened historical perspective, obscure the signs that predict the future. *The White Peacock* is full of children, but there is an ominous sense of historical impasse.

Ancestral ghosts, however, haunt the present. The Saxton family in *The White Peacock* feel this strongly:

'You do see yourself a bit ghostish –' said [George], 'on a background of your ancestors. I always think when you stop in an old place like this you sort of keep company with your ancestors too much; I sometimes feel like a bit of the old building walking about; the old feelings of the old folks stick to you like the lichens on the walls.' (200)

His father agrees – '"That's why I'm going to Canada"' – and adds: '"you stay in one place, generation after generation, and . . . keep on thinking and feeling the same, year after year, till we've only got one side"' (201). The conspicuous reversal here – the living are as thin as ghosts and reified as one side of a wall – expresses an anxiety that transmitted values are deadly. The weight of absent generations bears heavily in *The White Peacock*, emerging in ghostly ruins and insubstantial identities. 'I myself seem to have lost my substance,' remarks Cyril, 'to have become detached from concrete things . . . Onward, always onward, not knowing where, or why' (83). Feelings of personal emptiness and inhibition are widely distributed. They are accounted for by Lettie. '"I've been brought up to expect it"', she explains to George, '"– everybody expected it – and you're bound to do what people expect you to do – you can't help it. We can't help ourselves, we're all chessmen"' (120). This is the other side of Annable's brutalist materialism. Annable declares 'be a good animal'; Lettie declares 'be a good social cipher'. Annable spurns humanistic values, but others are imprisoned by their social and behavioural inheritance. *The White Peacock* deploys its inconclusive argument around this uncongenial choice.

The second novel, *The Trespasser*, dramatises what became major Lawrencean themes, including the need to seek release from inhibiting social obligations, the discovery of personal authenticity through sexual passion and an energising vision of the sexual body which avoids Annable's gross reduction. The novel is a philosophical melodrama in which potential growth (described as a vitalistic urge) collides with ensnaring circumstance. This was a popular theme (in E. M. Forster, for instance), but the distinctiveness of *The Trespasser* lies in the complications in both perspective and analysis introduced into the narrative. The lovers appear united, but are quickly divided by their natures. Lawrence examines a collision between old and emergent forms of being, but refuses to sentimentalise their defeat into sad romantic tragedy.

On holiday on the Isle of Wight, the lovers try to live outside time: '"There is *no* next week", she declared . . . "There is only the present"'; 'he wanted to . . . blaze up all his past and future in a passion worth years of living' (58–59). But what calls Siegmund, particularly, back into time are his obligations to his children. Meanwhile, off Spithead, battleships cruise through heavily defended waters, fronting rival European nationalisms during a visit by the Czar. They act as reminders of social time. Helena and Siegmund temporarily choose to be isolated from family and community. But children and warships, personal and social time, press them towards defeat.

This, however, is by no means all the story. Siegmund's brain is in traumatic disorder throughout: 'Thoughts came up in his brain like bubbles, random, hissing out aimlessly. Once, in the startling inflammability of his blood, his veins ran hot, and he smiled' (66). A grotesque simile is disconcertingly capped by a smile. It is one of many heavily materialised images used to describe Siegmund's and Helena's mental and emotional states. These are of various kinds: histological change (as we have seen), bodily wounds, the swarming of insects, the fertilisation of seeds, the running of machines and the smelting of metals.[22] The inconsistency of the group seems deliberate. It suggests the precarious uncertainty of their condition, but the images also subvert conventional descriptions of thought and the expected attributes of mind and body. Thus, blood possesses consciousness (p. 63). Or, when images are drawn from natural history, they do not suggest classifiable behaviour as they do when used by George Eliot, for instance. Instead, they have a rather ugly function, degrading individual significance or disempowering the human will (for an example, see pp. 165–66).

Such images make one uneasy. Is this description of Helena's transported state intended to be attractive or not? 'It seemed to her as if all the lightness of her fancy and her hope were being burned away in this tremendous furnace, leaving her, Helena, like a heavy piece of slag seamed with metal. She tried to imagine herself resuming the old activities, the old manner of living' (119). The passage is obviously thematically pertinent, but the image 'slag seamed with metal' is disconcerting. It shows a modernist appetite for defamiliarising the rhetorics of interior life, but this only partially accounts for it. Comparing states of feeling to industrial smelting certainly avoids stereotype, but the metaphor also implies that mind-states are dramatically material rather than spiritual, and that they have multiple products, including waste. Processes of refinement produce ashes and slag, and this doubleness is essential to Lawrence.

Such rhetoric has complicated effects. As early reviewers discovered, it unsettles. But, in a distinctive and original way, it joins contemporary debates about materialism in life processes. These images press their heavy substance, but they are also flauntingly metaphorical and encourage imaginative exploration of their conceptual implications. This impressed one early reader who exclaimed over the 'wonderful interfusion' of 'physiology, psychology, and splendid poetry' in *Sons and Lovers*.[23] Like these images, the mind in Lawrence's work is neither exclusively physical process nor autonomous consciousness. Just as his revisionary and dramatising intelligence works between polarised issues, the images negotiate implications without simplifying reduction.

In 'Study of Thomas Hardy', written from September 1914, Lawrence argued that 'generations of ultra-Christian training', producing a de-eroticised and patriarchal culture, explain Angel Clare's failure to cope 'when he finds that [Tess] has, in his words, been defiled' in *Tess of the d'Urbervilles*. Angel's hysteria, for Lawrence, is symptomatic of an epochal crisis which also includes

> the great scientists and thinkers of the last generation, even Darwin and Spencer and Huxley. For these last conceived of evolution, of one spirit or principle starting at the far end of time, and lonelily [*sic*] traversing Time. But there is not one principle, there are two, travelling always to meet, each step of each one lessening the distance between the two of them. And Space, which so frightened Herbert Spencer, is as a Bride to us. And the cry of Man does not ring out into the Void. It rings out to Woman, whom we know not. [24]

It was shrewd of Lawrence to note the masculine bias of nineteenth-century science.[25] But his main criticism of evolutionary materialism is not only that it is womanless and sexless, but that it lacks dialectical exchange. His vision of biological development is curiously abstract (and is written in a distinctively religious register), but he is imagining a complex, polarised interaction which is, above all, unfinished. He rejects reductions of human origins and development to a limited causality, and his career as a novelist, despite his dogmatic outbursts, is committed to this kind of multi-aspected, exploratory understanding.

So Helena is both slag and metal and the divided qualities of both lovers prevent *The Trespasser* becoming sentimental. Their relationship grows increasingly awkward and divided as the novel develops. Lawrence renders this by swift alterations of point of view and use of free indirect speech. The narrative dissolves into their separate, limited consciousnesses, most clearly when episodic chapters (17–19, for example) switch rapidly from one to the other to reveal, without commentary, the detached imagined worlds of their relationship. It is this that provides the literary energy of the novel.

Desire is solipsistic in *The Trespasser*. Helena, like Miriam in *Sons and Lovers*, wants a romantic lover: 'It was a gay, handsome boy she had to meet, not a man strange and insistent' (74). But, if she is troubled by grown-up desire, Siegmund's hopes of erotic translation are, in their way, equally dreamy: 'His dream was melted in his blood, and his blood ran bright for her. His dreams were the flowers of his blood' (64). Their separate, eventually conflicting, mental planes collude in fantasy. Helena is the 'Dreaming Woman' (p. 64), but it is Siegmund who 'awoke with wonder in the morning. "It is like the magic tales," he thought, as he realised where he was, "and I am transported to a new life, to realise my dream. Fairy tales are true after all"' (72). Torn between past and present, routine and potential selves, mind and body, duty and desire, social responsibility and fantasy, the lovers, like the characters in *The White Peacock*, have no clear vision of their aspirations.

Sons and Lovers: point of view and the unconscious

The manipulation of point of view and free indirect speech to expose the predicament of the isolated individual is also central to the narrative method of *Sons and Lovers*. It is used there with an assurance and precision only intermittently equalled in earlier work, as in this episode when Paul searches for his first job:

> And then, at ten o'clock, he set off. He was supposed to be a queer, quiet child. Going up the sunny street of the little town, he felt as if all the folk he met said to themselves: 'He's going to the Co-op Reading Room to look in the papers for a place. He can't get a job. I suppose he's living on his mother.' Then he crept up the stone stairs behind the drapery shop at the Co-op, and peeped in the reading room. Usually one or two men were there, either old useless fellows, or colliers 'on the club'. So he entered, full of shrinking and suffering when they looked up, seated himself at the table, and pretended to scan the news. He knew they would think, 'What does a lad of thirteen want in a reading room, with a newspaper', and he suffered.
>
> Then he looked wistfully out of the window. Already he was a prisoner of industrialism. Large sunflowers stared over the old red wall of the garden opposite, looking in their jolly way down on the women who were hurrying with something for dinner. The valley was full of corn, brightening in the sun. Two collieries, among the fields, waved their small white plumes of steam. Far-off on the hills were the woods of Aldersley, dark and fascinating. Already his heart went down. He was being taken into bondage. His freedom in the beloved home valley, was going now.
>
> The brewer's wagons came rolling up from Keston, with enormous barrels, four a side, like beans in a burst bean pod. The wagoner, throned aloft, rolling massively in his seat, was not so much below Paul's eye. The man's hair, on his small, bullet head, was bleached almost white by the sun, and on his thick red arms, rocking idly on his sack apron, the white hairs glistened. His red face shone and was almost asleep with sunshine. The horses, handsome and brown, went on by themselves, looking by far the masters of the show.
>
> Paul wished he were stupid. 'I wish', he thought to himself, 'I was fat like him, and like a dog in the sun. I wish I was a pig, and a brewer's wagoner.'
>
> (114–15)

Dense, lulling detail carries a passage like this, so much so that one only slowly becomes aware of the distinct point of view. But the consciousness embedded there is clearly Paul's rather than that of some impersonal

observer. The dogged procession of dispiriting detail and the anxious awareness of others follows the course of his mind. The self-pitying wistfulness and
anger is his too, as well as the painter's eye looking through the window to
observe the landscape as though it were a stylised picture of sunflowers, old
walls, corn fields and distant labour in which even colliery chimneys look
pretty and wave their steam like feathers. (The picturesque conventionality
makes a point about Paul's callowness.) There is no formal marking of this
transfer of voice and perspective; the point of view is simply and delicately
shifted around the mind of the precocious thirteen-year-old as decisively as
the baby-language of the opening page of Joyce's *Portrait of the Artist as a
Young Man* creates the consciousness of the infant Stephen Dedalus.

Sons and Lovers has been discussed before in these terms (most originally
by Louis Martz in his path-breaking essay 'A Portrait of Miriam'[26]), but the
temptation has always been to limit the novel's use of these techniques. In
fact they are permanent features of the style to which readers need to be consistently alert. But this is more than a technical achievement. These techniques are central to the novel's concerns, not least because they convey
complexity and avoid summative judgement. The passage describes Paul's
adolescent alienation from his community. But it also indicates the degree to
which he has internalised versions of many of its values. Thus his self-image
is poor when he sees himself through others' eyes (he thinks his masculinity
is compromised by 'living on his mother'). Though the passage opposes the
world of work to the world of art, the stylised nostalgia of Paul's vision com-
promises its preferential claims and suggests, in part, that art's value for Paul
lies in escape and imaginative mastery, a mechanism through which he might
feel not only released but superior. Like the sunflowers, he can look down
on those in whose presence he feels ashamed. Paul is squeezed between
native and aspirant cultures and so the episode ends in aggressive self-
loathing. Like Annable, he wishes himself an animal, a dog or a pig – but
also a wagoner. The shocking thing is that he sees the last as equivalent to
the first two.

The internalisation of the attitudes of others through the skilful manipulation of point-of-view and free indirect speech produces a subtle account of
how identity is formed interpersonally. This is a major concern. It is a development from the solipsistic self-absorption with which *The Trespasser* deals,
and beyond the boundaries of ethical and metaphysical enquiry set by the
debate over scientific materialism. *Sons and Lovers* continues to be concerned, very urgently, with the relations of mind and body and issues of sub-
social and impersonal determination, but an additional, thickly described
layer has been added. The novel is consistently attentive to psychological
conditioning through the interrelation of personalities, not least, of course,

in the relationship between Mrs Morel and her sons. Its dynamics include (as between Paul and Miriam) the interplay of desire and aggression, the adoption of postures of domination and deference, and the way in which potentially protean selves are reduced to smaller, more defensive entities.

One example concerns an aspect of the novel brought more vividly to light by the restoration of Lawrence's original text in the Cambridge edition. Among other material cancelled by Edward Garnett's editorial work on the original version of *Sons and Lovers* were substantial passages relating to Paul's elder brother William. This produced a more focused narrative and reduced the book's length, but unintentionally the patterns in the family dynamics are blurred. A two-page passage omitted from chapter 3, for instance, describes William attending a fancy-dress ball. He looks fine in his costume, but Mrs Morel disapproves for complex reasons. She has a compulsion to control a son growing up, jealousy of his girlfriends, fear that he might go 'the same way as his father' and a snobbery that the ball is held in 'a low town'. William attends the ball nevertheless, and enjoys himself, but '[h]e never knew how disappointed he was. The excitement of the moment, and of anticipation, was enough to carry him through the present. But all his hurt pride was built upon *her* seeing him. And afterwards, it always hurt him to think back on this ball' (76). There are several key issues here. There is William's need to project an image that his mother will approve of and authenticate; there is an account of the way pleasure turns to retrospective pain because that authentication is withheld; there is her manipulation of the situation. But above all there is the key point that all this develops *unconsciously*. William is not even aware of his own disappointment.

The subtlety of Lawrence's analysis is very telling, and over subsequent pages he builds a picture of the emotional structuration of William's personality through complex interpersonal interactions. Lawrence's images for this process are of grain-by-grain sedimentation, and the adding of small amounts to a mixture. It is a process described with great delicacy (as later for Paul) and it is important not to reduce or simplify what is happening as do cruder versions of psychoanalytic commentary. The formation of unconscious mental structures is exactly the issue, but Lawrence himself seems to me right to sense that psychoanalysis, like materialist determinism, is at best half a story. He resented Alfred Kuttner's early seizure of the book for psychoanalytic case-law and complained to a friend that '"complexes" are vicious half-statements . . . When you've said Mutter-complex, you've said nothing – no more than if you've called hysteria a nervous disease. Hysteria isn't nerves, a complex is not simply a sex relation: far from it. – My poor book: it was, as art, a fairly complete truth: so they carve a half-lie out of it, and say "Voilà". Swine!'[27]

As Fiona Becket's chapter elsewhere in this volume indicates, Lawrence's psychological modernity does not consist of fellow-travelling with Freud, though their coincidence in intellectual history is of serious significance. The unconscious in *Sons and Lovers* is a complex and delicately formed structure derived from multiple sources including an embattled sexuality. But the novel is open and exploratory in its account of this formation. Indeed, the very word 'psychological' (widely used by early reviewers of *Sons and Lovers*[28]) usually suggested in this period not psychoanalysis, but materialist psychology in the nineteenth-century tradition. William James used it this way in *Pragmatism*, the book that influenced Lawrence strongly in 1907, and Lawrence's sister Emily shared the association, though she valued it negatively, deploring her brother's 'psychological set at the University, who ridiculed religion'.[29] In trying to understand Lawrence's distinctive achievement in the early work it is to this context that we should turn as readily as to other more familiar ground as he negotiated new, complex forms and ideas in a period of intellectual and personal transition.

NOTES

1 See the reviews collected in *D. H. Lawrence: The Critical Heritage*, ed. R. P. Draper (London: Routledge, 1970).
2 Unsigned review, *Daily News*, 14 February 1911. Reprinted in *Critical Heritage*, p. 40.
3 *Critical Heritage*, p. 37.
4 *WP*, 247 (Colwick Hall), 260–61 (Crystal Palace).
5 *Daily Chronicle*, 10 February 1911. Reprinted in *Critical Heritage*, p. 38.
6 'E. T.' [Jessie Chambers], *D. H. Lawrence: A Personal Record*, ed. J. D. Chambers (London: Frank Cass, 1965), p. 117.
7 For discussion of the 'polarised' nature of Lawrence's thinking see Robert E. Montgomery, *The Visionary D. H. Lawrence: Beyond Philosophy and Art* (Cambridge: Cambridge University Press, 1994), but other critics also recognise its centrality. An important discussion of the general area is Michael Bell's *D. H. Lawrence: Language into Being* (Cambridge: Cambridge University Press, 1991).
8 [Chambers], *Personal Record*, p. 117.
9 William James's definition is helpful in a book that influenced Lawrence considerably in 1907: materialism is 'in the widest sense, explaining higher things by lower ones, and leaving the destinies of the world at the mercy of its blinder parts and forces. It is in this wider sense of the word that materialism is opposed to spiritualism or theism': *Pragmatism, A New Name for Some Old Ways of Thinking: Popular Lectures on Philosophy* (London: Longmans, Green, & Co., 1907), p. 93.
10 The literature on developments in evolutionary theory in the period is, of course, extensive but Peter J. Bowler, *Theories of Human Evolution: A Century of Debate, 1844–1944* (London: Johns Hopkins University Press, 1986), Robert J. Richards, *The Meaning of Evolution: The Morphological Construction and*

Ideological Reconstruction of Darwin's Theory (London: University of Chicago Press, 1992) and Robert M. Young, *Darwin's Metaphor: Nature's Place in Victorian Culture* (Cambridge: Cambridge University Press, 1985) are more than helpful.

11 [Chambers], *Personal Record*, p. 112.

12 John Worthen describes this milieu in Eastwood in his excellent biography: 'The process of questioning had begun almost a century earlier; but Lawrence was one of those people who came to consciousness in the earlier twentieth century with their Christian faith still untroubled. Religion in Eastwood's chapels was still an unassailable fact of life, its faith unquestioned and often unquestioning': *EY*, 173.

13 *SL*, 230, 256, 263, 267, 298–99, 314.

14 Useful commentary on Lawrence's interest in materialism includes Roger Ebbatson, 'The Spark Beneath the Wheel: Lawrence and Evolutionary Thought', and Christopher Heywood, '"Blood-Consciousness" and the Pioneers of the Reflex and Ganglionic Systems', both in *D. H. Lawrence: New Studies*, ed. Heywood (London: Macmillan, 1987), pp. 90–103, 104–23; Montgomery, *Visionary D. H. Lawrence*; Daniel J. Schneider, *The Consciousness of D. H. Lawrence: An Intellectual Biography* (Lawrence, KS.: University Press of Kansas, 1986); and *EY*, esp. ch. 7.

15 T. H. Huxley, 'Prolegomena' and 'Evolution and Ethics', in *Collected Essays*, 9 vols. (London: Macmillan, 1893–94), IX. 1–116.

16 Lawrence, 'Art and the Individual: A Paper for Socialists', in *Hardy*, 133–42 (p. 138).

17 See *Hardy*, xli–xlii, 271–75.

18 For commentary on Lawrence's reading in Schopenhauer see Bell, *Language into Being*; Montgomery, *Visionary D. H. Lawrence*; Schneider, *Consciousness of D. H. Lawrence* (note 14); and Allan R. Zoll, 'Vitalism and the Metaphysics of Love: D. H. Lawrence and Schopenhauer', *D. H. Lawrence Review*, 11 (1978), 1–20. For Schopenhauer's general influence see John A. Lester, *Journey Through Despair 1880–1914* (Princeton, NJ: Princeton University Press, 1968).

19 Arthur Schopenhauer, 'The Metaphysics of Sexual Love', in *The World as Will and Representation*, trans. E. F. J. Payne, 2 vols. (New York: Dover, 1966), II. 536.

20 Ibid., p. 534.

21 Ibid.

22 For examples see ibid., 162, 159, 165–66, 93 and 198–99 respectively. An example of the last type is discussed below.

23 Unsigned review in *Nation*, 12 July 1913. Reprinted in *Critical Heritage*, p. 70.

24 *Hardy*, 98.

25 For discussion see Evelleen Richards, 'Redrawing the Boundaries: Darwinian Science and Victorian Women Intellectuals', in *Victorian Science in Context*, ed. Bernard Lightman (London: University of Chicago Press, 1997), pp. 119–42; Adrian Desmond, *Huxley: Evolution's High Priest* (London: Michael Joseph, 1997).

26 Louis L. Martz, 'A Portrait of Miriam: A Study in the Design of *Sons and Lovers*' (1968). Reprinted in *Sons and Lovers: A New Casebook*, ed. Rick Rylance (London: Macmillan, 1996), pp. 49–73.

27 Lawrence to Barbara Low, 16 December 1916 (ii, 655). Alfred Kuttner's article – '*Sons and Lovers*: A Freudian Appreciation' – appeared in *Psychoanalytic Review* in 1916. It is reprinted in *D. H. Lawrence, Sons and Lovers: A Casebook*, ed. Gãmini Salgãdo (London: Macmillan, 1969).

28 See the reviews collected in *Critical Heritage,* pp. 58–80, and Helen and Carl Baron, 'Introduction' to *SL*, lxiii–lxxi.

29 For William James see *Pragmatism*, especially Lecture II 'What Pragmatism Means', where he distinguishes the study of psychology from rationalist philosophy. For Emily Lawrence see *EY*, 178.

2

MARIANNA TORGOVNICK

Narrating sexuality: *The Rainbow*

'The Lawrence problem'

It seems that everyone, or everyone of a certain age at least, has had experience of Lawrence. For many, their first experience of Lawrence comes in adolescence or early adulthood, in a setting fraught by the most personal of questions. Who am I, sexually speaking? What am I in the cosmic scheme of things? Lawrence's books ask such questions and often pose extremes as answers. So that everyone feels the need, at the outset, either to like him or to dislike him. There are other writers who produce a similar effect (one thinks, for example, of Lawrence's contemporaries, T. S. Eliot and Ezra Pound), but there are many more who do not. For we are talking, clearly, about more than just a literary judgement, though it may be partly that. We are talking about a judgement of the man, or rather of the man's effect on our life, and of a reaction that is almost visceral.

Although I am very far from being a single-author critic, I have been writing about Lawrence for most of my career, albeit always within larger contexts, such as primitivism. The fact that I have never been entirely free of Lawrence worries me a little, because critics, like readers, have a hard time maintaining distance from Lawrence: they feel compelled either to like or to dislike him, viscerally. Kate Millett, for example, in her landmark book *Sexual Politics* (1970) expressed a certain justifiable animus towards Lawrence – one it was easy to contextualise in the 1970s as feminist and, later on, as lesbian activist as well. But Millett's hostility is relatively unusual in criticism, even recent criticism, of Lawrence's works. The more usual tendency of Lawrence critics is to get caught up inside the author's theories and to judge experience in their terms. In fact, until very recently, reading Lawrence criticism sometimes felt like being caught in a time warp: when compared with criticism of other modern authors, there were relatively few references to theorists such as Foucault, Lacan or Bakhtin, and some critics wrote as though post-structuralism and feminism had never happened or were terrible mistakes. The tendency to admire Lawrence and to defend what is often termed 'the Lawrencean ideal', prevails even today, when many of Lawrence's sexual beliefs have long been thoroughly discredited.

My purpose in making these points is not at all to quarrel with any single critic, for there are many who read Lawrence in this way. Instead, my purpose is to show how hard it is to talk about Lawrencean themes such as marriage or sexuality without seeming to be Lawrence's partisan, anxiously measuring oneself and others against 'the Lawrencean ideal' – a phrase I quite deliberately surround by quotation marks. So, to take a random example, the critic Peter Balbert in an essay from an influential volume of Lawrence criticism, notes that, in its views of marriage, '*The Rainbow* is a testament to the conservative impulse in Lawrence that is at the heart of his apocalyptic doctrines.'[1] He is referring here to Lawrence's belief in monogamous marriage, and, as a conscientious critic, he is careful to use terms which suggest that certain views are Lawrence's, not the critic's own, or to suggest that such views are more generally espoused by the novel rather than by this particular reader. Nonetheless, Balbert has a great deal of trouble maintaining his distance from Lawrence's views.[2] So much so, that his essay ends with an unglossed citation from Lawrence's letters, in a way which suggests a far simpler and more laudatory perspective on Lawrence's relationship to marriage than the one with which the essay began. The citation is from a well-known letter Lawrence wrote to Frieda Weekley shortly after their elopement in 1912. Lawrence was writing to Frieda while she was briefly travelling in Germany and he was briefly lodged in Italy:

> Can't you feel how certainly I love you and how certainly we shall be married . . . Do you know, like the old knights, I seem to want a certain time to prepare myself – a sort of vigil with myself. Because it is a great thing for me to marry you, not a quick, passionate coming together. I know in my heart 'here's my marriage'.
> (i. 403)

The really fetching quality of the last sentence – 'I know in my heart "here's my marriage"' – makes the quotation function as a kind of cross-court shot, especially unglossed, and especially coming, as it does, right at the end of Balbert's essay. When all is said and done, the quotation implies, Lawrence was devoted to the ideal of monogamous marriage – just like most of his aspiring or happily married readers. But there are more than a few problems, of the simplest kind, in deploying the quotation, or similar ones, in this way.

Lawrence *was* ultimately devoted to his marriage, as was the three-times-married Frieda Weekley Lawrence Ravagli, in her fashion. But what do such statements mean, briefly given? Not much. In fact, when Lawrence wrote the letter I have just cited, he was in the act of coercing Frieda Weekley to become his wife, an act which was to have lifelong and dramatic consequences for them both insofar as the huge differences between them were a virtual guarantee of the trials and tribulations in male–female relationships recorded in Lawrence's fiction. In one of the most spectacular love letters ever sent to one's lover's husband, Lawrence notified Ernest Weekley of Frieda's adultery, calling her a 'giantess' whose nature, like that of all women, 'will break through everything' (i. 392). Yet the evidence suggests that Frieda wished to preserve the secret of her affair with Lawrence until she could figure out a way to retain custody of her three children – so that the letter, which was sent, apparently, without Frieda's knowledge or permission, forced her hand.[3] What is more, in the 'here's my marriage' letter, Lawrence was steadfastly ignoring Frieda's not-so-subtle hints that even if he wanted a monogamous marriage, like a knight of old, she did not – if, indeed, she wanted to marry again at all. Even as Lawrence wrote, Frieda was entertaining a new lover and her hints to him about this possibility were the occasion for his letter.[4] Lawrence's firm insistence in this letter upon a certain ideal of marriage is significant. But its significance can only be understood in the context of its being written to a woman who he knew had a different understanding of the married state from his own and who gave fair warning of that fact. Indeed, one might note the egoism of this letter, whose theme words are *with myself* and *for me*, and its relative indifference to Frieda's thoughts and feelings. A similar egoism appears in Lawrence's decisive letter to Ernest Weekley, which is arguably more about Lawrence's needs than Frieda's.

Lawrence's relationship with Frieda was, to say the very least, complicated. It included numerous psychological infidelities (with men such as John Middleton Murry and 'spiritual brides' such as H.D.), the occasional spousal beating, and fairly consistent sexual incompatibility which became complete after Lawrence became impotent with the full onset of active TB in the mid-1920s.[5] The relationship also included numerous sexual infidelities on Frieda's part and at least two possible physical infidelities on Lawrence's part (with William Henry Hocking in Cornwall and Rosalind Baynes in Florence) – infidelities with which neither partner felt comfortable or easy.[6] Many critics would like an author who projects strong sexual and marital ideals to have lived idyllically himself. That desire is understandable, but untenable in Lawrence's case. Still, it is hard for critics who admire Lawrence to write without affirming 'the Lawrencean ideal'. When they find that the ideal never really existed, they persistently invent it.

What Lawrence really represents for critics, I think, is not so much 'the Lawrencean ideal' as 'the Lawrence problem'. Few authors have had more effect on how people in our century think about male–female relationships, male–male relationships, sex and marriage than Lawrence. (The poet Philip Larkin quipped that the sexual revolution began 'Between the end of the Chatterley ban / And the Beatles' first LP', and there is at least something to be said for that.)[7] Yet few authors have been as heavy-handed as Lawrence sometimes is in the act of writing about sex, not to mention the unwitting comedy of some of his descriptions.

The 'Lawrence problem', then, is how to write about Lawrence in a way which acknowledges his power and his vibrancy when addressing the issues of sex and marriage, without surrendering one's sense that he was not just a deeply flawed writer but also a deeply flawed guide to experience. There are as many solutions to this problem as there are writers and writings. As this opening portion of the chapter may suggest, one that I have recently explored is that of thinking of Lawrence as one half of a couple and considering not just Lawrence's side of the story, but Frieda's. I have been spending a good deal of time with Frieda Lawrence and inhabiting, at times, her point of view.

But in the remainder of the chapter, I would like to explore some alternative solutions to 'the Lawrence problem'. First, I would like to examine some passages from *The Rainbow* to show how Lawrence writes about sex. Then I would like to glance, very briefly, at a few of the models for such writing available in Lawrence's time. My argument will be that Lawrence's claim to greatness – a claim which was not without its risks, and its failures – was his willingness to *narrate* sex rather than simply to evade it or to reduce it to a series of mechanical, repeatable or quantifiable actions.

The Rainbow

The Rainbow was written between 1913 and 1915 and was first intended to be part of the same novel as *Women in Love*. The book-in-progress started out as 'The Sisters' in 1913, becoming 'The Wedding Ring' in 1914. Then in 1915 *The Rainbow* as we know it separated from what would become *Women in Love* and was published in September of that year. By the end of October it had been suppressed on charges of obscenity and a month later it was banned. Its relatively early date places it in what I see to be the first phase of Lawrence's career, which is marked by the kinds of idyllic claims for male–female relationships and the married state that many Lawrence critics have stressed. Biographically speaking, this period was dominated by Lawrence's avid seeking of a wife, whom he found in Frieda Weekley, and by his attempt to perfect his relationship with her. *Women in Love*, finished in 1916 (though not published until 1920), marks the end of this early phase;

in it, a certain assertiveness about sexuality has replaced the open-hearted explorations of *The Rainbow*. Biographically speaking, these years correspond to what Lawrence calls 'the bitterness of war' and to the sensation of being a marked man (an issue discussed more fully by Hugh Stevens in chapter 3 of this volume). What I would characterise as the middle phase of Lawrence's career, from *Aaron's Rod* (1922) to *The Plumed Serpent* (1926), is more frankly suspicious of, and even hostile towards, women; many of the works of this period are more fully exploratory of male–male themes. Biographically speaking, this phase corresponds to Lawrence's distress and disillusionment after the First World War and to a period when Lawrence and Frieda were in trouble as a couple, and, I believe, actively considering whether they should, or should not, remain together. The late phase, which includes *The Virgin and the Gipsy* (written in 1926), *Lady Chatterley's Lover* (1928) and 'The Man Who Died' (first published as *The Escaped Cock*, 1928–29), is concerned not just with the graphic representation of sexuality (a misreading fostered by the notoriety of *Lady Chatterley's Lover*) but also with tenderness and surrender as the ultimate meaning of sexuality. Biographically speaking, it was marked by the need to confront illness and death.

Because *The Rainbow* is less hostile towards women than much of Lawrence's later work, it has remained one of the few Lawrence texts feminist critics admire, though that is not the reason for my interest in it here. My interest centres on the way in which sex is *narrated* in *The Rainbow*, though much of what I say here is also applicable to texts which are more overtly concerned with sex and sexuality, such as *Lady Chatterley's Lover*. In fact, I would argue, there is ultimately more connection between sexuality in *The Rainbow* and in *Lady Chatterley's Lover* than between *The Rainbow* and *Women in Love*, despite their temporal proximity and the characters the books share. This is not to overlook the many strengths of *Women in Love*. Indeed, that novel supports one of my primary points about Lawrence and sexuality: his innovation and courage. It broaches views of sexuality rarely discussed in fiction before its time: sado-masochism, wild fluctuations in emotions within the love and sex relation, and the awareness and torment of bisexual longings which cannot speak their name. But, although *Women in Love* has some claim to being the greatest of Lawrence's fictions, it falls short in the category I am considering here: that of *narrating* sexuality. Between completion of *The Rainbow* and completion of *Women in Love*, something had hardened in Lawrence. He had become in every way a less flexible man and, more important, he now had an agenda. Linda Ruth Williams entitled her 1993 study of Lawrence *Sex in the Head*, and the metaphor is peculiarly appropriate for many of the sex scenes in *Women in Love*.

Above all, sex in *Women in Love* is not integrated into the texture of experience as it is in *The Rainbow*, and it is this aspect of *The Rainbow* on which I wish to focus.

The first passage from *The Rainbow* I would like to examine bears direct comparison to *Lady Chatterley's Lover*. The passage occurs early in the marriage of Will and Anna Brangwen and describes a post-coital interlude during one morning of their honeymoon:

> It was so sweet and satisfying lying there talking desultorily with her . . . One day, he was a bachelor, living with the world. The next day, he was with her, as remote from the world as if the two of them were buried like a seed in darkness. Suddenly, like a chestnut falling out of a burr, he was shed naked and glistening on to a soft, fecund earth, leaving behind him the hard rind of worldly knowledge and experience. He heard it in the hucksters' cries, the noise of carts, the calling of children. And it was like the hard rind, discarded. Inside, in the softness and stillness of the room, was the naked kernel, that palpitated in silent activity, absorbed in reality.
>
> Inside the room was a great steadiness, a core of living eternity . . . here at the centre the great wheel was motionless, centred upon itself . . .
>
> As they lay close together, complete and beyond the touch of time or change, it was as if they were at the very centre of all the slow wheeling of space . . . They found themselves there, and they lay still, in each other's arms; for their moment they were at the heart of eternity, whilst time roared far off, forever far off, towards the rim. (R, 134–35)

The first thing to notice about this passage is something I mentioned rather casually in introducing it. Although there are phrases within the passage (the 'chestnut . . . naked and glistening') which might be read as suggestive of actual intercourse, this is a *post*-coital moment, like many moments in *Lady Chatterley's Lover* and the most striking moments in 'The Man Who Died'. Lawrence is among the first – and still among the rare – writers to focus upon this aspect of lovemaking as part of a continuum. Will, and the narrator, clearly relish the moments which follow intercourse as much as, and sometimes more than, the act itself. In fact, Will and Anna are described as being 'buried like a seed in darkness' – an image Lawrence strongly favoured and uses several times in his novels, always in situations separate from actual intercourse and always to suggest the division between earthly time and eternal time which is the primary burden of this passage. Anna and Will exist at the centre of the circle, in an 'unflawed stillness that was beyond time'. As in several novels by Virginia Woolf (*Mrs Dalloway*, *To the Lighthouse* and *The Waves*, for example), what Lawrence calls 'eternal time' is conceived of as 'reality'; 'social time' is a form of necessary but distracting illusion. The passage uses religious imagery, which could be Christian but also works well in the versions of Eastern religions current in Lawrence's time, such as theosophy.[8]

Will Brangwen is, loosely speaking, the focal point of this portion of the novel, through Lawrence's use of free indirect discourse; by the last paragraph quoted, though, the perceptions belong to both Anna and Will, and the shared quality of the perception is important. Will is a character of intense religious sensibility who is attracted all his life to Christian churches. But the contrast between motion and stillness, temporality and eternity, is also more broadly characteristic of Lawrence himself who, though neither a church-goer nor a believing Christian in adult life, never lost his spiritual temperament. In this passage, as in many others in *Lady Chatterley's Lover* and 'The Man Who Died', Lawrence asserts a spiritual dimension to sexuality: sex in all of these texts gives access to a sense of the eternal.

Such a view exists within many mystical traditions but has become rather alien in our time. 'Cheesy' ('corny', 'embarrassing'), students might call such passages, and I would partly agree. But they are also an interesting and bold attempt to render the ineffable surround of sexuality – those aspects which exceed physicality and often elude representation, literary or otherwise. Despite their frequent references to sex, few sex manuals or movies attempt to capture these more intangible aspects of sexuality. Indeed, relatively few novelists even attempt it. I would compare this passage to certain parts of, say, Vladimir Nabokov's *Lolita* (1955). Nabokov's narrator, Humbert Humbert, freely claims that nymphet love represents the quest for 'aesthetic bliss' and for moments which (as in Keats and Dante) transcend time. Humbert Humbert's assertions are often suspect, but we sense here a real intuition. Lawrence felt the same intuitions and narrates sexuality as both physical and symbolic.

I will turn now to a passage describing a later phase in this relationship, after Will and Anna have been married about eight years and have four children. It takes place after Will tries, half-heartedly and therefore unsuccessfully, to seduce a young woman he has picked up in town, and returns home to Anna. She senses something different about him and reacts immediately:

> He was the sensual male seeking his pleasure, she was the female ready to take hers: but in her own way. A man could turn into a free lance: so then could a woman. She adhered as little as he to the moral world. All that had gone before was nothing to her. She was another woman, under the instance of a strange man . . .
>
> She laughed, and kept him at arm's length, whilst apparently ignoring him. She watched him undress as if he were a stranger. Indeed he was a stranger to her . . .
>
> Strange was his wife to him. It was as if he were a perfect stranger, as if she

were infinitely and essentially strange to him, the other half of the world, the dark half of the moon. She waited for his touch as if he were a marauder who had come in, infinitely unknown and desirable to her. And he began to discover her. He had an inkling of the vastness of the unknown sensual store of delights she was. With a passion of voluptuousness that made him dwell on each tiny beauty in a kind of frenzy of enjoyment, he lit upon her . . .

He was quite ousted from himself, and sensually transported by that which he discovered in her. He was another man revelling over her.   (R, 218)

In contrast to the first passage, this one celebrates the art of foreplay, physical and mental, segueing mid-way into a somewhat mediated description of sex which is nonetheless intensely physical. The passage includes some irritating features which mark it as typically Lawrencean. Has there ever been another writer, for example, who would use words like 'strange' and 'stranger' so often, so repetitiously, without seeking a synonym? There is also a vaguely disapproving tone in this passage, which becomes more explicit as it continues: 'Their children became mere offspring to them', the third-person narrator observes, 'they lived in the darkness and death of their own sexual activities' (219). In such a sentence, one feels the novel becoming too didactic and preachy, asking and answering too simply the question of what is life-affirming and what is not. But still this is a remarkable passage. Like similar episodes in *Lady Chatterley's Lover*, it is keenly aware that each encounter between two people can have a very different emotional surround, a surround which is sometimes consistent with earlier encounters and sometimes dramatically different. The passage moves between Anna and Will as focal points of the narration in order to suggest that compatible fantasies motivate each: his mood is different, and so his body seems different to her; her attitude is different, and so her body exerts a new fascination for him, which is manifested in a fetishistic exploration of each bodily part. The passage is also keenly aware of the fact that intercourse can seem different for a long-established couple – even after they have been married for many years and are the parents of four children. This aspect of Lawrence's narration of sex, as with the first passage I looked at, points to the ineffability of sex and its resistance to codification and representation.

As this part of the novel develops, another aspect of Lawrence's narration of sexuality emerges. That is his awareness that every change in a sexual relationship affects a wide circle of those around it. Having alluded to the couple's four children, the narrator turns directly from the passage I have cited to one of those children, Ursula, and to the impact of her parents' relationship upon her. For Will Brangwen, his new immersion in raw physicality leads to a new way of being in the social world, a world he had ignored in the first years of his marriage. He begins teaching night classes in woodwork. And 'To Ursula, a child of eight, the increase in magic was consider-able . . . to Ursula, everything her father did was magic' (221). Some of the most evocative scenes in *The Rainbow* describe the ripple effect between the hidden sexual lives of two characters and an entire extended family. Or they describe the way that characters exist, within families, at multiple points in time – any one of which can be activated by memory. It would take too long to quote all such moments – for it is in the nature of this ripple effect that it stretches across large tracts of the novel – but I will point to just one sequence which shows Lawrence's awareness that sexuality both changes over time and affects those who are not active participants as it changes.

The sequence follows quite closely on from the passage I have just looked at. Its focus is on Tom Brangwen, Anna's stepfather, although that focus alters as Lawrence traces the widening circle of effects that spills from Anna and Will's sexual union. It begins by identifying a general alteration at the Marsh (the Brangwen family home) after Anna marries: 'So a change in tone came over the Marsh. Tom Brangwen, the father, as he grew older seemed to mature into a gentleman-farmer. His figure lent itself: burly and handsome' (224). But the passage moves, with extreme lability, to Tom's inner feelings as he realises his age; to those of his wife, Lydia; to Tom's eldest son (also named Tom) and a breach between father and son; and then, finally, back to Ursula who finds the young Tom, once he has left the Marsh, 'a romantic, alluring figure' (225). The cascading effects reflect an aspect of *The Rainbow* that has been much praised but not commonly con-nected to this issue of the narration of sexuality: the ability to capture the rhythms of family life. It is this aspect of the novel which, to my mind, dif-ferentiates it so clearly from *Women in Love*. The characters in *Women in Love* are vividly engaged in an attempt to break free of the 'nets' which enfold characters in *The Rainbow*: the nets of custom, family and loyalty between a single man and a single woman. Their attempt to break free shows at every point in the novel's rendering of sex, which has a 'snapshot' effect, one in which sexuality has been detached from the full continuum of life. When compared with *The Rainbow*, many of the sexual encounters in *Women in Love*, but especially those between Gudrun and Gerald, seem abrupt and isolated: they are marked by the absence of foreplay and post-coital glow, the absence of a spiritual dimension, the absence of family context.[9]

The last passage I wish to consider from *The Rainbow* comes from Ursula's half of the novel and describes an encounter with her cousin, Anton Skrebensky. This passage reflects a late revision to the novel, made after Lawrence had encountered the art of the Italian Futurists and was influenced by their imagery, and is among the most famous in *The Rainbow*:

She lay motionless, with wide-open eyes looking at the moon. He came direct to her, without preliminaries. She held him pinned down at the chest, awful. The fight, the struggle for consummation was terrible. It lasted till it was agony to his soul, till he succumbed, till he gave way as if dead, and lay with his face buried partly in her hair partly in the sand . . .

. . . It was a long time before he came to himself. He was aware of an unusual motion of her breast. He looked up. Her face lay like an image in the moonlight, the eyes wide open, rigid. But out of the eyes, slowly, there rolled a tear. (444–45)

For reasons that say as much about us as about Lawrence, this passage might be remembered by many as a typical Lawrencean sex scene. It includes a struggle over orgasm – his and hers, in which the man feels a certain resentment against the woman with her 'fierce, beaked, harpy's kiss' (444). The image of the harpy's beak to describe female sexuality and, most specifically, the female clitoris, carries over into the later Lawrence, where it inflects Mellors's denunciation of his wife, Bertha Coutts, and of women as lesbians in *Lady Chatterley's Lover*. Such images are rightly among those that have caused Lawrence's sex scenes to be denounced as erroneous and harmful. But whilst it might be tempting to read this passage as part of Lawrence's fear of female sexuality, I believe that would be too simple a reading. In the context of the novel, this scene is only the climax, so to speak, of a series of encounters in which Anton and Ursula use sex to skirmish with and control each other. Even in isolation, the scene seems to me to be wholly sympathetic neither to Anton nor to Ursula, both of whom exercise a will to power, and the narrator is at least as sympathetic to Ursula as to Anton. Indeed, Lawrence has already given us numerous reasons why Ursula might find Anton unsatisfying, reasons that may be expressed through sex but are not identical to it. Among those reasons is Anton's affiliation with the Boer War and with British colonial forces in India – and thereby with a whole set of militaristic, exploitative and conventional attitudes. Faced with Ursula's repeated displays of dissatisfaction, Anton finds himself suggesting, as a remedy, their immediate marriage: it is precisely the remedy a man of his background and temperament would suggest. Ursula has no vocabulary to express her needs, even if she fully understood them. But she senses that her acquiescence in sex will signify willingness to marry a colonial officer – and thereby to espouse a great many other things as well.

It is of course crucial that Ursula, in this and other scenes, is given a body and bodily needs. Indeed, both in *The Rainbow* and, more famously, in *Lady Chatterley's Lover*, Lawrence gives women's bodies and women's orgasms both a discernible place and a discernible name. He even attempts, sometimes too broadly, but always quite courageously, to describe the female orgasm – something virtually unmentionable in his time. Kate Millett was right to argue, back in 1970, that Lawrence shared Freud's views on this subject. But she underplayed the extent to which Lawrence is fascinated by women's bodies, and candid about his envy of the ecstasies he attributes to them. In his naming of women's bodily parts and his representation of female orgasm, Lawrence was highly unusual for his time.

Contexts

The words 'Lawrence was unusual' can serve as my hinge into the final part of this chapter. In the limited space that remains, I would like to address the following questions: what were the *usual* ways of representing sexuality when Lawrence wrote? Do those *usual* ways provide a solution to 'the Lawrence problem'? I believe that they do, by enabling us to see what is distinctive about Lawrence's approach without losing sight of its flaws.

The first and most obvious models available to Lawrence for the representation of sexuality were the novels of his own contemporaries. But when one compares Lawrence's treatment of sex with that of other novels of the period, it soon becomes clear to what extent other major novelists evade sex altogether or represent it in very oblique, aestheticised terms. This is perhaps not surprising given the climate of likely censorship. An example comes from Henry James's *The Golden Bowl* (1904):

> 'It's sacred', he said at last.
> 'It's sacred', she breathed back to him. They vowed it, gave it out and took it in, drawn, by their intensity, more closely together. Then of a sudden, through this tightened circle, as at the issue of a narrow strait into the sea beyond, everything broke up, broke down, gave way, melted and mingled. Their lips sought their lips, their pressure their response and their response their pressure; with a violence that had sighed itself the next moment to the longest and deepest of stillnesses they passionately sealed their pledge.[10]

The passage from which this extract is taken does contain hidden depths, including a sense of how sexuality affects and is affected by family dynamics. But its depths are hidden indeed. James represents the lovers' kiss straightforwardly enough – the seeking, pressure and response. But he evades the question of what else – if anything besides 'the longest and deepest of stillnesses' – seals 'their pledge'. Phrases such as 'this tightened circle', 'the issue of a narrow strait' and 'melted and mingled' suggest intercourse. But it all takes place within a highly evasive 'moment'. All in all, one suspects that the mechanics of heterosexual intercourse baffle or elude James in this passage.

A second example comes from Gertrude Stein's 'Melanctha' in *Three Lives* (1909):

> It was not from the men that Melanctha learned her wisdom. It was always Jane Harden herself who was making Melanctha begin to understand . . . Jane grew always fonder of Melanctha. Soon they began to wander, more to be together than to see men and learn their various ways of working. Then they began not to wander, and Melanctha would spend long hours with Jane in her room, sitting at her feet and listening to her stories, and feeling her strength and the power of her affection, and slowly she began to see clear before her one certain way that would be sure to lead to wisdom.
>
> Before the end came, the end of the two years in which Melanctha spent all her time when she was not at school or in her home, with Jane Harden, before these two years were finished, Melanctha had come to see very clear, and she had come to be very certain, what it is that gives the world its wisdom.[11]

Stein is no wallflower in her writing and, later in her career, will celebrate – if only obliquely – woman–woman sex (in, for example, *Tender Buttons* (1914)). This passage from 'Melanctha' also dallies around the issue of lesbian sexuality. It bears comparison to the Winifred episode in Lawrence's *The Rainbow* insofar as both present lesbian experience as a threshold or initiatory experience to heterosexuality. This is an interesting similarity, given that Stein was so much more affirming of lesbianism and homosexuality than Lawrence ever could be, given his ambivalent attraction to men, which remains one of his major blocks in narrating sexuality. But Stein's passage has some blocks of its own. The passage obscures its reference by repetition of – and play on – the word 'knowing', a euphemism that is both Biblical and novelistic. But it is hard, finally, for the reader to *know* what, if anything, ultimately happens in a passage like this one. And its opacity is typical of the various devices novelists evolved to describe sex in a cultural context of reticence and censorship.

The second possible model for Lawence in his own time is pornography. As Steven Marcus and others have shown, pornography was a flourishing industry in Victorian and Edwardian England. Collections like *The Pearl* give a fair example of the texts circulated at this time, which favoured slave girls with masters, pirates with captives, fathers with daughters, deflowerings, and so on. Partners change, but neither the acts nor the vocabulary used to describe the acts change much at all.[12] In his 'Afterword' to *Lolita*, Nabokov suggests that pornography can be distinguished from art because of its dependence on convention and repetition:

> In modern times the term 'pornography' connotes mediocrity, commercialism and certain strict rules of narration . . . in pornographic novels, action has to

be limited to the copulation of clichés. Style, structure, imagery should never distract the reader from his tepid lust. The novel must consist of an alternation of sexual scenes. The passages in between must be reduced to sutures of sense, logical bridges of the simplest design . . . which the reader will probably skip but must know they exist in order not to feel cheated.[13]

Pornography can only capture aspects of sex that are replicated from act to act, and the spaces in between these acts are, Nabokov argues, essentially dead spaces, 'sutures of sense, logical bridges' to be skipped over. Lawrence, on the other hand, as we saw with some of *The Rainbow* passages, represents fantasy and quotidian sexual experience simultaneously – as part of a flux and a continuum – and does so while striving for what escapes replicability, what cannot be fully captured in words, what makes sexuality more than the sum of its parts.

A third possible model for Lawrence in his time would have been sexology, which was a flourishing discipline by 1920, especially in Germany and Austria. Sacher-Masoch's *Venus in Furs* appeared in 1886; Krafft-Ebing published *Psychopathia Sexualis* in 1912 (it appeared in English in 1922). It is possible that Lawrence knew of such work through Frieda, who moved in intellectual and bohemian circles prior to her marriage with Lawrence. Frieda had also had a brief affair with Otto Gross, a renegade psychologist who espoused the cult of the Magna Mater (the Great Mother) which was based on the work of J. J. Bachofen. Bachofen had published a highly influential book entitled *Mutterrecht* ('Matriarchy' or 'Mother Right') in 1861. But Gross took Bachofen's theories in a new direction by recommending (as Bachofen had not) female promiscuity as a way of undermining the modern bourgeois state. In addition, as Fiona Becket discusses in chapter 12 of this volume, Lawrence was familiar with psychoanalytical theorists such as Freud and Jung, and wrote works on the unconscious himself.

The most accessible work of sexology for Lawrence, though, is likely to have been that of Havelock Ellis, the multi-volume *Studies in the Psychology of Sex* (1897–1928). A letter of 1925 indicates that Lawrence had been reading some of Ellis's work (v. 230–31), and there are a few further references to Ellis in the *Letters*. It is hard to tell exactly how much of Ellis Lawrence had actually read, but it is worth describing Ellis's methods briefly, since they reflect methods for discussing sex that were available in Lawrence's lifetime.

One of Ellis's standard methods is the description of animal or insect mating habits as possible analogues to human ones. Whether Lawrence learned this method from Ellis or from other, perhaps much older, sources, Lawrence *does* sometimes use animals or insects to spin miniature sex parables: the hens and chicks in *Lady Chatterley's Lover*, for example (113–15);

the cat, Mino, in *Women in Love* (148–50). But the use of animal analogues is fairly limited in Lawrence's representations of sexuality and even antithetical to his more rounded characterisations.

A second method used by Ellis is the verbatim reproduction of reports by anthropologists or travellers about the sexual habits of so-called 'primitive' peoples. As in Sir James Frazer's *The Golden Bough* (1890–1915), the anthropological narratives often favour macabre or violent episodes: the multiple intercourse which guests inflicted on brides for their first sexual experience; dances followed by sexual licence. These reports – as opposed to the ostensibly neutral presentation of biological data about insects and animals – immediately introduce a prurient element into Ellis's text. Indeed, at such moments, Ellis's sexology resembles Victorian pornography since the narratives he includes are often wildly unsubstantiated and read suspiciously like the stuff of western fantasy.

The anthropological method, too, appears at points – though only at points – in Lawrence's fiction. A novel such as *The Plumed Serpent*, for example, states its racialised theses quite clearly at times. It posits Lawrence's views, derived from theories circulating within his culture, of the fall and rise of races based upon energy and power. Lawrence's fear is specifically the fear that the white race will be supplanted:

> While the white man keeps the impetus of his own proud onward march, the dark races will yield and serve, perforce. But let the white man once have a misgiving about his own leadership, and the dark races will at once attack him, to pull him down into the old gulfs. To engulph him again.
> Which is what is happening. (*PS*, 148)

Perhaps the most spectacular example of the anthropological method is the use of African statues and the whole very odd theory of 'the African way' (in *Women in Love*), where Lawrence writes of 'the long, long African process of purely sensual understanding, knowledge in the mystery of dissolution' and of 'unsealed, sensual, mindless, dreadful mysteries far beyond the phallic cult' (*WL*, 253).

Finally, and perhaps most germanely, Ellis includes narration by individuals who agreed to talk with him, several of them homosexual, and many of them either lesbian or heterosexual women. Their stories of sexual initiation and experience are often (like the primitivist narratives) titillating. In Ellis's *Studies*, though, individual narrations are often made to bear too much weight: for example, Ellis describes how one man discovered his homosexuality as though this were typical of *all* homosexuals, a generalisation the single instance cannot adequately sustain.

Like Ellis, Lawrence sometimes uses his characters as 'types' of the universal male or the universal female: in *The Rainbow*, Ursula functions this way occasionally, and Winifred Inger becomes at times the 'type' of lesbian sexuality, with her 'fine, upright, athletic bearing and her indomitably proud nature' (*R*, 312). But it is the very essence of Lawrence's novelistic form to resist such universalising tendencies. And by and large, Lawrence's characters emerge as particularised, with histories and an emotional surround rather than just a 'typical' sexual history.

What is so striking about sexological writing is the way in which, paradoxically, it is curiously devoid of sex and of any sense of the many variables involved. Even into the 1990s, sexology can be devoid of sex, as the comparatively recent study *Sex in America* will attest.[14] Oddly enough, sexology is often incapable of *narrating* sex, and by 'narration' I mean the ability not just to tell a story and to create characters but also to include the mental components behind any action, to render a complex web of causality and affect, and to render those aspects of a situation which might be captured by mechanical instruments, such as a tape recorder or a camera, as well as those which could not. In this sense of the word 'narration', neither the novels written around the time in which Lawrence wrote, nor pornography, nor sexology could really narrate sex. That, for me, is the solution to why Lawrence is a great writer on the subjects of sex and sexuality, despite his many stylistic flaws and his even more egregious contentual ones. Lawrence investigated sex not just as mechanical, physical action, but as a tissue of thoughts, fantasies and emotions. Lawrence *narrated* sex. Few others have even tried.

NOTES

1 Peter Balbert, '"Logic of the Soul": Prothalmic Pattern in *The Rainbow*', in *D. H. Lawrence: A Centenary Consideration*, ed. Peter Balbert and Phillip Marcus (Ithaca and London: Cornell University Press, 1985).

2 See, for example, p. 59 of the essay, which describes Ursula's education as Birkin's future bride.

3 See *EY*, 383–84.

4 See *EY*, 405; i. 404, 406.

5 See *DG*, 163–64.

6 Biographers differ substantially in their accounts of Lawrence's physical infidelities; not all agree that the relationships with Hocking and Baynes were sexual love affairs. Mark Kinkead-Weekes argues that there was no actual physical relationship with Hocking (*TE*, 379–81) but suggests that there was with Baynes (*TE*, 601–6, 647–50).

7 'Annus Mirabilis', in *High Windows* (London: Faber and Faber, 1974), p. 34.

8 I discuss the influential role of such philosophies in Marianna Torgovnick, *Primitive Passions: Men, Women, and the Quest for Ecstasy* (New York: Knopf, 1997).

9 See for example, *WL*, 344–46, 401–02.

10 *The Golden Bowl* (Oxford: Oxford University Press, 1983), pp. 228–29.

11 *Three Lives* (Harmondsworth: Penguin, 1990), p. 73.

12 Anonymous, *The Pearl: A Journal of Voluptuous Reading / The Underground Magazine of Victorian England* (New York: Grove Press, 1969).

13 Vladimir Nabokov, *Lolita* (1955; Harmondsworth: Penguin, 1980), p. 311.

14 The survey published its results in two forms, popular and scholarly. See Robert T. Michael, John H. Gagnon, Edward O. Laumann and Gina Kolata, *Sex in America: A Definitive Survey* (Boston: Little Brown, 1994); and Edward O. Laumann, John H. Gagnon, Robert T. Michael and Stuart Michaels, *The Sexual Organization of Sexuality: Sexual Practices in the United States* (Chicago: University of Chicago Press, 1994).

3

HUGH STEVENS

Sex and the nation: 'The Prussian Officer' and *Women in Love*

It is not that I care about *other people*: I know that *I* am the English nation – that *I* am the European race – and that which exists ostensibly as the English nation is a falsity, mere cardboard. L'Etat c'est moi.

And I am English, and my Englishness is my very vision. But now I must go away, if my soul is sightless for ever.

– D. H. Lawrence, March and October, 1915[1]

Lawrence's subjection

Quoting Louis XIV, 'L'Etat c'est moi', Lawrence is also echoing Flaubert's celebrated dictum, 'Madame Bovary, c'est moi' – a phrase equating the writer's identity with his writing. In this formulation – a comic delusion of grandeur, of megalomania – Lawrence, his writing and England are a trinity become one.

Yet the writer who claimed to be the English nation and the European race was poorly treated by England's state institutions during the First World War.[2] If Lawrence was England, his wartime experiences show a nation at war with itself. The state restricted the distribution of his writing by banning *The Rainbow* in 1915. This cut Lawrence off from his audience, and his royalties were so reduced that he lived out the war years in poverty. The state restricted his rights of movement, expelling him from Cornwall under suspicion of espionage, and refusing to allow him to leave England. Most traumatically, the state 'pawed', scrutinised and mocked his naked body, a body not fit for military service. Lawrence was examined by military doctors three times. In his letters, and in the chapter of *Kangaroo* entitled 'The Nightmare', Lawrence portrays his treatment by military tribunals as a form of sexual assault.

If these measures were intended to make an obedient disciplinary subject out of Lawrence, they were spectacularly unsuccessful. Rather, his experiences of state authority brought his sense of his own Englishness and his intense identification with the English nation into crisis. In 1919 Lawrence left England, never to return except for brief visits. As Anthony Burgess writes, '[f]rom then on his estrangement was permanent'.[3]

Yet the wounds inflicted by the state *were* acts of subjection. Lawrence *was* subjected by the state, but not in ways the state had intended. Showing a 'contempt for martyrs', Lawrence did not believe in suffering in silence. 'Humanity spits me out, and I spit humanity out', he wrote in 1918 (iii. 281). The wounds inflicted on Lawrence during the war had lasting effects. They were taken into himself. Lawrence, at war with England, is also at war with himself; he has been disciplined and formed by that which he is rejecting. *Women in Love* differentiates between 'a resistance to authority' and 'liberty' (*WL*, 28); Lawrence cannot 'free' himself from England by resisting its authority. Accepted or rejected by England, accepting or rejecting England, he remains marked by England. From the beginning of the war years, we see Lawrence casting himself as an outcast, rejected by a nation which only his nurturing, caring and prophetic voice could save. 'If I have nothing, I will ask people for a piece of bread . . . it is like the prophet in the wilderness', he wrote to Lady Ottoline Morrell in September 1915 (ii. 389).

Lawrence's writing before the war had already figured an opposition between an industrial England and a pastoral, agricultural England. The war intensified this opposition. In Lawrence's eyes, the war was responsible for the passing of an old organic England, which is supplanted by modernity, an England of mechanised, inorganic alienation. In 'The Nightmare', Lawrence figures this passing in terms of gender, in terms of an injury to the English body: the war years are '[a]wful years . . . when the damage was done . . . when the world lost its real manhood' (*K*, 213); 'It was in 1915 the old world ended . . . London . . . perished from being a heart of the world, and became a vortex of broken passions, lusts, hopes, fears, and horrors' (216). This mad 'vortex of broken passions' is associated with 'people going mad about the Zeppelin raids' (216), and (in a subversive statement made by the novel's hero, Somers) the 'trench and machine warfare', which is 'a blasphemy against life itself' (221). Wartime England is portrayed as a totalitarian state – 'a reign of terror, under a set of indecent bullies' – ruled by 'the criminal mob' (212).

Lawrence figures himself as a sacrificial victim, even as he protests that he won't be made into 'a martyr of self-sacrifice' (iii. 286). His thirty-third birthday heralds his impending crucifixion: 'Today is my 33rd birthday – the sacred age. So today once more I receive a notice calling me up for medical reexamination' (iii. 281). The episode in 'The Nightmare' where Lawrence describes this third medical examination is, as Paul Delany notes, 'so saturated with contempt that Lawrence often loses control of the fictional tone and yields to pure rage'.[4] The prose has a frenzied hysterical tone: it proceeds in a breathless staccato rhythm, in which declarative sentences are replaced by mere phrases, and feels like notes for a fuller account which was never written. There is some humour, as when Somers thinks, of two men awaiting examination, that '[n]aked men in their civilised jackets and nothing else make the most heaven-forsaken sight I have ever seen' (252), but this does little to mitigate the overall effect of sinister violence: 'The place was full of an indescribable tone of jeering, gibing shamelessness' (253). The jeering is not just at the experience Somers undergoes, but at the inadequacies of his frail body – Somers's 'thin legs' and 'stalky, ignominious nakedness' make him vulnerable in an 'atmosphere of corrosive derision' (253). The examination is described in terms which might be used to describe a rape: Somers has his genitals examined and prodded by a 'chemist-assistant puppy', and is jeered at when forced to spread his legs so that the 'puppy' can 'look into his anus' (254). This shaming scene is like a trauma, and surfaces as a repressed memory, 'like a volcanic eruption in his consciousness' (259). This trauma has severed Somers from his nation; he is 'loose like a single timber of some wrecked ship, drifting the face of the sea . . . broken apart' (259).

Eros and brownness

How might subjection to a particular nation influence a writer's attitude towards other nations? Lawrence's writing strikingly blends eroticism and racial markings. Lawrence eroticises race, ethnicity and nationality, and fantasies of race, ethnicity and nationality feed into his representations of sex. Accounting for this dual movement – Lawrence's eroticising of race, and his 'racialising' of eros, sex and the body – is necessarily a complex and difficult task.

It is possible to relate Lawrence's idealisation and eroticisation – and, occasionally, his demonisation – of other races and other cultures to his alienation from England during the war. Yet I will be arguing that Lawrence's fascination with racial alterity begins before the war. Lawrence's wartime experiences might be seen as constituting a second, formative, Oedipal crisis in his life – a crisis in his relation to the nation state as father who brutally treated the wayward son, crucified him, marked him out as symbolic and sacrificial victim in order to consolidate its own militaristic, brutalising modernity and the psychotic discourse of modern nationalism. This is very much the story Lawrence himself tells, both in The 'Nightmare' chapter of *Kangaroo* and in his introduction to Maurice Magnus's *Memoirs of the Foreign Legion*, which he wrote in 1922. Here Lawrence claims that violence, hatred and war are deeply embedded in our culture, and that resistance to these forces cannot be straightforward as we are formed by the disease we need to cure: 'we have got to take this putrid spirit to our bosom . . . and cleanse it there'.[5]

In 'The Nightmare', Somers is crucially marked out, formed, subjected by the powers he wants to resist. Made to feel 'a foreigner' in his own land, Somers is yet 'intensely English', even if his 'passion' for England is 'a passion of hatred' (223). The following might be hypothesised: Lawrence's experience of abuse at the hands of state authority was peculiarly intimate, erotic and sexual, and was responsible for his belief that the possibilities of nurture and intimacy in England had been contaminated. During the war his writing portrays human relationships hyperbolically marked by plays of power and subordination, cruelty and violence, which might be seen to mimic his relationship with the English state and with the military. The war years see Lawrence idealising other cultures believed to have a masculinity and organicity England has lost. It seems Lawrence can admit the possibility of homoerotic bonds between men as long as they take place in other cultures. This is evident in the essays on American literature he began during the war. He writes, of *Moby Dick*, that 'Queequeg has opened again the flood-gates of love and human connection in Ishmael', and, discussing Whitman's 'adhesive love', judges it (in what reads like a perverse appropriation of St Paul's reasoning, in I Corinthians, 'Better to marry than to burn') even more sacred than marriage: 'If marriage is sacred, the ultimate comradeship is utterly sacred, since it has no ulterior motive whatever, like procreation.'[6]

During the war Lawrence was markedly homophobic when responding to scenes he saw as epitomising aspects of English life. Viewing soldiers at Worthing, he is reminded of lice, bugs or beetles – 'I like men to be beasts – but insects – one insect mounted on another – oh God!' (ii. 331). On a visit to Cambridge in the same month, the sight of John Maynard Keynes in his dressing gown awoke in Lawrence a 'horrible sense of frowstiness, so repulsive, as if it came from deep inward dirt – a sort of sewer' (ii. 320). At the time, Lawrence seemed to think that in other cultures men loving men might not inevitably be linked with beetles, dirt and sewers. To David Garnett he wrote: 'It is foolish of you to say that it doesn't matter either way – the men loving men . . . it matters so much, David, to the man himself – at any rate to us northern nations – that it is like a blow of triumphant decay, when I meet Birrell or the others' (ii. 320).

How do the northern nations differ from the imagined South? This North/South opposition recalls Sir Richard Burton's invocation of the 'Sotadic Zone' in his famous 'Terminal Essay' of *Thousand Nights and a*

Night (1885–88). Edward Said, in *Orientalism*, discusses the 'almost uniform association between the Orient and sex',[7] and André Gide's *L'Immoraliste* shows that northern Africa also appealed to the European imagination as a place of homoerotic permissiveness.[8] 'Sotadic', according to the *Oxford English Dictionary*, denotes a 'coarseness and scurrility' like that in the writings of the ancient Greek poet Sotades, and in Burton's 'Sotadic Zone', said to include southern Europe and northern Africa, 'the Vice [pederasty] is popular and endemic, held at the worst to be a mere peccadillo, whilst the races to the North and South of the limits here defined practise it only sporadically amid the opprobrium of their fellows who . . . look upon it with the liveliest disgust'.[9]

Frequently Lawrence plays upon oppositions similar to those invoked by Burton, but where the 'South' begins is open to question. Wondering, in a letter to Lady Ottoline Morrell, whether David Garnett is 'also like Keynes and Grant', he writes: 'It is enough to drive one frantic. It makes me long for my Italy. Sometimes I can't stand this England any more: it is too wicked and perverse' (ii. 319). Does he long for Italy because Italy is free of the 'triumphant decay' associated with 'men loving men'? He seems rather to feel that male homosexuality in Italy does not 'matter', as only in the North, to echo Burton, do 'fellows . . . look upon it with the liveliest disgust', whereas in Italy men *can* love men without the 'wrong . . . unbearable . . . inward corruption' (ii. 320) implicit in northern homoeroticism. In a letter to Henry Savage in 1913 Lawrence had stressed the 'freedom' of Italy as opposed to the repressed, fettered, life-denying condition of England: 'You should watch the free Italians, then you'd know what we've done. We've denied the life of our bodies, so they, our bodies, deny life unto us' (ii. 95). The 'Northern races', by contrast, have been overcome by a 'suicidal tendency' (ii. 101).

The war years certainly contributed to Lawrence's sense of an inevitable waste and corruption in homosexuality. However, his most virulent homophobic outbursts precede his brutal treatment by the state. His negative response to Bloomsbury homosexuality or to a perceived homoeroticism in the spectacle of soldiers predates the suppression of *The Rainbow*, his medical investigations and the persecution he experienced as a suspected spy. Lawrence's letters give the impression that seeing John Maynard Keynes in a dressing gown was as traumatic as, perhaps more traumatic than, the experience of state brutality – seeing Keynes was 'one of the crises of my life' (ii. 321). The erotic charge of his reactions to authority resembles his troubled and charged response to homoeroticism.

In addition, Lawrence was already involved in eroticising the foreign before the war years. England was in a sense already contaminated for him before 1914; before 1914 he was already exulting in a brown, foreign masculinity. Jessie Chambers records that during his college years Lawrence 'was vehemently of Schopenhauer's opinion that a white skin is not natural to man . . . "For me, a brown skin is the only beautiful one."'[10] Her younger brother Jonathan David Chambers writes that Lawrence 'was especially fond of dressing up my brother Alan in some oriental costume, as an Arab chief or a Jewish prophet, and I can see him standing back and admiring my brother's display of tanned neck and arms'.[11] This brownness was either foreign, or else could only be found in outdoor workers whose skin was browned by long exposure to the sun. In Lawrence's very first short story, 'A Prelude', he creates an erotic spectacle of Fred dressed as an Arab for a Christmas drama. Fred's 'eyes glittered like a true Arab's . . . the dark folds of the rug and the flowing burnous glorified this young farmer'.[12]

It is perhaps, then, more accurate to say that the war years made more intense and more troubling Lawrence's relations to ethnic alterity, to authority and to homoeroticism. These changing relations can partly be seen in texts which appear early in the war but were written before the war. Lawrence revised *Twilight in Italy* for publication in 1916, but the essays date from 1913. In the revised text, the pathos of the agrarian Italy of the past now threatened by modern industrial Italy is more explicitly related to the context of modern imperialism. The descriptions of wooden crosses in the Tyrol become more pronounced meditations on the fascination with 'death, physical violence, and pain'[13] which the war exemplifies for Lawrence, and show the beginnings of his interest in the symbolic role of sacrifice in human culture. In *Kangaroo* he makes connections between the violence of the war and the 'pre-christian human sacrifice' Somers thinks of as taking place in the 'pre-world' of the Cornish moors (238).

But an accurate picture of such tensions in Lawrence's writings would show the role they played before the war. Lawrence's story 'The Prussian Officer' appeared in the *English Review* in August 1914, the same month war was declared. The coincidence is uncanny, but certainly wasn't planned by Lawrence, who wrote the story in 1913.

Love and sacrifice

After Lawrence read Edward Garnett's play *The Trial of Jeanne d'Arc* in 1912, he wrote to Garnett claiming that '[c]ruelty is a form of perverted sex . . . sex lust fermented makes atrocity' (i. 469). Lawrence saw this cruelty as a product of all-male institutions such as the priesthood or army.

This letter might frame but not determine a reading of 'The Prussian Officer'. This story describes the disturbing relationship between a Prussian aristocratic officer and his orderly, a 22-year-old peasant. The two men are systematically opposed not only in terms of class, age and authority, but also in terms of colour: the 'light blue eyes' and 'cold fire' of the officer are opposed to the 'warm flame' of the 'swarthy' orderly.[14]

The orderly's name is 'Schoner', not quite but near enough to the German word for beautiful, *schön*. The officer is irritated by 'something so free and self-contained' in his servant, by 'the blind, instinctive sureness of movement of an unhampered young animal' (3). This irritation tips over into more extreme emotions: 'To see the soldier's young, brown, shapely peasant's hands . . . sent a flash of hate or of anger through the elder man's blood' (3). The officer becomes possessed by this brown peasant's hand, and is fixated in particular by 'a scar on [the] left thumb, a deep seam going across the knuckle' (4). He is also irritated by the fact that his orderly has 'a sweetheart, a girl from the mountains, independent and primitive' (5).

Lawrence describes the officer's feelings as a 'passion that had got hold of him', 'an agony of irritation, torment, and misery' (6). The officer begins to abuse his servant, flinging a heavy military glove into his face, lashing the servant's face with the end of a belt, and eventually kicking him repeatedly on the legs as he clings to the banister.

This is not just a story of repressed homoeroticism spilling over into vio-lence. Nor is it a story of a violence arising from the Captain's not having a woman, according to the psychic structure outlined in Lawrence's letter to Garnett. Lawrence writes there that '[c]ruelty is a form of perverted sex', and '[i]t is sex lust fermented makes atrocity', but the erotic cruelty in 'The Prussian Officer' is not described as a displaced heterosexual desire on the Captain's part. The eroticism derives both from the palpable attraction of the young man's free brown body and from the bond of authority which brings the two men together. There is a psychic life to the power the two men have over each other which is related to but also goes beyond the institu-tional relation which bonds them. The Captain wants to repudiate or banish his obsession with the young man, which exceeds their constitutional rela-tion; he feels '[h]is own nerves must be going to pieces', and is mortified by the 'thrill of deep pleasure, and of shame' he feels when seeing 'the pain-tears in [the soldier's] eyes and the blood on his mouth' (6). This shame is conta-gious and operates to intensify rather than weaken the intimacy between the two men; the shame is a secret shared, an intimacy between abuser and abused. Looking at his bruises, the soldier feels 'he did not want anybody to know . . . There were only two people in the world now – himself and the Captain' (10). The bruises mark the soldier as the Captain's property. Perhaps the Captain's irritation with the scar on the soldier's hand was an irritation at a mark he had not made himself; the Captain marks the soldier's flesh, inscribes the young man's flesh with authority's bruise. His anger derived from a sense that the young man was *not* subjected to him – the soldier would be leaving his service in two months' time, and returning to his 'sweetheart'. In bruising the soldier the Captain writes his own name on the soldier's body, and effaces other claims on that body.

This is a story of subjection. The soldier finds the Captain's authority difficult to resist, as he has been subjected by the Captain's power. The power penetrates and forms him: '[i]nside had gradually accumulated a core into which all the energy of that young life was compact and concentrated' (13). The soldier is aware, however, that he also has 'in the centre of his chest . . . himself, firm, and not to be plucked to pieces' (13). Yet he cannot avoid being plucked to pieces by walking away from the Captain, as the Captain is inscribed on his body and in his psyche. Resistance can only take a form which mimics the initial act of violent, erotic subjection. Like Lawrence's subjection by the English state authorities during the war, the subjection of the soldier is unsuccessful if assessed by its intent to produce an obedient disciplinary subject. When the Captain falls off his horse onto 'a sharp-edged tree-base', the soldier holds his master's chest down with his knee and pushes the officer's chin back over the tree-stump, breaking his neck. This struggle is intensely erotic, an eroticism tipping over into death and the pleasure of sacrifice. We are told that 'it pleased' the soldier 'to feel the hard twitchings of the prostrate body jerking his own whole frame' (15). The soldier is shamed by his act, which has only intensified his intimacy with the Captain: he cannot bear to see the Captain's 'long, military body lying broken', and hides the body under some felled tree-trunks. He wanders through the mountains, not eating or drinking, until he expires amidst 'the mountains as they stood in their beauty, so clean and cool, [which] seemed to have it, that which was lost in him' (20). He dies in hospital, where his bruises are observed silently by the doctors, and the story ends with a sentimental tableau of the two bodies together in the mortuary: 'the one white and slender, but laid rigidly at rest, the other looking as if every moment it must rouse into life again, so young and unused, from a slumber' (21).

The story recalls Lawrence's descriptions, in *Twilight in Italy*, of the wooden Christ figures in the Tyrol mountains. The Christ's 'whole body is locked in one knowledge, beautiful, complete. It is one with the nails . . . sure of the absolute reality of the sensuous experience'. The Christ figures exemplify 'the worship of death and the approaches to death, physical violence, and pain'. The peasant kneels 'in spell-bound subjection' before the Christ figure, but the Christ figure 'sits in utter dejection, finished, hulked, a weight of shame . . . his body is a mass of torture, an unthinkable shame' (13). Like the dead bodies of the Captain and the servant, the Christ figures become a spectacle for others to behold; they create 'a centre . . . of almost obscene worship' (13).

If the original versions of *Twilight in Italy* and the story 'The Prussian Officer' predate the war, it is interesting to see how Lawrence reworks this scene of homoerotic sacrifice in *Women in Love*, which he wrote in the war years. This novel ends with Rupert Birkin's discovery of Gerald Crich's corpse in the Austrian Alps, a death which might have been avoided, Birkin thinks, if Gerald could have found 'the great Imperial road leading south to Italy'. Lawrence goes on to question whether the road south could truly have led Gerald away from the death he associates with the 'northern nations': 'Was it any good going south, to Italy? Down the old, old Imperial road?' (478).

Eros and blackness

'I think Rupert means', [Gerald] said, 'that *nationally* all Englishmen must die, so that they can exist individually and –'

  'Supernationally –' put in Gudrun, with a slight ironic grimace.   (397)

The metaphorical entanglement of tropes of race, eros and death in *Women in Love* is extraordinarily dense. To understand these metaphors we need to appreciate the contradictions actively at work within them, most importantly the one that brings 'life' close to 'death', merging 'creation', 'fulfilment' and 'dissolution'. This metaphorical instability is most active in the racial opposition between black and white, African and northern.

With Gerald Crich, Rupert Birkin wants 'a further sensual experience – something deeper, darker than ordinary life could give' (252). He remembers an African statuette of a woman with a 'diminished, beetle face, the astounding long elegant body, on short, ugly legs, with such protuberant buttocks'. '[I]n these Africans', Birkin thinks, 'the desire for creation and productive happiness must have lapsed, leaving the single impulse for . . . mindless progressive knowledge through the senses'; this is 'knowledge such as the beetles have . . . within the world of corruption and cold dissolution'. Hence 'the Egyptians worshipped the ball-rolling scarab: because of the principle of knowledge in dissolution and corruption' (253).

This language makes it clear that Lawrence's homophobic association of homoeroticism and beetles stems from a linkage of beetles, shit, waste and death.[15] Yet the scarab, or dung-beetle, destabilises these metaphorical linkages, because it nurtures and hatches its eggs in its dung-ball, which it rolls. For the Egyptians the rolling of the dung-ball 'imaged the sun's passage and its function towards the earth' (*WL*, 548). The scarab, then, merges deathly dung with the life of eggs, birth and the sun. It functions like the phoenix for Lawrence, suggesting the possibility of life out of death, of rebirth. These possibilities cannot be found, the novel suggests, in northern Europe: 'this awful African process . . . would be done differently by the white races' (254). Dissolution in the North could only be 'death by perfect cold . . . universal dissolution into whiteness and snow' (254).

The 'protuberant buttocks' of the African statuette bespeak the attractions of anal eroticism for Rupert even as they associate this eroticism with blackness and the African. Yet anality has other racial and cultural connotations in the novel. Just as Lawrence writes to David Garnett that 'men loving men . . . to us northern nations . . . is like a blow of triumphant decay', in *Women in Love* he identifies two other cultures in which anal pleasure and decay are linked: Sodom and the decadent Roman Empire. Lawrence's homoerotic and homophobic imagination becomes prophetic and apocalyptic when he has Birkin tell Ursula that '[h]umanity is dry-rotten', that the 'myriads of human beings hanging on the bush . . . are apples of Sodom . . . Dead Sea Fruit' (126), or when he writes that a 'strange black passion surged up pure in Gudrun', who 'remembered the abandonments of Roman licence' (287). These metaphors suggest that the sodomitic practices of the European nations risk bringing on large-scale devastation.

In associating 'black' anal passions with Sodom and decadent Rome, Lawrence is also linking them with the apocalypse of the First World War. There are no dates mentioned in *Women in Love*, but it is evidently set in the 1910s before war has broken out.[16] In his 1919 Foreword to the novel, Lawrence said he wished 'the time to remain unfixed, so that the bitterness of the war may be taken for granted in the characters' (*WL*, 485). The novel's warning about the risks of sodomy is appropriate from a writer who figures himself as the prophet in the wilderness. Here, as often, attempts at interpreting what the novel is trying to say lead to a banality which is absolutely at odds with the novel's power.

This discrepancy should lead us to question the hermeneutic procedures we bring to reading Lawrence. Frequently, attempts to paraphrase the novel in political terms risk injustice to the compelling and disturbing force of the novel's poetic prose. Reading *Women in Love* as a political allegory means contending with the uncertain causality of its metaphorical structures, and the relationship between these structures and what Lawrence terms 'crisis'. Just as seeing Keynes in a dressing gown was 'one of the crises of [Lawrence's] life', so in the 1919 Foreword to *Women in Love*, Lawrence remarks, '[w]e are now in a period of crisis. Every man who is acutely alive is acutely wrestling with his own soul' (*WL*, 486). The relationship between crisis and war is not straightforward: it seems that the war itself is a mere side effect of a much greater crisis within our own souls. This would account for Lawrence's unmitigated pessimism when the war ended. David Garnett recalls that Lawrence told a gathering of Bloomsbury's inner circle celebrating the end of the war that 'the war isn't over. The hate and evil is greater now than ever . . . and will show itself in all sorts of ways which will be worse than war'.[17]

However accurate this apocalyptic strain in Lawrence's writing and political commentary might appear with hindsight, its value does not lie in its analysis of international politics, but in its acute and troubled perception of diseased human relations and of what Lawrence calls a 'disintegration' of the human self. The novel's power derives in part from its poetic merging of this troubled realm of intimacy with a picture of global chaos, so that if Gudrun and Loerke playfully compose a 'mocking dream' of a man inventing 'such a perfect explosive that it blew the earth in two' (453), this global splitting is only a natural consequence of such social milieus as the Pompadour Café, a 'small, slow, central whirlpool of disintegration and dissolution' (380).

Is such poetic power – the power of apocalyptic writing at its best, 'some new Mene! Mene! upon the wall' (413) – the result of profound political thought on Lawrence's part, or simply an aspect of Lawrence's very personal nightmare, a peculiar crisis of his own psyche? Both answers might hold valid. Indeed, the personal inflections of Lawrence's politics help us account both for his political perceptiveness and his political waywardness. Two especially important features might be identified in the portrayals of human relationships in *Women in Love*, both of which are important to the intensity and strength of the novel's poetic language. Firstly, the relationships in this novel are marked by intense power struggles which move towards destruction. They often consist of a relay of acts of subordination and domination, acts which are both critiqued and eroticised, made to appear peculiarly compelling. These aspects of relationships are examined in connection with the fundamental act of subjection which Lawrence sees as central to the modern crisis of Europe – our subjection to the nation state. Secondly, the novel contains a remarkable but extremely confusing exploration of anal eroticism. Anal eroticism in the novel is semantically and hermeneutically overburdened – hyperbolically, it is both a source of life and creative renewal, and a force which threatens death, disintegration and dissolution. Hence it is not correct to see the novel's concern with anality simply as slotting into a longer history of cultural associations of anal pleasure, shit and death.[18] Anal pleasure in the novel is both intently celebrated and described in alarmist, apocalyptic tones, but its celebration should signal the inadequacy of viewing Lawrence as priest of the phallus, or as puritan sexual moralist. If Lawrence is a prophet, he is not a puritan prophet in the Pauline tradition, worrying that non-marital, non-reproductive sex will result in burning fire. Rather, he celebrates a transgressive sexuality, even if this celebration is qualified by his own anxieties. This simultaneous celebration and repudiation has brought attempts to interpret certain aspects of the novel to an impasse.

The association of anality with either death or life has been a problem in criticism of the novel ever since John Middleton Murry argued that the novel's 'distinction between the "love" of Rupert and Ursula . . . the way of salvation . . . [and the love of] Gerald and Gudrun . . . the way of damnation' is opaque to the readers: 'To our consciousness, they are indistinguishable.'[19] A recent masterly reading of the novel by Christopher Craft concurs with this judgement. Craft notes the 'critical anxiety' which 'has proceeded largely from sheer cognitive frustration: with both couples lapsing apace, the language of the novel works perversely to block or intermit the fundamental binarism that organizes its plot'.[20]

I'd like to try and alleviate some of this cognitive frustration. It stems, I am sure, from a critical belief that the survival of one couple, Birkin and Ursula, and the demise of the other, Gerald and Gudrun (Gudrun, however, palpably survives), suggests the greater psychic health of the surviving pair. Yet the novel seems in fact to suggest the contrary. Its attitude towards anality recalls Lawrence's attitude towards the disease of war; the novel seems to suggest we 'have to take [anality] into our consciousness and let it go through our soul, like some virus'.[21] There are in fact perfectly plausible (but perhaps *too boring*) explanations for Gerald's death: it takes place after he feels abandoned for Loerke, whereas no such rivalry threatens Birkin and Ursula. Gudrun herself provides, but rejects, this explanation: 'let them have it as an example of the eternal triangle, the trinity of hate'. But for Gudrun this argument is only a front, a conventional, comforting explanation for the *real* 'fight' which was 'between Gerald and herself' (477). Loerke's presence 'was a mere contingency – an inevitable contingency perhaps' (477). Namely, Loerke exposes but does not cause a problem which was inherent in the relationship between herself and Gerald. It is not merely that the relationship is one of combat, in which '[o]ne of them must triumph over the other' (413). This combat arises not from a lack of health in Gudrun and Gerald's relationship, but from a lack of perversity: for Gudrun, Gerald is simply not perverse enough.

Whereas Ursula can take pleasure in Birkin's 'licentiousness [which is] repulsively attractive', in the '[d]egrading things . . . real, with a different reality', in the 'bestial' and the 'shameful' – 'How good it was to be really shameful!' (413) – Gudrun is left with the disappointing knowledge that Gerald, although he might 'reap the women like a harvest' (394), as she joyfully tells Ursula, is in the end only a boring Don Juan, and 'his Don Juan does *not* interest me . . . Nothing is so boring as the phallus, so inherently stupid and stupidly conceited' (463). Loerke, by contrast, 'could penetrate into depths far out of Gerald's knowledge'; Gerald 'had penetrated all the outer places of Gudrun's soul', but '[o]f the last series of subtleties Gerald was not capable . . . where his ruder blows could not penetrate, the fine, insinuating blade of Loerke's insect-like comprehension could' (451–52).

Although the novel amply avails itself of the vocabulary of degeneration, decadence and eugenics, it turns the logic of these discourses on its head. If the novel invokes Sodom and decadent Rome to suggest that anal practices might have apocalyptic implications, it more forcefully implies that the 'perversions' which signal, for Europe's most prominent writers on degeneration like Max Nordau, the impending decay of European culture and the European race,[22] need in fact to be recognised rather than repudiated, and that cultural survival is at stake in this recognition. Yet this argument is made with extraordinary inconsistency: the novel is clearly troubled by the very pleasures it advocates. Prudish Birkin, it seems, can be perfectly degrading, bestial and shameful with Ursula, but Birkin more than anyone else is shocked by Loerke, whose perversity he verbally outlines in quite startling detail, showing a perception which can only stem from a degree of identification and recognition. Loerke's degeneration does not mark him out for destruction, but for survival. Loerke represents, for Birkin, our evolutionary future: he is '[s]tages further in social hatred . . . lives like a rat, in the river of corruption . . . further on than we are . . . the wizard rat that swims ahead' (428).[23] At the end of the novel 'Gudrun went to Dresden', and Birkin is left melancholically rueing his failure to obtain 'eternal union with a man too: another kind of love' (481). Hence Birkin too suffers, not from having had too much shame, degradation and bestiality, but from not having had enough.

To understand the novel's advocacy and repudiation of non-phallic pleasures, we need to understand a basic ambivalence in its attitudes towards 'blackness' and cultural or racial otherness. Thinking of how the novel combines sex and the nation can help us discern that there is in fact more sense – or at least consistency – to the novel's metaphorical binarism than critics have suggested. *Women in Love* opposes the northern nations to an idealised Italy, and also to a West Africa which has 'gone beyond phallic knowledge', unearthed 'sensual, mindless, dreadful mysteries, far beyond the phallic cult' (253). Lawrence has (for some good reasons) relentlessly been associated with the phallic,[24] but the narrative of *Women in Love* embodies a feverish search for pleasures which are non-phallic.

In the 'Excurse' chapter, Ursula Brangwen and Rupert Birkin embrace in a parlour of the Saracen's Head, an inn in the Midlands town of Southwell. The inn's name suggests an oasis of Arabian or Oriental pleasures, and

Ursula's discoveries there recall Moses drawing water from a rock in the desert. Before they arrive in the inn, they have quarrelled furiously, Ursula unleashing a torrent of invective which makes Birkin the embodiment of anality, dirt and death – a 'scavenger dog . . . eater of corpses . . . a foul, deathly thing, . . . obscene and perverse . . . you don't want love. No, you want *yourself*, and dirt, and death' (307). Now that they have made up, however, she seeks out in Birkin 'the darkest, deepest, strangest life-source of the human body, at the back and the base of the loins', and 'rivers of strange dark fluid richness . . . passed over her . . . from the smitten rock of the man's body . . . further in mystery than the phallic source, came the floods of ineffable darkness and ineffable richness' (314). It sounds as if Ursula is being drenched by a sloppy bowel movement of Birkin's, and squeamish readers might find it distressing that the next paragraph has them going straight to a meal, of 'a venison pasty, of all things, a large broad-faced cut ham, eggs and cresses and beet-root, and medlar and apple-tart and tea' (314). (This clash of linguistic registers outraged John Middleton Murry, who asked, 'Why, in the name of darkness, "a venison pasty, *of all things*"?'[25]) Yet the rivers which emerge from the 'strange fountains of [Birkin's] body', 'marvellous fountains, like the bodies of the Sons of God who were in the beginning', are cleansing rivers, 'sweeping away everything and leaving her an essential new being, she was left quite free' (314).

Birkin and Ursula's liberating discovery of the 'fulness of dark knowledge' in part derives from their discovery of the 'immemorial potency, like the great carven statues of real Egypt'; their encounter with 'the rivers of strange dark fluid richness' makes them 'like the immobile, supremely potent Egyptians, seated forever in their living, subtle silence' (314, 318). Gerald, by contrast, has made no contact with the life-renewing warmth of the South, in which anality need not be a 'blow of triumphant decay'. Relentlessly northern and industrial, with 'his clear northern flesh and his fair hair [with] a glisten like cold sunshine refracted through crystals of ice' (14), he ends up 'frozen dead . . . frozen into a block of ice' (477). Birkin and Ursula sensibly leave the Alpine landscape of death, making a life-saving voyage into Italy, 'the south . . . land dark with orange trees and cypress' (434), into the safety of the Sotadic zone (just as the homosexuality of England, personified in Duncan Grant and John Maynard Keynes, makes Lawrence 'long for [his] Italy'). Gerald's death, on the other hand, takes place in the Alpine twilight, after he sees 'a half-buried crucifix, a little Christ under a little sloping hood' (473). Like the deaths of the Prussian officer and his orderly, Gerald's fate is 'to be murdered' like 'Lord Jesus' (473). Recalling the Alpine Christ figures Lawrence finds so fascinating in *Twilight in Italy*, Gerald's death is the necessary sacrifice, the expiation of the perverse pleasures which he himself is unable to enjoy. The end of the novel is a Wagnerian Triumph of the Perverts, who happily survive while the 'infant crying in the night, this Don Juan' with his boring 'inherently stupid and stupidly conceited phallus' is slain.

This reading might sound odd, as it shows the same Lawrence who responds so violently to Keynes as a positive proselytiser of perversion, and seems to sit uneasily alongside the censorious and phobic voices contained in the novel itself. But of course, the novel *is* an uneasy conglomeration of conflicting voices; this clash of voices is crucial to the novel's great crisis. And the baroque extravagance of the novel's argument is also that argument's implausibility. It should not be thought that the novel resolves the crisis of anality by invoking a benign spirit of racial alterity, of a foreign culture in which the human fundaments might be explored in ways that lead to creative rebirth rather than disintegration, or by a 'suggestion of primitive art' (448). I have tried to show that there is some sense in the novel's effort to think through differences between life-enhancing and life-threatening forms of anal eroticism, but this trajectory through cultures, races and nations which are thought to have certain sexual meanings and to enable or frustrate different sexual possibilities, is so extraordinarily complex that its success is at best tenuous. It is surely not that easy to escape the cultural associations of anal pleasure and death by voyaging down the old imperial road to the Hippocrene South, to sun-drenched Italy or to the Egypt of Burton's Sotadic zone.

Indeed, *Women in Love* might be seen to perform its own critique of the aspiration to escape through such idealisations of other cultures. The 'excurse' to the continent is partly an escape from the paternal law of England: '"Isn't it marvellous", [says] Gudrun, ". . . to be out of one's country . . . I am so transported, the moment I set foot on a foreign shore"' (395). Julia Kristeva suggests in her book on foreignness, *Strangers to Ourselves*, that 'Tearing oneself away from family, language, and country to settle down elsewhere is a daring action accompanied by sexual frenzy: no more prohibition, everything is possible.'[26] Birkin, however, thinks of the national subjection that accompanies the traveller even after the *patria* has been abandoned, remarking that love of England is 'like a love for an aged parent who suffers horribly from a complication of diseases' (395). Birkin asks the questions which throw the whole force of the novel's arguments into doubt: 'The south? Italy? What then? Was it a way out? – It was only a way in again' (478).

This escape from the paternal law into a world of licence brings on another crisis in the novel, the encounter with Loerke, the foreigner *in extremis* and 'little obscene monster of the darkness' (428) whose pronounced association with perverse pleasures, whether the polyglot pleasure of perverse interlingual talk, beating slight women under twenty or being beaten by big and powerful men (433–34), turns Birkin into the spokesman of the paternal law of prohibition he has endeavoured to escape. Strangely, Loerke can be identified in many ways with Lawrence, or, in the novel, with the Birkin who despises him. He is a powerful Lawrencean *alter ego*, with his 'thin legs' (422), his polyglot talk, his dislike of the Futurists, and admiration of 'the Aztec art, Mexican and Central American' (448), and his bohemian artist existence which is preferred by Gudrun to Gerald's achievements in 'a richly-paying industry out of an old worn-out concern' (418). Gudrun and Loerke, like Birkin, 'kindled themselves at the subtle lusts of the Egyptians or the Mexicans' (448).

This is perhaps the problem with the metaphorical structure of the novel: the novel attempts to imagine an escape from problems inherent in 'our' culture by recourse to 'other' cultures, but as our relation to those other cultures is conditioned by the very cultural framework we are trying to escape, contact with the other culture does not bring a release but only exposes the extent to which we cannot undo our national subjection. Lawrence was to keep on trying to escape from the problem that was England through a romancing of various other cultures and nations – whether America, Mexico, Italy or Etruria. Perhaps he never succeeded, and the openness to cultural alterity his quest implied was always compromised by forms of the law he carried within him, or by encountering in those other cultures the very problems he had hoped to leave at home. But this story of cultural crossing remains intriguing, and is still being digested.

NOTES

1 ii. 301, 414.
2 For full accounts of Lawrence's experiences during the war see Paul Delany, *D. H. Lawrence's Nightmare: The Writer and his Circle in the Years of the Great War* (Hassocks: Harvester, 1979), and *TE*.
3 Anthony Burgess, introduction to *D. H. Lawrence and Italy: Twilight in Italy; Sea and Sardinia; Etruscan Places* (Harmondsworth: Penguin, 1985), p. viii.
4 Delany, *D. H. Lawrence's Nightmare*, p. 375.
5 *Memoir of Maurice Magnus*, ed. Keith Cushman (Santa Rosa, CA: Black Sparrow Press, 1987), p. 100.
6 *Symbolic*, 238, 263. In the version of these essays eventually published as *Studies in Classic American Literature* in 1923, Lawrence is no longer so enthusiastic about Whitman, writing that his love of comrades 'always slides into death': *SCAL*, 178.
7 Edward Said, *Orientalism* (New York: Vintage, 1979), p. 188.
8 André Gide, *L'Immoraliste* (1902; Paris: Gallimard, 1976). See also Eve Kosofsky Sedgwick, 'Up the Postern Stair: *Edwin Drood* and the Homophobia of Empire', chapter 10 of *Between Men: English Literature and Male Homosocial Desire* (New York: Columbia University Press, 1985), pp. 180–200,

for a discussion of some nineteenth-century associations of the Orient with homoeroticism.

9 Richard Burton, 'Terminal Essay', pp. 63–302 in *The Book of the Thousand Nights and a Night*, trans. Richard F. Burton, 10 vols. (by private subscription: the Burton Club, 1885–88), x. 207.

10 Jessie Chambers, *D. H. Lawrence: A Personal Record* (London: Frank Cass, 1935), p. 111.

11 Jonathan David Chambers, 'Memories of D. H. Lawrence', *Renaissance and Modern Studies*, 16 (1972), pp. 5–17 (p. 12).

12 'A Prelude', in *Love Among the Haystacks and Other Stories*, ed. John Worthen (Cambridge: Cambridge University Press, 1987), p. 9.

13 *D. H. Lawrence and Italy*, p. 11.

14 'The Prussian Officer', in *The Prussian Officer and Other Stories*, ed. John Worthen (Cambridge: Cambridge University Press, 1983), pp. 2–3. Subsequent references are given in the text.

15 See Christopher Craft, 'No Private Parts: On the Rereading of *Women in Love*', in *Another Kind of Love: Male Homosexual Desire in English Discourse, 1850–1920* (Berkeley, CA: University of California Press, 1994), pp. 154–59, for a full exploration of Lawrence's deployment of the 'phantasmagoric pun' linking bugs and buggery.

16 Cultural references such as the Picasso reproductions in the Brangwen house and Hermione Roddice's home theatricals in the style 'of the Russian Ballet of Pavlova and Nijinsky' help us date the novel's action fairly precisely: drawings by Picasso were included in the first Post-Impressionist Exhibition of 1910.

17 David Garnett, *The Flowers of the Forest* (London: Chatto & Windus, 1955), pp. 190–91.

18 See Leo Bersani, 'Is the Rectum a Grave?' in *Aids: Cultural Analysis, Cultural Activism*, ed. Douglas Crimp (Cambridge, MA, and London: Massachusetts Institute of Technology Press, 1988), for an analysis of fantasies linking anality and death.

19 John Middleton Murry, *Son of Woman: The Story of D. H. Lawrence* (London: Jonathan Cape, 1931), p. 131.

20 Craft, 'No Private Parts', p. 168.

21 *Memoir of Maurice Magnus*, p. 100.

22 In Max Nordau's *Degeneration*, for example, Oscar Wilde is considered as an ego-maniacal example of a literary degenerate, in a chapter which attacks literary decadence for its failure to embody an ideal of healthy masculinity: *Degeneration* (London: William Heinemann, 1895), pp. 317–21.

23 Compare Lawrence on John Maynard Keynes: 'I can imagine the mind of a rat, as it slithers along in the dark, pointing its sharp nose. But I can never feel happy about it. I must always want to kill it. It contains a principle of evil . . . I saw it so plainly in Keynes at Cambridge, it made me sick' (to Morrell, ii. 311).

24 The major attack on Lawrence's phallicism is of course that made by Kate Millett in her *Sexual Politics* (London: Rupert Hart-Davis, 1971).

25 John Middleton Murry, review of *Women in Love*, in *Reminiscences of D. H. Lawrence* (London: Jonathan Cape, 1936), p. 224 (Murry's italics).

26 *Strangers to Ourselves*, trans. Leon S. Roudiez (Hemel Hempstead: Harvester Wheatsheaf), p. 30.

4

MARK KINKEAD-WEEKES

Decolonising imagination: Lawrence in the 1920s

Imagining – and its difficulty

For Doris Lessing, racism is an 'atrophy of the imagination'.[1] Many factors combine to block our responsiveness to people of other races and cultures: attitudes imbibed unconsciously at our mother's knee and from fathers and elders, peer-group pressure, the limitations of our education and of what we read, the conditionings of our post-colonial and still largely racist societies. If, however, as Lessing implies, imagination is antipathetic to racism, can a writer (sometimes) decolonise his vision? It would seem so; and no English-born author[2] of the early twentieth century went further in this than D. H. Lawrence, through his encounter with the native peoples of North America. However, in tracing this process, we must not fail in imagination ourselves, by condescending to the past. We need to see just how hard it could be (and is) to unscale one's eyes from the prejudices of the time, and how easy there-fore to relapse into a conventional self. Imagination could prove intermittent.

In 1915, for example, Lawrence the novelist could conceive anti-Raj sen-timents for his rebellious young Ursula in *The Rainbow* (R, 427–28).[3] Yet in 1922 we find him voicing Raj attitudes himself, after sailing to Ceylon and Australia on P&O liners with 'Old India hands'. He writes of his pride in being white and English and the fear of being swamped by coloured people; he is certain that 'corruption and chaos will follow' any British handover in India, and that 'the dark races *don't have* any sense of liberty in our meaning of the word' (iv. 234, 245–46).

Similarly, the Lawrence of *Women in Love* was able to imagine how encounters with the cultures of other races might supply defects in himself and his civilisation. In the final version of the novel (79, 253–54) he makes Birkin insist that West African carving is not barbaric but the product of another kind of civilisation.[4] In his wartime essay on Fenimore Cooper's 'Leatherstocking' novels, he not only praises the deep relationship imagined there between red man and white, but also finds behind it a psychic quest, novel by novel, to discover the lost 'Indian' within the self, a dimension of being that the defective white man desperately needs to recover, in order to achieve wholeness again.[5] The essay on Melville's *Typee* shows how the lost valley of the cannibals turns out to be not savage but a kind of Eden, though Melville is too much a Yankee to be able to stay there. Yet Lawrence was repelled in 1922 by his first actual encounters with 'dark' people, and was too habitually honest to pretend otherwise. Admittedly he had fallen ill in Ceylon and the exotic colours, sounds, tastes and smells of the tropics proved too much for someone feverish and nauseous – but this hardly accounts for his sense of the local people 'swarming', 'soft', 'boneless', with 'black bottomless hopeless eyes'. Like Forster, he sensed something muddy, antediluvian – and hostile and jeering too (iv. 217, 225–30). After calling at Tahiti on his way to New Mexico (at the invitation of a rich American, Mabel Dodge), a postcard to Compton Mackenzie put an end to their old dream of sailing the South Seas: 'If you are thinking of coming here, don't. The people are brown and soft' (iv. 286). When, some months after arriving in Taos in autumn 1922, he revised those earlier essays into the much more hard-hitting (but also less sensitive) *Studies in Classic American Literature*, the physical aversion is even more explicit – felt now for the very people whom Melville had made him imagine as Edenic. However rotten our civilisation may be, he now writes, the South Sea islanders are ages behind the white man in 'the struggle of the soul into fulness':

> There is his woman . . . I like her, she is nice. But I would never want to touch her. I could not go back on myself so far. Back to their uncreate condition.
> She has soft warm flesh, like warm mud. Nearer the reptile, the Saurian age.
> *Noli me tangere.* (*SCAL*, 145)

What brought this on, and the attack that follows on the renegade '"reformers" and "idealists" who glorify the savages in America'? The answer would seem to be three months of Mabel Dodge. It seems likely that Lawrence's febrile tension at their first meeting[6] came partly from sudden awkward feelings about miscegenation, in the shock of realising that she had a sexual relationship with the taciturn 'Indian'[7] Tony Luhan, whom she was later to marry, and to whom Lawrence never warmed. By December 1922 when he revised the Melville essay he had already had enough of close proximity to Mabel and her circle, and had moved out of the house she had provided.

Early encounters with American Indians

However, immediately after his arrival in Taos, Mabel had sent him off by car with Tony on a five-day trip to a gathering in the Jicarilla Apache reservation. She hoped he would write about Indians as powerfully as he had written in 1921 of the almost lost culture of ancient Sardinia. His 1920 essay 'America, Listen to Your Own' had called on white Americans to renounce their cultural enslavement to a decaying Europe, and to try instead to 'take up life where the Red Indian, the Aztec, the Maya let it fall', in their own continent. 'They must catch the pulse of the life which Cortes and Columbus' (and white America) 'murdered' (*P*, 90–91) – a logical extension of his essay on Fenimore Cooper. But once again, actual contact with indigenous people in September 1922 produced a response, in his first 'Indian' essay, that was strikingly different from his response to the 'Leatherstocking' novels, as he candidly acknowledged – and a considerable disappointment to Mabel.

For 'Indians and an Englishman' (*P*, 92–99), which begins in sardonic amusement at being suddenly plunged into the 'wild and woolly' American West, ends with a serious admission that there *can* be no going back of the kind that he had called for. Here, however, there is little sense of superiority or repulsion – even though the Apaches' taboo against washing means a smell 'that takes the breath from the nostrils'. For as soon as Lawrence begins to respond to the scene at dusk – 'tepees, and smoke, and silhouettes of tethered horses and blanketted figures' moving against the glowing camp-fires – his sensuous imagination comes alive. The pulses of the drums 'beat on the plasm of one's tissue'. The dancers' feet thud, 'pàt-pat, pàt-pat', as they move in opposite lines from the kivas in a strange stooped bird-like dance, sideways. The 'song-shout' of the chanting is interlined with whoops and gobbles produced 'from the deeps of the stomach' which surprise him to his 'very tissues' – a response less conscious or emotional than visceral, but vividly re-imagined as he writes of it now. The experience dwarfs his attempts to interpret it: 'It was not what I thought it would be. It was something of a shock.' He speaks of sounds 'pre-human' and 'pre-animal . . . full of triumph in life, and devilment . . . and mockery' and blood-thirstiness, but he knows perfectly well that he 'may have been all wrong'. Far from superiority, what he feels is 'an acute sadness, and a nostalgia, unbearably yearning for something', for a tribal past 'when man was dusky and not individualised'. But as he wanders later, through tourists and onlookers, to stand outside a kiva and listen to an old man reciting (he supposes) the history of the tribe and its gods, the question of what relation there can be between himself and the red man takes a new turn. In Ceylon he thought the natives were secretly mocking him; here too the impression of something jeering, 'a sort of unconscious animosity', grows. A young man warns him off: only Indians can approach the kiva. The sense of an unbridgeable gap deepens from his side too. For however much he 'trembles still alive to the old sound' or 'quivers to the old mystery', there can be no going back, nor even the wish to do so. A long process of developing consciousness separates him from them, and his blood flows 'always onward, still further', ahead; 'My way is my own, old red father; I can't cluster at the drum any more.'

The impression that Indians were also secretly laughing at him strengthened, in the first months in Taos; but this is actually a sign of potential decolonisation, a first crack in the armour of superiority, and a first inkling of how the colonised must feel towards the coloniser. That came vividly to mind when, in 'Taos' (*P*, 100–3), he recalled the San Geronimo festa he witnessed at the end of September – feeling the tensions between red and white Americans, but now placing himself as an 'outsider', to both. Now he sees the Pueblo as a kind of monastery preserving the human spirit, though he still feels 'the gulfs of time' between himself and it. Yet as the essay ends, imagination suddenly senses what lies behind the grimaces, which only seem like grins, of the red men dispersing through the tourists: the ordeal it must have been 'to sing and tread the slow dance between that solid wall of silent, impassive white faces'. Imagination confronts its absence. There is no doubt where sympathy lies.

Imaginative sympathy is one thing, however, political advocacy another. Pressed by Mabel to write against the Bursum Bill, that cynical attempt to open still more Indian land to white and Mexican settlement under the guise of bringing order and legality to a tangled situation, Lawrence complied with palpable awkwardness. 'Certain Americans and an Englishman' (*PII*, 238–43) begins with an unstable mix of would-be humour and irritation, and is only too visibly split between a sense of injustice, and dislike of the 'highbrows' who say 'Poor Indian, dear Indian! why, all America ought to belong to him', and stoke the Pueblo people up in ways that may make them still more vulnerable. (Lawrence reveals some paternalism here.) As he goes through the main provisions of the Bill, however, with tart comment on their implications, he does show up its brutal cynicism and injustice. Its passage would mean the end of the Pueblos. But he can only plead for a fair-dealing Indian Office or Commission, 'to shelter these ancient centres of life, so that, if die they must, they die a natural death'. And, he urges, let us try 'to see again as they see, without forgetting we are ourselves'. But 'what business is it of mine, foreigner and newcomer?' The essay is half-hearted, with imagination never in play. (In fact Lawrence was unaware that the real issue for the Taos Indians was not merely encroachment on the 17,000 acres around the Pueblo to which they had legal title, but the 30,000-acre watershed which contained their sacred Blue Lake. This was, and is, no mere water supply, but the place of their Emergence, the source of life and the retreat of souls after death, the home of the ancestors, and centre of religious ceremonies and training – to which the Pueblo only recovered title and control of access under Richard Nixon, in December 1970! Colonialism is not confined to Empires . . .)[8]

Mexico and 'Quetzalcoatl'

It was, however, Lawrence's experience of Mexico, from late March to early July 1923, that challenged his imagination to new depth and disturbance. After visiting Mexico City he settled on Lake Chapala, where the writing of the novel he called 'Quetzalcoatl' forced him to confront the racism and sense of superiority in himself and his culture, and his feelings of repulsion towards much that he saw and sensed in Mexicans – but also the imaginative challenge (behind colonial and revolutionary façades) of the religion of Old Mexico.

This novel has only recently become generally available[9] – and those who have read and responded (usually strongly, whether for or against) to the ideologically elaborated and much more assertive *The Plumed Serpent* which would grow out of it a year later, may find it hard to avoid coming to the earlier fiction through the later one. Yet it is no mere preliminary sketch, but a very different experience. Most of the later scenario is already there, but 'Quetzalcoatl' is only half as long and altogether more exploratory, being more consistently filtered through the questioning, and questioned, consciousness of Kate – whereas in the later novel the founders, and the foundation and elaboration, of a new religion and politics hold centre stage for long unquestioned stretches, and Kate seems certain to capitulate at the end. Indeed, if we could read 'Quetzalcoatl' without preconditioning, it might be easier to see how remarkably it anticipates anti-colonial writers like Chinua Achebe, Wole Soyinka and Ngugi wa Thiong'o, three decades and more ahead.[10]

For Lawrence imagines, in the growth of the movement led by Ramón Carasco (in this novel a brown man of mixed blood) and General Cipriano Viedma (pure Indian), many of the ways in which the later African writers would seek imaginatively to undermine colonialism, set native consciousness free from feelings of inferiority, and liberate a new sense of dignity and identity. Here, too, in these imagined Mexicans is an attempt to revivify an ancient pre-colonial culture and religion; a growing hostility to the Christian church as an agency of colonialism in unholy alliance with colonial exploitation; a gradual realisation that violence is both inevitable and indeed necessary for psychological as well as political decolonisation; an exposure of what is involved in the attitudes of those still caught in colonial mind-sets; and a felt need to revert, in the relations between men and women, to older frames of reference than that of modern 'western' feminism.[11]

All this is more sympathetically intelligible here than in the later novel, because it gradually develops out of the concrete situations of Ramón and Cipriano rather than springing as a full-blown dictatorial ideology from

Ramón's head. Both men have come through European educations that separate them from their roots, while leaving them sensitive to their skin-colour
and all the more conscious of the corruption and exploitation of Mexico
from without and within. Ramón has become disillusioned with left-wing
politics, as yet another form of materialism. But as he develops his sense that
what is needed is essentially a religious revolution in the psyche, by reviving
the old gods, there is always a robust awareness that he and Cipriano remain
flawed human beings, each needing the other's help to keep from falsehood
and evil, even as it is revealed that they do indeed have gods in them. The
new 'religion' *develops*, step by step, as does the gravity of the breach with
Christianity in reaction to the growing hostility of the Mexican church;
while Ramón's Christian wife is treated more humanely than she will be in
The Plumed Serpent. The realisation of the need for violence is gradual too,
both in response to the attempt on Ramón's life, and also to ensure that
change will be lasting, politically and psychologically (as Franz Fanon was
to explain).[12] This also relates to a growing sense in Lawrence of how the
jeering, cruelty, apathy and negation that Kate finds in Mexican peasants are
responses of the colonised and the have-nots to their poverty and lack of
power. There is no sentimentality or shirking. Kate may initially reflect her
creator's repulsions – but her self-image of racial and cultural superiority
suffers a series of jolts. Also, the 'liberated' *emancipée* is forced to confront,
in Teresa, a quite different concept of womanhood which she cannot despise,
try as she may. And disturbingly, under the pressure of Cipriano's desire for
her, Kate and her creator are made to expose, and begin to face up to, if not
yet to overcome, their deep-lying prejudice against 'mixed-blood' marriage.
Kate's last glimpse of Cipriano, naked and glowing red in the lakeside dawn,
is visionary – but though there is no physical repulsion now, she still cannot
but feel that blood-contact between them is unthinkable, and that blood-
mixture in marriage would be deadly, 'a kind of suicide'.[13] Indeed, in this
novel she never finally accepts Ramón's ideology either, nor will she take up
her role as Malintzi. She will go back to England, though she seems unlikely
to stay there. The novel is open-ended like the Indian weaving that Cipriano
praises because it leaves a gap for the soul to escape. It is easier to accept
what is psychologically revealing about Ramón's gods when Lawrence does
not require Kate (or us) to swallow them whole. Even the most worrying episodes are less so here than they will be later. Though Lawrence would soon
record his opposition to Fascism (*MEH*, 262–63, a view formed before the
rise of Mussolini and Hitler to dictatorial power), there is something uncomfortably dictatorial about the taking over of the church in Chapala by force
and the burning of its statues; about the salutes and ceremonies; and about
the arbitrary 'trial' and execution of the conspirators, already present in this

version. But readers who wince at these here will find their development in *The Plumed Serpent* even more rebarbative.

Kiowa essays

Between 'Quetzalcoatl' and its rewriting came a deeply disillusioning visit to England, and also a serious quarrel with Frieda and her near-betrayal of him with Middleton Murry.[14] Yet the Lawrences' return to make a home of their own on Kiowa ranch – albeit with Dorothy Brett in tow – led to one of the happiest and most productive periods of his life and an extraordinary imaginative effort to get *inside* Indian culture, seen now as in many ways superior to his own.

Up to *Women in Love*, dance had expressed for Lawrence either a state of individual being, or the relation between a man and a woman.[15] But now in 'Indians and Entertainment' (*MM*, 52–64), written at the ranch in April 1924, he absolutely opposes 'Indian' to 'European' as irreconcilable modes of consciousness because, he argues, Indian dance is not only essentially communal, but *all-communing*. Even the Hebridean (outermost European) feels himself, as human, a fraction distinct still from the world of nature that enters his wild song. Even the ancient Greek, performing a communal ritual, did so for a God conceived as watching, outside – which is why from that ritual could spring the whole of European drama, actors, audience, entertainment. But in the Indian dance the individual is lost in the tribe, which merges into the natural world; and there is no God separate from that world. God, the gods, are 'immersed in creation' and 'Creation is a great flood, for ever flowing, in lovely and terrible waves' (61), so everything, terrible or lovely, is godly. In the Indian dance, then, the drum is a heartbeat of communal blood, in which body and spirit reach out – no distinction there, either – to unite man, god and nature. In the corn dance, 'the spirits of the men go out . . . in waves . . . seeking the creative presence . . . seeking the identification, following on down . . . into the germinating quick of the maize that lies under the ground' to stimulate the power to grow (57). There are dances which mime single combat, power, heroism; but always the centre is the dance in unison, where men 'move with the soft, yet heavy bird-tread' as though from each separate existence the blood falls back – from mind, sight, speech and knowing – through the feet, to the great central source for renewal. In the same way, in the Deer Dance at New Year, the male dancers identify themselves with deer, buffalo, bear, wolf, coyote, following also the magical power of woman who leads the dance, and co-celebrating in wonder the godly creativity in all. Without sentimentality, the essay ends very differently from its beginning.

'Dance of the Sprouting Corn' (*MM*, 64–71), written soon afterwards, describes the great dance held annually in San Domingo Pueblo. This time Lawrence recreates the process of a watcher's immersion into the dance as the senses open: first the realisation that you have been hearing distant drumming before you actually hear it coming; then a distant vision of tossing boughs (held by the dancers) like a forest, in which the wind of song booms. Then the eye begins to realise the line of dancers and the cluster of singers near the drum, and the black and white jesters hopping in and out. The ear begins to distinguish the drums, the ripple of knee bells, the rattles; then the eye at last to see the dancers: their faces, costumes, rhythmic counterpoints of colour, foliage, flesh. 'Bit by bit you take it in.' Yet it is difficult to get a whole impression. For first you have to focus on the black-clothed women and the subtle sway of their movement; then to concentrate on the men, bent forward, foxtails swaying, the drive of their 'rhythmic hopping leap . . . as the strong heavy body comes down', down, down, bringing his life down, from mind to breast to knees, to ankles, plunging the feet into the red earth with which their bodies are smeared (67). All day long, dancers from the winter and the summer Houses alternate, dancing between the forces of the seasons, sky, and earth. They call, they command 'in that song, in that rhythmic energy of dance'; they partake 'in the springing of the corn' (70–71).

What the previous essay had talked of, the sensuous imagination now grasps and recreates: an experience which is a world away from the gulf at the end of 'Indians and an Englishman'. It remained to draw the contrast with the destructiveness of the white man, and to bring out the psychological damage of the colonisation of America, to white and Indian alike. The novellas of that summer and autumn are amongst the finest of Lawrence's works – and the more so when read together as they should be, for only accidents of publication separated them into different collections.

'The Woman Who Rode Away'

The story of a white woman who leaves husband and home in Mexico, falls in with a 'lost' tribe and is ritually sacrificed, has real power to disturb. It is often taken as an attack on feminism.[16] The woman is American, married to the owner of a silver mine who treats her as a treasure – but she lives in a stupor and her nerves are bad. She feels she must get away; and having heard of the 'lost' tribe of Montezuma, thinks it would be an 'adventure' to find their 'secret haunts'. But the Indians she meets in the mountains undermine her sense of identity. In their world, her riding breeches are cut away and her hair is undone. The drugs she is given make her passive. As she watches Indian men and women dance, she reads the Writing on the Wall: 'the quivering nervous consciousness of the highly-bred white woman was to be destroyed again, womanhood was to be cast once more into the great stream of impersonal sex and impersonal passion' (*WWRA*, 60). She is told how, for the Indian, man and woman must remain opposites, like sun and moon, and how cosmic fertility depends on each fulfilling their proper role. Her culture has subverted both maleness and femaleness, breeding anger and sterility. The symbolism of the ritual sacrifice emphasises once more the Lawrencean theme of sexual relation as source of life and creativity, but now (it seems) the condition is the death of individual independent personal woman, in order to regain 'The mastery that man must hold.'

Yet this Woman seems a poor example of liberation and independence. And to read the story as simply an anti-feminist tract is to blind oneself to highly significant things about both the Woman and the Indians. Her dissatisfaction is more closely connected with being a Gringo in Mexico than with being 'emancipated'.[17] The house and the mine lack any relation to the land or its people, and colonial life and economy are moribund. Romantic fantasy about wild Indians is only the tourist obverse of her husband's hard-bitten settler attitudes to 'savages'. The Woman rides 'away', not *to* anything. When asked where she is going she gives a tourist's answer, 'to visit', to 'see their houses and to know their gods' (47); a huge irony, fusing arrogance with ignorance. Her sense of identity comes from her whiteness and colonial status, and her 'womanhood' depends on these. When the Indians do not treat her as superior, she responds with 'the passionate anger of the spoilt white woman' (47); and then her social and sexual sense of herself proves hollow and collapses, even before she has to cross (without the horse of a Conquistador) the fearful rock-face into an uncolonised world. Though aware, there, of the 'purity' of the Chief's gaze and the reverence due to the ancient Cacique, she answers them falsely. There is *no* sense in which she has brought her 'heart to the god of the Chilchui' (51–52, 54). Talking down proves literally fatal.

Gradually, her consciousness is expanded until she can almost share the world-view of the Indians. It is her sense of being a separate imperial self, controlling her world, that blocks her off from the Indian sense of the human-in-the-universe. The drug is a purge, but it also restores what white consciousness has lost: relatedness to the cosmos through the senses, not in psychedelic hallucination, but heightening ordinary perception into an extraordinarily vital experience of harmony (56–57). In the rhythm of the dance; the life of animals and birds, the land and the elements are all brought into relation (59–60); and it is against *this* that the writing on the wall for the personal and individual kind of womanhood must be seen; it is no mere male chauvinism.

Most of all, we must look at the Indians – or rather, at the differences among them. Lawrence does not sentimentalise. He never lets us forget that the Woman is a prisoner, and his imagination brings out something terrible in the conflict of attitudes towards her. The older men show almost fatherly solicitude but also hide something ferocious. The young Indian seems kinder still, and talks with apparent candour, but he keeps back the most important things. All share a religious longing to restore, through blood sacrifice, the union of the great forces that create fertility but have been laid waste by the white man's ignorant irreligion; so the Woman must be cherished. But ever more clearly – and especially in the young man, who has been treated as an inferior in the white man's city – there is antagonism, even malignancy, the psychic backlash against the coloniser, the regaining of self-respect through hate, violence, revenge.[18] Moreover, as the last day comes, it is important to see how Lawrence ensures disturbance in the reader. He brings the Woman to the brink of Indian consciousness, but she can never fully understand what is done to her, or why. The young man's equivocation hides what lay behind the questions of his father and his grandfather: that she must *give* her heart. Only in the ancient Cacique is motive pure; but his last crucial speech to her is not translated, because the middle-aged are in conflict and the only one who speaks her language is the one who feels most hatred. So what are we to make of the ending? The old man's hand is raised 'to strike and strike home, accomplish the sacrifice and achieve the power. The mastery that man must hold, and that passes from race to race' (*WWRA*, 71). But what does that last sentence mean, suspended by itself? Whose conclusion is it? The old man's? Can we feel as he does – 'mastery' being, for him, the power to channel cosmic forces creatively, taken back from misuse by whites, without animus? (Yet he is deceived about the Woman's consent, he and his world are near death, and his glass-like eyes seem only to reflect our gaze back on us.) Is it the point of view of the other Indians? (But ritual killing is often the mark of acute anxiety; they lack the old man's confidence and their motives are mixed, including racial animus and desire to triumph.) Can it be Lawrence, when the story has carefully created such complexity and conflict (and is certainly about much more than an attack on feminism)? I think myself that the careful suspending of the sentence between the reader and the priest's arm, raised like a question-mark against the sun, together with the horror of what we know must happen but has not yet produced a decisive reaction, create a maximum of disturbance and questioning rather than conclusive judgement. What *is* the value of the white Señora's heart?

St. Mawr and 'The Princess'

At first sight, *St. Mawr* and 'The Princess' – though they pose that same question about their heroines, and end in the wild New Mexican landscape near the ranch – may seem to have little to do with native Americans and colonialism. Indeed, both are about a great deal more, which can only come into partial focus here. Yet the imaginative development and underlying structure of both stories spring from Lawrence's growing understanding of colonialism and of what it means, to those who profit by it, and to its victims.

Strikingly, all the main characters in *St. Mawr* are mentally either 'colonials' or 'colonised', and displaced. Colonial mentality typically feels its cultural home to be not in the colonial country, but in metropolitan Europe. Lou is an American expatriate turned metropolitan sophisticate, who belongs nowhere now, but lives the life of the Smart Young Thing at the expense of her nerves. Her Australian artist husband is fast becoming fashionable, as a purveyor of images to metropolitan society, a colonial type still very much with us. Her mother was raised in a slave-owning mansion in the American South – which is where the money comes from, though it is now invested in property in Texas. She turns a gunmetal sarcasm on everyone because she too belongs nowhere and can find nothing to believe in. Conversely, the mixed-race Phoenix and the Welsh groom Lewis are colonised people, showing the effects of this in different ways.

St. Mawr begins in splendidly laconic social satire as world-weary Lou and her subversive Mamma register the hollowness and the lack of true masculinity and femininity in their metropolitan circle; but this first phase turns on a striking contrast, a decolonisation of Lou's imagination in fact, when she confronts the beautiful but dangerous stallion of the title. St. Mawr's fiery life and luminous colour become for her a window into another 'darker, more spacious, more dangerous, more splendid world' (*SM*, 41), and a definitive measure of her world's sterility. As the scales fall from her eyes, she glimpses for the first time the 'God' burning in all things, Great Pan, before the Greeks reduced him to goatiness. Yet, maltreated, St. Mawr is dangerous, especially to the human ego that cares only for domination and display. The crisis comes with a ride to the Devil's Chair, a rocky outcrop in wild moorland 'where the spirit of aboriginal England still lingers' (*SM*, 73). There St. Mawr shies at a dead snake, Rico reacts in rage, pulling the horse over on top of himself, and a lashing hoof strikes a Bright Young Man coming to help. Imagination changes focal length now, in a way which can seem disconcerting, even excessive. For what comes to Lou suddenly is apocalyptic vision, looking behind the disaster to its ultimate cause. The wilful, brutal, but hollow rider and the rebellious violent animal image a deadliness always latent in the 'colonial' drive to *dominate* 'aboriginal' nature and native. But Lou now intuits something even deeper, darker, archetypal: a force seeking to undermine, pervert and finally *reverse* eternal living energy, into destruction. Lou's vision of Evil triumphant is the opposite of St John's in Patmos, which Lawrence had recently discussed with Frederick Carter in the Shropshire of the story. Through the particular image – that beautiful horse upside down, writhing and lashing, then half rising into a monstrous shape (hippogriff, dragon); with those young men, one corpselike, the other bleeding – comes a Revelation of something lurking everywhere, a horrible anti-life energy now suddenly released. When the aftermath seems to confirm her vision, in the plot to castrate St. Mawr, England becomes for Lou a deathland from which she must flee. (By now we have learned to see in Phoenix – part 'Navajo'/Dinee, part Mexican – and in Lewis the Welshman, the powerless half-life but also the potential for resistance and aggression of the colonised. For them too, no full life is possible in England.)

Once again the story changes key as St. Mawr, his work as catalyst of imagination done, is left behind in a Texas more spacious and natural for a horse but still, for Lou, colonial. By contrast, the ranch in the Rockies, looking out over the great plain of New Mexico, is an aboriginal place where 'god' becomes visible again, undistorted by man, and Lou can renew her life, though not ready yet for a new relationship. But the 'god' revealed in the great pine-tree, the alfalfa field, and the pack-rats on the roof of the log cabin, is no god of love. The place is untamed. It speaks of conflict, endless battle with bristling nature and squalor in striving towards further creation; but also of energy and vitality, a spirit that can save and regenerate. The clear implication is that only after true relation to the cosmos can there be integration of the self, and true relationship with others.

In contrast, 'The Princess' shows what happens when the 'spirit of place' – again wild, secret, very beautiful, and perhaps sacred too like the Blue Lake of the Taos Indians – is desecrated by human impotence, arrogance, lethal violence. Once more, however, as with 'The Woman Who Rode Away', one will not understand the nature and significance of the tragedy, the brutal rape and killing, until one grasps how it originates not merely in gender hostility but also in the impulses which underlie imperialism and colonial revolt. The heroine has been brought up to think of herself as a princess, with an imperial sense of belonging to a superior race. Her father's sense of his own identity is wholly bound up with his derivation from an ancient Scottish royal house, ante-dating the Stuarts who brought about the 'colonisation' of Scotland by England. His sense of superiority has no dependence on any kind of achievement but is racial, of the blood. (There are racisms other than those founded on skin-colour.) It allows him to father his child on a rich

American woman for whom he appears to feel nothing; and after her death to resist any claims of relationship, for the child as well as himself, with his wife's people or their land. Like Lou, he becomes a displaced person, travelling from country to country, with only the most formal acquaintanceship anywhere, and a constant change of nurse for his daughter, so that she has no sense of belonging or relationship other than with him. He teaches her not merely to think of herself as superior to all others, but further, to see everybody else as demonically self-centred under the skin. She is an apt pupil – sometimes mildly surprised by aggressive reactions in those to whom she unconsciously condescends. After her father's death she remains a wanderer, sometimes wondering abstractly about marriage, but virginal. No man has roused sexual interest in her, until she is 'intrigued' (*SM*, 167) by a guide on a dude ranch in New Mexico.

Domingo Romero is a Hispanic man who has lost out to whites, and is reduced to guiding tourists over the land his Mexican family took from the Indians. He has something of the heavy hopelessness and inertia of those whose lives have no meaning or self-direction; but in him there remains 'a spark of pride, of self-confidence, of dauntlessness . . . in the midst of the blackness of static despair'(*SM*, 168). Though silent and sometimes sullen-seeming, he not only is intelligent but shows her a male kindness, gentleness and helpfulness she has never known before. She persuades him to arrange a secret ride to a cabin by the mountain lake, with her woman companion, and when the latter's horse is injured, she trusts him enough to insist on going on with him alone.

As in the two other novellas, the journey is from one world to another, pre-colonial, and unspoilt. It recreates, in concrete immediacy, a ride Lawrence had taken with Dorothy Brett who had come to live with the Lawrences on the ranch,[19] but it is also a symbolic journey to an untamed psychological interior, beautiful but difficult of access for modern man and woman. There they may see wild nature, but must also confront their own, the deadliness they bring with them, so different from either the bobcat by the lakeside, or the two Indian hunters who pass by on their way back to the Pueblo. That night the tragedy begins when she cannot stand the cold, and begs him to warm her – only to find herself then 'given over' to something she may have willed to happen but never really wanted (*SM*, 188). The experience suffuses him with tenderness, pride, exultation, all the more so because of his background – but he is met the next morning by total rejection. Step by step the tragedy escalates through rape to death: she determined to retain possession of herself; his phallic pride exaggerated and intensified by the 'colonial' situation. Lawrence holds the balance true. Which is more to blame: her imperial *noli me tangere*, or his macho reaction to renewed humiliation? Rather we measure to the full a horror of mutual desecration; made still worse in the brisk callousness of the shooting of Romero by offi-cers of 'nature conservation', the Forestry Commission, which has made it a crime for Indians to kill deer for meat, on their own ancestral land.[20]

The challenge of the Hopi

One more challenge to imagination remained that autumn. 'The Hopi Snake Dance' (*MM*, 71–90) may suggest – to our privileged hindsight – how ima-gination needs knowledge in order to understand in full; but the sharply ironic contrast Lawrence draws between the 'grey', poverty-stricken, partly ruined and depopulated Hopi villages, and the hordes of tourists in long lines of automobiles, come to gaze on a 'circus performance', shows how far he is ahead of his time in his struggle to understand. The essay in *Mornings in Mexico* was in fact his second attempt. He had made the journey with Frieda, Mabel and Tony, and of course it was full of tension. He was dead tired, and had earache. In his first attempt at an essay,[21] imagination is wholly absent. Indeed the second version still begins depressingly, with a point of view markedly uninvolved. The first dance of the Antelope priests, described with physical accuracy but no comprehension, comes across as 'a brief, primitive performance' still (*MM*, 81) – even when prefaced by a lecture treating the animistic religion of *all* American Indians as an attempt to 'conquer' the great powers and potencies in nature and the cosmos. Ashy and black-smeared priests sway from side to side, thumping their feet in turn on an unexplained trapdoor in front of a patch of greenery. The dance has none of the sensuous or aesthetic appeal of the one at San Domingo; and despite his attempt to generalise about Indian animism Lawrence is well aware of how little he actually knows. The description is peppered with 'they say' and 'may be'.

Yet imagination does begin to stir as the strangeness of the 'low sombre, secretive chant-call' (to the dark underworld, he supposes, where snakes come from), and the deep concentration of the priests, conquer 'for a few seconds our white-faced flippancy' (*MM*, 80). Then the description of the Snake dance the next day sharply distinguishes his view from that of the tourists who can hardly wait for the preliminary 'mummery' to cease and only want to see the spectacle of men carrying snakes in their mouths. Sensuous imagination comes fully alive now: to the delicacy and beauty of the rattlesnakes, their birdlike heads so close to the cheeks of the snake-priests 'as if wondering or listening'; to the handsomeness of the bull-snakes; to the beautiful 'steering away' of snakes when released, and the gentle, rev-erent movements of the men who soothe them after recapture; to the anxious concentration of the old men 'dusting' with prayer-sticks the shoulders of the carriers. Sensuous imagination captures, truly, the creation of harmony with what is dangerous; the gentleness, reverence, quietening; the sense of communication (*MM*, 83–84).

Unfortunately – again from the privileged position of later knowledge unavailable to Lawrence – understanding still lags behind. Fresh from the sense of battle in the conclusion to *St. Mawr*, busy reading about the much more militaristic and terrible religions of the Aztec and Maya, it was easy for him to see the ceremony not only as communication with a nether world, but as an effort of 'conquest': the snakes like arrows carrying the human will, partly in love, but mostly to gain power, 'shot clean by man's sapience and courage, into the resistant, malevolent heart of the earth's oldest, stubborn core' (*MM*, 87). In fact the Hopi are not in ceaseless conflict with their gods, nor do they found their religion in the search for power and the will to conquer. Their name means 'The Peaceful People', and they claim to be the Anasazi, the most Ancient Ones whose passage left the ruins of cliff-dwellings and the petroglyph signatures of clan migrations across the canyons of Arizona, and who could find lasting refuge only in the inaccessible rocky mesas on which they still dwell. Almost more than any, they resisted colonial attempts to assimilate them to 'civilisation'; and it was a traumatic split between those who vowed to resist assimilation to the end, and those who could see a future only in compromise, that had led in 1906 to the exodus of the intransigents from Oraibi, and the foundation of Hotevilla, splitting the priest-clans in a deep psychological wound to a people already decimated by disease and persecuted by government. What Lawrence saw at Hotevilla and Oraibi was the aftermath of that disaster. (Typically of the Hopi, the bitter expulsion was done without bloodshed, by a kind of pushing contest.) If, however, Lawrence's understanding was inevitably incomplete,[22] much that his sensuous imagination detected was accurate, and knowledge adds even more resonance to the essay's concluding sense of something *really* poisonous: the engines of the white man, 'like the biggest of rattlesnakes buzzing' (*MM*, 90).

Mexico again – and a contrast

In October 1924, Lawrence went back to Mexico to rewrite 'Quetzalcoatl' into *The Plumed Serpent*. The nature of that rewriting is too big and complex a subject to be more than hinted at here. The return to England had left him with a sense of disillusion and betrayal, while Mexico seemed even more dangerous and unstable than before. He knew more now about its history and its ancient religion; and he felt even more strongly that only a religious revolution could arrest both European and colonial decadence – and change the symptomatic 'new woman' with (he thought) her self-centred sexuality. His imagination was caught up now in extending and elaborating the revolutionary ideas, hymns and ceremonies he had sketched in 'Quetzalcoatl'; and in intensifying his attack on the situation they sought to remedy. The new novel became more decisive and, in its chosen directions, more powerful; though readers inclined to question those directions will react the more strongly to what is now less exploratory and tentative, less questioned from within, altogether more dictatorial. Moreover there are times when imagination devoted to idea and symbol ceases to register human being and feeling. One example, and one contrast, must suffice to make the point and mark a difference. In *The Plumed Serpent* the attack on Christianity has become still more deliberate and intransigent, and in the chapter 'Auto da fe' the very title claims the authority of an Inquisition – by character and author alike, now – to pronounce on the nature of the Mexican peasant soul and its beliefs, and to burn away its idols for its own good. When, however, the culmination of this becomes Cipriano's vicious attack on Ramón's dying wife, something ugly has happened in the rewriting. It is no longer a question of the rights and wrongs of Christianity but of an imagination that has become so overwhelmingly ideological at this point as to be apparently quite blind to a suffering human being, whether judged inadequate or not. A hated idea has blinded author and character alike; and an inhuman exultance has taken the place of what has atrophied.

A smaller work may help as a measure of difference. *Mornings in Mexico* actually begins with self-mockery about author-ity. The author says 'Mexico', but really that comes down to a little town, a crumbly adobe house, and one person with a pen, scribbling in an exercise book. The treatment of the *mozo* Rosalino, in the essays that follow, demonstrates the need to keep humanising imagination awake. In 'Corasmin and the Parrots' the boy is sardonically diminished by the parrots' imitation. In 'Walk to Huapa' he is a 'dumb-bell' peasant, occasionally amusing in his stupidity. In 'The Mozo' Lawrence looks at him more closely; but seems divided between confident generalities about the soul of the peasant, and sudden moments of imaginative focus on the actual boy, such as the intuition, in a physical movement, of 'a certain sensitiveness and aloneness, as if he were a mother's boy' – like Lawrence. And by the end of this essay, Lawrence has convicted himself of superficiality. What has come into focus is what it means for such a boy to be separated from his own people; the difficulty of his lonely struggle to better himself; and the courage of his resistance to tyranny which explains what had looked like laziness and fear before. Yet Lawrence knew all that before he began to write the essay. He chose to *show*, in the writing, how it behoves one not to generalise too confidently, and to be imaginatively sensitive, even to an uneducated peasant boy. More effort to imagine the human implications of ideological 'necessity', in cases such as the cleansing of the temple, the execution of the conspirators, or the ban on female orgasm (to gesture towards a spectrum of the questionable) would have made *The Plumed Serpent* a much less rebarbative work. At least the horror of miscegenation has lapsed, since Kate will almost certainly marry Cipriano and become Malintzi now – though that also shows how much less questioning there is than before. Greater decisiveness has been bought at an imaginative price.

Yet Lawrence's later rejection of both the political and the sexual ideology of *The Plumed Serpent* allows the emphasis to fall in retrospect where it should do, not on blindnesses but on how much his imagination unusually enabled him to see, into colonialism and its victims, through his encounter with American Indians. His successes did not come easily, but are all the more precious, many years ahead of their time, and hardly recognised, even now.

NOTES

1 Preface to *Collected African Stories*. Vol. 1: *This Was The Old Chief's Country*, (St Albans: Triad Panther Books, 1973), p. 10.
2 The distinction is needed because of the rival claims of Kipling (in some works, though not others) and Conrad, both of whom had first-hand experience of other cultures. Forster is also a partial exception, though Lawrence pointed unerringly to an imaginative limitation of *A Passage to India* in dealing with an alien culture and religion, 'because he doesn't go down to the root to meet it' (v. 91, 142–43) – resorting to whimsy about Professor Godbole instead.
3 She had also sharply rejected Skrebensky's imperial arguments for *lebensraum* in the Sudan (*R*, 288). (Revised from the manuscript's 'Zululand', cf. 622.)
4 Moreover, Birkin explores the significance of the carving in terms that anticipate by decades the 'Negritude' of Léopold Sédar Senghor. For the influential ideology of President Senghor, what was black was sensuous, emotional, instinctive, rhythmic; what was white was cerebral, abstract, analytical, insentient; see for example his poems 'Black Woman' and 'New York' in *Prose and Poetry*, ed. and trans. John Reed and Clive Wake (London: Heinemann, African Writers Series, 1965).
5 *Symbolic*, chapter 5. See also his treatment of the significance of the friendship of Ishmael and Queequeg in Melville's *Moby Dick*, and of Dana and Aikane in *Two Years Before the Mast*.
6 Mabel Dodge Luhan, *Lorenzo in Taos* (New York: Knopf, 1932; repr. Kraus, 1969), pp. 36–39.
7 I am aware that this term is politically and geographically incorrect; but 'native' American is clumsy, and strikes an exiled South African as unpleasantly reminiscent of language under apartheid. It would be better to use each people's name

for themselves or their languages, but would readers relate 'Tiwa' to Taos Pueblo? Since Lawrence and his contemporaries of all races and persuasions used 'Indian', I shall too, for convenience. Readers may supply inverted commas if they wish.

8 For a full treatment of this long struggle, see R. C. Gordon-McCutchan, *The Taos Indians and the Battle for Blue Lake* (Santa Fé: Red Crane Books, 1991).

9 Ed. with an introduction by Louis L. Martz (Redding Ridge, CT: Black Swan Books, 1995).

10 E.g. Achebe's *Things Fall Apart* (1958) and *Arrow of God* (1964); Soyinka's *The Road* (1965) and *Death and the King's Horseman* (1975); Ngugi's *The River Between* (1965) and *Petals of Blood* (1977). All but Soyinka published in the Heinemann African Writers Series; Soyinka by Oxford University Press.

11 This last concern is less true of the later work of Ngugi, though his gradually developing conception of a 'new' African woman owes more to communist than to western feminist thinking.

12 cf. *Les Damnés de la Terre* (Paris, 1961) translated as *The Wretched of the Earth* (1965); London: Pelican Books, 1967); see especially chapter 1 'Concerning Violence'.

13 *Q*, 318–20, cf. also 215, 271–72.

14 cf. *DG*, chapters 6 and 7.

15 cf. Mark Kinkead-Weekes, 'D. H. Lawrence and the Dance', *Dance Research*, 10 (Spring 1992), 59–77.

16 See, especially, Kate Millett, *Sexual Politics* (New York: Doubleday, 1970), pp. 285–93, and, more temperately, R. P. Draper 'The Defeat of Feminism: D. H. Lawrence's *The Fox* and *The Woman Who Rode Away*', in *Critical Essays on D. H. Lawrence*, ed. Dennis Jackson and Fleda Brown Jackson (Boston: J. K. Hall, 1998), pp. 158–59.

17 For a fuller argument, see Mark Kinkead-Weekes, 'The Gringo Señora Who Rode Away', *DHLR*, 22 (Fall 1990), 251–65.

18 cf. Fanon, *The Wretched of the Earth*, p. 60: 'At the level of individuals, violence is a cleansing force. It frees the native from his inferiority complex and his despair and inaction, it makes him fearless and restores his self-respect.' See also his *Black Skin, White Masks* (Paris 1952, trans. 1968); and Derek Walcott's play *Dream on Monkey Mountain* (London: Cape, 1972) in which an old black woodcutter is made to feel like a deformed monkey by the apparition of a White Lady. He responds first with false messianism and then with fascist militarism; but it is only when he cuts Her head off that he can be free, accept himself and relate to his living world.

19 See Dorothy Brett, *Lawrence and Brett: A Friendship* (London: Secker, 1933), pp. 143–46.

20 This is why the Indians in the story deny having seen any game, despite their heavy bulging saddlebag. The bitter irony is that the most stubborn resistance to the claims of the Taos Indians to their ancestral territory came from the 'conservation' mentality of the Forest Commission, the foundation of which had seemed so progressive.

21 'Just Back from the Snake-Dance – Tired Out', *Laughing Horse*, 11 (September 1924); cf. *Lorenzo in Taos*, pp. 267–68.

22 Until fairly recently, powerful taboos prevented Hopi elders from explaining their

ceremonies. Earle R. Forrest, *The Snake Dance of the Hopi Indians* (Los Angeles: Westernlore Press, 1961), knows that the hole and sounding-board, on which the dancers stamp to alert the underworld, represents the *sipapu* from which the Hopi believe they emerged into this world, but offers no explanation of what the dances mean. Harold Courlander, *The Fourth World of the Hopi* (Albuquerque: University of New Mexico Press, 1987), relates the origin myth of the snake clan: a brave young man travels to the land of the snake people and returns with a bride and rain-making ceremonies, but is later expelled by an ungrateful people to their cost. But there is no explanation of the connection with the Antelope Clan. Only in 1963 did Frank Waters's *The Book of the Hopi* (1963; repr. Penguin 1973) offer an explanation of the Antelope–Snake Dance, based on the evidence of clan spokesmen. We learn of the marriage of Antelope Boy and Snake Maiden in the Antelope Kiva before the dances, anticipating harmony between the 'upper' and 'lower' worlds (both cosmic and within human beings) which the dances then go on to create, bringing the rains. Moreover, Waters draws an analogy (though with what basis in the original Hopi testimony is unclear) with the ancient Hindu neurology of *Kundalini*, the activation and harmonising of energy sources from the lower body upwards, which Lawrence had known and been profoundly influenced by since 1917. Accounts of the split in Oraibi and the foundation of Hotevilea appear in Forrest, *The Snake Dance*, pp. 65–71; Courlander, *The Fourth World*, pp. 194–200; Waters, *The Book of the Hopi*, pp. 301–5; and Harry C. James, *Pages from Hopi History* (Tucson: University of Arizona Press, 1974), pp. 130–45.

5

MORAG SHIACH

Work and selfhood
in *Lady Chatterley's Lover*

Lady Chatterley's Lover is famously, even notoriously, a book about sex. The novel is divided into three sections: the first seeks to register the nature and causes of psychic and social degradation; the second stages a series of sexual encounters between Lady Chatterley and the gamekeeper, Mellors; and the third considers the viability of their existence as a couple. Lawrence created three different versions of the novel, using a range of characters and circumstances to articulate its different forms of individual and social dysfunction, but the basic structure of degeneration, rebirth and consequent fragility remains intact throughout all of Lawrence's re-writing. What has less frequently been noted, however, is that *Lady Chatterley's Lover* is also a novel about work: about the alienation of industrial labour, the desperate compensatory quality of intellectual work, the inescapability of physical toil, and the imaginative and ideological work of narrative fiction. The novel begins with the observation that: 'The cataclysm has happened, we are among the ruins, we start to build up new little habitats, to have new little hopes. It is rather hard work.' It thus opens with the catastrophe and ruin which Lawrence aims to exemplify and to embody in the physical and psychic failings of his characters, but it also begins with the necessity for hard work.

The labouring self

The relations between work and subjectivity preoccupied Lawrence throughout his writing, though the ways in which he represented the social and psychic significance of labour were to develop significantly. In his 'Study of Thomas Hardy', written in 1914, Lawrence argues forcefully that work is a negation of the creative aspects of the individual self. Lawrence sees the human individual as caught between two opposing forces, one which is driven by fear and concentrates on self-preservation and another which is intense, transient, wasteful, but creative. Work, he argues, is securely placed on the side of self-preservation, fear of risk, and deadly repetition. Lawrence resists the tendency to elevate work as a moral or spiritual imperative and sees it rather as a destructive and inhibiting necessity. A man, and it is always a man in this essay, who is working is caught in the mechanical repetitions of a physical and intellectual habit 'repeating some old process of life, unable to become ourselves, unable to produce anything new' (*Hardy*, 45). For Lawrence work is 'simply, the activity necessary for the production of a sufficient supply of food and shelter: nothing more holy than that' (33), and it is a form of non-living or negation which every individual craves to escape. Though he indicts labour because of its repetitions and its basically mechanical character, Lawrence is at this stage willing to contemplate the idea that mechanisation could liberate us from the necessity of work. He insists that we can never go back to pre-industrial forms of artisanal labour, and thus sees the progressive reduction of working time as the only way to imagine greater resources of time and energy for wasteful, excessive and creative forms of being. Work may be a displacement activity for the 'unsatisfied soul', it may be a method of bringing aspects of life into our consciousness, but it is only ever the pre-condition of creative life and may in practice be its negation.

In his essay on the 'Education of the People', written in 1918, Lawrence is still concerned about the inhibiting effects of fear: 'if you can't cure people of being frightened for their own existence, you'll educate them in vain'.[1] He believes that fear of poverty grips everyone and drives them towards desperate and destructive strategies of self-preservation, in response to a threat that may well not be very substantial: this fear mechanism will reappear in *Lady Chatterley's Lover* as the bitch-goddess of success. But in 'Education of the People' Lawrence no longer sees work as a burden to be overcome, in fact he argues that it is irresponsible to educate children without considering the central role that physical and practical labour are likely to have in their adult lives. He condemns the idealism that 'sits decreeing that our children shall be educated pure from the taint of materialism and industrialism, and all the time it is fawning and cringing before industrialism and materialism' (93). He also sees the attempt to abstract a spiritualised notion of individuality from the simple material facts of labour as misguided, and even dangerous. Offering people some abstract future possibility of self-fulfilment or self-expression, beyond and apart from the world of work, is a kind of fraud: 'Away with the imbecile pretence of culture in the elementary schools. Remember the back streets, remember that the souls of the working people are only rendered neurasthenic by your false culture' (112). Against this idealism, Lawrence begins to construct his own versions of a materialism which seeks to ground the individual in the affective and physiological structures of the body. His rhetoric is brutal as he advocates seizing babies from their mothers, or beating children, as a necessary means to overcome the deleterious cultural and individual effects of spiritualised and idealised forms of selfhood. Thinking of ourselves as ideal cerebral beings we tend to reject physical work as degrading or menial, and so Lawrence insists that we must find a version of selfhood that encompasses our physicality. He sees work, in this essay, as 'a pleasant occupation for a human creature, a natural activity' (149). Work may provide the means for personal independence, and even liberty, but it should be undertaken in a spirit of pragmatism, in a fashion that is absorbed but mindless.

This concern with the development of a physical model of individual selfhood is much more fully articulated in *Fantasia of the Unconscious* (1922), where Lawrence tries to substantiate his ideas about the interaction of physical and nervous forces within the individual. Some notion of practical creativity remains central to his conception of human individuality, and in an analysis reminiscent of Marx's comments on work and species being, Lawrence asserts that 'It is the desire of the human male to build a world: not "to build a world for you, dear"; but to build up out of his own self and his own belief and his own effort something wonderful.'[2] Work then becomes an integral part of Lawrence's account of the interaction of individual and species: we are from the moment of conception individuals but we are also bound by the psychic and physiological laws of our species which drive us towards creative interaction with, and transformation of, the external world through the activity of labour. Lawrence's account in *Fantasia* becomes increasingly embattled and he returns to the pernicious effects of spiritual forms of knowledge and the domination of mental over physical life: twin manifestations of the distorted and destructive will. 'Will' here is associated with the spiritual, with the 'upper self', and with destructive egoism. As Lawrence will express it in 'A Propos of *Lady Chatterley's Lover*': 'Men only know one another in menace. Individualism has triumphed. If I am a sheer individual, then every other being, every other man especially, is over against me as a menace to me.'[3] This sense of being embattled, subject to threat and overwhelmed by the friction of other wills, will re-emerge in *Lady Chatterley's Lover*. In *Fantasia*, writing about dysfunction, danger and menace produces a violent supplement within the writing which again focuses on women and children. Lawrence argues that man's supreme responsibility is 'to fulfil his own profoundest impulses, with reference to none but God or his own soul, not taking woman into count at all' (124) and this task has become both more urgent and more violent by the end of the book:

> But fight for your life, men. Fight your wife out of her own self-conscious pre-occupation with herself. Batter her out of it till she's stunned. Drive her back into her own true mode. Rip all her nice superimposed modern-woman and wonderful-creature garb off her. Reduce her once more to a naked Eve, and send the apple flying.   (284)

This naked Eve, unlike the modern woman, is of course unlikely to work, or at least unlikely to be involved in waged labour outside the home.

By the end of the 1920s, Lawrence increasingly comes to see work as a point of resistance to excessively cerebral conceptions of selfhood: it may indeed be the residuum of the physical within social life, an activity whose materiality and temporality cannot be abstracted, despite the progressive tendency towards abstraction and alienation inherent in capitalist social and economic relations. When Lawrence recommends, in a letter written in 1927, that his wife's daughter should absorb herself in work, he does so out of despair over her capacity to engage in any other ways with the vital and dynamic processes he sees as integral to human subjectivity: 'it is better that she works. The young can neither love nor live. The best is that they work' (vi. 34).

The relations between the social degeneration and the psychic collapse Lawrence reads into contemporary idealisations of the self and the redemptive possibilities of manual labour are made even more explicit in the 1929 article, 'Men must Work and Women as Well'. Here he explicitly repudiates his earlier argument that material and mechanical progress could free us from the burden of toil, associating such inverted utopianism with 'great magnates of industry like Mr Ford'.[4] Indeed, the aspiration to free ourselves from physical labour becomes simply another manifestation of the repudiation of material forms of subjectivity. Having craved freedom from physical work, we are now doomed to resent all physical demands on our time and energies. Lawrence certainly condemns the pernicious effects of such fastidiousness, arguing that all that it has produced is angry and resentful individuals who are nonetheless still required to undertake a series of manual tasks. Yet his language suggests that his earlier aspiration to escape from the brute demands of physical labour has not entirely disappeared: 'the labouring masses are and will be, even if all else is swept away: because they must be. They represent the gross necessity of man, which science has failed to save us from' (587). Even allowing for the ironic tone in which he represents this 'gross necessity', it is hard not to hear some lingering regret over science's failure. As he tries to exemplify residual and necessary forms of physical labour, Lawrence is driven towards the ruthlessly and remorselessly gendered categories already in place in an earlier study such as *Fantasia of the Unconscious*. Women's labour is represented by cooking, cleaning and child care, while the epitome of male physical labour is revealed in the dark and sweaty body of the miner. Lawrence insists on the essential and originary distinction between men and women – 'A child is born with one sex only, and remains always single in his sex' (*Fantasia*, 140) – and he reads conflict between men and women as a symptom of the idealisation and repudiation of the physical, and specifically of physical labour.

Lady Chatterley's Lover, written in the late 1920s, engages in an imaginative mode with the ways in which work might express, repudiate or unsettle the destructive tendency towards idealism which Lawrence sees as most fully expressed through rapidly advancing industrialisation and mechanisation. Commercialism and industrialism are seen as dominating not simply economic relations between classes and between individuals, but also familial, sexual and cultural relations between all the characters in the novel. The novel is set in the industrial Midlands where Clifford Chatterley's country house is surrounded by the collieries that generate his wealth. This industrial landscape is consistently presented by the narrator as embodying broad social and ethical meanings:

> With the stoicism of the young she took in the utter, soulless ugliness of the coal-and-iron Midlands at a glance . . . she heard the rattle-rattle of the screens at the pit, the puff of the winding engine, the clink-clink of shunting trucks, and the hoarse little whistle of the colliery locomotives . . . when the wind was that way, which was often, the house was full of the stench of this sulphurous combustion of the earth's excrement. But even on windless days the air always smelt of something under-earth: sulphur, iron, coal, or acid. And even on the Christmas roses the smuts settled persistently, incredible, like black manna from the skies of doom. (13)

The movement of this passage is instructive. It begins with the tentative, even unconscious, recognition by Lady Chatterley of the ugliness of the landscape that surrounds her and it then creates through the insistent repetitions of its language an almost physical unease in the reader as it moves towards its conclusion with the skies of doom. That it should be Constance Chatterley who glimpses the ugliness that surrounds her is important for the narrative development of the novel, but so too is her incapacity at this early stage really to grasp the enormity and significance of such ugliness. The narrator drives us towards conclusions Constance Chatterley is far from reaching, while also letting us know that she will be capable of such perceptions in the future.

This industrial landscape dominates the lives of those who work in it, turning them from human flesh to soulless mechanism. Working people simply strive to do better within the industrial system: to earn more money. This mechanised greed, a form of 'prostitution to the Money-God', is condemned repeatedly in the novel but political alternatives to capitalism are represented as equally implicated in the logic of mechanism and system: 'You must submerge yourselves in the greater thing, the soviet-social thing. Even an organism is bourgeois: so the ideal must be mechanical . . . Each man a machine-part, and the driving power of the machine, hate: hate of the bourgeois! That, to me, is bolshevism' (*LCL*, 38). This remark brings together anxieties over mechanisation, objectification and submergence of self in what might seem like a relatively familiar sort of organicist nostalgia, but in fact the relations between mechanism and selfhood are far from stable in the novel as a whole. Representations of selfhood in *Lady Chatterley's Lover* draw on a series of minute but semantically and ideologically significant distinctions between self-consciousness, with its pathological manifestations in the will, and a pre-mental consciousness of self.

Thus, while one character can express anxiety about the ways in which communism necessitates a sacrifice of the self, other voices throughout the novel question the viability and the desirability of self-consciousness and its articulation through the will. Excessive self-consciousness, particularly a mental consciousness with no grounding in bodily experience, is ascribed to many of the characters in this novel. Michaelis, who is Lady Chatterley's lover in the early parts of the novel, is self-contained to the point of pathology: '"*Me* give myself away! ha-ha!" he laughed hollowly, cynical at such an idea' (27). Yet he also suffers from a 'sad-dog sort of extinguished self' (28). Clifford has a precarious sense of self – 'he needed Connie to be there, to assure him he existed at all' (16) – but also has a coercive, bullying self that seeks to eradicate disturbing or unpredictable elements of its own or in others. Constance Chatterley's sister Hilda seeks to intervene in her sister's life and is condemned as wilful by Mellors in generalising terms that move from character analysis to social dogma: 'A stubborn woman an' 'er own self-will: ay, they make a fast continuity, they do' (245). But it is in the sphere of sexual relationships where the dangers of self-assertion and self-consciousness are most powerfully asserted. Connie's early sexual experiences with a young German student, with whom her primary connections are 'philosophical, sociological and artistic', involve merely 'a queer vibrating thrill inside the body, a final spasm of self-assertion' (8). 'Thrill' and 'spasm' are terms which signal superficiality of experience throughout the novel and are associated with attempts to ward off the creative and the unpredictable. Thus Connie's self-assertion is read through her fearful conformity and the result is a neurotic spasm.

Lady Chatterley's Lover becomes increasingly forceful in its articulation of the forms of authentic selfhood which are desirable and possible. Beginning with a sense that Connie's early sexual experiences might have been transient and superficial but that she is still capable of change and development, the novel begins to see all manifestations of willed selfhood as pernicious and as irremediable. Mellors declares that 'when a woman gets absolutely possessed by her own will, her own will set against everything, then it's fearful, and she should be shot at last' (*LCL*, 280). Indeed Mellors has been given the power by the novel to distinguish between degenerate and empty forms of subjectivity, such as those associated with his ex-wife and with Clifford Chatterley, and creative forms of self-realisation. One of the first things we learn about Mellors is that he is 'sure of himself' and he is represented as intact and as separate to the point of hostility. For Connie, on the other hand, selfhood is a burden, a weight of mental consciousness that she carries from the opening pages of the novel until she 'could bear the burden of herself no more' (117). Connie's affair with Mellors leads to a loss of self which she both celebrates and fears ('she did not want to be effaced') and her will struggles against the forms of knowing associated in the novel primarily with the womb and the bowels: 'She had a devil of self-will in her breast that could have fought the full, soft, heavy adoration of her womb and bowels' (135–36).

Physical consciousness

Physical consciousness emerges, however fleetingly, as a key point of resistance to mechanisation and to the power of commerce in *Lady Chatterley's Lover*. This version of selfhood is explored physiologically and historically in Lawrence's two sustained engagements with theories of human subjectivity: *Fantasia of the Unconscious* and *Psychoanalysis and the Unconscious*. In these texts Lawrence argues that our conception of human subjectivity is partial, in that it interests itself only in our mental lives. For Lawrence this is a belated and contingent part of individual development. He prefers a psycho-biological model of selfhood which draws on networks of nerves to illuminate the particularities of human subjectivity. Lawrence insists that individuality is a given, though it is an attribute that may easily be lost. From the moment of conception the human infant is an individual whose development will depend on the particular balance of forces within distinct parts of the organism. Lawrence describes the forms of consciousness associated with areas such as the 'solar plexus' or the 'lumbar ganglion' and analyses the impact of these physical entities on the human individual. As in 'Education of the People', the imbrication of social policy, familial interaction and psychic life becomes increasingly troubling as Lawrence expresses his hostility not simply to the cerebral but also to the emotional. This may lie behind the brutality with which Mellors reprimands his daughter for weeping over the death of a cat: '"Ah, shut it up, tha false little bitch!" came the man's angry voice, and the child sobbed louder' (*LCL*, 58).

Lawrence's interest in a psycho-biological model of subjectivity was by no means eccentric, though some of his conclusions undoubtedly were.[5] Throughout *Lady Chatterley's Lover* we can find traces of a range of social and medical models of psychic life and of the forms and meanings of its failures. Clifford is to some extent a victim of war, the physical wound that paralysed him being a harbinger of subsequent psychological wounding: 'mentally he still was alert. But the paralysis, the bruise of the too-great-shock, was gradually spreading in his affective self' (49). The image of the bruise allows for the representation of a wound that is sudden, the result of a specific trauma, but also part of a slow, cumulative process. Clifford's loss of his affective self displays crucial attributes of 'traumatic neurasthenia', a medical condition widely discussed in the early years of the twentieth century.[6]

Neurasthenia was understood as a chronic condition, the result of exhaustion of nervous force, but it could also be the result of a more precise individual or social trauma. Clifford's nerves function erratically, creating imbalances of energy throughout the novel. At times he suffers from a collapse of nervous energy, or he wastes nervous energy through self-deception or obsession, and at other moments he is in a 'nervous frenzy'. When not braced up to work Clifford is reduced to 'a net-work of nerves' (139), a circulation of energy which serves simply to mask a dangerous void.

Clifford's condition is named variously. Early in the novel he is suffering from 'vacant depression', while in the later stages of the novel his behaviour is diagnosed as hysterical. Throughout, however, he is associated with wasteful and compulsive spending of nervous energy to no particular end. This lack of 'end' is given forceful, perhaps even crude, expression in his failure to procreate. But it also has more abstract meanings which are associated with his life even before the war. As the inheritor of the legacy of industrial exploitation he is bound to a system that can only accelerate both production and acquisition in an ever more frantic spectacle of industrial growth. As a young intellectual he is similarly caught in a discursive economy that knows no bounds: the intellectual discussions in *Lady Chatterley's Lover* are notably futile and rather prolonged. This forceful indictment of wasteful nervous expenditure sits rather uncomfortably with Lawrence's own fascination with excess and waste in his 'Study of Thomas Hardy', but in *Lady Chatterley's Lover* Lawrence displays a horror of non-productive, or non-procreative, expenditures of energy.

In the treatment of neurasthenia doctors recommended rest, but Clifford tries instead to overcome nervous and affective exhaustion by ever-increasing levels of work. His 'work' at the beginning of the novel is writing fiction, an activity that is treated with great scepticism. Joint participation in Clifford's work appears to offer Clifford and Connie some shared and meaningful activity and we are told that 'their interests had never ceased to flow together, over his work' (18). But this shared project is not long sustained: from the outset we are told that what they had shared was a 'vague life of absorption in Clifford and his work'. The vagueness already tells us about a lack of focus, a certain drifting, the absorption is a loss of self based more on fear and negation than on creative transformation, and finally the absorption is primarily in Clifford and only secondarily in his work which suggests that such collaborative labour cannot mask a more fundamental division. The sentence contrasts strikingly with the narrator's conclusion about Connie and Mellors after they have struggled together to push Clifford's wheelchair uphill: 'It was curious, but this bit of work together had brought them much closer than they had been before' (192), closer presumably than all the sexual intimacies they have shared at this stage of the novel.

Clifford's work is a frenzy of neurotic activity whose aim is worldly success. Connie's father tells us that as literary texts, his stories are 'void', a judgement that Connie herself will come to share. Connie also comes to resent Clifford's work as a symptom of his self-obsession: 'She wanted to be clear of him, and especially of his consciousness, his words, his obsession with himself – his endless treadmill obsession with himself and his own words' (93). The narrative voice here enacts the futile repetitions of the process it is describing, assaulting us with Clifford's selfhood and his language. Clifford's writing is simply an enactment of the futility of his speech, with its proliferation of words and its increasing incapacity to name or to know the world: 'when he was alone he tap-tap-tapped on a typewriter, to infinity. But when he was not "working", and she was there, he talked, always talked' (83). The inauthenticity of this form of labour is clearly signalled by the inverted commas, as aesthetic creativity is reduced to repetitive and mechanical tapping. Connie's role in this creative work is similarly reduced: 'the thrill had gone out of it. She was bored by his manuscripts. She still dutifully typed them out for him' (99). The creative capacity of language is here savagely removed from any concerns with the mode of its material production. As one considers the numbers of women who gave up time to struggle with the typing of Lawrence's own manuscript of *Lady Chatterley's Lover* this insistent degradation of the activity of typing strikes a particularly uncomfortable note.

Degeneration and industry

Clifford's work of literary production is, then, a self-deceiving and self-obsessed exercise in futility, and is indeed an activity he is pleased to renounce. As Connie's physical and mental health decline in the first section of the novel, Clifford acquires a nurse, Ivy Bolton, who will oversee the transference of his energies from literary to industrial production. Ivy Bolton is a strange and liminal character: she is the widow of a miner yet her education and professional training gain her an entry to the world of the Chatterleys. She has a fierce sense of class loyalty but also a fascination with the lives and mores of the upper class. As an independent working woman she is particularly susceptible to the corrosive effects of this novel's social and psychic categories which can only read her determination as pathological will. Ivy Bolton is introduced as a woman of some determination driven by a clear desire for economic independence: 'Ivy Bolton went to Sheffield, and attended classes in ambulance, special ambulance, and then the fourth year she even took a nursing course and got qualified. She was determined to be independent and keep her children. So she was assistant at Uthwaite hospital, just a little place, for a while' (*LCL*, 81). This training for independence actually leads her to economic, and later emotional, dependency on the Chatterleys. Her education separates her from the working classes, indeed leads her to a sort of contempt for them whilst at the same time identifying her with the progressive movements of industrial capital, if not exactly with progressive capitalists. Mrs Bolton encourages Clifford to shift his energies towards the development of his mines, pointing out in particular the importance of local labour for young girls: 'keep the men going a bit better, and employ the girls' (106). Clifford is pleased to transfer his energies from the 'populace of pleasure to the populace of work' which he finds grim and terrible, but also more substantial: 'the meat and bones for the bitch-goddess were provided by the men who made money in industry' (107). Under Mrs Bolton's influence, Clifford becomes increasingly absorbed in business and in his mines, in the 'brute business of industrial production'.

For Clifford, identification with the processes of industrial labour creates a harmony between labour and selfhood, even if this is a harmony of degradation. Industry and commerce sustain fantasies of potency and agency for Clifford which he had found in no other cultural sphere: 'he really felt, when he had his periods of energy and worked so hard at the question of the mines, as if his sexual potency were returning' (147). For Ivy Bolton, on the other hand, an increasing identification with the process of industrial production serves to disconnect her from her class and from any sustainable notion of 'independence'. By the end of the novel, however, both are destroyed and reduced to mutual dependence and perversity: 'And then he would put his hand into her bosom and feel her breasts, and kiss them in exaltation, the exaltation of perversity, of being a child when he was a man' (291).

The workers in his mines are also reduced and degraded by the results of

Clifford's feverish work, by the rapidity and momentum of industrial change. Lawrence is particularly forceful in his representation of the impossibility of creative forms of selfhood within the spaces of industrial labour. In other parts of the novel Lawrence works to construct the tension of dialogue between different characters and the narrative voice. Constance Chatterley's increasing identification with the terms and convictions embodied in the narrative voice develops slowly and hesitantly throughout the novel and is mediated by her exchanges with Mellors. The working classes, however, are not permitted to enter into such imaginative or intellectual dialogue, but are consistently objectified and offered as emblematic by the narrative voice: their meanings are always already given. This objectification draws to some extent on existing forms of language: the naming of the mine and its associated industries as 'the works' serves to evacuate conceptions of individuality from the process of labour by identifying activity and place. This is a form of abstraction which might be seen as fundamental to the social relations of industrial production under a capitalist economic system, but in a novel that seeks to undo such abstraction and objectification its easy reproduction is striking. Industrial labourers are 'weird distorted, smallish beings like men' (*LCL*, 153) whose degradation renders any notion of collectivity impossible. Their physical and moral state makes the idea of common humanity ridiculous, and at the sight of them Connie's 'bowels fainted' (159).

The working classes have been reduced, by industrialisation and by education, to false consciousness and coercive will. Connie overhears working-class children singing in their new school, a building which resembles both a chapel and a prison, and responds with horror:

> Anything more unlike song, spontaneous song, would be impossible to imagine: a strange, bawling yell that followed the outlines of a tune. It was not like savages: savages have subtle rhythms. It was not like animals: animals *mean* something when they yell. It was like nothing on earth, and it was called singing. Connie sat and listened with her heart in her boots, as Field was filling petrol. What could possibly become of such a people, a people in whom the living intuitive faculty was dead as nails, and only queer mechanical yells and uncanny will-power remained. (*LCL*, 152)

We can have no access to what this sort of singing exercise might mean to these children, or to whether they might elsewhere do other sorts of singing. Rather, they are condemned to represent the corrosive effects of industrialisation on human intuition and creativity. Working men are also read as expressive only of a system that contains them absolutely, 'men not men, but animas of coal and iron and clay' (169). They are identified completely with the materials and with the mechanism of industrial production while working women are barely perceptible at all. Working people are determined by the system that produces the forms of their labour, and the details of their work are thus profoundly insignificant.

There is, apparently, no redemption from the destructive effects of industrial labour. Certainly, the elderly Squire Winter suggests that industrial work may in fact be the saving of the race when he says to Clifford: 'you may again employ every man at TeTershall. – Ah, my boy! – to keep up the level of the race, and to have work waiting for any man who cares to work! –' (150), but since this comment is made in the course of a speech in which the Squire congratulates Clifford on his future paternity its perspicacity is in some doubt. Mellors tells us, on the other hand, that working for money has turned men 'into labour-insects, and all their manhood taken away, and all their real life' (220).

Physical labour

The hopelessness of this analysis continually disturbs the narrative and imagery of *Lady Chatterley's Lover*, but the possible recovery of 'manhood' through labour is imagined, through the activities of the gamekeeper, Oliver Mellors. We learn very early in the novel that Mellors maintains his own domestic space through his own labour. He has handed the daily care of his daughter over to his mother, but tends to his own garden and does his own housework. His domestic work is the condition of his separateness and allows him to control his environment and the rhythms of his day. Mellors's 'little railed-in garden in the front of the house' is also a measure of his control of his own environment. Interestingly, it evokes a markedly less sensual engagement with gardening than Connie is to experience later in the novel: 'Connie especially felt a delight in putting the soft roots of young plants into a soft black puddle, and cradling them down. On this spring morning she felt a quiver in her womb, too' (162).

Connie discovers Mellors in the woods: drawn by the sound of his hammering she finds him in his shirt-sleeves, kneeling and at work. He resents the intrusion, but she is apparently fascinated by the spectacle. She enters his hut and sees a carpenter's bench, tools and nails, an axe, a hatchet and 'things in sacks': the paraphernalia of artisanal labour. She then settles down to watching 'the man at work'. This fascination carries with it its own forms of objectification, with Mellors imagined simply as 'the man', but this is surely abstraction to an essence rather than reduction to an emblem. For Connie, her earlier glimpse of Mellors washing merges with her attentive observation of his labour:

> So Connie watched him fixedly. And the same solitary aloneness she had seen
> in him naked, she now saw in him clothed: solitary and intent, like an animal
> that works alone, but also brooding, like a soul that recoils away, away from
> all human contact . . . It was the stillness, and the timeless sort of patience, in
> a man impatient and passionate, that touched Connie's womb.   (*LCL*, 89)

Such stillness contrasts markedly with the fevered toiling of Clifford or the mechanised repetitions of industrial labour. Mellors's labour is individual and artisanal, and his intentness is distinct from the 'vague absorption' of intellectual labour. Mellors is the son of a collier, who after receiving an education at Sheffield Grammar School becomes a clerk. He later 'chucked up my job at Butterley because I thought I was a weed clerking there' (201) and found work instead as a blacksmith on the pit-brow. As a blacksmith he is curiously placed in relation to mechanised labour since the blacksmith points both backwards to a vanishing form of agricultural production and forwards to the dependence of labourers on a functioning machine. He spends some time in the army, displaying a particular knack for working with horses and winning the support and affection of one of his officers. He gains a commission, but following the death of his friend gives up army life to return to manual labour. This narrative of Mellors's career stresses his agency, his capacity to choose particular places and forms of labour, and Connie's observation that 'he seemed *so* unlike a gamekeeper, so unlike a working-man anyhow' (68) captures something of this anachronistic quality.

But how are such forms of work possible within an economic and moral system that seems so destructive of productive labour? The answer may lie in some theory of uneven development, with Mellors emerging as an anachronistic figure whose very oddness might provide a resource for utopian imaginings, the kind of figure of medieval labour that Lawrence had indeed specifically disavowed in his 'Study of Thomas Hardy'. Certainly there are suggestions at a number of points that physical and manual labour were not always the alienated thing that they appear to be in *Lady Chatterley's Lover* as a whole. At one point we are told that in the late Victorian period miners were 'good working men', though Mellors himself sees the decline as rather earlier: 'it's a shame, what's been done to people these last hundred years: men turned into nothing but labour-insects'(220). This uncertain periodisation is not simply a matter of carelessness, but a symptom of the particular interactions of myth and history within the novel: it is necessary for *Lady Chatterley's Lover* to imagine more integrated forms of labour, but not really to examine how or when they might have been realised.

Mellors's version of work is pre-industrial and he insists that 'I know nothing at all about all these mechanical things' (187), although as a trained blacksmith that is likely to be a question of willed ignorance. He extricates himself imaginatively from the economic relations and industrial forms of production that dominate the world around him: 'bit by bit, let's drop the whole industrial life an' go back' (219). Since working for money can only lead to physical and moral deformity, and there is no solution to the 'wage squabble' except not to care, Mellors 'refused to *care* about money' (148).

Yet in the sphere of labour, it is far from clear how these transformations can possibly be brought about. We have already been told that the 'individual asserts himself in his disconnected insanity in these two modes: money and love' (*LCL*, 97), and without dwelling on the disconnected insanity we can indeed see that money and love are privileged modes of experience and relationship within *Lady Chatterley's Lover*. The transformative possibilities of sexual relationship can be figured within the novel as a matter of unique and private forms of human relationship and as the outcome of the work of writing. It is certainly true that sexual behaviour is constantly metaphorised and pathologised in the novel and given public meanings, but, nonetheless, it is possible for two individuals, Connie and Mellors, to create forms of intimacy and passion that the novel represents as transformative and transgressive. In some sense the novel draws on the 'privacy' of sexual relations which it elsewhere denies in order to render alternative moral and sexual economies imaginable. It also builds up the symbolic and affective meanings of a series of terms, such as 'blindly', 'intuitively' and 'queer' in order to allow for the imaginative apprehension of new modes of selfhood. I do not intend to suggest that *Lady Chatterley's Lover* constructs some sort of sexual utopia: Mellors's hatred of 'mouth kisses', his murderous dislike of lesbians, and his distaste for black women who are 'a bit like mud' (204) all suggest that fear and phobia continue to circulate within his sexual fantasies and knowledges. Equally, Connie's increasing horror of other women ('to be free of the strange dominion and obsession of *other women*. How awful they were, women!' (253)) suggests that her new ways of knowing and experiencing the world are not without their rather brutal exclusions. Nonetheless, it remains the case that the novel can, through its own literary work, construct another version of sexual relationship with a freedom that is simply unavailable in the case of economic relations.

At the end of the day, and at the end of the novel, Mellors has to have a job: 'I've got to work, or I should die' (167). This need is not a matter of economic stringency, since he has an army pension, but is a question of having something to keep him occupied and 'working with the immediate quiet absorption that was characteristic of him' (198). He has to work in order to function creatively as an individual and he has to work for someone else in order to have the discipline of labour, but he refuses to participate in the 'wage-struggle'. The dilemma is simply exacerbated by his relationship with

Connie who could, after all, keep both of them financially secure, but Mellors makes it clear that his involvement in productive and waged labour is a condition of the viability of their relationship.

There is never any question that Connie might need work as a culmination of her selfhood since the narrative of her life is created out of affective and domestic relationships. It is pregnancy which delivers her from inertia, and motherhood is set to become her primary occupation. For Mellors, however, his life must have some sense of movement and purpose which is connected to his role as productive labourer: 'Living is moving and moving on . . . a man must offer a woman *some* meaning in his life, if it's going to be an isolated life, and if she's a genuine woman. – I can't be just your male concubine' (*LCL*, 276).

By the end of the novel Connie and Mellors are living apart, presumably temporarily. She is waiting to have their baby and he is learning to become a farmer:

> And for six months he should work at farming, so that eventually he and Connie could have some small farm of their own, into which he could put his energy. For he would have to have some work, even hard work, to do, and he would have to make his own living, even if her own capital started him.
>
> (*LCL*, 298)

Connie's capital sits uncomfortably beside Mellors's desire to make his own living because the acknowledgement of the need for capital allows social relations and economic structures to intrude into the unmediated exchange of work and individual selfhood that Mellors projects. Mellors ends by invoking the 'great groping white hands' (300) that will seek to crush all those who would live outside the norms of money and will, but in the face of the novel's incapacity really to imagine any such space except in the most abstract terms, these white hands become ghostly and even fantastical. The work of the novel has taken us so far from the contingencies and materiality of productive labour that even its vivid fears and passionate denunciations begin to feel less solid. The symbolic invocation of degeneration and decline cannot sustain its rootedness as we are taken from the physicality and economic contingency of labour to the ghostly abstraction of those groping white hands.

NOTES

1 D. H. Lawrence, 'Education of the People', in *RDP*, 85–166 (p. 91).
2 Karl Marx, *Economic and Philosophic Manuscripts of 1844*, ed. Dirk J. Struik (London: Lawrence and Wishart, 1970), p. 113; D. H. Lawrence, *Fantasia of the Unconscious* (New York: Thomas Seltzer, 1922), p. 3.

3 D. H. Lawrence, 'A Propos of *Lady Chatterley's Lover*', in *LCL,* 513.
4 D. H. Lawrence, 'Men Must Work and Women as Well', in *PII,* 582–91 (p. 583).
5 See Frank J. Sulloway, *Freud, Biologist of the Mind: Beyond the Psychoanalytic Legend* (Cambridge, MA: Harvard University Press, 1992), for an account of late nineteenth-century psycho-biology.
6 See, for example, Clifford Allbutt, 'Neurasthenia', in A System of Medicine, ed.Clifford Allbutt and Humphry Davy Rolleston (London: Macmillan, 1910), VII. 727–91.

6

CON CORONEOS AND TRUDI TATE

Lawrence's tales

Lawrence wrote more than sixty tales. His first published work, 'A Prelude', won the 'most enjoyable Christmas' section of a local short-story competition in 1907. His last published work, a long tale entitled *The Escaped Cock*, appeared in 1929. In the intervening years he wrote stories in a wide variety of forms – sketches and novellas, naturalistic tales, fables, apologues, satires and ghost stories. Many of these pieces were collected in the five volumes of stories published in his lifetime: *The Prussian Officer and Other Stories* (1914), *England, My England* (1922), *The Ladybird, The Fox, and The Captain's Doll* (1923), *St. Mawr together with The Princess* (1928) and *The Woman Who Rode Away and Other Stories* (1928). Most of the others appeared in three posthumous volumes: *Love Among the Haystacks & Other Pieces* (1930), *The Lovely Lady* (1933) and *A Modern Lover* (1934).

The remarkable achievement of this body of writing is often overshadowed by Lawrence's novels. Dozens of books have been written on the longer fiction but only a handful on the tales.[1] The disparity reflects both the relative prestige of the genres and the terms on which the stories were produced. Lawrence himself often represented his tales as a way of making 'running money' (i. 431) – in effect, of subsidising the longer works which consumed his attention. The vogue for the short story in the early part of the century opened a reasonably lucrative market, and Lawrence managed to have stories placed in a range of English and American literary journals and magazines, among them Ford Madox Hueffer's *English Review*, the *Nation & Athenaeum* (for which Leonard Woolf was reviews editor), the *Dial*, the *Metropolitan*, the *Century* and, at the popular end of the market, *Hutchinson's Story Magazine*. If a particular tale was then reprinted in one of his collections, Lawrence would benefit from it twice. These financial possibilities of short fiction were always significant for Lawrence; early on they strengthened his resolve to break with school-teaching and later they helped him keep financially afloat through a creative life on four continents.

In return, the novels have often been seen as subsidising the tales with ideas. There is an obvious truth in this. Throughout Lawrence's career, the tales keep in close touch with the geography and philosophy of the novels. *The Prussian Officer* and *England, My England*, set predominantly in the Midlands among the rural and working classes, share the early preoccupations with 'modern love' in *Sons and Lovers* and *The Rainbow* and, in the case of the second volume (although more tenuously), *Women in Love*. The three novellas in *The Fox* collection have affinities with *Aaron's Rod* while 'The Woman Who Rode Away' and *St. Mawr* follow *The Plumed Serpent* into New Mexico. In these cases, the novels take precedence not only because of their developed exploration of ideas but because of the process by which the volumes of tales came about. Unlike Joyce's *Dubliners*, published in the same year as *The Prussian Officer*, Lawrence's volumes of stories were rarely (with the important exception of the volume of three novellas, *The Fox, The Captain's Doll, The Ladybird*) designedly written. They tended to draw upon whatever material was available, and the result was sometimes eccentric. Only two stories in *The Prussian Officer*, for example, are on 'military' themes. It was, in fact, Edward Garnett who (to Lawrence's annoyance) changed the title of 'Honour and Arms' to 'The Prussian Officer', named the collection after it, and, it seems likely, determined the order of the stories. More to the point, the volumes represent Lawrence bringing his work 'up to scratch' (iv. 126). The stories available to us today have often been heavily revised within a brief period of time for volume publication – revised, in more cases than not, in the light of creative ideas gestating or achieved in the novels.[2]

But creativity finds many forms. According to F. R. Leavis, an early champion of Lawrence, his tales embody 'creative work of such order as would of itself put Lawrence among the great writers – not merely among the memorable, but among the great'.[3] It is a striking tribute from a critic who is, at least ostensibly, writing on *D. H. Lawrence: Novelist*, and claiming Lawrence for his own 'Great Tradition' in the English novel. As it happens, Leavis selects just two novels as making Lawrence worthy of inclusion in *The Great Tradition*: 'I want the stress to fall unambiguously on *The Rainbow, Women in Love*, and the tales . . . If I had thought it good policy to take more space, I should have spent my additional pages on other tales' (15–16).[4] The significance of his comment derives not only from the quality of his discussion – which remains one of the finest accounts of Lawrence's tales – but also from what it only half recognises: namely, the increasing dominance of the tales in Lawrence's creativity. On the one hand, these are the tales of a naturalistic novelist. They are praised for their grainy detail, the fine unsentimentality, the reach of sympathy and recognition, the rendering of community. These pieties of Lawrence criticism construct a writer who could have been the great novelist of the working class. But the tales for which Leavis reserves his greatest praise are those written in the 1920s. They are the work of a writer who has been seduced into the role of dogmatist and prophet, whose novelistic imagination has failed, and who has been transformed from *D. H. Lawrence: Novelist* into *D. H. Lawrence: Story-teller*. Many critics have shared this view. It represents an extraordinary transformation, and to discuss Lawrence's tales *as* tales, rather than as the off-cuts of great novelistic schemes, it will be necessary to make formal sense of this change.

'Queer dark corners': the early tales

Let us begin towards the end of Lawrence's career with 'Smile' (1926) – an ostensibly slight work of no more than a few pages, but one which will help bring into focus some of the concerns here. A man travels through the night to attend his sick wife. He is too late, and now stands in a stupor by her deathbed in the convent of the Blue Sisters. And yet as he gazes at the dead woman's face, 'something leaped like laughter in the depths of him, he gave a little grunt, and an extraordinary smile came over his face' (*WWRA*, 73). Looking up, he catches a responsive glimmer in the faces of the three nuns opposite. The smiles emerge differently: one 'with a touch of mischievous ecstasy', the second 'a pagan smile, slow, infinitely subtle in its archaic humour', while a smile 'grew, grew and grew' over the face of the Mother Superior. And then suddenly the man stops smiling and 'a look of super-martyrdom took its place' (*WWRA*, 73–74). Reflecting on the past, on marital discord and the melancholy possibility of his own imperfections, he can feel his wife 'nudging him somewhere in the ribs, to make him smile'. He mustn't smile, he must escape. Meanwhile, the nuns, peering closely, note for the first time 'the faint ironical curl' at the corners of the dead woman's mouth. The husband, now forlorn, takes his leave 'and never was man more utterly smileless' (74–76).

Lawrence's agent had some difficulty in placing this story with the magazines. Editors 'were afraid of it'[5] and it is easy to see why. But the reader who is able to get past the combination of death, laughter and nuns might still struggle to place 'Smile'. It may help to be familiar with the rise of the cryptic short story – Maupassant, Chekhov, the epiphanies of Joyce, the mannered artfulness of Mansfield. It may also help to be familiar with the psychological disposition of modernist writing, and especially perhaps with the figures of ambivalence and hysteria. And, closer to home, it may help to know something of Lawrence's soured relationships with John Middleton Murry and with Katherine Mansfield, whom Murry visited in the last days of her illness at the Gurdjieff Institute outside Paris in 1923. These are useful contexts for thinking about the story's historical possibility – reasons for its appearance in 1926 and not a hundred years earlier. What we are still left with, however, is an unsettling quality which arises not merely because of a line crossed from laughter to death but because that line is important to Lawrence. It is implicated in his whole relation to writing which is why there is often something to make us afraid of it.

For reasons which will emerge, this ability to disconcert is characteristic of the tales. Reviewers of Lawrence's first collection, *The Prussian Officer*, expressed admiration for the unsettling power of the volume, but complained of the author's 'morbid' tendency, his inclination to 'a hideous form of naturalism', his preoccupation with 'the queer dark corners' of life and 'the cruder and more instinctive side of humanity'.[6] 'The critics really hate me', Lawrence wrote with pleasure to Amy Lowell. 'So they ought' (ii. 243). What is perhaps most obviously unsettling is the kind of extreme sexual experience intimated in the title story of the collection (which Hugh Stevens discusses at greater length in chapter 3 of this volume). A young Prussian orderly, bullied by his captain, verbally abused, kicked black and blue, is finally driven to a moment of lucid distraction and strikes back:

> And in a second the orderly, with serious, earnest young face, and underlip between his teeth, had got his knee in the officer's chest and was pressing the chin backward over the farther edge of the tree-stump, pressing with all his heart behind in a passion of relief, the tension of his wrists exquisite with relief. And with the base of his palms he shoved at the chin, with all his might. And it was pleasant too to have that chin, that hard jaw already slightly rough with beard, in his hands. He did not relax one hair's-breadth but, all the force of his blood exulting in his thrust, he shoved back the head of the other man, till there was a little 'cluck' and a crunching sensation. Then he felt as if his heart went to vapour.
>
> (*PO*, 14–15)

The unpleasant power of this scene – the eroticism of the hard, rough chin, the passion, the release from tension, the dispassionate registering of position, touch and sound – encourages attention to those queer dark corners, but perhaps more attention should be paid to the significance of the words 'his heart went to vapour'. In 'The Thorn in the Flesh', the second of the two military stories in the volume, there is a more radical sense of the vertiginous – that is, the sensation of whirling or sinking, of the ground shifting beneath one's feet – on which Lawrence pauses in detail. Bachmann, a young German soldier with a fear of heights, is ordered to join in 'scaling practice':

> He placed his ladder with quick success, and wild, quivering hope possessed him. Then blindly he began to climb. But the ladder was not very firm, and at

every hitch a great, sick, melting feeling took hold of him. He clung on fast. If only he could keep that grip on himself, he would get through. He knew this, in agony. What he could not understand was the blind gush of white-hot fear, that came with great force whenever the ladder swerved, and which almost melted his belly and all his joints, and left him powerless. If once it melted all his joints and his belly, he was done. He clung desperately to himself. He knew the fear, he knew what it did when it came, he knew he had only to keep a firm hold. He knew all this. Yet, when the ladder swerved, and his foot missed, there was the great blast of fear blowing on his heart and bowels, and he was melting weaker and weaker, in a horror of fear and lack of control, melting to fall . . .

There came into his consciousness a small, foreign sensation. He woke up a little. What was it? Then slowly it penetrated him. His water had run down his leg. He lay there, clinging, still with shame, half conscious of the echo of the sergeant's voice thundering from below. (*PO*, 25)

In the other tales in the collection, the quality of the vertiginous is frequently expressed within domestic encounters. A man driven mad by the pain of a 'burst bladder' shouts he will kill his wife ('A Sick Collier'). A wife laying out the body of her dead husband suddenly experiences a nausea of distance from him and terror of his alien quality ('Odour of Chrysanthemums'). A man enraged by his flirtatious wife grasps her by the throat ('The White Stocking'). What is thus figured within the precise, lucid terms of Lawrence's early naturalism is a loss of control, and it is this, rather than poking into queer dark corners, which defines the state of sexual panic within the tales. The connection is suggested in the outcome of Bachmann's terrifying experience. Hauled over the rampart in disgrace, he strikes back at his bullying sergeant and flees the scene. Finding refuge in a private house, he falls for the virginal Emilie who is 'probably of some gipsy race' (*PO*, 31). Eventually the military authorities will find him out, but before this he will 'give' Emilie her sexual awakening: he is 'restored and completed', 'escaped, liberated, wondering and happy' (34); she, in turn, 'died in terror, and after the death, a great flame gushed up, obliterating her' (33). The earlier terms of vertigo – 'the blind gush', 'melting weaker and weaker', 'melting to fall' – are transferred into sexual experience. For this reason, the vertiginous in Lawrence is never simply good or bad; the terror of being out of control is also ecstasy, the pleasure of falling, when it is part of a liberation from false control – that is to say, from repression.

There are, of course, moments of panic or red mist in Lawrence's novels as well. The situation in 'Smile' has a precursor in *Sons and Lovers* where Paul Morel and his sister giggle over the body of their dead mother. But in the novel that scene is pulled back into the structure of the work, and diffused through the extensions of plot and characterisation. The vertiginous lends itself to short fiction, and perhaps especially to the trick-ending short story which suspends the reader over an ironic twist. Lawrence is never as cheap as this, and his moments of vertigo usually occur somewhere within the story, not at its end. These are important moments for Lawrence. They help him to escalate the significance of experience, to move between super-ficialities of existence and deep underlying necessities, to escape from the windless closure of naturalism into psychologically intense, symbolic or mythical modes. And vertigo itself, as a psychic or a physical condition, is available to metaphysical complications – issues surrounding order, repres-sion, freedom, falling, the Fall. Lawrence's recourse to the vertiginous, then, raises both formal and philosophical questions. The lucid precision of his early naturalist mode dictates a certain form of control. 'Smile', with its superb lightness of touch, could not have been written in this mode. Such a · story depends not merely on a more practised hand but on an altered rela-tion to the nature of writing.

The new development is just visible in the next collection of stories, *England, My England*. Although this collection appeared eight years after *The Prussian Officer*, it seems at first glance rather similar. The main setting is the Midlands, the prevalent mode is naturalism, there are the now familiar attractions and repulsions between men and women, and the customary sexual panics. Although the date of the collection is 1922, two of the stories were written before 1914, and three during the war itself. A number of the stories are set during or shortly after the war: the title story 'England, My England', 'Tickets, Please', 'Monkey Nuts', 'Hadrian', 'Samson and Delilah', 'The Thimble', 'Wintry Peacock' and 'The Blind Man'.[7] In the first of these, the protagonist joins up and is killed. In 'Tickets, Please' the tale revolves around the changing sex relations between newly empowered women-in-work and the men on the Home Front. Both 'Wintry Peacock' and 'The Blind Man' contain returned soldiers damaged by the war. Although these tales tend to depict domestic and personal intensities, they do so against a trans-formation in Lawrence's own circumstances – under suspicion from the authorities, confined with his German wife Frieda to England, this is the period of Lawrence's 'nightmare'.[8] All the more striking, then, is the comic quality of 'The Blind Man'. Maurice, the central character, is the returned soldier who has been blinded in combat. He and his wife now run a portion of a farm; he is 'fulfilled' while she is dissatisfied. An old friend of hers, a short, clever, ironical Scottish lawyer called Bertie (perhaps an oblique refer-ence to the philosopher Bertrand Russell with whom Lawrence was in contact during the war), has come to visit. An encounter in the barn brings the two men together and the lawyer panics, first as he is gently 'felt' by Maurice and then as he is compelled in turn to feel the 'scarred eyes' of the blind man:

Then suddenly Maurice removed the hand of the other man from his brow, and stood holding it in his own.

'Oh, my God', he said, 'we shall know each other now, shan't we? We shall know each other now.'

Bertie could not answer. He gazed mute and terror-struck, overcome by his own weakness. He knew he could not answer. He had an unreasonable fear, lest the other man should suddenly destroy him. Whereas Maurice was actually filled with hot, poignant love, the passion of friendship. Perhaps it was this very passion of friendship which Bertie shrank from most.

'We're all right together now, aren't we?' said Maurice. 'It's all right now, as long as we live, so far as we're concerned?'

'Yes', said Bertie, trying by any means to escape.   (*EmyE*, 62)

This depiction of sexual panic strikes a new note in Lawrence's work which will be more completely realised in later tales. In the early 1920s he remarks in a letter: 'Why not laugh, and spit in the eye of love. Really, why not laugh? . . . Kick the posterior of creeping love, and laugh when it whinges' (iii. 734). In the same letter, commenting on a work by Cyril Kay Scott called *Blind Mice*, he remarks: 'what a very good satire [it] would have made if CKS would have grinned up his sleeve'. This attitude had already emerged much earlier in 1915 in a letter to Bertrand Russell – 'I am ashamed to write any real writing of passionate love to my fellow men. Only satire is decent now' (ii. 283) – as had Lawrence's own developing habit of grinning up his sleeve. 'The Blind Man' is an early fruit of this habit, and it represents the development of a mode which distances him from his own panic. A related development occurs in the title story, 'England, My England', originally written in 1915 as a considerably shorter work. Like the title story in the *Prussian Officer* collection, it was also the last revised for the volume in which it appeared, and like that story it also strikes the newest note: there is a strong sense that it has been brought 'up to scratch'. Egbert is a young man of good birth who lives in the country, partly on a private income, partly off his father-in-law, and potters about doing nothing. His character degenerates along with his domestic situation. He drifts into the army and is killed. The whole story is thus a rueful, half-despairing cry over England which seems congruent with Lawrence's own state of mind at the time. But in fact, 'England, My England' appears in two versions. The earlier, written in 1915, was a considerably shorter work and ended with Egbert (Evelyn in the first version) lying on the battlefield, shot and slashed by the foe:

The German cut and mutilated the face of the dead man as if he must obliterate it. He slashed it across, as if it must not be a face any more; it must be removed. For he could not bear the clear, abstract look of the other's face, its almost ghoulish, slight smile, faint but so terrible in its suggestion, that the German was mad, and ran up the road when he found himself alone.

(*EmyE*, 232)

In the revised version, Lawrence abandons objective, naturalistic presentation and that eruption into panic. He merges, instead, with Egbert's consciousness:

To forget! To forget! Utterly, utterly to forget, in the great forgetting of death. To break the core and the unit of life, and to lapse out on the great darkness. Only that. To break the clue, and mingle and commingle with the one darkness, without afterwards or forwards. Let the black sea of death itself solve the problem of futurity. Let the will of man break and give up.

What was that? A light! A terrible light! Was it figures? Was it legs of a horse colossal – colossal above him: huge, huge?

The Germans heard a slight noise, and started. Then, in the glare of a light-bomb, by the side of the heap of earth thrown up by the shell, they saw the dead face.   (*EmyE*, 33)

The 'ghoulish, slight smile' has disappeared, as has the contrived ending of panic. Both these things, in the course of rewriting, have entered the work as a whole, under the terms of a new control. What this means is at once a naturalistic mode full of pitiless irony and an extension of the scope of short fiction which is indispensable to that new formal control.

'A new manner': the novelettes

The development is consolidated in Lawrence's third collection of tales, *The Fox, The Captain's Doll, The Ladybird*. In 'The Ladybird', the bohemian Count Dionys lies badly wounded in an English prisoner-of-war hospital where he is discovered by Lady Daphne, a beautiful woman and the wife of a rising politician who is now in the army. At first indifferent to the count, she gradually finds herself falling under his spell. Her husband returns, but he is now only her day-time husband. Count Dionys is her master in the dark. In 'The Fox', a man stumbles upon a farm run by two women, Banford and March. When he first appears, he is partly identified with the fox that has been preying on the chickens; an outside force, he introduces discord between the two women, though at first he doesn't recognise this. After killing the fox, he encounters the hostility of the frail Banford and realises that he can never marry March while Banford is still about. He must also kill Banford; he does so in a contrived 'accident' and at the end he and March are left meditating on the possibilities of a future together. Hepburn, the captain in 'The Captain's Doll', falls in love with a German woman Hannele while stationed in occupied Germany. But he is married and shows little inclination to make up his mind about the situation. The wife conveniently dies, but this does not immediately clear the way. Hannele at first feels that Hepburn can never be reached emotionally and leaves him; bereft of all relationships, he thinks through his attitude, seeks her out, and sets forth the terms on which she must come back to him – as in the other stories in the volume, terms of submission and total obedience.

The element of sex antagonism and will-to-male-dominance are characteristic of Lawrence's philosophy and novel-writing at this time, but these tales mark a formal development which Lawrence immediately recognised. Both 'The Fox' and 'The Captain's Doll', he remarks, are 'so modern so new: a new manner' (iv. 131–32). In the first place, these are long stories, much longer than the 'short' story favoured by the magazines. As in the case of 'England, My England', each had been greatly expanded by Lawrence from earlier works: 'The Mortal Coil' (1913) at 5,000 words was the (somewhat loose) basis for 'The Captain's Doll' at 20,000 words. 'The Thimble' (1915) at 6,000 words became 'The Ladybird' at 25,000; and the first version of 'The Fox' was expanded from 8,000 to 20,000 words, largely by virtue of what Lawrence called 'a strange and fiery brush' (iv. 126). In terms of plot rhythm and development, these stories do not resemble the 'short' stories of the magazines. Lawrence chose a new/old term for them – the 'novelette'. This term, as Lawrence would have been aware, recalls the disreputable form of publication towards the end of the previous century, the kind of soft-focus, trite romance which Joyce parodies in the Nausicaa section of *Ulysses*. The term is used frequently in Lawrence's correspondence in the early 1920s: 'These I call the three novelettes' (iv. 148); 'I think I'd better let [Martin Secker, his English publisher] have these little stories – not the three novelettes' (iv. 143–44); 'then I have written two novelettes' (iv. 121); 'of the two novelettes'; 'I have just finished the third of the novelettes' (iv. 150); and then a little later, when writing in New Mexico and with the success of the earlier volume in mind, he refers to 'the novelette "St. Mawr"' (v. 136) and thinks about another book of novelettes. What he means by this is nothing dogmatic. Rather, like the Jamesian *nouvelle* – a more supple term than short novel or novella – it describes a form which is appropriately ample. It is a matter not of length but of mode and rhythm – Leavis calls them 'dramatic poems' – and this amplitude informs a number of the subsequent novelettes: *St. Mawr*, 'The Man Who Loved Islands', *The Virgin and the Gipsy*, 'The Princess' and 'The Woman Who Rode Away'.

There are intimations of this rhythmic amplitude early in Lawrence's writing. The editor of the Cambridge edition of *The Prussian Officer* helpfully glosses 'clommaxed' as a Nottinghamshire word which means 'moved clumsily'. Lawrence himself puts it in clumsy inverted commas to mark its foreignness for the non-local reader he seems to have in mind, and after reading the later works there seems to be something 'clommax' about much of the volume. Despite the quality of the writing, the stories are too self-dramatisingly 'short stories' which authorise themselves by ending on a theatrical or portentous note, rather in the manner of Katherine Mansfield. An example is the ending of 'Odour of Chrysanthemums': 'She knew she submitted to life, which was her immediate master. But from death, her ultimate master, she winced with fear and shame' (*PO*, 199). Moreover, a number of the stories in *The Prussian Officer* have a tendency towards a greater amplitude than is typically associated with the idea of 'short story'. One indication of this is external structure. Both 'The White Stocking' and 'The Shades of Spring' are divided into three numbered parts; 'Goose Fair' and 'The Prussian Officer' are in four parts; 'The Thorn in the Flesh' is in six parts; and 'Daughters of the Vicar' consists of fifteen numbered sections. This might suggest a narrative impulse in Lawrence which was primarily novelistic. But this is not the case either, at least if we accept that view of the novel – 'the one bright book of life', hostile to dogma and thesis – expressed by Lawrence himself. Many critics have agreed with Leavis that the novels after *Women in Love* represent a deterioration in Lawrence's novel-writing powers; for Raymond Williams 'willed and abstract' writing such as occurs in *The Plumed Serpent* is 'the only form of an extensive kind still available to his imagination'.[9]

The novelette is a way of by-passing this problem. It belongs to a new creative field which involves a change in mode, away from the naturalism of the Midlands stories towards the ghost story – 'The Borderline', 'Glad Ghosts', 'The Last Laugh', 'The Rocking-Horse Winner' – and works in fabulous and allegorical modes such as 'The Man Who Loved Islands', 'The Woman Who Rode Away' and 'The Man Who Died'. Here, for example, is the fairy-tale opening to 'The Man Who Loved Islands':

> There was a man who loved islands. He was born on one, but it didn't suit him, as there were too many other people on it, besides himself. He wanted an island all of his own: not necessarily to be alone on it, but to make it a world of his own.
>
>   An island, if it is big enough, is no better than a continent. It has to be really quite small, before it *feels like* an island; and this story will show how tiny it has to be, before you can presume to fill it with your own personality.
>
> (*WWRA*, 151)

The fabulous-symbolic mode of these works wilfully ignores the claims of gritty naturalism. It moves with ease between levels of significance and information, effortlessly integrating the most occult concepts with everyday gossip and malice concerning Lawrence's immediate acquaintances – Compton Mackenzie (portrayed in 'The Man Who Loved Islands'), Lady Cynthia Asquith ('The Rocking-Horse Winner' and 'Glad Ghosts') and of course Katherine Mansfield and Middleton Murry (the Murry stories include 'Jimmy and the Desperate Woman', 'The Last Laugh' and 'Smile'). Inconvenient characters are easily dispensed with by an act of will. In 'The Captain's Doll', the wife of Hepburn falls out of a window. In 'The Fox', a tree falls on the frail Banford. In *The Virgin and the Gipsy*, a flood carries away Granny, that oppressive force last seen bobbing up like a 'strange float, her face purple, her blind blue eyes bolting, spume hissing from her mouth'.[10]

Laughter and bathos

Especially notable in these examples is a development of the kind of comedy already mentioned in the case of 'The Blind Man'. Lawrence is quite conscious of this, and draws attention to it in letters: 'I've just done "The Blind Man" – the end queer and ironical' (iii. 302–3); 'I wrote the fox story – rather odd and amusing' (iii. 307); and he describes 'The Captain's Doll' as 'a very funny long story' (iv. 109). There are also, of course, light and comic moments in some of the 1920s novels, in particular *Aaron's Rod*, but it is the shorter works of the period that formally sustain a satiric, mischievous element which flatly opposes T. S. Eliot's claim in *After Strange Gods* (1934) that Lawrence lacked a sense of humour. Leavis recognised that humour in the tales and wrote about it at length, and recently it has again intrigued Lawrence's critics, perhaps as part of a more general critical tendency to redeem modernists by rediscovering their playfulness. John Bayley argued this line in the case of Lawrence more than thirty years ago; nowadays, Bakhtinian theory is often brought into the equation, and the Lawrence who thus emerges is merry, subversive and carnivalesque.[11]

The laughter of Lawrence no doubt contains such qualities, but this 'passion without a name', as Hobbes called the emotion that triggers laughter,[12] is often more complex and 'queer' than it first appears. In his numerous discussions of laughter, Georges Bataille, the French critic and surrealist writer and Lawrence's near-contemporary, often returned to the case of the young woman who burst out laughing every time one of her relatives died. The reason might be 'shock', but then what is shock, and why should it result in laughter? Such tricky questions also seem to have something to do with Lawrence's laughter, and for thinking about them Bataille is perhaps more useful than Bakhtin. Although the author of *The Story of an Eye* would probably have offended Lawrence's notion of cultural hygiene, Bataille's preoccupation with the anthropological and cultural significance of sacrifice, with the idea of excess, with the sun, resurrection and the eroticisation of death is remarkably similar to elements in Lawrence's own thought. The problem of laughter is among these resemblances. For Kant, laughter 'is an affection arising from a strained expectation being suddenly transformed into nothing'; it is a sudden descent, a fall into the void.[13] For Bataille, however, this fall provides the joyous recognition of one's sovereign being. It is a way of becoming divine in the very act of acknowledging the emptiness of all things, the final, brutal absence of the sovereign good – that good, in other words, which is 'good for nothing'. Only the death of my fellow-man can reveal to me, by stealing it away from me, my own death. And for this reason the husband's smile in 'Smile' is the essence of all laughter. It is the 'laughter of being'.[14]

The suggestiveness of such ideas in Lawrence is connected with the issues of form and the vertiginous already raised. In returning to them it is helpful to remember that one laughs *at* Lawrence as well as *with* him – that the risibility of aspects of his work around this time seems to increase along with his own satiric powers. The notorious examples are usually drawn from his later novels, but the tales too have their moments. A case in point is 'Glad Ghosts' (1926) which is set in a kind of Lawrencean 'House of Usher'. Lord Lathkill, a member of a decaying aristocracy, unhappy in marriage, oppressed by his mother, is 'a corpse with consciousness' who is restored to life by supernatural forces. This tale was solicited for a book of ghost stories by Lady Cynthia Asquith who then rejected it, presumably after finding herself caricatured as 'Funny old Mother' in the following scene. A long quotation is necessary for the full flavour:

> Lord Lathkill threw up his arms, and stretched, quivering.
> 'Oh, pardon, pardon!' he said, stretching and seeming to grow bigger and almost splendid, sending out rays of fire to the dark young woman. 'Oh Mother, thank you for my limbs, and my body! oh Mother, thank you for my knees and my shoulders at this moment! Oh Mother, thank you that my body is straight and alive! Oh Mother, torrents of spring, torrents of spring, whoever said that!'
>   'Don't you forget yourself, my boy?' said his mother.
>   'Oh no, dear, no! Oh Mother dear, a man has to be in love in his thighs, the way you ride a horse. Why don't we stay in love that way all our lives? Why do we turn into corpses with consciousness? Oh mother of my body, thank you for my body, you strange woman with white hair! I don't know much about you, but my body came from you, so thank you my dear. I shall think of you tonight!'
>   . . . Lady Lathkill hurried past her son, with head ducked. But still he laid

his hand on her shoulder, and she stopped dead.

'Goodnight, Mother, mother of my face and my thighs! Thank you for the night to come, dear, mother of my body.'

She glanced up at him rapidly, nervously, then hurried away. He stared after her, then switched off the light.

'Funny old Mother!' he said. 'I never realised before that she was the mother of my shoulders and my hips, as well as my brain. Mother of my thighs!'

(*WWRA*, 207)

The effort required to read this in sympathy is large if not impossible. Orlando Williams, a perspicacious early reviewer, observes that Lawrence often falls 'into bathos or into a kind of irritable prosiness, when judged from the worldly, superficial, even the purely aesthetic point of view'.[15] But compare this with the scene in 'The Captain's Doll' when Hepburn and Hannele discuss their relationship while descending the mountain in a noisy bus:

'In fact', he shouted, 'I realised that, as far as I was concerned, love was a mistake.'

'*What* was a mistake?' she screamed.

'Love', he bawled.

'Love!' she screamed. 'A mistake?' Her tone was derisive.

'For me personally', he said, shouting.

'Oh, only for you personally', she cried, with a pouf of laughter.

(*Fox*, 149)

This is often seen as one of Lawrence's finest comic moments. What makes it incongruous in the 'right' way? How do we know that the passage in 'Glad Ghosts' is not intentionally bathetic? Is it possible that Lawrence really does not sense the risibility of 'Mother of my thighs' or grin up his sleeve at the absurd tableau of the two contrasted figures? The point is not to give Lawrence credit where it is not due, but to recognise a structure at work which binds together contrasting possibilities, rather like the pleasure and unpleasure of vertigo.

For these effects, the word 'bathos' seems exactly right. Alexander Pope employed the term in *Peri Bathous* (1728) to describe the 'art of sinking' in poetry: it applies to the kind of poetry which in risible attempts to become 'profound' – to achieve the sublime – truly becomes profound: that is, sinks to the depths. In Lawrence's later writing, there is both unintentional bathos of this kind but also another bathos, more willed, calculated, a kind of prosaic 'art of sinking'. The reader might expect the great flood in *The Virgin and the Gipsy* (1926) – a flood which carries away half of Yvette's father's house as well as her oppressive grandmother, and brings her into naked contact with the gipsy – to build into a grand symbolic climax. Instead, the gipsy disappears and the tale ends with him sending a *letter*:

> Dear miss, I see in the paper you are all right after your ducking, as is the same with me. I hope I see you again one day, maybe at Tideswell cattle fair, or maybe we come that way again. I come that day to say good-bye! and I never said it, well, the water give no time, but I live in hopes. Your obdt. servant Joe Boswell.
>
> And only then she realized that he had a name. (90)

The return to everyday idiom and the sense of normalisation thus achieved is characteristic of a deflation of the sublime which takes many forms in Lawrence's later tales. In 'Things' (1926), for example, two American idealists, in love with European culture, live in Paris, become dissatisfied, move to Italy, become dissatisfied, move back in high dissatisfaction to America where the life of cultivation exists only in the old and beautiful 'things' they have collected in Europe – splendid if shabby mahogany furniture. Europe has failed, even after one more try, and the man – Erasmus – is forced to take up an academic post. He has given in. He is now 'in the cage', full of fury, dissatisfaction, baffled, frustrated: 'His eyes grew more beady, and his long, queer face grew sharper and more rat-like, with utter baffled fury. He was forty, and the job was upon him.' But a half-contentment settles upon him and he becomes (dangerously) reconciled to his new life. Now he can show off the furniture, remarking to his wife as he looks at her with the queer, sharp eyes of a rat:

> 'Europe's the mayonnaise all right, but America supplies the good old lobster – what?'
>
> 'Every time!' she said, with satisfaction.
>
> And he peered at her. He was in the cage: but it was safe inside. And she, evidently, was her real self at last. She had got the goods. Yet round his nose was a queer, evil, scholastic look, of pure scepticism. But he liked lobster.[16]

In this case the bathetic is also figured in the structure of the narrative: the idealists are constantly recontextualised, each context part of a process of reduction, rather like the quest of the man who loves islands for an ever-smaller island or the Gulliver-like renunciation of English civilisation in *St. Mawr* for the true human companionship of a good horse in New Mexico. In many of the quest tales, in fact, the structure is a mischievous degenerative spiral, a progressive dismantling of idealism, as if *Pilgrim's Progress* meets *Candide*. But it is that descent down the mountain in 'The Captain's Doll' which best captures the bathetic in the later Lawrence. There are many mountains, many sublime heights, many expressions of the sovereign good, from which his writing must descend. In deflating the sublime, the panic of vertigo is wilfully brought to heel. Behind Lawrence's controlled falling is the tone of the question asked by Nietzsche's Zarathustra after he has come down the mountain and encountered the saint: 'Could it be possible? This old saint in the forest has not yet heard anything of this, that *God is dead*?'[17]

What is left when the sovereign good – God, or for that matter modern love – has disappeared, is no longer thinkable? The answer is only partially disclosed in the metaphysical failures and annunciations of Lawrence's later writing. Its fuller expression is the act of narrative itself: what makes it still possible to write and what it means to do so. It is fitting that the last story to appear in Lawrence's lifetime was *The Escaped Cock*, renamed 'The Man Who Died' in its extended version in *Love Among the Haystacks* (1930). 'I wrote a story of the Resurrection', Lawrence says to Earl Brewster, 'where Jesus gets up and feels very sick about everything, and can't stand the old crowd any more . . . begins to find what an astonishing place the phenomenal world is . . . and thanks his stars he needn't have a "mission" any more' (vi. 50). In the second part of the story the man who has renounced the sovereign good meets a priestess of Isis and for the first time in his life stirs with desire. He is born again, this time into the flesh. Lawrence makes him rediscover the sublime and, in a final turn on bathos, announce it triumphantly to his Father: 'I am risen!'

NOTES

1 Studies of the tales include: Kingsley Widmer, *The Art of Perversity: D. H. Lawrence's Shorter Fictions* (Seattle: University of Washington Press, 1962); Janice Hubbard Harris, *The Short Fiction of D. H. Lawrence* (New Brunswick, NJ: Rutgers University Press, 1984); and Weldon Thornton, *D. H. Lawrence: A Study of the Short Fiction* (New York: Twayne, 1993).

2 For accounts of the processes of composition and revision, see the editors' introductions to the Cambridge University Press editions of the collections of tales.

3 F. R. Leavis, *D. H. Lawrence: Novelist* (1955; Harmondsworth: Penguin, 1976), p. 295.

4 F. R. Leavis, *The Great Tradition: George Eliot, Henry James, Joseph Conrad* (1948: Harmondsworth: Penguin, 1972).

5 See the editors' introduction to *WWRA*, xxix.

6 For an account of the reception, see the editor's introduction to *The Prussian Officer and Other Stories* (Cambridge: Cambridge University Press, 1983), xxxiii–xxxvi.

7 On aspects of Lawrence's literary engagement with the war, see Trudi Tate, *Modernism, History and the First World War* (Manchester: Manchester University Press, 1998), pp. 102–9.

8 See Paul Delany, *D. H. Lawrence's Nightmare: The Writer and his Circle in the Years of the Great War* (Hassocks: Harvester, 1979). See also Hugh Stevens's chapter in this volume.

9 Raymond Williams, *The English Novel from Dickens to Lawrence* (London: Chatto & Windus, 1973), p. 181.

10 *The Virgin and the Gipsy* (Harmondsworth: Penguin, 1970), p. 82.

11 T. S. Eliot, *After Strange Gods: A Primer of Modern Heresy* (London: Faber and Faber, 1934), p. 58. On the general issue, see Paul Eggert and John Worthen (eds.), *Lawrence and Comedy* (Cambridge: Cambridge University Press, 1996). John Bayley's essay in this volume, 'Lawrence to Larkin: A Changed Perspective', develops points he first made in *The Uses of Division* (1976). The relevance of Bakhtin (especially the ideas in *Rabelais and His World*, trans. Helene Iswolsky (Cambridge, MA: MIT Press, 1968) is discussed in the editors' introduction, pp. 11–14.

12 Hobbes, *Human Nature* (1650; Oxford: Oxford University Press, 1994), ch. IX, para. 13: 'There is a passion that hath no name; but the sign of it is that distortion of the countenance which we call laughter.'

13 Immanuel Kant, *Critique of Aesthetic Judgement*, trans. James Creed Meredith (Oxford: Clarendon Press, 1911), p. 199.

14 This account of Bataille draws substantially on the extraordinary and complex discussion of 'The Laughter of Being' by Mikkel Borch-Jacobsen, *Modern Language Notes*, 102, 4 (September 1987), 737–59.

15 Cited in the Cambridge edition of *The Woman Who Rode Away and Other Stories*, ed. Dieter Mehl and Christa Jansohn (Cambridge: Cambridge University Press), p. xlviii.

16 *The Princess and Other Stories*, ed. Keith Sagar (Harmondsworth: Penguin, 1971), pp. 219, 220.

17 Friedrich Nietzsche, *Thus Spake Zarathustra* (1883–85), trans. Walter Kaufmann (New York: Viking, 1954), prologue to pt I.

7

HELEN SWORD

Lawrence's poetry

Although he is remembered and celebrated today primarily as a novelist and short-story writer, Lawrence first saw publication as a poet, wrote poetry throughout most of his life, and granted a privileged status to poetic language and vision: 'The essential quality of poetry', he declared in a 1928 essay, 'is that it makes a new effort of attention, and "discovers" a new world within the known world.'[1] That he was far too prolific and undiscriminating a poet, few readers would dispute: the posthumously published *Complete Poems*, at more than 1,000 pages long, functions better as a doorstop than as light bedtime reading. That a great many of his poems are didactic, prosy, irrational, undisciplined, sentimental, obscene, ranting, whiny or otherwise virtually unreadable, critics have agreed at least since 1919, when the rawly emotional marriage poems of *Look! We Have Come Through!* prompted Lawrence's sometime friend Bertrand Russell to snort, 'They may have come through, but I don't see why I should look.'[2] Lawrence's less fortunate poetic efforts do occasionally have value, if not as aesthetic masterpieces, then at least as historical documents of artistic struggle. His most memorable poems, however, stand alongside the finest poetic efforts of the twentieth century and are still widely anthologised and admired by readers today.

Lawrence's evolution as poet – from Imagist to confessionalist to nature poet to satirist to death-affirming mystic – enacts in microcosm much of the history of literary modernism. In 1909, Lawrence's girlfriend Jessie Chambers sent three of his poems to Ford Madox Hueffer (later Ford), who printed them in the *English Review* and later helped arrange for the publication of Lawrence's first novel, *The White Peacock* (1911). In an era of poetic 'isms', Lawrence was labelled first in temporal terms, as a 'Georgian poet', then in formal terms, as an 'Imagist' (a number of his early poems appeared in *Georgian Poetry* anthologies and in Amy Lowell's 'Some Imagist Poets' series). Characteristically, however, his work refused to fit into either of those categories very precisely, and it would continue to elude easy classification through most of his poetic career. Like many of his modernist contemporaries – among them T. S. Eliot, H.D., Ezra Pound, William Carlos Williams, and the Italian Futurists, with whose work he undertook a brief flirtation – Lawrence soon cast off what he called the 'shackles' of rhyme and metre[3] and became a fervent proponent of free verse instead; formally, then, he was very much a modernist, an iconoclastic practitioner of Pound's famous dictum, 'Make it new.' At the same time, however, Lawrence's oracular tone, visionary pretensions, lyrical cadences, overt sentimentality, highly personal subject-matter, and lack of irony (except in its most primitive form, sarcasm) earned him the antipathy of many members of his modernist cohort, including even those who claimed to admire his novels. 'Too much body and emotions', declared H.D. of his erotic love poetry; Virginia Woolf likened his aphoristic *Pansies* to 'the sayings that small boys scribble upon stiles to make housemaids jump and titter'; Richard Aldington compared the Lawrence of *Pansies* and *Nettles* to 'a little Blake raving, but without the fiery vision'; and T. S. Eliot might just as well have been writing of *Look! We Have Come Through!* or *Birds, Beasts and Flowers* when he excoriated Lawrence's 'distinct sexual morbidity' and his 'extraordinarily keen sensibility and capacity of profound intuition – intuition from which he commonly drew the wrong conclusions'.[4]

Lawrence, then, was a modernist poet who cultivated what at times seems to have been a distinctly anti-modernist stance. In his experimentation with free verse and his attention to the poetic image as a concrete vehicle for abstract emotion, he resembles modernist contemporaries such as Pound, Williams, H.D. and even Eliot. As an unabashed visionary, he fits into a Romantic lyrical tradition stretching from Blake, Wordsworth and Shelley through Whitman, Hopkins and Yeats. As a confessional poet, he forms a link in an unbroken chain that reaches from Whitman, Meredith, Hardy and Yeats through Robert Lowell, Sylvia Plath and Anne Sexton. And as a careful observer and awed explicator of nature, he finds common ground not only with twentieth-century 'thing-poets' such as Williams, Marianne Moore, Rainer Maria Rilke and Francis Ponge, but also with more recent writers such as Seamus Heaney and Ted Hughes, the latter of whom shares with Lawrence, as Edward Lucie-Smith notes, an 'insistence on the mystery and darkness to be found at the heart of the experience which is being described'.[5] Lawrence's poetry occupies, in other words, a central and enduring position in the history of twentieth-century literature.

Rhyming Poems

The poems from Lawrence's first four published volumes – *Love Poems and Others* (1913), *Amores* (1916), *New Poems* (1918) and *Bay* (1919), later collected as 'Rhyming Poems'– are far more conventional in their language, form, and subject-matter than most of his later verse. Already in these early works, however, we can see traces of a distinctively Lawrencean diction, ideology and imagery. In the preface to his 1928 *Collected Poems*, Lawrence recalls the Sunday afternoon on which, aged nineteen, he 'perpetrated' his first two poems:

> Any young lady might have written them and been pleased with them; as I was pleased with them. But it was after that, when I was twenty, that my real demon would now and then get hold of me and shake more real poems out of me, making me uneasy . . . A young man is afraid of his demon and puts his hand over the demon's mouth sometimes and speaks for him. And the things the young man says are very rarely poetry. So I have tried to let the demon say his say, and to remove the passages where the young man intruded. So that, in the first volume, many poems are changed, some entirely rewritten, recast. But usually this is only because the poem started out to be something which it didn't quite achieve, because the young man interfered with his demon.
>
> (*Poems*, 27–28)

R. P. Blackmur, in a famous 1935 critique, pounced upon this passage when he denounced Lawrence's poetry as 'hysterical', declaring Lawrence's 'young man' to be 'the poet as craftsman', while the demon is 'exactly that outburst of personal feeling which needed the discipline of craft to become a poem'.[6] Lawrence, however, clearly intended to invoke something far more complicated than mere 'personal feeling' when he described the demon – or, in an earlier draft, the 'ghost' or 'apparition' (*Poems*, 849) – that haunts his most effective work. For him, the demon is what liberates the poet from conventions of form and expression and prods him to explore his own darker side, bringing about what Lawrence, in a 1913 letter to Henry Savage, describes as a veritable explosion of visionary energies: 'It seems to me a purely lyric poet gives himself, right down to his sex, to his mood, utterly and abandonedly, whirls himself round . . . till he spontaneously combusts into verse' (ii. 115).

Few of the early 'rhyming poems', to be sure, have the spontaneous, combustive quality that Lawrence would strive to achieve a few years later in the rolling cadences of his Whitmanesque free verse. Most, instead, are carefully crafted – Lawrence was a supple prosodist when he chose to be – and filled with the metaphoric precision, exquisite detail, and sensitivity to form, colour and emotional nuance that one might expect from an Imagist poem of the same period. In 'Baby Running Barefoot', for instance, the poet employs evocative flower metaphors to describe the tiny, tender feet of a friend's baby daughter: 'Cool as syringa buds in morning hours, / Or firm and silken as young peony flowers' *(Poems*, 65). And in 'Piano', a frequently anthologised piece about the 'insidious mastery' of memory over emotion, he compactly telescopes present and past, sound and image, into a single, wrenching moment of nostalgia:

> Softly, in the dusk, a woman is singing to me;
> Taking me back down the vista of years, till I see
> A child sitting under the piano, in the boom of the tingling strings
> And pressing the small, poised feet of a mother who smiles as she sings.
>
> (148)

Other early poems, however, move beyond such delicate sentimentality to offer a more troubling view of both nature and human nature. In 'Cherry Robbers', Lawrence's depiction of a cherry-picking expedition (similar scenes can be found in *The White Peacock* and *Sons and Lovers*) conveys an unmistakable hint of sexual violence, as images of natural beauty – the trees, the cherries – are exoticised and eroticised. Green branches become 'long dark boughs', cherries first become jewels and then blood drops, and a laughing girl with 'cherries hung round her ears' is implicitly compared, like the tree itself, to an oriental seductress:

> Under the long, dark boughs, like jewels red
> In the hair of an Eastern girl
> Hang strings of crimson cherries, as if had bled
> Blood-drops beneath each curl.   (36)

In 'Snap-Dragon', similarly, a stroll through the 'mellow sunlight' of an Edenic garden becomes charged with libidinous energy, as a young woman's sadistic manipulation of a flower – '"I like to see"', she says, '"The snap-dragon put out his tongue at me"' – becomes a vivid metaphor for the sexual power she wields over the fascinated young suitor who accompanies her:

> She laughed, she reached her hand out to the flower,
> Closing its crimson throat. My own throat in her power
> Strangled, my heart swelled up so full
> As if it would burst its wine-skin in my throat,
> Choke me in my own crimson.   (123)

'Cherry Robbers' and 'Snap-Dragon' are only two among a number of the 'Rhyming Poems' which, despite their seeming sedateness of form, give voice to the demon of erotic violence lurking within so much of Lawrence's most powerful writing. Another such work is 'Love on the Farm', a gripping 1913 poem whose original title was, more accurately, 'Cruelty and Love'. From the poem's opening lines onward, we can hardly help observing that the narrator, a young farmer's wife, sees virtually everything around her in nature as brutal and threatening: 'What large, dark hands are those at the window / Grasping in the golden light . . . ? Ah, only the leaves!' Her morbid outlook is explained when she describes her husband, whose 'calm and kindly' eyes belie the terrifying force of his 'large, hard hands': upon finding a frightened rabbit in a trap ('Piteous brown ball of quivering fears!'), the handsome farmer matter-of-factly strangles it, then returns home to caress his wife with fingers that 'still smell grim / Of the rabbit's fur!' By this point in the poem, we are primed for the wife's revulsion and revolt; but her response instead is one of fascinated submission, as she confesses to the fatal attraction of her husband's power over her:

> God, I am caught in a snare!
> I know not what fine wire is round my throat;
> I only know I let him finger there
> My pulse of life, and let him nose like a stoat
> Who sniffs with joy before he drinks the blood.
>
> And down his mouth comes to my mouth! and down
> His bright dark eyes come over me, like a hood
> Upon my mind! his lips meet mine, and a flood
> Of sweet fire sweeps across me, so I drown
> Against him, die, and find death good.   (42–43)

'Love on the Farm' is, for some readers, a wonderfully romantic poem about love, desire and the primacy of sexual passion over rational thought. For others, however, it is a highly disturbing work, not only because of the gender ideology it espouses but also because of the narrative tactics it deploys in espousing them: much as he does in later novels such as *The Plumed Serpent* and *Lady Chatterley's Lover*, Lawrence uses a woman's voice and consciousness to convey the message that women should submit physically and emotionally to men. Numerous readers, both male and female, have praised Lawrence's insights into the female psyche: Anaïs Nin extolled his 'complete realization of the feelings of women', arguing that 'he wrote *as a woman* would write'; Henry Miller claimed that women 'adored' and 'worshipped' him 'because he revealed them to themselves in their nakedness'; Norman Mailer declared that 'Lawrence understood women as they had never been understood before'; and Mabel Dodge Luhan, in her adulatory biography of Lawrence, even offered a little free-verse ditty on the subject:

> Why do women like Lorenzo?
> They *do*.
> Maybe because no one, so well as he, knows
> How to stick in his thumb and pull out the plum
> Of their available, invisible Being.

Other commentators, however, have taken precisely the opposite position, acknowledging Lawrence's effectiveness in appropriating women's voices but criticising his hidden motives: Kate Millett calls him not only 'the most talented and fervid of sexual politicians', but 'the most subtle as well, for it is through a feminine consciousness that his masculine message is conveyed'; Simone de Beauvoir acidly observes that he spent his life writing 'guidebooks for women'; and H.D., in her thinly fictionalised novel *Bid Me To Live*, admits that Lawrence 'could write elaborately on the woman mood, describe women to their marrow in his writing' but calls his ability to do so 'diabolical'.[7] Lawrence's famous 'demon', then, at least for some readers, is a creature more devious than deviant, more wily than wild, an agent of and spokesman for the theme of sexual conflict that was soon to become one of Lawrence's major poetic preoccupations.

Look! We Have Come Through!

When Lawrence went off to Germany in 1912 with Frieda von Richthofen Weekley, the wife of his former modern languages tutor, he ushered in not only a new stage in his romantic life but also what he would call a 'new cycle' in his poetry (*Poems*, 28). The very title of his 1917 collection *Look! We Have Come Through!*, with its ringing injunction to attention and its adamant exclamation points, gives some indication of the visionary tone and emotion-laden content of these rhythmically free but often loosely rhymed poems – some rapturous, some anguished, but all deeply personal – in which he chronicles the early years of his tumultuous relationship with Frieda. Originally entitled *Man and Woman* or *Poems of a Married Man*, the volume takes as its major theme the emotional ambivalence of a man who is deeply in love with his wife but fears a 'mixing, merging' of identities, an annihilation of his autonomous self by what he calls 'the terrible *other*' ('Manifesto', *Poems*, 267).

While contemporaneous prose works such as *The Rainbow* and *Women in Love* explore the themes of love, marriage and sexual conflict through fictional characters and situations, Lawrence's poetry from the years 1912 to 1917 is for the most part deeply personal, comprising what the poet himself called 'an essential story, or history, or confession, unfolding one from the other in organic development, the whole revealing the intrinsic experience of a man during the crisis of manhood, when he marries and comes into himself' (*Poems*, 191). In keeping with his own later assertion that 'Even the best poetry, when it is at all personal, needs the penumbra of its own time and place and circumstance to make it full and whole' (28), Lawrence introduces the poems of *Look! We Have Come Through!* with a brief autobiographical gloss:

After much struggling and loss in love and in the world of man, the protagonist throws in his lot with a woman who is already married. Together they go into another country, she perforce leaving her children behind. The conflict of love and hate goes on between the man and the woman, and between these two and the world around them, till it reaches some sort of conclusion, they transcend into some condition of blessedness. (191)

Reprinting this opening 'Argument' a decade later, Lawrence would excise its final phrase – 'they transcend into some condition of blessedness' – perhaps because he had by then come to recognise that his continually escalating 'conflict of love and hate' with Frieda would lead, in the long run, neither to transcendence nor to blessedness. Nevertheless, *Look! We Have Come Through!* stands as a lasting document of Lawrence's short-lived sexual optimism during the early years of his marriage, his new-found belief, as he put it in several letters from 1913 to 1914, that 'sex is the fountainhead, where life bubbles up into the person from the unknown' (ii. 102):

I think the only re-sourcing of art, re-vivifying it, is to make it more the joint work of man and woman. I think *the* one thing to do, is for men to have courage to draw nearer to women, expose themselves to them, and be altered by them: and for women to accept and admit men . . . Because the source of all life and knowledge is in man and woman, and the source of all living is in the interchange and the meeting and mingling of these two: man-life and woman-life, man knowledge and woman-knowledge, man-being and woman-being. (ii. 181)

Some of *Look!*'s most impassioned poems enact the pure romantic ardour of a man determined, as Lawrence puts it, to 'draw nearer' to his wife, to 'expose' himself to her and 'be altered' by her. In 'Gloire de Dijon', for instance, his affectionate description of Frieda bathing – 'She stoops to the sponge, and her swung breasts / Sway like full-blown yellow / Gloire de Dijon roses' – becomes suffused, towards the end, with a visionary gleam, as woman, sunlight and roses all become one:

> She drips herself with water, and her shoulders
> Glisten as silver, they crumple up
> Like wet and falling roses, and I listen
> For the sluicing of their rain-dishevelled petals.
> In the window full of sunlight
> Concentrates her golden shadow
> Fold on fold, until it glows as
> Mellow as the glory roses. (217)

Other poems, however, employ similar imagery to a much more ominous effect, as in 'River Roses':

> By the Isar, in the twilight
> We found the dark wild roses
> Hanging red at the river; and simmering
> Frogs were singing, and over the river closes
> Was savour of ice and roses; and glimmering
> Fear was abroad. We whispered: 'No one knows us.
> Let it be as the snake disposes
> Here in this simmering marsh.'   (217)

Here, the domesticated yellow roses of 'Gloire de Dijon' have become dark, wild and blood-red, as bright morning sunshine gives way to the eerie atmospherics of twilight. The song of the frogs, 'simmering' rather than melodious, and the concealed presence of the snake hint that this wild, marshy landscape contains danger as well as beauty. Thus Lawrence's poetic demon rears its sinister head once more, introducing a note of 'glimmering fear' into the poet's Eden of sexual bliss.

Again and again, in fact, the poems of *Look! We Have Come Through!* focus not just on the ecstasy of married love – 'Between her breasts is my home, between her breasts' ('Song of a Man Who Is Loved', 249) – but also on love's ambivalences and anguish: 'The pain of loving you / Is almost more than I can bear' ('A Young Wife', 215). In 'Bei Hennef', the 1912 poem that opens the long poetic sequence about his married life, Lawrence's proclamations of sexual happiness and eternal love are tempered, towards the end, by a note of uncertainty and pain:

> You are the call and I am the answer,
> You are the wish, and I the fulfilment,
> You are the night, and I the day.
>> What else? it is perfect enough.
>> It is perfectly complete,
>> You and I,
>> What more –?
> Strange, how we suffer in spite of this!   (203)

In poems such as 'Mutilation' and 'Both Sides of the Medal', Lawrence dwells even more explicitly and unflinchingly on the dark side of desire – 'And because you love me, / think you you do not hate me?' (235) – while in 'Song of a Man Who Is Not Loved' he contemplates the emptiness and horror of a world without love: 'I hold myself up, and feel a big wind blowing / Me like a gadfly into the dusk' (223). And even in seemingly celebratory poems such as 'Song of a Man Who Has Come Through', in which the poet promises to 'be a good fountain, a good well-head' for 'the wonder that bubbles into my soul', he introduces, inevitably, a sudden note of anxiety at the end:

> What is the knocking?
> What is the knocking at the door in the night?
> It is somebody wants to do us harm.
>
> No, no, it is the three strange angels.
> Admit them, admit them.   (250)

The 'three strange angels', implicitly likened to the three messengers who appear to Abraham in the Old Testament with news of Sarah's fertility (*Poems*, 994), can be seen as yet another manifestation of Lawrence's poetic demon, the force of mystery that he fears but also desires to admit into his poetry.

'I know I am compound of two waves', confesses Lawrence in his 1915 essay 'The Crown'; 'I am framed in the struggle and embrace of the two opposite waves of darkness and of light.'[8] At their best, the poems of *Look! We Have Come Through!* illuminate and celebrate this eternal struggle between antithetical forces: darkness and light, man and woman, desire and fear, love and hate. In his 1914 'Study of Thomas Hardy', Lawrence even suggests that poetry itself partakes of such an oppositional embrace, a fruitful marriage between emotional energy (the 'will-to-motion') and formal structure (the 'will-to-inertia'):

> The very adherence to rhyme and regular rhythm is a concession to the Law, a concession to the body, to the being and requirements of the body. They are an admission of the living, positive inertia which is the other half of life, other than the pure will-to-motion. In this consummation, they are the resistance and response of the Bride in the arms of the Bridegroom.   (*Hardy*, 91)

With his next volume of poems, however, Lawrence would advocate a new verse form liberated from all such finality, fixity and consummation. As he explains in his 1919 essay 'Poetry of the Present', which heralds the radical new direction that his poetry is about to take:

> This is the unrestful, ungraspable poetry of the sheer present, poetry whose very permanency lies in its wind-like transit. Whitman's is the best poetry of this kind. Without beginning and without end, without any base and pediment, it sweeps past for ever, like a wind that is forever in passage, and unchainable.
>
> (*Poems*, 183)

Rejecting rhyme and regular metre altogether, Lawrence would abandon almost entirely his earlier conception of poetry as a balance of universal forces, 'the resistance and response of the Bride in the arms of the Bridegroom'. At the same time, he would shift his thematic attention as well, turning from 'the conflict of love and hate' between a man and a woman to the relationship between mankind and the natural world.

Birds, Beasts and Flowers

Although *Birds, Beasts and Flowers*, published in 1923 and composed in locations as diverse as Italy, Ceylon, Australia and New Mexico, ostensibly focuses not on men and women but rather on birds, beasts, trees, fruit and flowers, many of Lawrence's meditations on nature turn out to offer thinly disguised commentaries on human nature as well, and particularly on human sexual conflict. Significantly, however, the oppositional structure that characterised *Look! We Have Come Through!* – man and woman 'balanced . . . in strange conjunction' (*Poems*, 236), love and hate poised in eternal conflict, emotional energy steadied by formal constraints – is largely absent from *Birds, Beasts and Flowers*. Instead, like the three 'leadership' novels from the same period (*Aaron's Rod*, *Kangaroo* and *The Plumed Serpent*), many of these poems, and particularly those concerned with sexual politics, are dogmatic and one-sided, urging mindless subservience – of female to male, of nature to mankind – rather than a balanced equilibrium of opposites.

Other poems in the volume, to be sure, offer such vivid and poignant descriptions of the natural world that *Birds, Beasts and Flowers* remains, on the whole, Lawrence's most memorable and influential book of poetry. In his most successful poems, rather than using plants and animals to illustrate the ills of humanity, Lawrence makes a concerted effort to submit instead to the power of nature, admitting to the sometimes disconcerting otherness of the creatures he observes rather than attempting to describe and subdue them via brute poetic force. In 'Fish', for instance, the poet humbly confesses his inability to depict a fish in human language or to comprehend it according to human categories of judgement: '*I am not the measure of creation. / This is beyond me, this fish*' (339). In 'Mountain Lion', the killing of a wild creature by two 'foolish' Mexicans causes him to reflect, in full sympathy with nature rather than with human culture, that 'we might spare a million or two of humans / And never miss them. / Yet what a gap in the world, the missing white frost-face of that slim yellow mountain lion!' (402). And in poems such as 'The Mosquito' ('Queer, with your thin wings and your streaming legs, / How you sail like a heron, or a dull clot of air', 332) and 'Kangaroo' ('Her little loose hands, and drooping Victorian shoulders', 393) he offers visual descriptions so precise and accurate that even W. H. Auden, who admitted to disliking most of Lawrence's poetry, calls *Birds, Beasts and Flowers* 'the peak of Lawrence's achievement', a volume in which Lawrence's often 'turgid and obscure' writing becomes 'so transparent that one forgets him entirely and simply sees what he saw'.[9]

One of the best-known and most widely anthologised poems from *Birds, Beasts and Flowers* is 'Snake', in which Lawrence sensitively describes his encounter in Sicily with a golden serpent, which he frightens with a log – 'The voice of my education said to me / He must be killed' – but later regrets having chased away: 'I thought how paltry, how vulgar, what a mean act! / I despised myself and the voices of my accursed human education' (349–51). The poem's seemingly simple narrative incorporates rich allusions to classical mythology (the snake is 'like a god' and 'Like a king in exile, uncrowned in the under-world'), Romantic poetry (the poet compares himself to Coleridge's Ancient Mariner, who killed an albatross for no reason) and the Old Testament (the snake recalls the serpent that tempted Eve in the Garden of Eden; in trying to slay it, the poet listens to his 'accursed human education', the voice of Christian orthodoxy, rather than trusting his initial, pagan instinct to welcome the snake). 'Snake' contains, moreover, a strong undercurrent of sexuality: the phallic snake disappears into a 'dreadful hole', causing the poet to be over-come with 'a sort of horror' reminiscent of Lawrence's fear, in *Look! We Have Come Through!*, of 'mixing, merging' with 'the terrible *other*' ('Manifesto', 267). Only afterwards does he apparently acknowledge that the 'horrid black hole', the 'dark door of the secret earth' could be a place of mystery, beauty and otherworldly power to which the snake, had he welcomed it, might have granted him access. Although the poem ostensibly focuses on man's relation-ship to the natural world, then, it also explores, subtly and without didacti-cism, such issues as religious prejudice, the limitations of formal education, the lure of the forbidden, and the temptations of sexual knowledge.

Other poems in the volume, however, are not so balanced and complex in their approach either to nature or to human relationships. In his prose intro-duction to the 'Reptiles' section of *Birds, Beasts and Flowers*, Lawrence asserts (quoting from John Burnet's 1920 *Early Greek Philosophy*) that 'in the tension of opposites all things have their being' (348), a statement seem-ingly reflecting his gender ideology in *Look! We Have Come Through!*, where he focused on the fruitful 'conflict of love and hate' between a man and a woman. But in *Birds, Beasts and Flowers*, despite his oppositional rhetoric, Lawrence more frequently engages in a poetics of tyranny than in one of generative tension. In the 'Fruits' section that opens the volume, for instance, he declares that 'fruits are all of them female, in them lies the seed. And so when they break and show the seed, then we look into the womb and see its secrets' (277). Rather than positing a 'tension of opposites' – a bal-anced equilibrium either of man and woman or of mankind and nature – he suggests instead that physical penetration is the key to discovering the 'secrets' of both fruit and female. Thus, in 'Pomegranate', he praises the gaping 'fissure' through which one can glimpse the 'glittering, compact drops of dawn' inside the otherwise impenetrable fruit: 'It is so lovely, dawn-kaleidoscopic within the crack' (278–79). And in 'Purple Anemones', shifting his focus from fruits to flowers, he portrays Persephone's cyclical return from the underworld as a domestic drama of pursuit and capture; Pluto, 'Proserpine's master', allows his 'enfranchised' wife to escape from hell once a year only so that he might have the pleasure of hunting his 'white victim' down again: 'Poor Persephone and her rights for women' (307–9).

In 'Figs', noting that the Italians associate figs with the female genitalia, Lawrence condemns modern women for desiring to take control of their own secrets, to 'burst into affirmation' like ripe fruit:

> Ripe figs won't keep, won't keep in any clime.
> What then, when women the world over have all bursten into self-assertion?
> And bursten figs won't keep? (282–84)

One could easily argue, however, that what Lawrence decries here politically he enacts poetically, bursting into ideological self-assertion rather than main-taining a sense of mystery, exposing his own secrets like an over-ripe fig (or an emancipated modern woman) rather than allowing the poem to reveal them gradually and delicately. Indeed, he follows all too closely his own advice in 'Poetry of the Present', where he advocates 'the incarnate disclo-sure of the flux, mutation in blossom, laughter and decay perfectly open in their transit, nude in their movement before us' (*Poems*, 182). Such 'incar-nate disclosure' is meant to convey, no doubt, expressive energy and emo-tional candour; yet public nakedness – whether of bodies, emotions or political sentiment – is not necessarily a sight that every reader welcomes.

Lawrence himself asserted in a 1923 letter that he considered *Birds, Beasts and Flowers* to be his 'best book of poems' (iv. 380), and most critics, despite its failures and excesses, have concurred with that assessment. On the whole, the volume successfully captures the spontaneity, vigour and mantic energy that Lawrence calls for in 'Poetry of the Present': 'In the immediate present there is no perfection, no consummation, nothing fin-ished. The strands are all flying, quivering, intermingling into the web, the waters are shaking the moon' (182). Certainly Lawrence provides here enough moments of beauty, humour and even visionary insight – from his otherworldly self-absorption in 'Medlars and Sorb-Apples' to his all too down-to-earth observations about the sex life of tortoises in his 'Reptiles' series – to make up for infelicities elsewhere. He offers with this volume, moreover, a model for writing poetry that has proven enormously influen-tial throughout the twentieth century. Although few proponents of free verse would claim that their poetry operates entirely without principles of sound, metre or structure – 'no *vers* is *libre* for the man who wants to do a good job', as T. S. Eliot reportedly told Ezra Pound[10] – Lawrence is one modern poet who really does seem to have embraced with gusto, at least for

a time, Wordsworth's famous axiom that 'all good poetry is the spontaneous overflow of powerful feeling'.[11] (Like Wordsworth, to be sure,
Lawrence subjected most of his poems to elaborate revision; what he really
valued was the illusion of spontaneous expression rather than spontaneity
itself.) Subsequently, for better or for worse, the poems of *Look! We Have
Come Through!* and *Birds, Beasts and Flowers* have inspired and validated
the efforts of the millions of amateur poets throughout the English-speaking world for whom writing and emoting are a single, simultaneous gesture,
for whom freedom of form equals sincerity of expression, and for whom
virtually anything, from the ache of love to the sting of a mosquito, can be
an appropriate subject for poetry.

Lawrence's late poetry

Following the appearance of *Birds, Beasts and Flowers* in 1923 and until his
death in 1930, Lawrence continued to write poetry as prolifically as ever
(although, inevitably, in fits and starts), eventually producing *Pansies* (1929),
Nettles (1930) and the posthumously published *Last Poems* and *More
Pansies* (1932). Lawrence himself noted that his 'Pansies', or *pensées*,
stemmed 'as much from the heart and the genitals as from the head' (*Poems*,
417). Richard Aldington, however, attributed their origins to an even less
cerebral source: 'It seems to me that nearly all these Pansies and Nettles came
out of Lawrence's nerves, and not out of his real self' (*Poems*, 595). Although
many of Lawrence's gripes about the ills of the modern world are accurate
and justifiable – he complains, for instance, that 'sex in the head' has
replaced physical eroticism and that mankind's worship of the machine has
replaced our appreciation of nature – Lawrence's 'demon' manifests itself
here more often as an impish gadfly or petulant scold than as a force of universal mystery.

There are, to be sure, many notable exceptions among the hundreds of
verses that make up these four volumes: poems that explore contradictions,
cast doubts, set up paradoxes or simply evoke appreciative laughter. In some,
disturbing images of violence, blood and male leadership are undercut by
admissions of anxiety towards such potentially deadly forces, which appear
in the forms of powerful heroes and gods ('The Argonauts', 'For the Heroes
Are Dipped in Scarlet'), threatening swans ('Swan', 'Leda', 'Won't It Be
Strange –?') and even new scientific theories ('Relativity'). In others, especially throughout *Last Poems*, Lawrence tempers his sometime misogyny
with a renewed emphasis on female beauty ('The Man of Tyre'), female
mystery ('Invocation to the Moon') and the pleasures of sexuality ('They Say
the Sea Is Loveless', 'Whales Weep Not!'). And although Lawrence is gener-

ally too heavy-handed in his social criticisms to be a successful satirist, his dialect poems attacking bourgeois hypocrisy, middle-class values and the evils of censorship are often quite hilarious, as in 'Red-Herring', where he speaks as the morally conflicted son of a down-to-earth collier father and a socially 'superior' mother:

> O I am a member of the bourgeoisie
> and a servant-maid brings me my tea —
> But I'm always longing for someone to say:
> 'ark 'ere, lad! atween thee an' me
>
> they're a' a b—d— lot o' —s,
> an' I reckon it's nowt but right
> we should start an' kick their —ses for 'em
> an' tell 'em to —   (490–91)

Perhaps the most memorable of Lawrence's late poems, however, and certainly the best-known, are the ones that he wrote in the final months of his life, as his failing health forced him to confront head on the spectre of his own mortality. Whereas Dylan Thomas, several decades later, would famously beseech his dying father to 'Rage, rage, against the dying of the light', Lawrence admonishes us in 'The Ship of Death' to prepare ourselves quietly for the 'last journey' that we all must someday take:

> Oh build your ship of death, your little ark
> and furnish it with food, with little cakes, and wine
> for the dark flight down oblivion.   (718)

In several lengthy drafts of the poem, he emphasises the physical agony, spiritual pain and paralysing uncertainty of that voyage:

> There is no port, there is nowhere to go
> only the deepening black darkening still
> blacker upon the soundless, ungurgling flood
> darkness at one with darkness, up and down
> and sideways utterly dark, so there is no direction any more.
>   (719)

Eventually, however, in the much shorter and more coherent version that may well represent his last (though not necessarily final) draft, he excises virtually every negative image from the poem, replacing existential doubt with a serene sureness of purpose:

> Oh build your ship of death, be building it now
> With dim, calm thoughts and quiet hands
> Putting its timbers together in the dusk,

Rigging its mast with the silent, invisible sail
That will spread in death to the breeze
Of the kindness of the cosmos, that will waft
The little ship with its soul to the wonder-goal.

Ah, if you want to live in peace on the face of the earth
Then build your ship of death, in readiness
For the longest journey, over the last of seas. (965)

What is surprising here is not so much Lawrence's resignation in the face of death – this is a poet, after all, who always welcomed even the most disconcerting of personal demons into his poetry – but rather his new tone of almost euphoric calm, so unlike anything since his rapturous love poetry nearly two decades earlier in *Look! We Have Come Through!* The sprawling free-verse cadences of the poem's earlier drafts are now perfectly paced, lyrical but controlled, as the 'insurgent naked throb of the instant moment' ('Poetry of the Present', 185) gives way instead to a measured composure of style and sentiment.

A similar sense of joyous acceptance pervades 'Bavarian Gentians', another late poem that describes death as an exhilarating journey into the unknown, not outward across invisible oceans but downward into the murky underworld of Greek and Roman mythology:

Reach me a gentian, give me a torch!
let me guide myself with the blue, forked torch of this flower
down the darker and darker stairs, where blue is darkened on blueness
even where Persephone goes, just now, from the frosted September
to the sightless realm where darkness is awake upon the dark. (697)

Throughout his poetic career, as we have seen, Lawrence invoked flowers for a variety of imagistic purposes: in his early 'Snap-Dragon', they illustrate the thralldom of youth to the lure of sexuality; in 'Gloire de Dijon', they evoke ripe, voluptuous womanhood; and in 'Purple Anemones', in a new and surprising twist, they become emblems not of femininity but rather of male domination, symbolising the power of Pluto over Persephone and, more broadly, the dominion of Death even in the realm of the living:

When [Persephone] broke forth from below,
Flowers came, hell-hounds on her heels.
Dis, the dark, the jealous god, the husband,
Flower-sumptuous-blooded. (308)

Now, in 'Bavarian Gentians', Lawrence revisits the Persephone myth once again; but this time he has transformed Pluto's rape of Persephone from a jealous act of possession into a mystical act of passion:

and Persephone herself is but a voice
or a darkness invisible enfolded in the deeper dark
of the arms Plutonic, and pierced with the passion of dense gloom,
among the splendour of torches of darkness, shedding darkness on
the lost bride and her groom.   (697)

The blue gentians of the poem's title function at once as female and male symbols: having been borne, like Persephone, from the world of the living to the world of the dead, they pierce Pluto's gloomy underworld with phallic splendour. Thus, far from merely positing a glib union of opposites, Lawrence's flower imagery acknowledges the intricacies and nuances of all metaphoric language: in contrast to the 'two opposite waves of darkness and light' that Lawrence invoked, in 1915, to describe his own conflicted nature, here he gives us only degrees and layers of shade, 'blue darkened on blueness', 'darkness invisible enfolded in the deeper dark'. Ideologically, too, the poem is far more vexed and complex than many of Lawrence's earlier works. Feminist readers might well balk at Lawrence's portrayal of Persephone's rape as a conjugal consummation voyeuristically enjoyed by the male poet: 'I will go to the wedding, and be wedding-guest / at the marriage of the living dark', he writes in an alternate version of the poem (960). It is worth noting, however, that the poet takes on Persephone's role rather than Pluto's when he follows her 'down the darker and darker stairs' to the underworld and allows himself, in a sense, to be ravished by the mystery of death.

André Maurois has noted that, whereas the German poet Goethe is said to have asked on his deathbed for 'More Light', Lawrence might well have asked for 'More Darkness' instead.[12] Much of his work, after all, concerns the difficulty of admitting darkness into one's life, of achieving access to the forces of universal mystery (in nature, in sexuality, in the self), of welcoming one's poetic demons without succumbing also to passion, anger, fears and other overwrought emotions. In many cases, Lawrence falls short of the mark, clapping his hand quickly and firmly over his demon's mouth. In others, he mistakes intensity of feeling for mystical revelation, smothering the demon in a mire of rhetorical excess. An impressive number of his poems, however, composed in a range of poetic styles and on an astonishing variety of subjects, do successfully incorporate demonic energies and emotions even while maintaining a sense of expressive control. Like the torchlike flowers of 'Bavarian Gentians' – 'black lamps from the halls of Dis, burning dark blue, / giving off darkness, blue darkness' (697) – these are poems that illuminate by casting shadows, by 'shedding darkness' on the world in which we live.

NOTES

1 'Chariot of the Sun, by Harry Crosby', in P, 255.
2 Quoted in Harry T. Moore, The Priest of Love: A Life of D. H. Lawrence (London: Heinemann, 1974), p. 369.
3 'Poetry of the Present', in Poems, 185.
4 H.D. (Hilda Doolittle Aldington), quoted by Lawrence in a letter to Catherine Carswell, iii. 102; Virginia Woolf, 'Notes on D. H. Lawrence', in The Moment and Other Essays (London: Hogarth, 1981), p. 79; Richard Aldington, 'Introduction to Last Poems and More Pansies' (1932), in Poems, 595; T. S. Eliot, After Strange Gods: A Primer of Modern Heresy (London: Faber and Faber, 1934), p. 58.
5 Edward Lucie-Smith, 'The Poetry of D. H. Lawrence – With a Glance at Shelley', in D. H. Lawrence: Novelist, Poet, Prophet, ed. Stephen Spender (London: Weidenfeld & Nicolson, 1973), p. 227. For further commentary on Lawrence's relationship to earlier poetic traditions, see especially Sandra M. Gilbert, Acts of Attention: The Poems of D. H. Lawrence (Ithaca: Cornell University Press, 1972), and Ross Murfin, The Poetry of D. H. Lawrence: Texts and Contexts (Lincoln: University of Nebraska Press, 1983).
6 R. P. Blackmur, 'D. H. Lawrence and Expressive Form', in Form and Value in Modern Poetry (Garden City, NY: Doubleday, 1957), p. 255.
7 Anais Nin, quoted in Hilary Simpson, D. H. Lawrence and Feminism (London: Croom Helm, 1982), p. 13; Henry Miller, The World of Lawrence: A Passionate Appreciation (London: John Calder, 1985), p. 133; Norman Mailer, The Prisoner of Sex (London: Weidenfeld & Nicolson, 1971), p. 131; Mabel Dodge Luhan, Lorenzo in Taos (New York: Kraus Reprint, 1969), p. 245; Kate Millett, Sexual Politics (London: Rupert Hart-Davis, 1971), p. 239; Simone de Beauvoir, quoted in Millett, Sexual Politics, p. 239; H.D., Bid Me To Live (A Madrigal) (London: Virago, 1984), p. 62.
8 Lawrence, 'The Crown', in RDP, 265.
9 W. H. Auden, 'D. H. Lawrence', in D. H. Lawrence's Poetry: Demon Liberated. A Collection of Primary and Secondary Material, ed. A. Banjeree (Basingstoke: Macmillan, 1990), pp. 239–40.
10 Entry on 'Free Verse', in A Handbook to Literature, 7th edn, ed. William Hannon and C. Hugh Holman (Upper Saddle River, NJ: Prentice-Hall, 1996), p. 225.
11 William Wordsworth, 'Preface to the Lyrical Ballads' (2nd edn), in English Romantic Writers, ed. David Perkins (New York: Harcourt Brace Jovanovich, 1967), p. 321.
12 André Maurois, Prophets and Poets, trans. Hamish Miles (New York, London: Harper Brothers, 1935), p. 271.

8

JOHN WORTHEN

Lawrence as dramatist

For a writer never much regarded as a writer of plays in his own time – only three of his eight full-length plays were published before he died, and his plays were so substantially forgotten afterwards as to leave even competent scholars doubtful about what he had written[1] – Lawrence has achieved a surprising posthumous success as a dramatist. Three of his plays (*A Collier's Friday Night, The Widowing of Mrs. Holroyd* and *The Daughter-in-Law*) have, since the middle 1960s, entered the English repertory of theatre, radio and television, and another (*The Fight for Barbara*) has received occasional performances; while all eight of his full-length plays, even *The Married Man* (which at some point lost its first five pages in manuscript), have been staged.[2]

This is the more remarkable because Lawrence – although an avid theatre-goer – had no practical experience of theatre. He never saw a play of his own on the stage, never went back-stage, and until 1924 had only a passing acquaintance with actors.[3] What is more, living abroad a good deal, he was only distantly concerned with the small number of performances his plays received while he was alive.[4]

He was, however, aware from an early age of what the theatre of his own time was doing, and how his own dramatic work might fit into it; and this knowledge in turn derived from his constant attendance at the theatre and the opera, especially before he left England at the age of twenty-six. One of his very earliest childhood memories was of seeing *Hamlet* at Teddy Rayner's travelling theatre in Eastwood, the Midlands town where he was born. His mother, disapproving of most of Eastwood's entertainments, must have sanctioned a visit to what she doubtless thought of as an educational event. And Lawrence never forgot how, when the Ghost solemnly pronounced ''Amblet, 'Amblet, I *am* thy father's ghost', a voice from the audience dryly remarked 'Why tha arena, I can tell thy voice.'[5] References to theatre-going and opera-going turn up constantly in memoirs of his early life and in his own correspondence. He saw numerous plays, both known – *Man and Superman* (i. 377) and

Ghosts (i. 495) stand out – and others now quite unknown: *Proud Prince* by Justin McCarthy (i. 138) and *Don* by Rudolf Besier (i. 141), for example. Especially after moving to Croydon in 1908, he went to the theatre and opera-house as often as he could, his teacher's salary being his only restriction. His visitors from Nottingham regularly got taken to the London theatre; Tom Smith saw *Don* (i. 143), Alice Dax saw *Electra* (i. 157 n. 5), Jessie Chambers saw *The Making of a Gentleman* (i. 146 n. 5), he hoped (with Louie Burrows) to see Puccini's *La Fanciulla del West* (i. 277), his brother George saw the wordless play *Sumurun* performed by Max Reinhardt's company (i. 310), and a friend of George's visiting London also expected to go to the theatre (i. 327). Lawrence also constantly read plays: Ibsen and Synge by 1909 (i. 113–14, 142), Hauptmann by 1910 (i. 164–65, 168, 171), Euripides and Sophocles in 1911 (i. 261), Galsworthy also in 1911 (i. 326), Chekhov in 1912 (i. 385); he directed his own school class in a Yeats play in 1910 (i. 186).

Without, therefore, any specialist knowledge of theatre, Lawrence felt well positioned to do what many aspiring writers of the period did: write plays. It was not an accident that writers like Arnold Bennett, John Galsworthy and Joseph Conrad, not thought of today as playwrights, all wrote plays in the same period. Although none of them had any lasting success in the theatre, the medium was both voracious in its demand for material, and immensely rewarding for those who were successful.[6] Its temptation to an impoverished and aspiring writer was irresistible.

Beginning as a dramatist

It was thus not a coincidence that, towards the end of 1909, Lawrence wrote his first play, and that he wrote five more in the course of the next three-and-a-half years. In 1909 he was the author of a single, much-revised but still unpublished novel (which in 1911 would appear as *The White Peacock*), a handful of short stories (only one of which had been published), a couple of unpublished essays, and a considerable number of poems, four of which had just been published (he had been writing poetry since 1905). His immediate reason for turning to drama was probably the influence of Ford Madox Hueffer, the editor of the *English Review*. Hueffer's attention had been drawn to Lawrence's poetry in the late summer of 1909: he had met Lawrence in September, had agreed to publish four poems, and had told him that his writing should draw more on his own Midlands and mining back-ground.[7] Until the autumn of 1909, Lawrence's writing in all its genres had been resolutely middle-class in both subject and expression; he had grown up believing that, if he were to make a career as a writer, it would be by writing fiction and poetry which a middle-class audience would enjoy.

Almost immediately after meeting Hueffer, however, Lawrence wrote his short story about the death of a miner, 'Odour of Chrysanthemums', which – significantly – Hueffer mis-remembered as the work which drew his attention to Lawrence in the first place. Only a few weeks later, Lawrence wrote his very first play, *A Collier's Friday Night*, set in the Midlands and about the problems of a miner's family; in this case the action is compressed into the crucial Friday evening (pay night) when so many tensions within the family come to a head. Within six months Lawrence had also written the first draft of his play *The Widowing of Mrs. Holroyd*, which has close links with the story.[8] Lawrence of course sent both the plays and the story to Hueffer, who had many contacts in the publishing and theatre worlds.

We do not now know what the 1910 *Widowing* was like; but *A Collier's Friday Night* survives in its 1909 form and gives us a good idea of the experience of a working-class writer using what he knew intimately from his early life but which was hardly ever expressed in fiction or on the stage. What passed at that period for naturalistic drama about working people can be exemplified in Galsworthy's famous play *Strife*, written earlier in 1909, and staged in Nottingham in September: Lawrence saw it with Jessie Chambers.[9] *Strife* was a 'problem play' of industrial relations whose working-class figures are the stock characters of melodrama: the firebrand workers' leader Roberts contrasted with (but seen as equivalent to) the equally determined old owner Anthony: both men are destroyed by their refusal to compromise. When Lawrence wrote his own play about the industrial working class only a couple of months after the Nottingham debut of *Strife*, he chose, however, not to write a drama of industrial conflict, with managers, workers, union leaders and board members all offering their points of view, but a play set entirely in the kitchen of a miner's family: a room entered only by family and neighbours (Roberts's kitchen in *Strife* is visited by Anthony's daughter). Lawrence also chose a minimal plot and an unresolved conclusion, both very different from *Strife*. The Galsworthy play forms a kind of omnipresent alternative version of what a play about industry might be like; Lawrence was deliberately contrasting his own understanding of the industrial working class with Galsworthy's. *A Collier's Friday Night* might have been an exercise in the straightforward naturalism of the so-called Manchester school[10] if it had not also introduced many of the themes and situations which would re-appear in *Sons and Lovers*: in particular, the intellectual youth with the uneducated and violent (if also warm and loving) father, and the emotionally supportive (but also subtly dominating) mother.

The play's naturalism is in its setting, its detailed stage directions and actions, the extraordinarily skilled bringing-together of characters in ordinary situations, and above all in its dialogue. Here, an ingenious blend of dialect elements and standard English creates a version of Midlands working-class speech which never endangers the audience's capacity to understand it. The girl from next door, Gertie Coomber, for example, at one point sympathises with the old collier Mr Lambert, who is warming his trousers (brought down from upstairs) in front of the fire: his own daughter Nellie objects to his language, and also to Gertie's sympathy. Gertie's language is markedly less rich in local speech forms than Mr Lambert's, and Nellie's even less so, as she attempts to define her distance from her father:

> NELLIE LAMBERT *(much irritated)*: Isn't he a nasty-tempered kid?
> GERTIE COOMBER: But those front bedrooms are clammy.
> FATHER *(gratified)*: They h'are, Gertie, they h'are.
> GERTIE COOMBER *(turning to avoid NELLIE LAMBERT's contempt, and pottering the fire)*: I know the things I bring down from ours, they fair damp in a day.
> FATHER: They h'are, Gertie, I know it. An' I wonder how 'er'd like to clap 'er 'arce into wet breeches.[11]

This creation not just of a version of regional speech which can be immediately understood, but also of significantly different varieties showing (for example) the children's differences from their parents, was something Lawrence would frequently use in his fiction, over the years. It is significant that he should have developed it so early; but the speech of the Midlands would play a part in all his plays except one. It would, however, be another four years before – in *The Daughter-in-Law* – he wrote a play fully exploiting the possibilities of the varieties of speech hinted at in *A Collier's Friday Night*.[12]

The play's main difference from the fiction to which it is at times extremely close, however (it contains versions of two episodes which would be used in *Sons and Lovers*), is that the dramatic form required Lawrence to be more objective and less judgemental about these characters (all of whom would haunt him for years) than he would be in any of his early fiction. And it was plain from the start that his incomparable ear for idiom, for the incoherence of spoken anger, and for the subtlety of the voice which wheedles and manipulates love, were all operating in his dramatic work long before his fiction could be freed from conventions and awkwardness. He never seems to have revised *A Collier's Friday Night* after first writing it in 1909 (he apologetically referred to it in 1912 as 'most awfully green'[13]) but it stands as one of the major achievements of his early years.

The Widowing of Mrs. Holroyd, written a few months later, exploits the same kind of situation, and the same range of language, in a more overtly dramatic way: Holroyd (an uneducated, violent and drunken miner) is killed, which prevents his wife eloping with Blackmore, an electrician. The surviving text of the play, however, dates only from 1913, when Lawrence was in some ways a different kind of writer, with *Sons and Lovers* – and two re-writings of 'Odour of Chrysanthemums' – behind him, so that we cannot really judge what use he was making of such material, dramatically, in the spring of 1910.[14] The next play he wrote, however, in the autumn of 1910, does survive in its original form, and should probably be seen as a deliberate attempt to develop his range as a dramatist. Having first written a naturalistic play, and then a tragic melodrama, and having got nowhere with either of them (Hueffer managed to mislay both manuscripts for months, but none of the people he gave them to – including his friend the writer, director and producer Harley Granville-Barker – showed any interest[15]), Lawrence turned to comedy. He set *The Merry-go-Round* in the Midlands, but with a mixed cast of working-class and middle-class characters, and produced an extraordinary play: witty, long, at times rambling, full of opportunities for 'character acting', which is today almost unknown. *The Merry-go-Round*, as its title suggests, shows events and expectations going full circle; no-one comes out well, but nearly everyone gets married. Lawrence challenged staging conventions from the start, with a live goose called Patty on the stage as a crucial part of the action; while the slightly cumbersome development of the piece towards an ending parodic of *As You Like It*, in its likely and unlikely pairing-off of couples, is a literary device to be admired by the connoisseur rather than a dramatic resolution. But the play is full of good things; its dominating and bed-ridden mother, Mrs Hemstock, is one of those terrifyingly powerful, astringent women whom Lawrence created so well, full of epigrammatic good sense ('a man's knee's a chair as is soon worn out'[16] is one of her comments on marriage) and whose speech is rich in vivid images: 'I'm nowt but noggins o' bone, like iron bars in a paper bag' she says of herself.[17] The minor characters, such as Job Arthur Bowers (the baker) and the unhappy, grieving son, Harry Hemstock, are wonderfully characterised; Rachel Wilcox ('she's one would fuss round a pair of breeches on a clothesline rather than have no man'[18]) is seen as cruelly exploited by the men round her, yet also as having an eye to the main chance ('She fair pines for our Harry, yet she'd have Job Arthur for fear of getting nobody'[19]); she gets Harry in the end. The comic German vicar and his wife are not very amusing, but there is a great deal else in the play, which Lawrence wrote at the bedside of his own dying mother in the autumn and winter of 1910; its version of the dying mother and the troubled, loving son watching her 'dying by inches' is as good as anything he wrote in these years, and well in advance of what he would do with the characters of Mrs Morel and Paul in the proto-type *Sons and Lovers* of 1911. The play manipulates its large cast ingeniously and affectionately, and it is surprising that it is not more often staged.

During 1911, Lawrence wrote no plays; but in the spring of 1912, in one of the great liberating phases of his life and work (he was writing the version of *Sons and Lovers* which took the novel for the first time into a deep analysis of Paul's problems with his mother) he wrote a comedy which he thought 'middling good' (i. 386): another almost unknown play, *The Married Man*, about a schoolmaster who tries to escape the responsibilities of his marriage through his relationships with other women. What may be the main interest of the play today is the fact that Lawrence introduced into it a recreation of Frieda Weekley, as Elsa Smith: Frieda (whom Lawrence had met and fallen in love with in March 1912) was the wife of the Professor at Nottingham University College who had taught Lawrence French. Lawrence wrote the play in April, less than a month before he went away to Germany with Frieda, and it is the first example of Frieda's influence on his writing. In the play, Elsa Smith is a rather unconvincing *dea ex machina* who has good advice about relationships for everybody but who otherwise plays almost no part in the action.

This sudden creation of a new play in April 1912 was, however, probably as much influenced by the publisher's reader Edward Garnett – now advising Lawrence on his literary career – as it was a result of meeting Frieda. Garnett had sent one of Lawrence's plays – probably *A Collier's Friday Night* – to the actor, producer and director Ben Iden Payne.[20] Payne was not only the country's foremost exponent of the Manchester school of theatrical realism, but had produced Garnett's play *The Feud* in Manchester. Lawrence was, naturally, enthusiastic about Payne's reading his play. He told Garnett:

> It is huge to think of Iden Payne acting me on the stage: you are like a genius of Arabian Nights, to get me through. Of course I will alter and improve whatever I can, and Mr Payne has fullest liberty to do entirely as he pleases with the play – you know that. And of course I don't expect to get money by it. But it's ripping to think of my being acted. (i. 384)

It was in this expectant mood that he wrote *The Married Man*; there was some point in writing plays if productions might result.

A meeting with Payne in London was arranged for 25 April 1912 but a production was not as likely a prospect as Lawrence's optimism had led him to believe. He met the producer at the Managers' Club in Wardour Street (i. 386–87), but Payne – rather than discussing a production – offered to mark up Lawrence's manuscript with suggestions for changes. A week later Payne returned the manuscript without any specific suggestions: 'He rather amuses me – He was going to show me what he wanted altering, but now says I know what wants doing without his troubling. So I do' (i. 389). It seems likely that Payne had not been encouraging enough about the play to make it worth Lawrence's while to work on it again – particularly when he had other things on his mind (he was going to Germany with Frieda in a few days). So far as we know, he never looked at the play again; it did not reach the stage until 1938.[21]

Garnett's relationship with Payne might have launched Lawrence as a playwright, just as Hueffer's relationship with Granville-Barker might have done. But Payne, although interested in new plays, was turning away from the realism of the Manchester school. He would soon be invited to America and would consequently dissolve his acting companies.[22] Lawrence's work had come to his attention too late. As it was, Lawrence left the manuscripts of his (now) four plays in Garnett's safe-keeping, abandoned the fictional Elsa Smith for the real Frieda Weekley, and went to Germany with her on 3 May 1912.

Lawrence and the theatre of his time

It goes without saying that he and Frieda had, of course, gone to the theatre together almost as soon as they met; they saw *Man and Superman* in Nottingham in April 1912 before they left, they saw a passion-play in Bavaria at the end of May (i. 411), Ibsen's *Ghosts* in Munich during the summer of 1912, and a play in Bad Tölz while passing through on their way to Italy in August. Lawrence may possibly have sketched out a preliminary version of *The Fight for Barbara* in July 1912 – he was working on 'a comedy' in July (i. 427) – but it was not until October that, as a break from writing the final *Sons and Lovers*, he wrote the play.

In this, Frieda was transformed far more interestingly than she had been in *The Married Man*. Barbara's marriage has broken down and she has gone away with a young working-class Englishman, Jimmie Wesson. Her husband Dr Tressider pursues her to Italy, as do her parents, Lord and Lady Charlcote. Ian Clarke has shown how conventional such a plot is;[23] and although some of the play was based on what had actually happened between Lawrence, Frieda, her husband and her mother Anna von Richthofen, Lawrence had clearly learned about conventional play-making from his long hours in the London theatre between 1908 and 1912, and here used the conventions perfectly happily. And yet the dialogue in which he created this series of confrontations is absolutely unconventional; and its full power has never been revealed in the heavily cut text in which the play has up to now been known and performed.[24] The quarrels, in particular, are like nothing else in the drama of the period, and there is a wonderfully risky kind of realism in the ways in which characters who are supposed to be reaching crucial decisions about their future simply fail to do so. They posture, demand, throw temper tantrums, dive deep into self-pity, dissolve into help-lessness, kiss, and leave. After one such encounter with Tressider, who is pleading with her to return to him, Barbara is confronted by her mother, who naturally enough demands 'What have you decided?' And Barbara can only answer 'I don't know.' The conversation which follows may appear incon-sequential, but it relates directly to the way in which each character is pur-suing her own train of thought.

> LADY CHARLCOTE: That's no answer. Have you decided nothing?
> BARBARA: No.
> LADY CHARLCOTE: I hope he won't go and jump in the lake.
> BARBARA: He won't, will he?
> LADY CHARLCOTE: It all depends what state you left him in.
> BARBARA: I said I'd see him tomorrow.
> LADY CHARLCOTE: Then he won't be such a fool. He'll probably be hanging round for me, so I shall have to go. How did he behave?
> BARBARA: Oh don't talk about it Mama.[25]

If the play had, by some extraordinary means, been either printed or acted in Lawrence's lifetime, it would have done a good deal to show his range as a writer: a writer whom his contemporaries stereotyped as obsessed with sexuality and with the darker passions of relationship. It is a gripping comedy of an often very painful kind, written in just three days; once again it suggests just how good a dramatist Lawrence could have been if he had been encouraged to apply himself to the job.

Lawrence wrote his sixth play, *The Daughter-in-Law*, during the first twelve days of January 1913. What had happened between him and Edward Garnett in the winter of 1912, however, profoundly affected the way in which it would be considered. At this stage of his career Lawrence was wholly dependent upon Garnett's support and advice, and early in December 1912 Garnett had announced that *Sons and Lovers* was still far too shape-less, and would have to be radically cut: he had undertaken the job himself. Lawrence had been dismayed – 'I sit in sadness and grief after your letter. I daren't say anything. All right, take out what you think necessary' (i. 481) – but also grateful; and it was at exactly this point that he made his single reference to *The Daughter-in-Law* in his surviving correspondence. On 12 January 1913 he told Garnett:

> I am going to send you a new play I have written. It is neither a comedy nor a tragedy – just ordinary. It is quite objective, as far as that term goes, and though no doubt, like most of my stuff, it wants weeding out a bit, yet I think the whole thing is there, laid out properly, planned and progressive. If you don't think so, I am disappointed.

> I enjoy so much writing my plays – they come so quick and exciting from the pen – that you mustn't growl at me if you think them waste of time. At any rate, they'll be stuff for shaping later on, when I'm more of a workman. And I look at the future, and it behoves me to keep on trying to earn money somehow . . . I must see to the money part. I *do* think this play might have a chance on the stage.
>
> (i. 500–1)

Lawrence obviously feared that Garnett would dismiss the play for the same reasons as he had objected to the novel: for being written too fast, and for being badly constructed. So Lawrence felt obliged to argue that the play would be useful material for working over again, later on, even though he also hankered after the idea that it might make him some money now, if only someone would take it up. But he felt he could not press Garnett on that; Garnett was already being enormously helpful to him.

He must have sent the manuscript of *The Daughter-in-Law* to Garnett shortly after writing this letter. His next surviving letter to Garnett, of 1 February, begins by thanking Garnett for returning him *The Merry-go-Round*, *The Married Man* and *The Fight for Barbara*, all of which he had asked in November to be sent back for possible reworking. We therefore do not know what Garnett's reaction to *The Daughter-in-Law* had been. Lawrence presumably did not ask for *A Collier's Friday Night* or *The Widowing of Mrs. Holroyd* because – after Granville-Barker's and Iden Payne's comments – he did not think there was anything he could do to improve their chances significantly. They were also both serious plays and he may well have decided to try and concentrate on comedies for the moment, while waiting for *Sons and Lovers* to be published. He badly needed an income, and attempted during the spring of 1913 to write fiction, too, in a more popular and commercial vein (i. 530, 536).

However, it was in February 1913 that Lawrence made one of his very rare statements about contemporary British theatre, and how his work might fit into it; and, in its own way, this was also a kind of response to Garnett's criticisms of his plays.

> I'm sure we are sick of the rather bony, bloodless drama we get nowadays – it is time for a reaction against Shaw and Galsworthy and [Granville-]Barker and Irishy (except Synge) people – the rule and measure mathematical folk. But you are of them and your sympathies are with your own generation, not with mine. I think it is inevitable. You are about the only man who is willing to let a new generation come in. It will seem a bit rough to me, when I am 45, and must see myself and my tradition supplanted. I shall bear it very badly. Damn my impudence, but don't dislike me. But I don't want to write like Galsworthy nor Ibsen, nor Strindberg nor any of them, *not* even if I could. We have to hate our immediate predecessors, to get free from their authority.
>
> (i. 509)

JOHN WORTHEN

Those remarks almost certainly refer to *The Daughter-in-Law*: a naturalistic dialect play, combining psychological and class insight, which was very different from the work of most contemporary British and European dramatists. Lawrence was freeing himself from authority in many forms during 1912–14 and would end by freeing himself from Garnett too. Furthermore, if Garnett had actually thought highly of any of Lawrence's early plays – and it appears that the only one he cared much for was *The Widowing of Mrs. Holroyd* – he would also have been aware (as a dramatist himself) that if producers like Granville-Barker and Payne did not want them, trying to do anything with them on the English stage was pointless. The regional speech of *The Daughter-in-Law* had moved away from the selective blend of speech registers which had characterised Lawrence's earlier theatre pieces and would have been impossible for many actors to speak and for most audiences to understand; while the unashamedly working-class concerns of *A Collier's Friday Night*, the odd comedy of *The Merry-go-Round*, the slightness of *The Married Man* and the possibly libellous quality of the recreation of Professor Ernest Weekley in *The Fight for Barbara* would have been thoroughly off-putting, even to enlightened theatre managements. These considerations, coupled with the plays' general refusal to create typically 'dramatic' confrontations, would have ruled them out for most commercial theatres. More than twenty years later, when Lawrence's was a household name, *The Daughter-in-Law* would still be regarded by theatrical managements as unacceptable unless rewritten by a professional dramatist (which is what happened to it in 1936). In 1913, things were even more difficult.

At some stage – perhaps in February 1913, but more likely rather later – Garnett returned the manuscript of *The Daughter-in-Law* to Lawrence. There was nothing he could do with it. In spite of Lawrence's hopes of using his plays as something to revise and develop for an appropriate audience, it was clear to him by the spring of 1913 that there was nothing else which could be done without either a publisher or a producer taking them up. He was fortunate with *The Widowing of Mrs. Holroyd*, because Garnett liked it and the American publisher Mitchell Kennerley took it for his series of 'Modern Drama'; Lawrence was able to revise it in the autumn of 1913 and turn it into a play which embodied something of what he had learned during his revisions of his story 'Odour of Chrysanthemums'. But whereas he might have been known as the author of that mordant, shocking and brilliant work *The Daughter-in-Law*, the play vanished for twenty years and was not even published until 1965. In so far as he was known as a playwright, Lawrence was the author of *The Widowing of Mrs. Holroyd*, a gloomily tragic play about the industrial Midlands. His versions of the dramatic and of the comic were left to find alternative routes through his writing, some of which I shall discuss below.

146

1918–1925

Lawrence only wrote two more full-length plays, neither of them successful nor very characteristic. In 1918, with his novel *Women in Love* still unpublished (three years after being written) he used some of its characters in his play *Touch and Go*, which he wrote very fast in the autumn in the belief that the mining district was likely to erupt into violence, and he could effectively – and profitably – dramatise its problems. This time, at least, the play found its way into print fairly quickly; but it was not staged. It contains some powerful scenes, but as a writer Lawrence was caught between a number of different aims: to use the Crich family material from *Women in Love*, to stage a play addressing itself to an industrial situation which might become tragically violent, and also to work out a love affair between Gerald and the Gudrun character, Annabel Wrath. A Birkin-like figure, Oliver, acts as commentator on the action, but is dramatically unpositioned; and though the last scene in particular (Gerald is almost murdered by the mob) might work well if effectively staged, much of the rest of the play – including the very open ending, in which Gerald simply walks away from the very problems with which the second half of the play had been concerned – is profoundly undramatic. Unlike Lawrence's first six plays, *Touch and Go* is the play of a writer of prose fiction rather than of someone thinking dramatically; it is, if anything, reminiscent of *Strife*.

If its dramatic qualities are the weakness of *Touch and Go*, they are almost completely the problem with *David*, which Lawrence wrote in the spring of 1925 as he recovered from the very serious illness he had suffered in Mexico after finishing *The Plumed Serpent*. *David* was actually written for an actress, Ida Rauh,[26] but in no other respect was it addressed to the theatre of the time, only to what Lawrence thought the theatre of his time *ought* to be. And when Ida Rauh found out what the play was like, she was quick to rule out any possibility of acting in it, while the American company to which she recommended it turned it down, too. A Bible play in sixteen scenes, it is driven by a Lawrencean philosophy linked directly with *The Plumed Serpent*: the old world (characterised by Saul), with its mystery, power and capacity for belief, gives way to the modern world characterised by David, with his sharp intelligence, mental energy and cunning. But this dichotomy is only really apparent when one knows that the play is a work by Lawrence. To most readers (and probably all playgoers) it is a play written in a pastiche of the King James Bible, at times incomprehensible, and extremely long. It was performed, catastrophically, in the spring of 1927 by the Stage Society in London, and not everything which went wrong can be attributed to its having been allotted too short a rehearsal time. It is one of the small number of works by Lawrence which now feels thoroughly dated, belonging as it does to a conception of theatre as a place of intense artificiality; while the saving and creating grace of the rest of Lawrence's plays, the extraordinarily vivid dialogue, is ruled out by the Biblical diction. The only parts which remain impressive are the speeches of Saul as he goes mad; Lawrence had always written well about extreme states of mind, and these speeches are no exception. Scholars can enjoy the play's links with Lawrence's other writing, but as a piece of drama it is a non-starter. That in turn suggests how little (by the end of his life) Lawrence was prepared to work *with* the theatre of his time. It can only make one the sadder that he had not been able to establish any profitable links with the theatre back in 1912–14, when he would have had much to bring to it, and would have been capable of learning, too.

Lawrence's only two other works in dramatic form date from the same period: a fragmentary forerunner to *David*, also in the diction of the King James Bible, *Noah's Flood*, of which only two scenes were ever written; and an unusual *jeu d'esprit* in the fragment *Altitude*, dating from the summer of 1924. Lawrence had gone to Taos in 1922 at the invitation of the society hostess Mabel Dodge Sterne, and though he had fairly quickly moved out of her orbit in Taos, up to a ranch on Lobo mountain, he and Frieda continued to pay visits to Mabel and her guests. In the first scene of *Altitude*, the guests (Ida Rauh among them) assemble for breakfast; in the second scene, Mabel's daughter and a young man fail to reach any understanding of each other. Both scenes are sharply observed and at times wickedly satirical; both were apparently written during an actual visit, with contributions made to the text by the guests themselves. They reveal a potentiality in Lawrence for a kind of realism, sardonic and comic, which he exploited nowhere else in his dramatic work, but which did find its way into his later fiction.

The 1960s

What happened in the English theatre after 1956 has been well documented in a number of places;[27] suffice it to say that plays in the realist tradition concerned with ordinary (at times working-class) life became fashionable and desirable, and Lawrence's rediscovery as a dramatist was at last made possible. This time, the accidents of fortune played a useful part. Television drama was reaching a steadily increasing audience, and it too employed predominantly naturalistic means. In 1961, *The Widowing of Mrs. Holroyd* became the first Lawrence play to be produced for television, even though the adaptation reduced the play to one hour's duration (less commercials). It was nevertheless well received, a review in the *Daily Telegraph* linking it directly with contemporary theatre by describing it as '"Kitchen Sink" D. H. Lawrence'.[28]

What made the crucial difference to Lawrence's reputation as a dramatist happened four years later, in a momentous first professional performance of *A Collier's Friday Night*. Peter Gill, an assistant director at the Royal Court Theatre, had heard 'astonished reports' of the 1961 television *Widowing of Mrs. Holroyd* (which he had not seen himself) and had planned a Sunday night production without decor (the English Stage Company's usual practice for trying out new work not deemed commercial). Gill sent for a copy of the text; but what came back, by accident, was *A Collier's Friday Night*, which so impressed him that he decided to produce it instead. It proved so successful, on Sunday 8 August 1965, that it was repeated the following Sunday. Two years later, *The Times* would claim that the production had 'exploded the idea that Lawrence the dramatist could safely be ignored'.[29]

This influential stage production was, by a fortunate coincidence, followed just four months later by the publication of all eight of Lawrence's full-length plays and the two fragments in Heinemann's edition of the *Complete Plays*. This came at exactly the right moment. *The Daughter-in-Law* was published at last, the three full-length plays which had only appeared in magazines now became widely available, and the other four plays came back into print. Anaïs Nin, in the *New York Times Book Review*, suggested that, in his plays, Lawrence respected the need for action, dialogue and direct expression – and consequently avoided the exploration of emotions and the unconscious so characteristic of his prose fiction. Instead, he was 'content to present a lifelike portrait of instants. He makes no attempt to break with conventions of the theater, as he did with those of the novel.'[30] These judgements were shortly to be tested by audiences' experiences in the theatre; while just at the right moment to help the long-delayed revival of interest in Lawrence as a dramatist, Granada Television transmitted thirteen of his short stories as television plays between January 1966 and June 1967. The stories lent themselves extremely well to dramatisation and filming, and Lawrence's dramatic gift quickly became known to a very wide audience; while *The Widowing of Mrs. Holroyd* was also staged in Leicester in the summer of 1966.

The final act in his rehabilitation as a playwright happened at the Royal Court Theatre in London in 1967. Whilst not staging the first performance of *The Daughter-in-Law* (that honour went to Edinburgh: the play was also broadcast on the BBC Third Programme), Peter Gill directed it using some of the actors from the 1965 *A Collier's Friday Night*, and directors, critics and audiences quickly realised that this was the Lawrence play they had been looking for. Frank Marcus in *Plays and Players* wrote that 'it seems hardly credible that a play of the quality of *The Daughter-in-Law* could have remained unperformed', but he also made some pertinent points:

Was D. H. Lawrence a great dramatist? No, but he might have become one if he had been able to see a performance as good as this. The marital rows come blazingly to life; he could have built on that. He could have re-written the curtain lines; he could have ventured beyond strict naturalism. He knew that he was offering emotional truth: he could have learned to express it in dramatic terms.[31]

If *The Daughter-in-Law* does more with its characters, its language and its tragic sense of the dominant mother than any other of Lawrence's early plays, it is partly because he had learnt from the experience of writing them; the real tragedy was that he was not able to build on that knowledge.

Dramatic interplay, dramatic character and the dramatic narrator

What happened in the 1960s will not now be repeated; plays by Lawrence have become part of the theatre's repertory of early twentieth-century work, and there is no need for him to be discovered as a dramatist again. However, the qualities in his writing which made him a good dramatist – and might have made him an excellent one – have not similarly been identified in his writing of prose and poetry, and I would like to conclude by suggesting what two of these are.

In the first place, Lawrence's dialogue in his plays has always struck readers and actors as witty, idiomatic, self-assured, with an excellent sense of an individual voice within it, and as particularly tough and hard-hitting in argument and quarrel. Exactly the same is true of his dialogue in his fiction; a reader only has to glance (for example) at the long exchange between Hepburn and Hannele, as they come down the mountain by bus in 'The Captain's Doll', to become aware of the touches of self-consciousness, petulance, selfishness and self-importance in both characters, beautifully offset by the lurching of the bus round the corners and the fact that the journey is so loud that they have to shout to make themselves heard.[32] It is clear that Lawrence could have written extremely effective stage comedy.

Secondly, Lawrence's range of narrative voices in his prose fiction is essentially dramatic. The changes of narrative point of view from character to character, and from narrator to character and back again, in the course of passages which in other writers would be wholly narratorial, are often richly dramatic, even when no character is actually speaking. We hear the character's own voice articulating his or her attitude, from his or her point of view; we hear that implicitly judged by the way it is immediately juxtaposed and thus contrasted with another point of view; while the point of view may shift several times in a paragraph. It is, at times, extraordinary how little independent narration there is in Lawrence's prose. In *Sons and Lovers*, for example,

Paul goes with Miriam to see a rose tree by which she has been deeply impressed. I have given the sixteen sentences superscript numbers for ease of reference.

(1) Paul looked into Miriam's eyes. (2) She was pale and expectant with wonder, her lips were parted, and her dark eyes lay open to him. (3) His look seemed to travel down into her. (4) Her soul quivered. (5) It was the communion she wanted. (6) He turned aside, as if pained. (7) He turned to the bush.

(8) 'They seem as if they walk like butterflies, and shake themselves', he said.

(9) She looked at her roses. (10) They were white, some incurved and holy, others expanded in an ecstasy. (11) The tree was dark as a shadow. (12) She lifted her hand impulsively to the flowers, she went forward and touched them in worship.

(13) 'Let us go', he said.

(14) There was a cool scent of ivory roses, a white, virgin scent. (15) Something made him feel anxious and imprisoned. (16) The two walked in silence.

(SL, 195–96)

Only sentence (16) arguably comes from an impersonal narrator; all the other sentences come from either Miriam's or Paul's particular point of view. The passage begins with the articulation – in sentence (1) – of how Paul looks at Miriam, and how he sees her: sentence (2) is not then an impersonal narrator's comment, but descriptive of how Paul looks and observes. Sentence (3) is a transition from our consciousness of Paul to our consciousness of Miriam, but comes far more fully from her awareness than from his. Sentence (4) marks our definitive arrival in Miriam's point of view, and sentence (5) confirms our new situation, as it tells us exactly how Paul's look satisfies Miriam. In sentence (6) we switch suddenly away from Miriam's self-satisfaction, and observe instead how Paul reacts to *her*; so that his turning away from her, and to the bush in sentence (7), seem part of a rather desperate turning away from her demands on him, not just a neutral action.

Paul's extraordinary remark in sentence (8) should thus be seen as his attempt not just to say something to Miriam about her rose bush, but to say anything at all, to get away from her impassioned look. What he says is both confused and pretentious: he would like to be an artist, producing impressive aesthetic reactions to his experience, but his confused (and highly sexualised) response comes out with almost a parody of an aesthetic reaction. Sentence (9), with its satisfied adjective 'her' applied to the roses, confirms that we are back with Miriam; and we remain with her for the rest of the paragraph, seeing as she sees and feeling as she feels. The paragraph break at sentence (13) marks Paul's decisive attempt to escape from what is, to him, Miriam's oppressive possessiveness: one which we ourselves have experienced while trapped within her narrative consciousness. We therefore read sentence (14) as Paul's, not Miriam's, perception; but he is not as aware as we are of what he is trying to escape from. Sentence (15) maintains 'his' perception, but he does not know (as we do) what is oppressing him. Finally, in sentence (16), an impersonal narrator tells us what they both do.

Such a range of dramatic interplay is common in the narrative of Lawrence's fiction, and it is time that critics responded to its richness. Thinking about Lawrence as the dramatist he undoubtedly was, in his prose as much as in his plays, may encourage such an awareness. Lawrence's finest work as a dramatist may indeed turn out to be not in his plays at all, but in the narrative of his fiction, and in the creative and self-creating brilliance and range of his letters. Encouragement for *The Daughter-in-Law* in 1913, however, might have led him into a career in which drama played a far larger part than it did. The experiences of audiences from the 1960s to the present day have shown that he had a genuine ability as a theatre writer to hold an audience and to give actors parts they enjoyed working with. What he lacked was the encouragement, in the period 1910–13, to develop for the stage the kind of 'ordinary' drama of which he could have been such a master.

NOTES

1 The drama critic Eric Bentley remarked that Lawrence 'wrote three plays' (*The Playwright as Thinker: A Study of Drama in Modern Times* (New York: Meridian Books, 1946, pp. 280, 76); Harry T. Moore's pioneering book *The Life and Works of D. H. Lawrence* listed six plays and a fragment and included *The Daughter-in-Law* only as an unnamed 'unfinished play' (London: Allen & Unwin, 1951, pp. 330–31); early in 1965 the distinguished bibliographer James G. Hepburn engaged in unfounded speculations about non-existent lost plays (*Book Collector*, 14 (1965), 78–81).

2 See Introduction, *Plays*, c–cxi.

3 See i. 144 n. 5, for details of how, in 1911, he briefly met the well-known variety actress Ellaline Terriss. In 1924 he became friends with the American actress Ida Rauh in Santa Fe; he wrote her into his play fragment *Altitude*, performed charades with her, and finally wrote his play *David* for her. See *Plays*, lix–lxxiii.

4 He met Robert Atkins (at that stage, director of *David*) and Phyllis Whitworth in September 1926, and subsequently gave the latter detailed advice about costumes. See *Plays*, lxxix–lxxxii, lxxxiv–lxxxix.

5 See *TI*, 149.

6 In *Kipps* (1905), by H. G. Wells, Chitterlow makes an immense fortune from a single play; his success typifies the popular fantasy of the unexpected wealth which could be gained from the theatre. Arnold Bennett also made a good deal of money from individual plays; see, e.g., *Milestones* in 1912, which 'ran for more than a year, bringing in about £60 a week': Margaret Drabble, *Arnold Bennett* (London: Weidenfeld & Nicolson, 1974), p. 189. See too *Letters of Arnold Bennett, Volume I: Letters to J. B. Pinker*, ed. James G. Hepburn (Oxford: Oxford University Press, 1966), pp. 167, 171.

7 See *EY*, 216–18.

8 Within a year, he also started his 'colliery novel' 'Paul Morel', which would become *Sons and Lovers*.

9 See E. T. [Jessie Chambers], *D. H. Lawrence: A Personal Record* (Oxford: Oxford University Press, 1935), p. 109.

10 See below, p. 142.

11 *Plays*, 11:22–29.

12 He did compose a small number of dialect poems in the period 1909–11; see, e.g., 'Whether or Not' and 'Violets'.

13 Warren Roberts, *A Bibliography of D. H. Lawrence*, 2nd edn (Cambridge: Cambridge University Press, 1992), E74a, p. [1]; the manuscript's pages are not numbered.

14 All manuscript materials (including the 1910 version) are lost. See *Plays*, xxxviii–xli.

15 See *Plays*, xxx.

16 See ibid., 121:21–22.

17 Ibid., 117:31–32.

18 Ibid., 170:25–27.

19 Ibid., 170:29–30.

20 (1881–1976): he had moulded the first true British repertory theatre in Manchester at Miss Horniman's Gaiety Theatre (1907–11).

21 See *Plays*, xxviii, xxii, xcvi.

22 B. I. Payne, *A Life of the Wooden O: Memoirs of the Theatre* (New Haven, CT: Yale University Press, 1977), pp. 114–16.

23 See '*The Fight for Barbara*: Lawrence's Society Drama', in *D. H. Lawrence in the Modern World*, ed. Peter Preston and Peter Hoare (Basingstoke: Macmillan, 1989), pp. 47–68.

24 The text was cut for its magazine publication in 1933; the full text has been published for the first time in *Plays*, 237–99.

25 *Plays*, 291:17–28.

26 See n. 3.

27 See, e.g., Katharine J. Worth, *Revolutions in Modern English Drama* (London: G. Bell, 1972), and Christopher Innes, *Modern British Drama 1890–1990* (Cambridge: Cambridge University Press, 1992).

28 24 March 1961, p. 16.

29 28 January 1967, p. 13.

30 10 April 1966, pp. 4, 33.

31 'The Dominant Sex', *Plays and Players*, 14 (May 1967), 19.

32 See *Fox*, 148–50.

2

CONTEXTS AND CRITICAL ISSUES

9

PAUL EGGERT

The biographical issue: lives of Lawrence

Aesthetic autonomy *versus* biography: the 1930s and after

T. S. Eliot famously argued in 'Tradition and the Individual Talent' (1919) for a perfect division between 'the man who suffers and the mind which creates'.[1] Only thus could artists find the appropriate form for dealing with the problem or issue with which they were tussling; only thus would the necessary impersonality be achieved. In taking a very different path, D. H. Lawrence would pay a price but also find a rewarding freedom. Appreciating the implications of this changes one's understanding of virtually everything he wrote.

Eliot's desideratum articulated what would become a widely held cultural position. Contemporary reviewers and critics found indifference to Lawrence's flouting of it impossible. Trenchant, occasionally vitriolic, disagreements resulted; and the dispute gave rise to nearly a dozen biographical studies in the decade after Lawrence's death in 1930. In addition, many of the reviews of Lawrence's posthumous publications, and essays and books about his whole oeuvre, took a biographical turn. John Middleton Murry staked out one side of the argument, and Catherine Carswell the other. Lawrence was either the mother-dominated and then sex-crucified man whose confused intellectual writhings only intermittently permitted his unquestioned sensitivity to natural beauty and spirit of place to find expression (Murry). Or he was the late-Romantic genius who wrote from his daimon; the life-affirming hero who struggled against an unpropitious upbringing and a sickly body to articulate the spiritual sickness of modern society (manifested disastrously in the First World War) and who offered a vision of rebirth by means of a new openness to impulse and feeling (Carswell). Many more commentators joined the debate, focusing the murmurings of discontent and the praise that had been voiced during Lawrence's lifetime.[2] Both Lawrences – the intellectually perverse heretic and the Romantic genius – were inextricably intertwined with the writings, whether for good or bad.

More ambitious biographies were needed if the issue were to be better understood, and after the Second World War they began to appear: Piero Nardi's (in Italian) in 1947, Richard Aldington's in 1950 (he described it as 'a portrait and not a detailed exhaustive biography'), and then Harry T. Moore's in 1954. Unlike Aldington and the 1930s memoirists, Moore had not met Lawrence but was approaching the subject as a literary scholar in a period when the study of twentieth-century authors was still barely respectable. The biographical resources available to Moore were limited; most of the Lawrence letters had not been published, and of those that had (principally by Aldous Huxley in 1932) some had had references to particular people removed and some passages excised. Edward Nehls's compilation of his three-volume *Composite Biography* (1957–59) – a chronologically arranged selection from published and newly solicited memoirs, and from Lawrence's letters, relating to each successive period in his life – was a breakthrough; it remains an important source-book. But the scholarly interest it signalled (and that of Emile Delavenay in 1969 on the sources of Lawrence's ideas and on his reading) would have to wait for its day.[3] Literary criticism rather than scholarship was in the ascendant.

The critical reception of Lawrence had also been shifting. Chris Baldick shows (in chapter 14 of this volume) how the posthumous Lawrence went through successive incarnations in the lives of his readers as his writings responded to or resisted the broader cultural currents of the day, and as influential critics articulated his relevance.[4] In the 1930s Lawrence attracted acolytes and scoffers in about equal numbers. The former had a mission to perform in the 1950s and 1960s, and they performed it in the name of a humanly central and normative Lawrence; that gave way to feminist debunkings of the patriarchal-misogynist Lawrence in the 1970s; but in the 1980s the scoffers, by and large, went on to other challenges. Lawrence was no longer a primary battlefield. French post-structuralist theory was gaining the moral–intellectual high ground in English departments around the anglophone world, among other things challenging the basis of author-centric interpretation.

Roland Barthes's catchphrase in his essay 'From Work to Text' (originally in French, 1971) was: 'the work is held in the hand, the text is held in language'. For him, the author's life offered no point of origin for texts and therefore no hope of explanation of them. Existing only in language, texts could have neither origin nor closure. Given that their fate was to be 'traversed' again and again by readers, texts could be experienced only as 'an activity, in a production', and were therefore irreducibly plural.[5] Participating in larger cultural flows of meaning, they were not stable objects. This would be an influential position which signally rejected the existing understandings. The New Criticism in North America and the practical criticism movement in Britain and the Commonwealth in the 1950s and 1960s had opposed biographical criticism on different grounds. Both these movements tended, in varying degrees, to insulate works from their contexts, especially biographical ones (thus avoiding the so-called 'intentional fallacy'): there was no question about the aesthetic autonomy of the work of art. So Harry T. Moore, writing from Southern Illinois University in the expanded 1974 version of his Lawrence biography of 1954, wished to claim no more than that knowledge of Lawrence's life 'helps to illuminate his writings': there should be no seepage from one category (the life) into the other (the work), since the work of art had to exist on its own terms for close reading and intensive reflection. And this was despite Moore's awareness that Lawrence was even more 'intensely autobiographical' than similarly inspired writers.[6] That belief in autonomy was swamped in the 1980s and 1990s by a transferral of theorists' interest into the psychological and political workings of socially circulating discourses. At the popular level, however, the two decades saw author biographies and interviews with authors flourish as never before.

This situation calls out for a clarification in relation to Lawrence. The present chapter offers a reconsideration of the ways in which it remains meaningful (and important) to say that Lawrence wrote 'from' his living, and to show why this matters in the changed cultural climate of today. Biographies of Lawrence are clearly relevant to this task, and a large section will be devoted to the scholarly, three-volume Cambridge biography (1991–98). I offer this not by way of a review, but rather as a next-stage reflection of where understanding of the life–writings nexus, in Lawrence's case, might go.

Biographers have to balance the pertinacity of their collation and analysis of relevant documents against the need to provide their anticipated readership with a story of a life, preferably a new story of a life. The popular and the scholarly biographies have recently, in the case of Lawrence, struck very different balances. Brenda Maddox's *D. H. Lawrence: The Story of a Marriage* is an example of a successful trade biography. Maddox exercises the prerogative of a novelist or a features journalist to create a story that is likely to catch the eye of her 'nonacademic reader'[7]: she creates a scene in Lawrence's life, then backtracks chronologically, darting ahead if the story needs a lift. One is aware of her dramatising hand throughout. She starts her Part Two *in medias res*, relating as fact the story that Frieda had Lawrence in her bed within twenty minutes of meeting him. Nice if it were true; but, as Mark Kinkead-Weekes shows in the second volume of the Cambridge biography, the two extant sources are contradictory and the balance of probabilities is very much against the one Maddox chooses.

Again, she claims on page 136 to know the exact problem in Lawrence and Frieda's lovemaking in their first year together, 1912. Perhaps she is right in claiming that it was Lawrence's annoyance at Frieda's capacity to delay her orgasm and then to achieve it 'easily and insistently' – who knows?; who *could* know? – but she fails to reconcile her hunch with a quotation from a Lawrence letter also of 1912 which she quotes seven pages later: 'I do love, and I am loved – I have given and I have taken – and that is eternal. Oh, if only people could marry properly, I believe in marriage' (i. 441).

Maddox's failure to ponder the implications of the evidence, and to reconcile conflicting statements in it, makes one lose confidence – a situation that is worsened when one realises that the biography is not consistently reliable at the level of fact and simple description.[8] The work is littered with twinkling but stranded *aperçus* that don't connect. Her genuine fascination with the problem of understanding Lawrence is mixed with a condescension that she cannot quite contain, so that she has little time for his ideas or their dynamic. The work's subtitle, 'The Story of a Marriage', in any case declares the centre of her interest: this is not a biography of a *writing* life. The three-volume Cambridge biography, on the other hand, *is*.

The young Lawrence reconsidered

The great virtue of the first volume (by John Worthen) is, indeed, the easy and unstrained commerce it conducts between Lawrence's fictional writings, letters and his life: the effect as one reads is of writings weaving around writings, weaving in and out of the life. In identifying far more precisely than ever before the various stages and emotional colourings of the young Lawrence's relationships with Jessie Chambers, Louie Burrows and Alice Dax, Worthen's refrain is how continuously Lawrence wrote out of himself, how little was wasted.

Worthen shows how, in the comparatively late autobiographical essays 'Return to Bestwood' and 'Getting On', written after revisiting his home-town of Eastwood in summer 1926, Lawrence would re-cast the balance of sympathies he had struck in *Sons and Lovers* (1913). There, the balance had been weighted in favour of Mrs Morel, the character based on Lawrence's mother. In 1926, the class ambitiousness of his mother (who, as Lawrence puts it, 'has captured [her son] and in whom he implicitly believes')[9] comes off badly in comparison with his father's intuition and naturalness (*EY*, 500). This was in keeping with where Lawrence had arrived by the time of his writing *Sketches of Etruscan Places* and *Lady Chatterley's Lover*: the position is, indeed, the familiar Lawrencean one. But it forgets the far more guarded, self-conscious and spiritualising young man he had once been.

Worthen comments that 'he was a tremendous role player' (*EY*, 146), leaving different impressions on those who knew him. Lawrence's account in 1908 of hearing Sarah Bernhardt sing shows a fear of giving himself away emotionally, yet a desire to do so – and to relive both the fear and the desire in writing what is a memorable letter (i. 59). In another letter of the time, he wrote: 'in the moments of deepest emotion myself has watched myself' (i. 39). He had been deeply influenced by the example of his mother's self-control and the no-nonsense reserve cultivated within the Lawrence family. This helps explain the succession of narrators in Lawrence's pre-*Sons and Lovers* fiction who, growing out of 1890s literary stereotypes, adopt roles of aesthetic, sensitive observers at the cost of any capacity to get outside themselves and to love. Lawrence said of *The White Peacock* that he needed the gamekeeper Annable because otherwise the novel would have been, in the character of Cyril, 'too much *me*'.[10] Jessie Chambers describes in her memoir, *A Personal Record*, the extraordinary education she and Lawrence gave one another over a number of years, the refined tastes this gave him (the son of a miner), and the sensitivity to one another's feelings it cultivated. Their relationship, a sort of intellectual communion, seems to have been quite asexual until 1906 (by which time Lawrence was twenty), at which point his family forced him to become aware that he was monopolising Jessie and diminishing her chances of marriage.

Until reading this biography, I had never really taken the young Lawrence seriously: I had always found much of the early work stylistically overblown and emotionally forced, at times embarrassing to read. I had seen the early narrators being replaced (healthily) by the third-person narrator suitable to the dramatic realism Lawrence was developing for the mining-life stories: he had come under the influence of Ford Madox Hueffer and then Edward Garnett, upon moving from Eastwood in 1908 to teach at Croydon outside London. From 1912, under the additional influences of Frieda and living in Italy, Lawrence could probe the question of how the spiritual ecstasies Paul Morel finds with Miriam in *Sons and Lovers* disable him from loving her. In this view of things, Lawrence's creative effort in writing 'The Wedding Ring' (an early version of *The Rainbow*) in early 1914 at Fiascherino in Italy laid the ground for his imagining a renovating otherness in his revision of the *Prussian Officer* stories in July 1914 (particularly 'Odour of Chrysanthemums' and 'Daughters of the Vicar'). But this narrative of personal progress and organic growth was, it now seems to me, mistaken or at least simplistic.

What those early sensitive observer-narrators testify to in Lawrence did not simply evaporate as he grew up as man and artist – Worthen makes one see this. Rather, there is a continuity. In the post-*Sons and Lovers* work, Lawrence's need to live out, on the page, through his characters, the intensities of experience (as he so remarkably does in *The Rainbow*) represents, among other things, a determined attempt to shake off that old temptation of uninvolved self-consciousness. Spiritual intercourse, and specifically the substitution of sexuality for it, would be vilified in Lawrence's later writings (as exemplified in a character like Hermione in *Women in Love*) partly because the young Lawrence knew at first hand the terrible attractiveness – the spiritualising lure – of a woman's sexless devotion to him.[11] In 1911, he described himself as 'intense and concentrative' (i. 332). In later writings, the workings of mentalised knowing would be polarised against the knowledge of touch and the spontaneous life of the senses. But it would be the subtle and subtlised instrument of *verbal* consciousness that Lawrence had painstakingly developed that would serve as the vehicle for the exploration. Lawrence would swap roles, determined to have experience of both kinds of knowledge – and perhaps finding a sustaining personal integration only at moments. So the habit of polarising which he develops from 1914, the extremes to which he would characteristically push emotions and states of knowing and being, almost certainly had a biographical basis, one that *can* be reduced to evidence of a psychological condition (as John Middleton Murry, T. S. Eliot and others did) or be seen (as I will show) as the stimulant for an exploratory art of unaccommodating but clarifying extremes.

Worthen brings a new and welcome astringency to this crucial early period of Lawrence's life. He believes that Lawrence's mother was 'the only person who had ever really succeeded in breaking down his reserve and getting a whole-hearted loving response from him' (*EY*, 347). She died in December 1910. Earlier in that month he had become engaged to Louie Burrows; it was a desperate assertion of his capacity to be an ordinary man. But, as the biography shows, he conveniently dissociated the role he played for her benefit from the spectator–artist who was not benevolent or loving. While his mother was ill, he had also begun a first version of 'Paul Morel' (now lost), another in March 1911 with which he struggled throughout the year, and then in November 1911 a third version, interrupted when he contracted pneumonia – an illness which his elder brother Ernest had died of. He emerged from the illness a changed man, and he discovered for the novel that would become *Sons and Lovers* a more biographical and autobiographical subject. He began to write Jessie, and to some extent his mother, *out* of himself. The life fed the writing, and the writing reshaped his understanding of the life; but he also altered it to suit the needs and narrative strategies of the prose. He broke off his engagement to Louie Burrows in February 1912 and left Jessie Chambers 'devastated'. (He had begun to see her again in 1911 after he returned to Eastwood – *EY*, 266.)

The brutal honesty to which he committed himself in the analysis of others, but especially of himself, would remain a constant feature throughout his writing life. Frieda later said that 'his courage in facing the dark recesses of his own soul . . . scared me sometimes'.[12] The violent arguments that he would periodically have with her, and which so shocked others, stemmed not only from her conscious rejection of repression (she had had an affair in 1907 with Otto Gross, one of Freud's disciples, and she had none of the puritanism of Lawrence's upbringing about her); they also stemmed from his determination to be truthful to his feelings and direct in acting from them, no matter what they might be. Self-restraint tied to self-consciousness was a sickness he evidently, at some level, believed he had to overcome. He would do it in words.

The Lawrence of the war years

Worthen's volume has a pleasing movement: the biographer is prepared to chance his hand to find a shape in the life that, after careful and strenuous analysis, remains consistent with the (necessarily incomplete) sources. The writing is evidence for the life, but the newly textualised life we are given is, inevitably, 'made up'. In volume II (covering 1912–22), we enter different territory: not only is the textual and contextual archive for Lawrence larger after 1912, but the biographer Mark Kinkead-Weekes is canvassing and embodying a more ambitious approach to biography. In an essay, 'Use of Sources', offered as a reflection on his practice, Kinkead-Weekes states:

> This biography has tried . . . to 'live' with Lawrence week by week and month by month, avoiding hindsight and its patternings, not in the hope of some impossibly definitive truth, but trying for some sense at least of what it may have been like to live as Lawrence did: and live a writing life . . . [I]t is vitally important to get back to the versions written at the time, behind the often much revised and rewritten later ones with which we may be familiar . . . [I]t was in his writing that Lawrence perhaps lived most intensely (and spent much more time than in quarrelling with Frieda). Biography [must accept] the challenge to deal, sensitively, with the relationship of living man to creative 'manuscript'. (*TE*, 758–59)

This is biography as the literary-critical quintessence of the editorial theory of the late 1980s and early 1990s: the call was for editions that would document the 'process' of works of art as they were written and revised, rather than, as traditionally, for editions that would stabilise a single-text, ideal 'product' based on final authorial intention and representing the work in its purest achievable form.[13] The recovery of the circumstances surrounding the writing, revision, production and early reception of the Lawrence works in each of the Cambridge critical editions was feeding into the new movement, even as the general-editorial policy of the series respected the traditional goal.[14] Kinkead-Weekes edited *The Rainbow* for the Lawrence Works series (1989). Here, in the biography, he frequently and to great effect deals with the versions tucked away in appendices in the Cambridge editions or recorded in their textual apparatuses.

The reward for his approach is palpable: the works are, at every point in their development, unravelled into the life; they are measured and compared against all the contemporaneous evidence of letters, anecdotes and memoirs. Rather than simply repeat the dubious gossip of previous memoirists and biographers, Kinkead-Weekes and his fellow biographers investigate the primary material as never before. Although it is no part of their aim to challenge the traditional distinction between literary criticism and biography, they create nevertheless an author-centric intertextuality with a vengeance – and with a new authority. Its achieved seamlessness presupposes and depends upon the sheer apparatus of Lawrence scholarship that had come into being by the end of the 1980s – as well as demonstrating a mastery of it on the part of the biographer. Nearly all of this archive focuses on Lawrence in his time: neither the critical editions nor these biographies spend much time sifting the opinions, speculations and interpretations generated by the shelves of literary-critical and other studies of Lawrence's writing that have been published since, for the great bulk of them lacked this archival resource. Given the expansive, relativising mood which reception histories of Lawrence are apt to set off, one can only be grateful. Nominating a target time at which to aim brings a sharpness of focus to the debate in all three volumes of the Cambridge biographies. Barthes's quip that texts write the author, when taken seriously as here, doubles around on itself and leads, strangely, to an author-centric conclusion.

But there is a corresponding cost, especially noticeable in volume II. A doubling or tripling of the size of the archival evidence needing to be brought under biographical control has led to what is, in its word count, a veritable *War and Peace* of biographies, even without the other two volumes. In spite of a reduction in the size of the type, the volume comes out at 989 pages. Its chronologies and index are heroic.

Kinkead-Weekes's approach to biography is served by an attuned sympathy towards his subject. Both require much room to move; but the upshot is a remarkable patience and care in elucidating Lawrence's unsystematic philosophical writings, alongside his letters, where others would throw up their hands. This is a substantial contribution. Kinkead-Weekes's interpretation of Lawrence's two elusive letters about the Futurists (of June 1914), for instance, is masterly (ii. 180–84; *TE*, 121–25). Impressive too are his summary of Lawrence's attitudes to homosexuality from 1913 to late 1915 (*TE*, 303–5), his authoritative rejection of the idea that Lawrence was 'making furtive homosexual love in Cornwall' with William Henry Hocking in 1917 (380), his capacity to summarise confidently what the lost 'Goats and Compasses' manuscript of 1916 must have been about (303–5), and the wonderful balancing of information and disciplined speculation that allows him to defend Lawrence over his infamous letter to Katherine Mansfield, 'stewing in . . . corruption', when she was dying of tuberculosis (559–64).

Nevertheless there are, as I see it, some harder things to say as well, and they are not said. This is partly because the avowed aim is to attempt to '"live" with Lawrence' in a sort of re-created present. Readers like me will be grateful for the continuity of insight afforded by this approach but will inevitably also want to test it out against their larger picture of Lawrence (which *will* include 'hindsight and its patternings'). So one notices that Lawrence is criticised by Kinkead-Weekes, but only for his behaviour or poor judgement or bad temper – as one responds to and judges a friend. His behaviour is not seen as symptomatic of any fundamental or indelible psychological constraints; but this is not true of the other people in his life. Indeed, Frieda and John Middleton Murry come into focus for me as never before in Lawrence studies, and the treatments of Ottoline Morrell and Katherine Mansfield are not far behind. Kinkead-Weekes has a tendency in the biography to internalise and then reflect Lawrence's characteristic phrasing, and so accept the existence of a concept he ought (I believe) ideally to be resisting or at least translating. This is a problem, say for 1915, when Lawrence was going through a phase of tortuous and obscure philosophising: certainly his friends could not understand what 'The Crown' was about.

My reservation can be put another way. While instinctively knowing, as scholar, the importance of 'process' for telling the story of Lawrence, Kinkead-Weekes uses Romantic and Lawrencean metaphors of organic growth towards an achieved form to conceptualise and protect that process: for example, 'Each work will . . . have to find its own living form, though this may require repeated spontaneous reconceiving' (*TE*, 79). This sounds as if the work was, all along, meant to be the way it ended up – but meant by whom?[15] Lawrence worked very hard with his writing in the *Rainbow – Women in Love* period, and the feeling of discovery would have been strong for him. But the extant documents testify more obviously to change and variation, response to accident: each work could have gone in numerous directions, had the circumstances bearing on Lawrence been different. In fact, some of the most striking moments in the biography occur when Kinkead-Weekes stops to ask this very question.

In pursuing this line of commentary I find myself impelled – as I try to reconfigure my own 'larger picture' – to mix biographical and literary-critical understandings in ways that the biographers themselves resist: literary criticism, they might say, is for the written whereas theirs is a biography of a *writing* life'. Yet their attention to the documents from which they weave the textile of that writing life is so fine and complete that (it seems to me) the traditional wariness about the biography – literary criticism divide need no longer be maintained, at least with Lawrence. The biographers have created a sort of plateau for others to walk on with confidence, and to see what has changed in the Lawrence landscape.

From this vantage point one can say confidently that, had the war not broken out, *The Rainbow* would have been different from the novel we now have. When Lawrence returned to London in 1914, it was as the newly successful author of *Sons and Lovers*. He began mixing in literary circles, meeting Gilbert Cannan, Rupert Brooke, S. S. Koteliansky ('Kot'), Catherine Jackson (later, Carswell), and renewed acquaintance with Ezra Pound, Murry, Katherine Mansfield, Richard Aldington, H.D., and Edward Marsh. Having sloughed off Edward Garnett's literary mentorship while writing 'The Wedding Ring', he must have had the sense of writing for an audience that he could attune to his way of seeing things. He thought of himself, still, as essentially English.[16] The war put paid to all of this; the climate changed utterly in a frenzy of nationalistic and warlike fervour. It would drive Lawrence back on his own inner resources, applying a pressure that would only increase when *The Rainbow* was banned in November 1915. Money would be hard to come by, and there would be no continuity of contentment or stability within his usually fraught marriage to fall back on. (Murry said at this time that 'Frieda just squanders his nervous energy' – *TE*, 155.)

When Lawrence was revising *The Rainbow* in early 1915, he was extending the story chronologically backwards to 1840 to include the account of Tom and Lydia Brangwen. As he explored anew, with a language and style forged for the purpose, the psycho-sexual lives of the characters, he struggled with only partial success to find a way of differentiating the stages of fundamental growth and reaction in each generation. Biblical motifs (especially of death and rebirth) helped provide the amplitude, but he could afford only to gesture at a changing social world since its changes were of marginal relevance to his central proceeding. F. R. Leavis first noted that the use of repetition and variation of similar experiences across the three generations functions as a structuring device. This is true, but it only restates the problem and avoids the more obvious conclusion that Lawrence never finished, in the sense of clarifying, *The Rainbow*.

This criticism is also a measure of Lawrence's ambition – but it does, I believe, need saying and can be sustained. Kinkead-Weekes shows how, in rewriting the novel in early 1915, Lawrence was plumbing the new significances in his life as his acquaintances changed in his moves from Chesham to the Meynells' estate in Sussex in January and as he was taken up by Bloomsbury and began forming an attitude about the meaning (as opposed to the practice) of its homosexuality. His rapid, fertile development of an intensely idiosyncratic apprehension of the forces underlying the familiars of personality, speech and behaviour was, in a sense, artificially stopped by his need to get *The Rainbow* published so that he could earn money (the high hopes of late 1914 having largely evaporated). To expect that he could simultaneously pull off an analysis of the social history of the past three generations in England, and that this could provide the novel with a clarifying structure, is too much. All of Lawrence's novels from *The White Peacock* to *The Rainbow* took years to mature; all have unresolved elements which, in retrospect, belong to the next novel or stage of work. Only in the third generation of *The Rainbow* does a polarisation of life-directions, such as would structure *Women in Love*, begin to emerge: Winifred and Uncle Tom Brangwen align, in Lawrence's thinking, with the Futurist cluster of excessive intellectuality, mathematics (expressed in the enthusiasm about the colliery) and homosexuality;[17] Skrebensky, 'the most invented of all the main characters' (*EY*, 200), is lured to the self-extinction of devoting himself to the service of the state; but Ursula is spared to see a vision of a new wholeness symbolised by the rainbow.

What meaning are we to give to this vision? Many of Lawrence's friends remarked upon his sudden intuitiveness about personality and emotion; he extended it habitually to larger arenas. This, together with his powerful vocabulary of the psychological underlife, allowed him to build a mental world and a heterodox philosophy which he trusted to, even amidst its gradually changing conclusions. 'They say I cannot think' (ii. 380), he complained; the charge would recur in the 1930s, and it is the one that Leavis expended most energy in combating. Philip Heseltine remarked in late 1915 that Lawrence was 'too metaphysical, too anxious to be comprehensive in a detached way' (*TE*, 298). In biographical fact, Ursula's vision of rebirth and a new wholeness (versions of which are expressed in Lawrence's letters) would not long outlast his bruising arguments with Bertrand Russell in mid 1915 and his reading of John Burnet's *Early Greek Philosophy* (1892) – which, Lawrence would report in July, has 'clarified my soul' (ii. 364).

In allowing Lawrence to get in behind the tradition of idealism that comes from Plato, the early Greeks offered a clean sweep that was a natural for a man who had begun to see the war as the unleashing of passions of destruction that a century's ideology of selflessness had made inevitable as a last, desperate assertion of being. I have argued elsewhere that it was the fragments of Empedokles rather than Herakleitos (whom Lawrence names – ii. 364) that gave Lawrence the confidence to reject his sustaining hope in Ursula's vision of wholeness and move forward with the polarising he had tentatively begun to employ in the last part of *The Rainbow*. The polarising is immediately evident in the revisions to *Twilight in Italy* carried out later in 1915, and most importantly it orders the thematics of *Women in Love*.[18]

As Kinkead-Weekes tellingly observes, the novel needed a Hermione and a Pussum – female extremes (*TE*, 333–34). It would achieve in 1917 the clarification that *The Rainbow* misses: extremes of corruption and creation would be traced, and a diagnosis of the past and a prognosis for the future powerfully offered within the polarised field created by the extremes; but without the muddying of definition, the sameness of intensity in nominally different experiences, and the claustrophobia of *The Rainbow*.[19]

In *Women in Love*, Lawrence's art of extremes found its most powerful expression. But in this – to use James Joyce's image in *Portrait of the Artist* – Lawrence was no author paring his fingernails above the fray, and readers would not find that comfort available to them either: 'whoever reads me', Lawrence later warned, 'will be in the thick of the scrimmage' (v. 201). His by-now instinctive habit of stripping back to what he intuited as the changing essentials that needed to be brought to bear upon the situation in hand amounted (as I show below) to what might be called a projective fundamentalism. And it was deeply subjective (an allied thing) in that his changing relationship with Frieda often dictated the terms of his fictional explorations: from the struggle to win her commitment and loyalty early in the relationship, to Birkin's positing of the notion of a star-equilibrium between the partners (in *Women in Love*), to various 1920s protagonists' need to win a woman's acknowledgement of their male purposiveness. In July 1919, he told Cynthia Asquith: 'Love is heavily overweighted. I'm going to ride another horse' (iii. 368). Lawrence was never afraid to generalise, courageously, from his own predicaments and insights. They were the fuel of his art.

The later Lawrence

Lawrence's imagination could be so powerfully projective partly because circumstances were cutting him off from the feedback loop of a more fully socialised existence. In a famous letter in June 1914 to Edward Garnett, he had predicted: 'I shall get my reception, if not now, then before long' (ii. 184). By 1917 that hope was out the window: 'One's old great belief in the oneness and wholeness of humanity is torn clean across, for ever', Lawrence wrote (iii. 84), and with it went, implicitly, his own role in articulating it. Even the Lawrence of 1915 had been 'so absorbed in his own thought processes that they often came pouring out [in his letters] . . . with little sense of how they might seem to their recipient' (*TE*, 192). He professed to ignore, but was nevertheless sometimes affected by, the reviews he received. Those of *The Lost Girl* were arriving as he was writing the second, unfinished half of *Mr Noon* in December 1920 – his combative relations in the novel with his 'gentle reader' are surely a response; and, as David Ellis remarks in volume III of the biography, the new flippancy of tone and manner in his revision of his 1917–18 essays for *Studies in Classic American Literature* (1923) reveals a 'lurking despair over whether his audience would ever understand'.[20]

Nevertheless, the social arena operated at too low a heat for Lawrence to work suavely towards the minds and affections of readers whose resistances he could foresee and mollify (as the chameleon Middleton Murry could) or for whom, on a more serious level, he could speak. He did not *represent* them, no matter how English he had once felt. The war had heavily discounted that loyalty.[21] No wonder, too, that he had so many spectacular fallings-out with friends in the wartime years, for he characteristically miscalculated them. The initial burst of hope they each represented to him would in due course be shattered; new societies would be the same in the 1920s, as he travelled the world from Italy to Ceylon and Australia, the USA and Mexico. At a low point in March 1918, he had said that he could not now stand 'the presence of anybody else – barring Frieda, sometimes' (iii. 224).

Part of that alienation was Lawrence's deepening sense that his civilisation had become corrupt and hollow. If so, then its obliteration was a healthy and literal necessity: Birkin's imagining of just such a thing in *Women in Love* was not a passing fancy, as much of his writing from 1917 would show. Ellis comments strikingly that 'one needs to realise how completely and passionately Lawrence believed he was living in the modern equivalent of the Dark Ages' (*DG*, 152). It explains his interest in the occult and mysticism from 1917. What he would take away from what he read would typically be selective, and he would actively adapt and re-imagine it. Nevertheless, somewhat like a counter-culturist of the 1960s and after, he was looking for an alternative source of wisdom as a way of addressing what he saw as the present crisis. His so-called primitivism (from the African carvings in Halliday's flat in *Women in Love* to his 1920s interests in 'primitive' and ancient societies) is an allied response. Ellis's approach to these matters is nicely sceptical while refusing interpretative closure.

Few of Lawrence's friends agreed with his assessment of England's hopeless situation. They were having babies or affairs or earning a living or painting or writing; they were more receptive than he to the everyday currents of opinion, and more solicitous than he about their own families and careers. He was interested in the underlying continental drift of life: his alertness throve in the psychological realm, specialising in making normally unseen connections. Murry, who had set up the *Adelphi* as a mouthpiece for Lawrence in June 1923, refused to print Lawrence's first, acerbic essay upon his return to England from Mexico in January 1924:[22] Murry knew his readers and would not alienate them. Lawrence expected far more and was usually disappointed. This does not mean that he was a humourless prophet. Indeed, as the three biographers show, there is ample contemporary testimony to his high spirits, his sense of fun, his love of charades, his cheerful house-cleaning and cooking, his spells of work repairing the house on the Lobo ranch (renamed Kiowa) above Taos, New Mexico, which Mabel Luhan gave the Lawrences in 1924. He loved children, treating them as equals, although they were at first usually afraid of him for his similarity, in his skinny, red-bearded appearance, to Sunday-school images of Christ. Throughout his life he offered to teach poor children he knew – mathematics in one case, Spanish in another. He died game, as Ellis says, writing until the end, having consistently refused to acknowledge the inevitable dominion over his body that his tuberculosis (diagnosed in February 1925) had been gradually, ineluctably securing.

Some reflections on the new Lawrence

What emerges clearly and convincingly in these Cambridge volumes – and for the first time for me – is a Lawrence who is, at one level, an ordinary man with a range of problems, suffering from too early an acculturation into a conscious (and self-conscious) awareness of the feelings of his mother and then of Jessie Chambers, finding release in a relationship with his wife but pushing it harder than it could finally bear, not as monogamous as we had assumed,[23] depressed and solipsistic, but also wickedly joyous, outward-looking and fearless in the most intellectually ambitious ways. None of the Cambridge biographers surrenders to the intoxication of, say, an Aldous Huxley in his influential introduction to his *Letters of D. H. Lawrence* (1932). None of them offers to pigeon-hole Lawrence; he keeps eluding the satisfactory summary (as Frieda and the others do not). Dethroned from his position as the Lawrence-as-prophet of the 1950s and 1960s, distanced from the furies of 1930s disputation and returned to the period of his own life so convincingly, this Lawrence emerges as far more impressive when we recognise the conditions of his own personal history – when we appreciate how limitations transformed into stimulants, how he wrote from his life and how he lived in his writing.

His behaviour could by ordinary standards, as Ellis observes, seem wildly inconsistent without, from his own point of view, necessarily being so. Trigant Burrow's *The Social Basis of Consciousness* (1927) explains human behaviour as our adaptation to the images of ourselves that our upbringing has persuaded us to accept. For Lawrence, in his review of the book, this meant the death of spontaneity: all so-called normal behaviour was therefore neurotic. His taking of only a minimal interest in the peer pressures that shape conventional lives (a shaping that could be dealt with parodically, as

at the start of *St. Mawr*) gained, late in the day for him, a sort of justification. For Ellis, this is evidence of Lawrence's solipsism, and he sees
Lawrence's strong desire for collective action (in *Kangaroo* most obviously)
as an antidote; under this reading, Frieda's habitual sarcasm in the face of
his would-be world-renovating politics was equally necessary.

Lawrence's conscious incorporation in his fiction of this tension between
his intellectual projection and Frieda's disillusioning reception must mean
that he was aware that almost everything he wrote was only a provisional
solution or articulation. He must have known in some part of himself that
there were brackets around his truth-claims; but he could not write as if there
were. It would have been paralysing. He knew he might rewrite tomorrow
in a different mood, that the opportunity for revision was in any case not far
away; meanwhile he would take the insight wherever it would go, however
unbalanced it might seem to someone else.

A test-case occurs in Lawrence's writing of the second-last chapter of *The
Boy in the Bush* in November 1923: aware that his schemes have come to
nought and after his bigamous proposal to Mary has been rebuffed, Jack
Grant spews bile on all and sundry in an extended interior monologue.
(Significantly, Frieda was in Europe, and not with Lawrence in Mexico, as
he wrote this.) Ellis's refreshingly unprotective approach impels him to ask
the needful question: whether the collapsing of the distance maintained early
in the novel between Lawrence-as-narrator and Jack indicates that Jack's
paranoia here was an expression of Lawrence's:

> one of his strengths as a novelist is certainly the fairly direct attribution to his
> protagonists of feelings of his own which in most of us go unavowed. When
> he is writing at his best however, such feelings are given a critical context: other
> characters contest their validity, or their unreasonableness is demonstrated in
> the unfolding of events. 'One sheds ones sicknesses in books', Lawrence
> famously said on *Sons and Lovers* (ii. 90), but in traditional literary criticism
> at least, there is an important difference between writers working out their
> problems and merely displaying them.   (*DG*, 138)

This is fairly stated: it shifts the charge from a psycho-biographical one
(where one is reduced to speculation) to a literary-critical one (where one has
at least one's responses as a member of a reading community to go by). My
view, however, is that the 'traditional' distinction is not adequate to the
Lawrencean case, not sensitive enough to the dynamic of his writing. Even
in Jack's rant, there is a repressed half-consciousness of what is being so wilfully excluded.[24] Lawrence was letting himself go just as he had in the
superb, mood-driven 'Nightmare' chapter in *Kangaroo*, when his resentful-
ness at his wartime treatment bubbled up to the surface and required to be

given voice. And when Lawrence shortly afterwards returned to London from Mexico, he did add the present last chapter, in which a very different tone is struck. It is another example of the provisionality of his writing.[25]

Lawrence's peculiar unfetteredness by the conventional prepared him for the experience of unnervingly foreign places and cultures. In 1928 he recalled his first coming to New Mexico in 1922: 'the moment I saw the brilliant, proud morning shine high up over the deserts of Santa Fé, something stood still in my soul, and I started to attend . . . In the magnificent fierce morning of New Mexico one sprang awake.'[26] The full effect was not instantaneous. Revising *Studies in Classic American Literature* in 1922–23, he defined his culture's necessary progression as a 'great swerve' to take in primitive life in order 'to gather up again the savage mysteries' without 'going back on ourselves'.[27] The use, here, of the first person plural is revealing. The ideology of race in Lawrence's period was very strong; during the nineteenth century it had become interwoven with that of Empire and its civilising benefits. For Lawrence, it connected more with blood than Empire, but it balanced against his belief that what his race had produced, socially and psychically, did not deserve to stand.

The Indian Tony Luhan's presence at Taos as Mabel's husband raised for Lawrence the problem of sexual relationship between races, miscegenation (*DG*, 60), and at first he doubted the chance of 'any real reconciliation, in the flesh, between the white and the red':[28] Kate in 'Quetzalcoatl' (written 1923) cannot betray her race by marrying the Mexican-Indian Cipriano, but in *The Plumed Serpent* (finished 1925) she does. Comparison of Lawrence's first essays on Indian culture written in 1922 (e.g. 'Certain Americans and an Englishman') against 'The Hopi Snake Dance' of 1924[29] (which he sent to E. M. Forster) shows a deepening receptiveness that is very different from the alternative approaches towards aboriginal cultures in white societies of his day: dying-pillow liberalism on the one hand or eugenic extermination on the other. Lawrence could *take* the primitive connectedness to the land and the elements partly because of the authenticity of his rejection of the values of his own culture. (Mark Kinkead-Weekes discusses these issues in detail in chapter 4 of the present volume.) But Lawrence would not duck the integral part that violence played in primitive cultures, not wanting to sentimentalise them. (See, for instance, his short story 'The Woman Who Rode Away'.) He admired Forster's *A Passage to India* (1924) but felt it did not go far enough: 'you are the last Englishman', he told him, 'And I am the one after that' (iv. 584). And he declared in another letter: 'The day of our white dominance is over' (v. 77).

Rebecca West, writing in 1928, did not agree. In 'The Classic Artist', she praises Willa Cather in *Death Comes for the Archbishop* (set around Santa

Fe, published 1927) for not forcing the bishop to participate in an Indian consciousness: 'There is no attempt to fit the key into the lock. That door will not open.' In comparison, West argues, Lawrence is querulous in insisting that it can be done and that it means 'the death of our consciousness'. Cather's work, on the other hand, 'has not that air of claiming to cover all the ground'.[30] West had a point. When, in *The Plumed Serpent*, Lawrence tries to project a whole society renovated by a new religion, the pretension and strain become evident. Lawrence's disavowal of English culture and its ways of arriving at knowledge and truth is, however, strangely prescient in view of the validation of native cultures and the dislodging of the European from its central epistemological position in recent political debate.

That Lawrence should have such a relevance to agendas at the beginning of the twenty-first century is a consequence of what I have called his projective fundamentalism: his fearless determination to think his way through to extreme, often polarised, psychological positions and ways of being (which he had intuited in the first place and then projected) in the hope of new clarification. Lawrence had read deeply in Nietzsche when at Croydon; and, as Michael Bell has shown, there are parallels between Lawrence's idea of knowledge in the body and his contemporary Martin Heidegger's concept of Being-in-the-world.[31] A rejection of the tradition of Judeo-Christian idealism underlying the philosophical traditions of rationality coming down to the present from the Enlightenment is common to all three. Jacques Derrida (b. 1930) is Heidegger's philosophical descendant in this, and his philosophy of deconstruction (and the various kinds of post-structuralism generally) extend the rejection. Someone of such strongly projective imagination as Lawrence, who had not internalised dominant paradigms of knowledge of his own period, is likely to keep cropping up with newfound relevance in ours.

In Lawrence's essays on the novel written in June 1925 ('Art and Morality', 'Morality and the Novel' and 'The Novel'), the idealisms of Christianity, philosophy and scientific laws are said to nail down the living: in the novel, where morality means maintaining the 'trembling instability of the balance', a rigidifying, according to Lawrence, typically sets in.[32] The novel should be revealing the fluidity of life, just as he had said (in 'Poetry of the Present', 1919) that it was the poet's business to respond sensitively to the creative upwellings of the moment without imposing a conscious shaping and metrical form. His essay 'John Galsworthy', written in February 1927, opens with a denunciation of 'critical twiddle-twaddle about style and form', a continuation of an objection he had shown as early as 1913 to the 'carefully plotted and arranged developments' of the novels of Flaubert and Thomas Mann.[33] Having finished his translation of Giovanni Verga's

Cavalleria Rusticana in September 1927, he wrote an introduction minimising the importance of Verga's conscious *verismo* technique and drawing attention to Verga's attentiveness to the achronological, unplanned workings of the inner mind.[34] In 'Making Pictures' (1929), he recalls his taking up the brush again in 1926–27 after many years, learning to paint 'out of instinct, intuition and sheer physical action';[35] and in his memorable, longest sentence (in his essay 'Introduction to these Paintings', written in 1928–29) beginning 'He knew technically all there was to know about pictures', Lawrence mocks the young painter who has substituted technical knowledge for intuitive apprehension.[36] The line is consistent. It is based on the opposition of intuitive knowledge (where the mind is following the promptings of the body and the feelings) and mentalised knowing where the mind is in control and body-knowledge is repressed. His famous rejection in 1914 of 'the old stable ego of the character' had also been done under the sign of the body (ii. 183).

The argument is a magnificently confident *half*-truth: polemical, daring one to disagree, half-conscious of its own repression of the alternative. In fact, Lawrence very frequently had his finger in the pan of his novels' scales (witness his sarcasm, stridency, extremist postures); his paintings show a beginner's technique of being very tight – of failing to allow the surface and the paint to become expressive – in his determination to retain control of the paintings' meaning; and throughout his life he carefully revised earlier versions of his writings, only sometimes abandoning the earlier version and starting again. He could never copy out his own work without altering it in the process – which, in his introduction to his *Collected Poems* of May 1928, leads to a jesuitical explanation of why his earlier poems needed his later help to become fully spontaneous!

His post-Romantic aesthetic is saved, however, by the very process of his writing and rewriting: by the courage of its subjective propulsion, its projection of risk-taking polarisations and extremes, its contradictoriness and refractoriness. We all write and rewrite, but not with the energy of personal exposure nor with the energising effect that Lawrence habitually did. His intellectual swoops gather up so *very* much, in their polarised trajectories, but also too much to be convincing for long: their 'truth' exists temporarily in the intellectual space of the polarised apprehension that we are invited to share. His fresh and unembarrassed intellectual risk-taking will always appeal, although not to everybody. The confronting intensities, and his forceful conclusions that seem to fill and sometimes clog the narrative space, are always in a fraught balance with the (redeeming) provisionality of the writing, its liability to revision under new stimulus, its tricksiness, its sardonic comedy, its idiosyncrasies. Lawrence is no moral guide, but travelling the imaginative distance with him – watching the versions develop and work unfold into work – is to participate in the most chastening and invigorating of experiences. You are not the same afterwards; you see differently.

NOTES

1 T. S. Eliot, *Selected Essays*, 3rd edn (London: Faber and Faber, 1951), p. 18.

2 See chapter 14 for a discussion of John Middleton Murry's *Son of Woman: The Story of D. H. Lawrence* (1931) and of Catherine Carswell's answer, *The Savage Pilgrimage: A Narrative of D. H. Lawrence* (1932), as well as F. R. Leavis's early part in the disputes over Lawrence's person and his importance as an artist. Other significant, at least partly biographical responses from the 1930s include: Frederick Carter, *D. H. Lawrence and the Body Mystical* (London: Archer, 1932); Aldous Huxley's introduction to his edition, *The Letters of D. H. Lawrence* (London: Heinemann, 1932); E. T. [Jessie Chambers], *D. H. Lawrence: A Personal Record* (1935; Cambridge: Cambridge University Press, 1980). See also John Heywood Thomas, 'The Perversity of D. H. Lawrence', *Criterion*, 10 (1930), 5–22; and T. S. Eliot (editor of *Criterion*), review of Murry's *Son of Woman*, *Criterion*, 10 (1931), 768–74: they defined Lawrence's heretical way of thinking and rejected his intellectual procedure. (See also the related comments of Rebecca West, discussed in the fifth section of the present chapter.) In *D. H. Lawrence and Susan his Cow* (New York: Columbia University Press, 1939), William York Tindall would perform the scholarly debunking.

3 Piero Nardi, *La vita di D. H. Lawrence* (Milan: A. Mondadori, 1947); Richard Aldington, *Portrait of a Genius, But . . .* (London: Heinemann, 1950), p. v; Harry T. Moore, *The Intelligent Heart* (London: Heinemann, 1955); Edward Nehls, *D. H. Lawrence: A Composite Biography*, 3 vols. (Madison, WI: University of Wisconsin Press, 1957–59); Emile Delavenay, *D. H. Lawrence: L'Homme et la genèse de son oeuvre . . . 1885–1919* (Paris: C. Klincksieck, 1969; in English, London: Heinemann, 1972).

4 For an early, historiographical sketch of Lawrence criticism, see Paul Eggert, 'Opening up the Text: The Case of *Sons and Lovers*', in *Rethinking Lawrence*, ed. Keith Brown (Milton Keynes: Open University Press, 1990), pp. 38–39. Much useful information can be found in Peter Preston's 'Lawrence in Britain: An Annotated Chronology: 1930–1998', in *The Reception of D. H. Lawrence around the World*, ed. Takeo Iida (Fukuoka, Japan: Kyushu University Press, 1999).

5 Roland Barthes, 'From Work to Text', in *The Rustle of Language*, trans. Richard Howard (Oxford: Basil Blackwell, 1986), pp. 57–58.

6 Harry T. Moore, *The Priest of Love* (London: Heinemann, 1974), p. 10.

7 (New York: Simon & Schuster, 1994), p. 11. Other post-1960s biographical studies include: Paul Delany, *D. H. Lawrence's Nightmare* (Hassocks: Harvester, 1979); Keith Sagar, *The Life of D. H. Lawrence* (London: Eyre Methuen, 1980) and *D. H. Lawrence: Life into Art* (Harmondsworth: Penguin, 1985); John Worthen, *D. H. Lawrence: A Literary Life* (London: Macmillan, 1989); Jeffrey Meyers, *D. H. Lawrence: A Biography* (London: Heinemann, 1990); and a three-volume biography in Japanese, *Hyouden D. H. Lawrence*, by Yoshio Inoeu (1992–94).

8 E.g., she gives Lawrence and Frieda's route over the Alps in summer 1912 as it

is reported in *Twilight in Italy* (1916). In fact, their route was different, and Maddox quotes letters written during that walk from places which, had she consulted a map, she would have seen were not on the stated route. She fails to use the essays Lawrence wrote in Metz and Trier in May 1912, preferring to use the racier version he provides in *Mr Noon*. Apparently from the fact that Lawrence was for a short period in Catania in 1920 (the home town of Giovanni Verga, the Sicilian master of *verismo* fiction), she concludes that Lawrence met Verga, even though the surviving letters point the other way. Again, Maddox comments, by way of setting a scene, that when Lawrence visited Australia in 1922 it had a population of only 7 million. In fact, it did not reach that figure till 1939. She describes the escarpment above Thirroul in New South Wales where Lawrence wrote *Kangaroo* as 'a long, low, black rock' (298) when, as the novel makes plain, it is a dominating geographical feature: the coastal towns, only villages in 1922, hug the coast in its afternoon shadow. Maddox's citations are eccentrically presented as if they were an afterthought; the quotations from Lawrence's writings are not sourced; and although the seven volumes of the Cambridge *Letters of Lawrence* are used as basic sources, the standard critical editions of Lawrence's works with all their accompanying textual–biographical information have been mostly ignored.

9 'Getting On', unpubld, qtd in *DG*, 340. 'Return to Bestwood' in *PII*.

10 E. T., *Personal Record*, p. 117.

11 See *EY*, 266.

12 Frieda Lawrence, '*Not I, But the Wind . . .*' (New York: Viking, 1934), p. 57.

13 See, e.g., chapters by Peter Shillingsburg, Paul Eggert, Philip Cohen and David H. Jackson in *Devils and Angels: Textual Editing and Literary Theory*, ed. Philip Cohen (Charlottesville: University Press of Virginia, 1991).

14 See further Paul Eggert, 'Reading a Critical Edition With the Grain and Against: The Cambridge D. H. Lawrence', in *Editing D. H. Lawrence: New Versions of a Modern Author*, ed. Charles L. Ross and Dennis Jackson (Ann Arbor: University of Michigan Press, 1995), pp. 27–40.

15 Cf. Kinkead-Weekes's comment on Lawrence writing, in 1918, the early version of the essays that would form *Studies in Classic American Literature*: 'as always, imaginative exploration came before ideas' (*TE*, 439). This accepts a lead that Lawrence gives, privileging the creative act over abstract thought. But, as the introductions to the various Cambridge critical editions show, Lawrence wrote the philosophical chapters of 'Study of Thomas Hardy' before he wrote the commentary chapters retelling Hardy's stories as Lawrence believed they should have been written; the philosophical additions in 1915 to the early versions of the first four essays in *Twilight in Italy* precede the writing of the new, more creatively observed ones from 'Il Duro' to the end; 'The Crown' and the lost 'Goats and Compasses' precede the writing of 'The Sisters III' (the forerunner to *Women in Love*) in 1916; and the writing of 'The Reality of Peace' in 1917 precedes and feeds into the *Women in Love* of 1917.

16 See *TE*, 146, and n. 21 below.

17 See ii. 182–83 for the Futurist meaning.

18 See *TI*, xlix–lviii. For an early case about Lawrence's art of 'articulate extremity' (ii. 661), see Eggert, 'Lawrence Criticism: Where Next?', *Critical Review*, 21 (1979), 72–84.

19 See further Paul Eggert, 'The Half-Structured Rainbow', *Critical Review*, 23 (1981), 89–97.

20 *DG*, 77. Lawrence revised the essays from November 1922 to January 1923. See also his amused exasperation at his critics in 'Accumulated Mail' in *RDP*. His three essays on the novel (in *Hardy*) were another response to criticisms – in articles by Carlo Linati, Edwin Muir and Dr Joseph Collins (a psychoanalyst): see *DG*, 249–50.

21 In 1921 he wrote 'I am an Englishman – but good God, I am a man first' (iv. 133). His refusal in 1929 to assist Dorothy Trotter of the Warren Gallery in a legal action to force the return from the authorities of his confiscated paintings (which would have created a useful precedent) when there was an easier option to secure their return and when failure of the action might have meant their destruction shows that by then Lawrence had put his 'manhood and [his] sincere utterance' before his nationality (vii. 369).

22 'On Coming Home', in *RDP*.

23 See *TE*, 603, for his brief affair with Rosalind Baynes in September 1920 and its effect on the 'Tortoises' and 'Fruit' poems.

24 As he wrote this penultimate chapter, Lawrence was running out of room in his last notebook. The handwriting becomes much smaller than usual so as to fit the available space. But the chapter is remarkably free of revision: this chapter definitely came with a rush. (The ms. is at the Bancroft Library, University of California at Berkeley.)

25 For an argument that this provisionality is a form of comedy, see Paul Eggert, 'Introduction' and 'Comedy and Provisionality: Lawrence's Address to his Audience and Material in his Australian Novels', in *Lawrence and Comedy*, ed. Paul Eggert and John Worthen (Cambridge: Cambridge University Press, 1996), pp. 1–18, 131–57.

26 'New Mexico', in *P*, 142.

27 New York: Seltzer, 1923; first English edition, London: Secker, 1924, p. 139.

28 Ibid., p. 41.

29 Respectively in *PII* and *Mornings in Mexico* (1927).

30 Rebecca West, *The Strange Necessity: Essays and Reviews* (1928; London: Virago, 1987), pp. 222, 227.

31 Michael Bell, *D. H. Lawrence: Language and Being* (Cambridge: Cambridge University Press, 1992). See also Anne Fernihough, *D. H. Lawrence: Aesthetics and Ideology* (Oxford: Oxford University Press, 1993). The influential phenomenology of Edmund Husserl (1859–1938) was the point of departure (and rejection) for Heidegger (1889–1976); Bertrand Russell's embodiment of the rationalist traditions of analytic philosophy was Lawrence's. He had not read Heidegger who wrote in German, most notably *Sein und Zeit* (1927).

32 *Hardy*, 172.

33 Respectively in *P*, 218–22 (as 'The American Edition of *New Poems*, by D. H. Lawrence'); 537; 313 (in a review, 'German Books: Thomas Mann').

34 In *P*. In May 1927, Lawrence had also written an introduction (collected in *PII*) for Cape's reissue of his 1922 translation of Verga's *Mastro-don Gesualdo*.

35 In *PII*, 603.

36 In *P*, 582–83; cf. also v. 629 on Alberto Magnelli's paintings.

10

MICHAEL BELL

Lawrence and modernism

The word 'modernism' raises two immediate problems. It usually refers not to modern literary consciousness at large but to the more specific and self-conscious avant-garde movements associated with such writers as Ezra Pound, T. S. Eliot, James Joyce, Wyndham Lewis and Virginia Woolf. Furthermore, even these writers had different, sometimes competing, conceptions which are still a matter of controversy. Yet there is a distinctive set of cultural and artistic concerns shared by these writers and Lawrence stands in a peculiarly significant relation to them. He is usually seen as being at best marginal to the modernism which these figures came largely to define, and they were almost uniformly hostile or condescending to him. But once it is properly understood, his apparently marginal position becomes critically central. For Lawrence provided then, and still provides, one of the most significant critiques of modernism arising from the same historical context and concerns.

Lawrence's relation to these modernist writers is most clearly illustrated by the case of his co-eval Ezra Pound. Lawrence's initial friendship with Pound on first coming to London soon led to a mutual disenchantment. Yet even when Pound afterwards referred to Lawrence as a 'detestable person', he continued to acknowledge that Lawrence had discovered, before he had, the 'proper treatment of modern subjects'; perhaps the highest compliment Pound could make to anyone.[1] This is the important point: Lawrence was not just outside this, partly retrospective, grouping of modernists, he was engaged in a parallel project, both creatively and critically, which is vital to the proper appreciation of these other writers. Their very blindness, and in some cases hostility, to him are a vital part of his meaning, and theirs, since he radically disagreed with their understanding of the same important questions concerning art, feeling and the nature of human being.

Something of what is at stake can be seen in the concern of all these writers to define their own work according to an existing tradition since, although they sought, in Pound's words, to 'make it new', this involved, as T. S. Eliot explained in a classic essay of the period, the prior existence of a tradition within which anything truly new could occur.[2] Hence the most influential writers of the period staked out the varying versions of the 'tradition' within which their own works achieved their significance. Examples of this are Eliot's own reading of English seventeenth-century poetry and Dante; Pound's of late classical and Provençal poetry; Yeats's Anglo-Irishry; and Woolf's tracing the line of her female predecessors. Lawrence's sense of his own tradition was just as strong but not so programmatically polemical. His critical reaction to the tradition of the English novel was no less radical for being from the inside. He modelled his first novel on the fiction of George Eliot and, although the sequence was not planned in that way, his preparation for an unpublished book on Thomas Hardy proved to be a way of thinking through the central expression of his metaphysical vision: *The Rainbow* (1915) and *Women in Love* (1920).[3] While working on those novels he was also preparing a set of lectures, later published as *Studies in Classic American Literature* (1923), which is one of the first, and still important, attempts to understand the neighbouring tradition of American literature as a powerful and distinctive one. Lawrence was to become in some measure an adoptive American writer just as his American *émigré* contemporaries, including some of the moving spirits of modernism, became European.

Modernism, following the Victorian and the symbolist/aestheticist moments, was in part a third-generation assimilation of Romanticism although in the conscious form of a classicising reaction against the perceived dangers and errors of Romanticism itself; an emphasis signalled in the title of Joyce's *Ulysses* (1914–22). Hence also the desire in Eliot and Pound to pick up the literary tradition from an earlier point, and their occasional disparaging comments about the Romantic spirit.[4] But Lawrence, who when he first arrived in London astonished Ford Madox Hueffer with his knowledge of nineteenth-century literature, understood the philosophical and psychological power, as well as the problems, of the Romantic tradition from within.[5] Lawrence's transformation of his Romantic inheritance was his central life's work and he did so as one who had absorbed Nietzsche and was a contemporary of Martin Heidegger.[6] Like these philosophical thinkers, Lawrence understood the central problems of modernity as a complex of psychological, cultural and ultimately ontological questions – questions, that is, about the nature of being, which could be understood only by an imaginative recovery of the pre-Socratic world such as Lawrence read of in John Burnet's *Early Greek Philosophy* in 1915. On this interpretation, the dominant western desire for knowledge, classically associated with Socrates, and the linked desire to control the world, involve a loss of what Heidegger's translators always capitalise as 'Being'. Briefly, this refers not to individual beings, but to the underlying mystery of Being at all. Our practical relations of knowledge and power with the beings we encounter in the world lead to a forgetfulness, or blindness, towards Being.

Heidegger's philosophical concern with Being parallels Lawrence's critique of modernity, and his invoking of very early Greek culture helps to bring Lawrence's primitivism into focus, for Lawrence was at once the major modern primitivist and the most radical critic of primitivism. The modernist generation was strongly affected by contemporary anthropology, especially by James George Frazer, who was still expanding his life work, while versions of Lucien Lévy-Bruhl's notion of a 'primitive mind' were common currency. The final abridged edition of Frazer's *The Golden Bough* was published as late as 1922 and Lévy-Bruhl's *Primitive Mentality* in 1923.[7] The conception of a universal primitive mind anterior to civilisation, and therefore still to be encountered in 'primitive' peoples around the world, was rejected by a later, more scientific, anthropology, and Frazer had already been seriously criticised, notably by Andrew Lang, for some decades.[8] Yet as Eliot affirmed in his 'Notes' to *The Waste Land* (1922), Frazer profoundly affected this literary generation. To some extent, therefore, the belief in an archaic mythic sensibility is a sentimental myth of the period and Lawrence's relation to it requires careful discrimination. He was making a philosophical statement about Being rather than a historical statement about cultural development and he saw exotic primitivism as precisely a symptom of modern alienation. He was capable, particularly in his later moods of desperate isolation, of confusing these levels himself, as in *The Plumed Serpent* (1926), but in his central works, such as *The Rainbow* and *Women in Love*, he both expressed his positive sense of Being and diagnosed some classic modern nostalgias; whether colonialist, as in the soldier Anton Skrebensky's exotic fascination with the 'strange darkness' of Africa (R, 413), or aesthetic, as in the artist Loerke's interest in 'the West African wooden figures, the Aztec art, Mexican and Central American' (WL, 448).

Lawrence risked sentimentality in seeking to express his vision within the language, sensibility and world-view of modernity which he did not wish, in any simple sense, to 'reject'. He was successful in a variety of genres ranging from lyric poetry, through stories, fables and drama, to cultural and literary criticism. But in so far as the novel as a genre attempts a comprehensive conception of the world and society, it involved a fundamental contradiction between Lawrence's ontological vision and the experience of the alienated modern individual in a fragmented social order. Not surprisingly, the very genre of the novel increasingly disintegrated under the strain. Once again, this puts Lawrence in a relation of significant parallel to dominant currents of modernism. The realist novel had been under question since the last two decades of the previous century as the high Victorian synthesis gave way to narrower conceptions such as naturalism and aestheticism – a break-up which also reflected the increased awareness of the partial nature of any particular perception of society as the viewpoints of women, or of the working class, came to be recognised as significantly, perhaps incommensurably, different. The bolder spirits of modernism found ways of expressing this subjectivity and relativity in new narrative forms; in Joyce and Woolf, for example, the confident voice of the omniscient narrator was no longer tenable. Yet Lawrence, as has already been noted, did not start with a radical formal departure so much as discover the need for it in process.

Modernism, then, was a crisis of representation in two related senses. First, there was the conscious desire to express a greater range of social and psychic experience, and this in turn threw into question the mode of imitation. Modernism is, therefore, characterised in all the arts by a self-conscious focus on its own medium; to the extent at times that this is the primary significance of the work. It is also clear that Lawrence shared this formal consciousness, and for the same reasons, yet never wore it on his sleeve as self-consciousness. His formal concern was only an aspect of the job in hand. For this reason it is helpful to expand on some of the modern themes already touched on in Lawrence which in other writers were the self-conscious, almost the defining, features of modernism. To reduce complex questions for a moment to simple headings, these concerns may be listed as: time, personal identity, artistic impersonality, gender, and history and myth.

Time

The modernist generation was a complex of partly overlapping, partly competing, visions and by the late twenties it was apparent that several writers who had felt a strong sense of collegiality in the teens were actually pursuing radically different courses. Percy Wyndham Lewis's *Time and Western Man* (1927), for example, already looked back on the period to criticise what he saw as its obsessive, and unhealthy, privileging of the dimension of time. He saw this in the philosophy of Henri Bergson and A. N. Whitehead, and in the science of Einstein, as well as in novelists such as Joyce and Proust. As a practising artist and sculptor he found a sense of reality in the tactile, spatial medium in contrast to a ghostly and idealising tendency in the intellectual and literary privileging of time. Although we inhabit a longish span of time, traditionally three score years and ten, we do so, beyond the infinitesimal present, only in the imaginative modes of memory and anticipation so that, in Lewis's view, the emphasis on time went with a preoccupation with the inner processes of consciousness at the expense of a grasp on the external world. As often, Lewis had a point despite much reductiveness and misappreciation of the writers in question. Undoubtedly, he identified one of the distinguishing features of modernism, both thematically and formally. What he missed was the way modernism privileged time in order to overcome it. These writers were seeking to face the problem rather than just perversely inventing it.

Lawrence also thematised time, along with modernists such as Thomas Mann, Joyce, Proust and Woolf, but less overtly than they. In *The Rainbow*, for example, Lawrence uses the simple past and continuous tenses in fluid ways which, almost subliminally, allow the characters' inner lives to pause, to omit, to circle or to repeat according to the emotional occasions.[9] The larger generational structure takes its force from the way characters relive, and modify, their forebears' experiences as well as their own. To speak of someone as being personally 'rooted' is metaphorical but not meaningless, and refers essentially to a mode of existence in time whereby the past lives actively in the present. Not surprisingly, when the story passes to the more alienated world of *Women in Love*, it is precisely this depth of consciousness of time which disappears from both the characters and from the narrative. It ceases to be a governing category of their world. Yet few readers will be conscious of this aspect of the narrative, still less think of it as a 'theme' or 'technique'. By contrast, it is in the more strident, and desperate, rhetoric of *The Plumed Serpent* that a stopped church clock, or the heroine Kate Leslie's desire to remove her watch, make the question of time an overt theme (*PS*, 132, 288). In Lawrence's view, it was precisely the quality of modern self-consciousness which constituted the mischief. The formal self-consciousness of modernist art and writing, therefore, was for him only a further, indulgent symptom of the condition. Hence, he sought subliminal ways of rendering the experience of time including what he called the one 'realm we have never conquered: the pure present. One great mystery of time is terra incognita to us: the instant. The most superb mystery we have hardly recognized: the immediate instant self.'[10]

Personal identity

It is appropriate that Lawrence should speak here of the 'instant *self*' since the thematising of time in such writers as Joyce, Proust and Woolf is inseparable from their conceptions of identity. Modernism represents a double crisis in the historical construction of personal identity. Historians of culture seeking the starting point for the creation of subjectivity have found it a notoriously moveable feast. It has no doubt been underway since the beginning of culture, but the evolution of the European novel since the eighteenth century reflects a distinctive modern phase of the story. Over this period, the importance of the individual, in increasing contrast to that of the social order, continued to rise to the point where society might be valued in so far as it serves the fulfilment of the individual rather than the other way round. Joyce's Stephen Dedalus catches the spirit of this when he refuses to sign a student petition for the nationalist cause.[11] Or if the political context makes that instance too specific, Lawrence's Ursula Brangwen makes it more general when she expresses her first intuition of the essential dissatisfaction with her lover, Anton Skrebensky, which makes her eventually leave him. He offers a purely social explanation of his own existence in terms of 'duty' and 'service' leading her to say 'It seems to me . . . as if you weren't anybody – as if there weren't anybody there, where you are. Are you anybody, really? You seem like nothing to me' (*R*, 289). Ursula, clearly speaking for Lawrence at this moment, affirms individuality, or sheer individual being, as the crucial value. Lawrence is of his cultural moment in this respect.

Yet the rise of the individual as a value went along with its increasing disintegration as a category. As the idea of the Christian soul was discarded, it was able to live on for some time as a cultural habit, like the smile of the Cheshire cat, but the fundamentally unstable and ungrounded nature of individuality became more and more evident with an understanding of the social and biological processes of which it was a part; a development which had its literary reflection in late-nineteenth-century naturalism. Finally, with the generation of Freud, the ego became a partial, perhaps illusory, function of the psyche. Although most of the literary modernists, apart from such as Thomas Mann and H.D., kept a wary, or critical, distance from Freud, this was because they were committed to some comparable model of the psyche. Lawrence's own quarrel with Freud is discussed by Fiona Becket in chapter 12, but he shared the sense of the human personality as a process to be understood in 'inhuman' as well as 'human' terms. In a famous letter to Edward Garnett, he criticised the Italian Futurist writer, Filippo Marinetti, for separating the 'phenomenal' aspect of the woman's laugh from the personal dimension (ii. 182–83). For Lawrence, it has to be both, and perhaps the most important aspect of this is his puritan insistence that the dissolution of the category only makes the responsibility of the individual even more vital. This is not so much moral responsibility, in a narrower sense, as responsibility for one's own being. Yet there is a connection between ethical and ontological responsibility as Skrebensky illustrates. He is a good citizen, and carries out his colonial functions in Africa and India, but he has no resources within himself to question contemporary social ideology and ask what he is doing there at all.

Artistic impersonality

If there is a paradox in the simultaneous dissolution and responsibility of the self, it may be understood partly as a matter of taking responsibility for aspects of the self which fall outside the conscious ego. In fact, any mere assertion of ego is likely to be compensatory, a substitute for this fuller awareness, such as we find in Gerald Crich, a more developed version of Skrebensky. This kind of limited ego awareness, a more typical form of individuality, is what Lawrence had in mind with his remark that 'Hate is not the opposite of love, individuality is.'[12] Hence the understanding of personality in Lawrence rapidly modulates into an understanding of 'impersonality', something beyond the immediately conscious, or Cartesian, ego. The question of impersonality is perhaps the most crucial point of contrast between Lawrence and the typical proponents of modernism. As a way of understanding the relation of the 'human' and the 'inhuman' standpoints it is truly the heart of the matter.

In their anti-Romantic, anti-sentimental aspect, major modernist writers sought a quality of emotional impersonality. Ezra Pound's praise of the early Joyce was that he 'deals with subjective things, but he presents them with such clarity of outline that he might be dealing with locomotives or with builders' specifications'.[13] Joyce himself went on in *Ulysses* to thematise the significance of artistic impersonality, and to demonstrate it in the progressively depersonalising techniques of the episodes. But the most famous, and problematic, statement of this theme came in the second part of T. S. Eliot's essay on 'Tradition and the Individual Talent' (1919) where he refers to his own argument as an 'Impersonal theory of poetry'.[14]

The second part of this essay, as Eliot moves from the general question of tradition to the personal dimension of creation, suffers a striking fall in its quality of insight, and indeed of its impersonality. Like Lawrence in his letter to Garnett, where he was also concerned with impersonality, Eliot appeals to a chemical image: platinum and the catalyst instead of Lawrence's carbon and its allotropic states. But whereas Lawrence uses the image to define the character's state within his fiction, Eliot uses it for the poet's own emotional state in writing a poem. Although it is offered as a universal formula, there is a highly personal note in Eliot's insistence that poetry is not 'a turning loose of emotion', it is 'an escape from emotion'. The stark choice between 'turning loose' and 'escape', without the intervening possibilities of expression or understanding, gives a broader clue to the modernist concern for impersonality. The anti-sentimental reaction of the period, quite understandable and necessary in itself, was likely to expand into a broader attack on the Romantic heritage, and throw the baby of feeling out with the bathwater of sentimentalism. Seen in this way, the overt concern for impersonality reveals itself, in Eliot's case, as a compensatory symptom of its felt lack; where there *is* impersonality it may rather be taken for granted. This is, of course, to put the case at its most negative. In practice, the modernist writers were arguing, as Eliot is here, against the common assumptions of their culture and signalling the significance of their own innovations. Once again, Joyce's *Ulysses* is the classic instance with its lucidly demonstrative thematising of its own achievement in this regard. But the general point stands that modernist impersonality is rather programmatically conceived and the formal correlative of this is the belief that it can be achieved by technical means, that the right technique will produce it.

Lawrence shared the concern for impersonality from the opposite end of the question. He virtually never discusses his own literary technique *per se* but places a quality of impersonality at the centre of his understanding of the emotional life. Moments of crisis and transition, moments of recentring of the self, repeatedly involve a transcending of the immediate, conscious ego, not, as might be the case in George Eliot, for the sake of a moral imperative, but through an imperative of emotional truth which may well, on occasion, challenge the moral order. Impersonality in Lawrence is not just to be defined negatively as the anti-sentimental; it is the non-moral awareness of a 'beyond self' which provides the ultimate imperative for all life decisions, the non-teleological 'purpose' of existence. Of course, in order to express this within his characters, Lawrence does need technical means but these seem rather to grow out of the subject-matter than to be consciously applied as technique. His own 'formal' awareness can usually be seen indirectly through his discussions of other writers and his reviews of Giovanni Verga's *Mastro-don Gesualdo* and *Cavalleria Rusticana* express what he means by impersonality with comprehensive lucidity. Whilst admiring Verga, Lawrence criticises him, and modern Italian literature generally, for taking literary cues from elsewhere in Europe 'and then letting loose a lot of emotion in a borrowed vision' (225). That Lawrence should speak just as critically as Eliot of 'letting loose . . . of emotion' sharpens the contrast between them. In Lawrence's case, it is not a general remark about emotion but an internal discrimination of emotional quality. Verga, as Lawrence says in another review, looks absurd when momentarily adopting a consciously Flaubertian pose of impersonality, but he was nonetheless a great writer because he had real objectivity reflecting that of his characters: 'Gesualdo didn't have feelings about the soul. He was remorselessly and relentlessly objective' (*P*, 229). Lawrence himself was not writing about Sicilian peasants but he tried to touch a similar level of emotional being in his characters, and to be equally remorseless in his objectivity.

Gender

The common modernist view that feeling requires discipline is also highly gendered. Ever since the movement of sentiment in the eighteenth century, which brought into consciousness the long-term affective changes which had been coming over modern culture, as discussed by social historians such as Lawrence Stone, sentiment has been associated with the female.[15] The mid-eighteenth-century 'man of sentiment', and later heroes of sensibility, such as Henry Mackenzie's Harley in *The Man of Feeling* (1771), were 'feminised' males. Even if some of these figures, like Harley or Goethe's Werther, were seen ironically by their authors, this was not usually recognised at the time since they corresponded to powerful new formations in the culture at large.

Pound, Eliot and Joyce saw this movement to have run to seed in Victorian sentiment, and to have affected political culture rather than 'just' the arts. The First World War in 1914–18, for example, was a crucial and crystallising event for many of these writers, and they saw how it was powered and defended by a miasma of sentimental patriotism. The critique of sentimentality, therefore, had good grounds, but in the literature of modernism, and, even more importantly, in the long-lasting influence of modernist criticism, the gendered assumptions about feeling are a pervasive subtext. Of course, this could often accompany a celebratory view of the female, as in Joyce's Molly Bloom, but what is at stake is the conception, if not to say the stereotypes, of the female in her characterisation. Likewise, Pound praised, as a leitmotif of the *Cantos*, Eleanor of Aquitaine whose name is made to rhyme with the mythical, divinely descended, Helen. Yet this presentation of Eleanor through the eyes of Provençal poetic conventions elides her historical existence as a cultured woman and patron of the arts.[16] Of course, Pound could create whatever figure he needed for his poetry. Historical accuracy is not the point here but the way in which the male modernist celebration of sexuality was often linked to mythical or sterotypical conceptions of 'Woman' compatible with a condescending view of women.

The question of gender in modernism, not just at the level of characterisation and overt attitude but at the level of its implicit discursive formations, has now been opened up more explicitly by feminist critics, and Lawrence becomes a significant case in question. His obvious male insecurity, and reactive misogyny, clearly come from a man with a strong female identification which has creative as well as personal dimensions. Early reviews assumed him to be female, and Lisa Appignanesi has noted the cooption of femininity, by several male modernist writers, as a vital element in their creativity.[17] Lawrence struggled with the question of sexual difference internally as well as creating a variety of strong and complex female characters. If Lawrence had not had problems, he would not have had the insights, and hard-won sanities, for which he is still read. By avoiding the ideological correctnesses both of his own day and of later generations, he continues to raise some of the unresolved predicaments of individuals and of our culture. But the primary emphasis here is on the larger question of feeling as a matter of permanent struggle for realisation and responsibility. Lawrence attacked sentimentality with no less vehemence than other modernists, as can be seen in his essay on John Galsworthy, to be discussed later. His own language was impersonal in so far as it served a continuing emotional discrimination in the lives of his characters, and this is also the standpoint from which to understand the last two of the general terms in which Lawrence stands in significant contrast to modernism: history and myth.

History and myth

A controversial feature of modernist literature from the outset was its conscious turn to myth as a mode of structural organisation. This could be seen either as a rejection of history, or just as a different way of understanding it. A rich discursive account of the issues at stake had been given some years earlier by Friedrich Nietzsche in his essay 'On the Uses and Disadvantages of History for Life' (1872). Here he reflected on the historical sense which had become so powerful, and so institutionalised, in the nineteenth century as to become in itself as much a problem as a mode of understanding. Nietzsche, along with others, argued it is possible to be over-conscious of history, to have a surfeit of information, whereby history ceases to clarify and inform action in the present.[18] The capacity to recognise living purpose through the mingled forgetting and concentration of historical knowledge is what, in *The Birth of Tragedy*, published in the same year as the essay on history, Nietzsche defined as myth: a 'concentrated image of the world'.[19] In a comparable spirit, modernist writers, such as Eliot, Pound, Joyce, H.D. and Thomas Mann turned to myth not as a flight from history but as a concentration of its meaning; or to put it differently, as a recognition that, although values are produced in history, history does not ground them. Myth is a way of looking at history in the critical light of trans-historical values made self-conscious. The complementary Darwinian and Edenic myths of *The Rainbow*, and the competing world-views between the poles of Nordic and African in *Women in Love*, are to be understood in precisely such a spirit. In novels with a dense sense of history, they seek to illuminate or affirm fundamental values for the understanding of history.

In *The Rainbow*, for example, which was arguably the first mature expression of his ontological vision, he traces the loss of this vision in the historical period leading up to modernity. Lawrence, in his own way, shared the influential belief of the early T. S. Eliot in a lost unity of being; a belief that modernity had involved a progressive 'dissociation of sensibility' by which thought and feeling came apart.[20] Whereas Eliot gradually moved the historical location of this change from Donne back to Dante, and eventually abandoned the idea altogether, Lawrence, like Yeats in his *A Vision* (1925), saw that it was essentially a mythic, or a philosophical, rather than a historical intuition and therefore placed the whole novel under the mythic sign of the Biblical rainbow. At the same time, this was not to ignore history.[21] Lawrence seeks to honour both the historical and the mythic dimensions of his theme without confusing them. Combining Darwinian and Edenic myths of origin, he is not making a statement about literal cultural development so much as defining the complementary motives of rootedness and progress in the human psyche at any time. Appropriately, therefore, he adapts a traditional form of the family saga novel using it, as it were, in brackets since it is not so much his own chosen form, as it might be in, say, Arnold Bennett, but rather the form expressive of the period which it covers. The three generations of the Brangwen family act as a compressed analysis of a much longer process of cultural evolution which lives on as an unconscious history within the modern.

The family saga form is also bracketed for the more fundamental reason that this 'realist' history is itself enacted within the philosophical or mythic backdrop already mentioned. If he were Thomas Mann or Joyce, Lawrence might overtly ironise the earlier narrative form but that is not the spirit of his relation to it. It is never so formally self-conscious as in those authors and is rather a way of focusing the emotional material. Similarly, Lawrence lyricises the characters' emotions with a narrative mode of shifting subjectivity yet at the same time impersonalises their individual experience by seeing it as part of a larger process. In doing so, he avoids the level of immediate authorial judgement and fulfils his ambition, expressed in the letter to Edward Garnett already cited, to represent what is 'physic, non-human, in humanity' rather than the 'old-fashioned human element' (ii. 181–82). His use of a traditionary form, then, serves a specific purpose and it is noticeable that it is precisely as the novel, in its third generation, approaches modernity, that Lawrence's capacity for such an impersonal narrative viewpoint wears thin and his relation with his now central figure, Ursula Brangwen, becomes more identificatory and less testing.

In *Women in Love*, by contrast, he switches to the spatial form which Joseph Frank, many years ago, identified as a feature of modernist narrative.[22] Whereas *The Rainbow* is about promise within a long evolutionary process, and therefore uses a form accentuating historicity, *Women in Love* concerns the conflicting world-views of a number of modern characters grouped within the geographical, spatial metaphor of the Nordic and the African. The novel's 'authorial' figure, Rupert Birkin, is himself subjected to the overall relativity of viewpoint. Once again, it is not so much that Birkin is ironised as that he is used to explore, sometimes through rhetorical extremes, possibilities of feeling and attitude to which the novel is not necessarily committed even as it supports the emotional quest. This internal relativism has more recently been understood through the 'dialogic' conception of the Russian critic Mikhail Bakhtin whose writings, including *Dostoevsky's Poetics* written in the early 1920s, only became widely known in the west in the 1980s. Readers of Lawrence hardly need Bakhtin to explain him but the underlying historical parallel is suggestive. Bakhtin developed his dialogic conception of the novel from an apparent paradox he detected in Dostoevsky. This author's most dogmatic views, when expressed through a character, became part of a testing, independent dramatic life. Almost contemporaneously, Lawrence was critically assimilating the Russian novelists for his own creative purposes, and especially Dostoevsky who had a great British vogue in the teens of the twentieth century, including the study *Fyodor Dostoevsky* (1916) by Lawrence's then close friend, John Middleton Murry. Indeed, another way of expressing the difference between *The Rainbow* and *Women in Love* is as a shift from the Tolstoyan to the Dostoevskean. For, like Dostoevsky, *Women in Love* uses a group of extraordinary, articulate, slightly perverse, yet representatively modern, characters to conduct an in-depth psychological investigation of their own authenticity. It privileges the 'struggle into conscious being' rather than the Tolstoyan commitment to the traditionary and the unconscious.[23]

Bakhtin's sense that the authorial intrusions and philosophising in Dostoevsky's novels are actually converted, by the dramatic power of the narrative, into dramatic elements tested in the larger play of values, applies even more clearly to *Women in Love*. Yet that was not how Lawrence saw Dostoevsky. He came to see Dostoevsky as suffering a sickly spirituality and perverse hyper-consciousness. Far from reading him in a Bakhtinian way, Lawrence objected to both the doctrine and the whole tone of Dostoevsky's fiction.[24] Nonetheless, the narrative mode of *Women in Love* is 'Bakhtinian' in its effect and the very features of modernity which led Lawrence to adopt it, the incommensurability of viewpoints and the consequential loss of authorial authority, are part of the gradual break-up of the Lawrencean novel.

He saw his next published novel, *Aaron's Rod* (1922), as a thematic sequel to *Women in Love* although there is no narrative continuity. Reacting against his wartime confinement in England, Lawrence began a series of novels in which characters go around the world in search of places and cultures which would exemplify, or provide insight into, his sense of being. At the same time, his underlying perception, in the preceding novels, that love relations are always also power relations became a more general investigation of the power motive as a hidden or suppressed dimension in culture, including the political realm. This was an important point of parallel with other modern writers, such as Yeats, Pound and Wyndham Lewis, all three of whom became tainted, in varying degrees, with fascistic leanings.[25] Lawrence did not live to be tested by the 1930s to see whether he would have proved to be another of what the historian Jeffrey Herf has called 'reactionary modernists'.[26] Yet it seems clear that after his sequence of novels, *Kangaroo* (1923) and *The Plumed Serpent*, which treat the motive of political authoritarianism with increasing, though still quite critical, sympathy, he turned strongly away from the 'leadership' ideal not just with *Lady Chatterley's Lover* (1928), which was something of a retreat into the personal sphere, but more significantly perhaps with the posthumously published *Sketches of Etruscan Places* (1932).

In this speculative account of the ancient Etruscans written after visiting their tombs, Lawrence contrasted what he saw to be their sensitivity, their capacity to be 'in touch', with the relative brutality of the Romans. For cultures, as for species, the Darwinian survival of the fittest did not necessarily mean the survival of the best, and Lawrence's regret at the passing of the Etruscan world was with an eye to the literal contemporary revival of those same Roman values in Mussolini's fascist movement. In this respect, we can see the contrast, once again, between a sentimental modern primitivism, now enacted in the political sphere, and an archaic culture truly sensitive to Being. It is suggestive, however, that *Sketches of Etruscan Places*, along with a fable such as 'The Man who Died' (1929) – originally called *The Escaped Cock* – and poems such as 'The Ship of Death', should represent the late Lawrence more effectively than his last novel. For his novels of the early and mid twenties are personal, hybrid forms including a large element of travel writing mixed with speculative essayistic investigation, while *Lady Chatterley's Lover* itself is partly a mixture of fable and lay sermon. It is as if Lawrence, as he became more isolated from official and mainstream culture after the war, lost interest in consummate formal command over a long fiction, the command that led him to say, while working on *Sons and Lovers*, 'it has got form – *form*' (i. 476). Seen alongside the dissolution of realist form in modernism, the break-up of the Lawrencean novel under its own internal logic is peculiarly instructive.

Lawrence's struggle with form is the attempt to express a vision which is indeed prophetic but has a philosophical edge. It is useful to call this vision mythic although there is a danger here of reifying myth, turning it into an externally applicable technique rather than a mode of being and perceiving. Such a reification lurks in T. S. Eliot's approving remarks on Joyce's use of the 'mythic method' as a technique which others will be able to use after his example.[27] Individual modernist writers used myth differently, and its use also changed as the decades went by.[28] Generalisations are, therefore, misleading but an important clue to the significance of myth in Lawrence is that it is often most crucially present not by allusion to traditional myths, or through the invention of new ones, or by the elaboration of special literary techniques, but in a mythopoeic mode of attention which may occur in the most ordinary and modern circumstances.

The difference between 'using' myth and being mythopoeic can be seen in Lawrence's story 'The Horse-Dealer's Daughter' (1922).[29] A young doctor, who cannot swim, saves a desperate young woman as she attempts to drown herself in a farm pond. Both characters nearly drown and both undergo an emotional resurrection through this experience. The pond, which is square and artificially dug, can be seen in the imagery of the story as a grave as well as a womb from which the doctor delivers the woman. But to read the story as mythic for this reason is to reduce it to an idea, to miss the true sources of its power. The narrative is more importantly constructed on a growing discrimination in the quality of vision, attention and feeling, in the characters. This entirely realistic discrimination of feeling, by which it is rather the woman who delivers the doctor from his former life, is the true mode of mythopoeic consciousness in the story. Myth is a mode of being, not a technique, and used as a conscious technique it can run directly counter to mythopoeic sensibility. For Lawrence, myth typically emerges at those moments of crisis in which characters pass beyond their everyday, or most conscious, selves to touch what he called the impersonal, and in that respect it leads back to the question of feeling.

Truth of feeling

Lawrence's significance does not lie in doctrines which can be extrapolated from his writing. In that respect, he was at one with those other modernists who were suspicious of ideas.[30] But the reason in his case was that he saw 'ideas' as largely epi-phenomenal to the life of feeling which was his true concern. As he put it: 'My field is to know the feelings inside a man, and to make new feelings conscious' (*PII*, 567). His whole oeuvre was motivated by the recognition that, as he put it in an essay entitled 'The Novel and the Feelings', 'We have no language for the feelings' (*Hardy*, 203). Although Lawrence had a strong and subtle formal sense for his purposes, his exploratory mode did not lend itself to formal perfection in longer works. The exploratory nature of his novels makes them almost necessarily open-ended and they are all in some measure unsatisfactory although they are also, perhaps for related reasons, the principal source of his cultural impact.

Following his own lead on the importance of the novel form, he is rightly thought of primarily as a novelist. But several of his plays, many of his short stories and novellas, and much of his poetry are consummately achieved by following an emotional action isolated as an episode. In other words, their formal concentration and closure do not deny the underlying relativity, the on-going struggle, in the life of feeling. Plays such as *The Daughter-in-Law* (1912) and *The Widowing of Mrs. Holroyd* (1914), which take such a struggle as their theme, were, as John Worthen notes in chapter 8 of this volume, virtually undiscovered till the 1960s.[31] Had they been the exemplary cases of naturalistic theatre, naturalism might have had a better name as the inner emotional logic of these plays makes a work like Strindberg's *Miss Julie* (1888) seem comparatively synthetic.

It is clear, then, that Lawrence does not answer to the view of modernism which, even as the conceptions promoted by Eliot and Pound have been increasingly questioned, still largely governs the perception of it. Eliot, Joyce, and Pound in particular, were tireless and skilful propagandists, not just in promoting their own work, but in creating a climate of reception. Lawrence was not part of this, and his commitment to the life of feeling made him seem naive and irrelevant, as well as hostile, to much of this programme. His own way of writing about literature, although it took on the same enormous themes as the work of these writers, did so in an apparently informal, localised manner, which always went for an emotional issue or discrimination and eschewed the academic manner of a writer such as T. S. Eliot. Hence, although his reviews show a wide, considered reading in English, American and European literature, for example, he is not commonly thought of as a critical guide, or as offering a new principle of criticism. Unless perhaps his central dictum from *Studies in Classic American Literature* is taken in that light: 'Never trust the artist. Trust the tale' (*SCAL*, 8). This is undoubtedly a central principle for later criticism, and is often quoted. What is generally missed even here, however, is Lawrence's nose for the emotional question. At the latter end of the twentieth century, the distrust of the author takes the more typical form of ideological exposure, the work being judged by its ideological tendency rather than by the quality of life in it; which might well throw a testing light on the reader's own ideological preconceptions. Lawrence's opening statement in his essay on 'John Galsworthy' that 'Literary criticism can be no more than a reasoned account of the feeling produced upon the critic by the book he is criticizing' (*Hardy*, 209) seems impossibly naive now to many academic readers who have imbibed the lessons of critical theory largely derived from the modernists. Yet, as the essay proceeds, Lawrence's critique of Galsworthy proves penetrating and significant in its analysis of sentimentality and false feeling in the culture Galsworthy reflects.

To take feeling as the true question, in the direct way that Lawrence did, is as uncomfortable now as it was then. The struggle in his work is for emotional acknowledgement, and the frequent hostility and condescension expressed towards Lawrence by his modernist contemporaries, and which continues in our own day, is itself largely a problem of acknowledgement on the part of the reader. For all his own moments of absurdity, he is the repressed conscience of modernism and of its postmodern avatars.

NOTES

1 *The Letters of Ezra Pound*, ed. D. D. Paige (New York: Harcourt, Brace and World, 1950), p. 17.

2 See *Make it New* (London: Faber; New Haven: Yale University Press, 1934); 'Tradition and the Individual Talent', in T. S. Eliot, *Selected Essays* (London: Faber, 1961), pp. 13–22.

3 Lawrence used George Eliot's model of the 'two couples' for his first novel *The White Peacock*. See 'E. T.' (Jessie [Wood] Chambers), *A Personal Record* (London: Cape, 1935), p. 103.

4 Pound, for example, refers dismissively to 'nature worship' in *The Spirit of Romance* (London: Peter Owen, 1952), p. 228, and Eliot defines the Romantic as the 'fragmentary', the 'immature' and 'chaotic' in 'The Function of Criticism', *Selected Essays*, p. 26.

5 Ford Madox Hueffer's phrasing further exemplifies the slighting attitude of modernists to Romanticism: 'I have never known any young man of his age who was so well read in all the dullnesses that spread between Milton and George Eliot.' Cf. *EY*, 122.

6 Friedrich Nietzsche, German philosopher 1844–1900, whose radical critique of western culture anticipated and influenced the modernist generation. Lawrence read him closely in 1908. Martin Heidegger, German philosopher 1889–1976, was unknown to Lawrence but his major work, *Being and Time* (1927), and later essays on art and language, parallel Lawrence's concern with Being.

7 *The Golden Bough: A Study in Magic and Religion*, abridged edn (London: Macmillan, 1922); *Primitive Mentality*, trans. L. A. Clare (London: Allen and Unwin, and New York: Macmillan, 1923). For a critique of Frazer's influence on modern writers, see Marc Manganaro, *Myth, Rhetoric and the Voice of Authority: A Critique of Frazer, Eliot, Frye and Campbell* (Princeton: Princeton University Press, 1990).

8 Originally sympathetic to Frazer, Lang attacked the 1900 edition of *The Golden Bough* in the *Fortnightly Review*, February 1901, and in his *Magic and Religion* (London: Longman, 1901).

9 I discuss this more closely in *D. H. Lawrence: Language and Being* (Cambridge: Cambridge University Press, 1992), pp. 67–73.

10 'Introduction' to American edition of *New Poems* in *P*, 222.

11 *A Portrait of the Artist as a Young Man*, ed. Chester G. Anderson and Richard Ellmann (New York: Viking, 1964), pp. 201–3.

12 'Love was once a Little Boy', in *PII*, 444.

13 *Literary Essays of Ezra Pound*, ed. T. S. Eliot (London: Faber, 1954), p. 399.

14 *Selected Essays*, p. 18.

15 For a general history, see Lawrence Stone, *Family, Sex and Marriage in England 1500–1800*, rev. and abr. edn (London: Penguin, 1990). For a study of sentiment and gender, see G. J. Barker-Benfield, *The Culture of Sensibility: Sex and Society in Eighteenth-Century Britain* (Chicago and London: University of Chicago Press, 1996).

16 Philip Grover has developed this point in an unpublished essay.

17 See *D. H. Lawrence: The Critical Heritage*, ed. R. P. Draper (London: Routledge, 1970), p. 3, and Lisa Appignanesi, *Femininity and the Creative Imagination: A Study of Henry James, Robert Musil and Marcel Proust* (London: Vision, 1973).

18 See, for example, F. H. Bradley, *The Presuppositions of Critical History* (1873; Bristol: Thoemmes, 1993); Benedetto Croce, *History: Its Theory and Practice* (1917), and *Meaning in History: Dilthey's Thoughts on History and Society*, ed. H. P. Rickman (London: Allen and Unwin, 1961). For a good general account, see James Longenbach, *Modernist Poetics of History* (Princeton: Princeton University Press, 1987).

19 *The Birth of Tragedy out of the Spirit of Music*, trans. Walter Kaufmann (New York: Random House, 1957), p. 135.

20 This idea, partly borrowed from Rémy de Gourmont, was first proposed by Eliot in his essay on 'The Metaphysical Poets'. See *Selected Essays*, pp. 286–88.

21 See Mark Kinkead-Weekes, 'The Sense of History in *The Rainbow*', in *D. H. Lawrence and the Modern World*, ed. Peter Preston and Peter Hoare (London: Macmillan, 1989), pp. 121–38.

22 'Spatial Form in Modern Literature', in *The Widening Gyre: Crisis and Mastery in Modern Literature* (New Brunswick, NJ: Rutgers University Press, 1981).

23 From the 'Foreword', *WL*, 486.

24 Lawrence criticised Dostoevsky sharply in reviews of *The Grand Inquisitor* and V. V. Rozanov's *Solitaria*. See *P*, 283–91, 367–71.

25 Yeats supported for a while the Irish 'Blueshirts'; Pound was charged with treason for his wartime broadcasts in support of Mussolini; Wyndham Lewis wrote a book supporting Hitler.

26 *Reactionary Modernists: Technology, Culture and Politics in Weimar and the Third Reich* (Cambridge: Cambridge University Press, 1984).

27 '*Ulysses*, Order and Myth', *Dial* 75 (1923), 483.

28 I treat this topic in *Literature, Modernism and Myth: Belief and Responsibility in the Twentieth Century* (Cambridge: Cambridge University Press, 1997).

29 Originally written in 1916 as 'The Miracle', and revised for publication in 1922, the story is discussed closely in *Literature, Modernism and Myth*, pp. 97–111.

30 See, for example, 'An idea has little value apart from the modality of the mind which receives it' – Ezra Pound, *Literary Essays*, p. 341 – and T. S. Eliot's obituary compliment to Henry James that he 'had a mind so fine that no idea could violate it': *Egoist*, 5, 1 (1918), p. 2.

31 A 1961 television adaptation of *The Widowing of Mrs. Holroyd* partly initiated the serious discovery of Lawrence as a dramatist mainly through Peter Gill's productions at The Royal Court Theatre. See *A D. H. Lawrence Handbook*, ed. Keith Sagar (Manchester: Manchester University Press, 1982), pp. 300–22. See also John Worthen's chapter in this volume.

11

DREW MILNE

Lawrence and the politics of sexual politics

Introduction: the priest of love?

If sex has replaced religion as the opium of the people, how are we to assess the self-appointed priests? In a letter written on Christmas Day, 1912, D. H. Lawrence declared, 'I shall always be a priest of love' (i. 493), a resonant phrase later adopted by Harry T. Moore for the title of his biography of Lawrence.[1] The phrase captures some of the contradictions of authority in Lawrence's work, suggesting that awkward combination of the didactic and the prophetic which has so troubled Lawrence's critical reception. His writing unsettles aesthetic judgement by cutting across the relative autonomy of life and art to explore new experiences of feeling and belief. In *The Love Ethic of D. H. Lawrence* (1955), for example, Mark Spilka argued: 'that Lawrence was a religious artist, and that all his work was governed by religious ends'.[2] Kate Millett's very different critique echoed this characterisation: '*Lady Chatterley's Lover* is a quasi-religious tract recounting the salvation of one modern woman . . . through the offices of the author's personal cult, "the mystery of the phallus"'.[3]

Even if it makes sense to consider his novels as an art of secular scripture, Lawrence's non-conformist moralism nevertheless pits the art of the novel against religion. As Lawrence put it in 'Morality and the Novel': 'The novel is a perfect medium for revealing to us the changing rainbow of our living relationships. The novel can help us to live, as nothing else can: no didactic Scripture, anyhow' (*Hardy*, 175). In this sense, his writing does not offer propositions for public debate, but an aesthetics of life. Although Lawrence's writing is argumentative, then, his exploration of life through art asks for a qualitatively different kind of analysis. This chapter suggests that the politics of his writing has been misrecognised in the conflation of politics with sexual politics.

As Michel Foucault has suggested in *The History of Sexuality* (1976), sexuality has become a secular discourse which takes over the mediations of

197

power associated with religion, perhaps most notably in the priesthood of psychoanalysis.[4] While religion has ceased to provide the dominant moral language of love and sexual conduct, the emergence of a secular moral language remains incomplete. Lawrence was critical of Freud, and many have seen similarities between Lawrence and Nietzsche, though the extent of Nietzsche's direct influence on Lawrence remains obscure.[5] These writers reflect profound disturbances of morality in modern secular society, but the consequences for their conceptions of writing are very different. The difficulty, then, is to negotiate the needs and desires reflected in these disturbances without being seduced into rhetorics which mystify the conflicts involved.

From ethics of love to aesthetics of power these disturbances have been focused on sex and sexuality. Where religion once mediated the supposedly private and domestic spheres of birth, death and marriage, sexuality has become the site of conflicts between the individual and the state. The awkward relation between public and private conduct, so graphically dramatised by President Clinton's affairs, disturbs the secular meaning of moral and political distinctions. Struggles for love and empowerment are symbolised as moral actions which are in turn understood as representations of political conflict. Lawrence addressed such questions with unusual intensity in both his life and his writing. He wrestled with a critique of existing society which nevertheless failed to find a social position on which to ground or substantiate his critique. His novels investigate the moral and existential choices open to individuals in this society, but as a literary form the novel formalises lived experience as ideological representation. If sexuality has replaced religion as the opium of the people, 'sexual politics' risks being a contradiction in terms, a reduction of politics to an ideological emphasis on particular aspects of experience. This emphasis nevertheless highlights the role of sexuality in the misrecognition of political interests. In broad terms, recognition is the problem of achieving self-respect and legal personhood through the acknowledgement of others. If politics is the struggle for the recognition of human interests through the legal, economic and emotional organisation of society, then ideology organises the misrecognition of human interests. This chapter seeks to show how Lawrence's writing can help to illuminate the dynamics of recognition and misrecognition.

Mistrusting the tale: the novelist and the novel

Lawrence's experience of alienation from capitalism through the crises and utopian possibilities of personal relations has been widely shared by adolescents and adults of both sexes. Many readers have noted marked differences

prophet of sexual liberation, Lawrence has always provoked political controversies. But the legal and moral focus on Lawrence's representations of sex and sexuality has made it difficult to develop analyses that relate class and gender both politically and through an awareness of the detailed dynamics of literary texts. Lawrence's position as more or less the only writer of working-class origin accorded canonical status in the study of English literature has also been controversial outside academic and educational contexts, not least because his novels offer a provocatively anti-academic mode of self-education. His notoriety as a writer much obsessed with sex has piqued many a reader in search of dirty bits and has provoked widespread moral debate beyond conventional academic terms. As a representative of white, working-class male consciousness, a deeper logic of political debate involving class and gender can be discerned in Lawrence's critical reception.

In *Paleface* (1929) Wyndham Lewis accused Lawrence of a politically unconscious mindlessness: 'Mr Lawrence is, in full hysterical flower, perhaps our most accomplished english communist. He is *the natural communist*, as it were, as distinguished from the indoctrinated, or theoretic, one.'[10] From an opposing, self-consciously communist position, Christopher Caudwell discerned 'a clear artistic, i.e. *emotional*, analysis of the decay of bourgeois social relations'.[11] This analysis, according to Caudwell, remains within a revolutionary bourgeois individualism which collapses into self-contradictory fascist appeals to abandon consciousness. There are echoes of this in Terry Eagleton's more recent critique.[12]

In *After Strange Gods*, Eliot pursued a less overtly political attack, but criticised Lawrence as a moral heretic. The awkward status of argument in Lawrence's rhetoric is reflected in the way Eliot accused Lawrence of having a 'lack of the critical faculties which education should give' and 'an incapacity for what we ordinarily call thinking'. The class basis of Eliot's hostility extends to finding a 'distinct sexual morbidity' in Lawrence's 'insensibility to ordinary social morality'.[13] Beneath debates about sex, these attacks suggest how responses to Lawrence have also been framed by awareness of the class dynamics of argument and education. Lawrence was no communist, mindless or otherwise, but the association with communism is a measure of the threat he posed to the class consciousness of the self-elected moral elites of literary modernism.

F. R. Leavis defended Lawrence as a great novelist of the English tradition, claiming that *St. Mawr* has a 'creative and technical originality more remarkable than that of *The Waste Land*'.[14] But Leavis obscured Lawrence's rejection of English class politics by assimilating Lawrence within a moral, humanist account of the English novel: 'class is a major fact . . . but attention focuses on the essential humanity this fact conditions'.[15] Both Eliot and

Leavis reveal the difficulty of separating class consciousness from Lawrence's challenge to the conventions of representation. In short, long before Lawrence became an object of feminist censure, his writings were censured as political and moral heresy.

The central heresy in Lawrence's writing is the importance accorded to sex. For Lawrence, as Frank Kermode suggests, 'sexual reform becomes the key to cultural and economic reform'.[16] In this way Lawrence prefigures the 'sexual politics' of the 1960s. But if the turn to sexuality reflects frustration with the failures of radical politics, then the politics of sexuality risks being a utopian and politically indeterminate rejection of politics. Recognition that sexuality is central to the ideological reproduction of patriarchy and capitalism does not mean that political change can be achieved through sexuality. As Lawrence suggested in his critique of Freud, sex may be our deepest form of consciousness, but 'a sexual motive is *not* to be attributed to all human activities'.[17]

This suggests why Lawrence has become a privileged object of analysis for sexual politics. But the terrain of argument shared by Lawrence and his critics obscures the political conditions of these arguments. Raymond Williams argued against isolating sexual experience from Lawrence's response to capitalism:

> The real meaning of sex, Lawrence argues, is that it 'involves the whole of a human being'. The alternative to the 'base forcing' into the competition for money and property is not sexual adventure, nor the available sexual emphasis . . . The final emphasis, which all Lawrence's convincing explorations into the 'quick of self' both illumine and realize, is his criticism of industrial civilization.[18]

For Williams, Lawrence's tragic social exile should not be repeated by isolating sexuality from the capitalist divisions of work and life. Placing the truth of sex within a critique of capitalism suggests one way of contextualising the politics of sexuality. But the subsumption of patriarchy within capitalism allows the peculiarities of Lawrence's representation of sex to be glossed over. A different emphasis is suggested by Simone de Beauvoir's assessment of Lawrence: 'in his works woman serves as a compensation myth, exalting a virility that the writer was none too sure of'.[19] The difference between understanding sex as a compensation for damaged class consciousness and understanding it as a compensation for individual sexual insecurity marks the need for a politics of sexual politics.

Sexual politics: the personal *versus* the political

The term 'sexual politics' has been current since the 1930s, when Wilhelm Reich employed it.[20] But Reich's idiosyncratic account differs in important respects from that made popular by Kate Millett's book *Sexual Politics* (1970). Millett attacks Lawrence as 'the most talented and fervid of sexual politicians' (239) whose analysis is inadequate and influence pernicious, but acknowledges him as 'a great and original artist, and in many respects a man of distinguished moral and intellectual integrity' (xii). She argues that sex has a frequently neglected political aspect, taking politics to refer to power-structured relationships. Millett uses literary representation to illustrate her theory, but the status of literature as that which sustains patriarchy remains ambiguous within her claim that sexual dominion is 'perhaps the most pervasive ideology of our culture and provides its most fundamental concept of power'(25). Millett acknowledges that the relation between class and patriarchy is complicated, claiming that 'women tend to transcend the usual class stratifications in patriarchy' (38) while also claiming that 'the position of women in patriarchy is a continuous function of their economic dependence' (40). She claims, moreover, that literary misogyny is not a continuous feature of patriarchal socialisation, but has reemerged in twentieth-century writing. Millett cites Engels with approval to the effect that only with the end of male economic dominion 'will sexual love cease to be barter in some manner based on financial coercion' (125), but criticises Marxist theory for failing to 'supply a sufficient ideological base for a sexual revolution' (169). She gives priority to the struggle to radicalise consciousness through the critique of ideological representations of sexuality. Millett's critique opened up ideological implications that critics had either ignored or implicitly supported. The risk, however, is that 'sexual politics' redefines 'politics' by repeating Lawrence's own subsumption of political criticism within textual representations of sexual morality. Although their positions appear diametrically opposed, the shared centrality accorded to sexual politics obscures the ongoing political redefinition of gender relations within capitalism, giving a surprising primacy to literature and literary criticism over political analysis. According to Millett:

> *Lady Chatterley's Lover* is a program for social as well as sexual redemption, yet the two are inextricable . . . While a sexual revolution, in terms of a change in attitudes, and even in psychic structure, is undoubtedly essential to any radical change, this is very far from being what Lawrence has in mind. His recipe is a mixture of Morris and Freud, which would do away with machinery and return industrial England to something like the middle ages. Primarily the thing is to be accomplished by a reversion to older sexual roles.   (242)

While Millett rejects his social programme, both Lawrence and Millett link sexual awareness to radical social change. There are passages in the novel which support Millett's interpretation, but her assertions about Lawrence's authorial ideology obscure the status of novelistic representation in the move from literary criticism to ideology critique.[21] Isolating programmatic statements from the dynamics of the novel is one way of responding to Lawrence's often provocative characters and narrators. Even if more subtle distinctions are made between what his characters and narrators say, the more important misrecognition is the authority ascribed to the author and to the novel.

It is surprising, then, that, despite her stringent rejection of Freud, Millett ascribes Lawrence's basic positions to his personal negotiation of what she calls his 'well-documented Oedipus complex' (280). Millett's polemical emphasis reads Lawrence as a sophisticated opponent of feminism whose consciousness was shaped by unconscious personal difficulties and a consciously defensive relation to feminism. Although Millett acknowledges Lawrence's 'life-long hatred of industrialism' and his utopian search for radical political transformation, Lawrence's class consciousness is subsumed within the primacy of patriarchal consciousness. Millett notes that *The Rainbow* develops an 'original species of psychic narrative which is Lawrence's major technical achievement' (257) but she collapses these narratives into positions. The polemical need to schematise Lawrence's literary consciousness reduces the novel to an undialectical relation between the personal and the political.

Within the terms of Millett's critique, then, it is difficult to explain how Lawrence's novels become both 'representative' of sexual politics and yet reducibly personal as expressions of Lawrence's authorial ideology. Sexual politics is construed by Millett as a master narrative which explains the exploratory negotiation of existential questions in the novel in the reductive terms of opposing positions within patriarchy. This both displaces the politics of interpretation in the critical reception generated by Lawrence's novels and makes it difficult to analyse the dynamics of women's subordination through capitalism's sexual divisions of labour. Paradoxically, Millett confirms the terms of Lawrence's attempt to replace politics with patriarchal narratives.

Evidence of the strained coherence of Millett's critique is provided by her account of differences between Lawrence's novels. Working backwards Millett suggests that: 'With *Lady Chatterley*, Lawrence seems to be making his peace with the female, and in one last burst of passion proposing a reconciliation for the hostilities embarked upon with the composition of *Aaron's Rod* in 1918' (238). She sees a development, accordingly, from the moving record of the formative love for his mother in *Sons and Lovers* through a transition from mother to mistress and the campaign against the 'new woman' in *The Rainbow* and *Women in Love*. It is possible to see continuities between *Women in Love* and *Lady Chatterley's Lover*, but it is difficult to sustain this as an account of the intervening novels. Millett sees these novels as displaced reflections of more essential questions of patriarchal power: 'For all the excursions into conventional political fascism that occupy the middle and late period of his work, it was the politics of sex which had always commanded Lawrence's attention most, both as the foundation and as a stairway to other types of self-aggrandizement' (245). After *Women in Love*, Millett sees *Aaron's Rod* as a watershed: 'Lawrence is here repudiating his early work's concern with love and personal relationships, dedicating himself to the power urge that dominates his late fiction' (278).

Millett interprets the exploration of the will to power in *Aaron's Rod* and the subsequent novels *Kangaroo* and *The Plumed Serpent* as being based in the rejection of heterosexual love:

> In Lawrence's mind, love had become the knack of dominating another person
> – power means much the same thing. Lawrence first defined power as the
> ability to dominate a woman; later he applied the idea to other political situations, extending the notion of *Herrschaft* to inferior males mastered by a superior male. (269)

Millett nevertheless acknowledges that *Aaron's Rod* concerns two versions of Lawrence's negotiation of class – 'Aaron Sisson, the artist as escaped proletarian, turning his back on his class, and Rawdon Lilly, also a refugee among the middle classes, but now a successful writer and social prophet' (269). Despite evidence of a shift away from personal relations between men and women towards questions of male privilege, politics and public life, Millett sees this as being overdetermined by the way sexual politics is the foundation of all his other social and political beliefs (281). Millett is surely correct to claim that Lawrence turned his back on feminist claims to human recognition. But she discounts too quickly the way Lawrence's critique of power in struggles of recognition also engages questions of class, race and social being. Millett is left with an account of Lawrence as an insecure, self-aggrandising working-class boy with a poorly worked-out Oedipal complex. Construing Lawrence in this way, she underestimates the social forces against which Lawrence set himself, and the utopian tendencies within the political negativity of his aesthetics of life.

Return to Bestwood: *St. Mawr* and the displacement of realism

Lawrence's understanding of the novel as the most refined medium for understanding living relationships amounts to an aesthetic rejection of more overtly political modes of representation. Many of Lawrence's characters and narrators, including his apparently omniscient narrators, reject political forms of identification in favour of more individualised ideas of life. The process of rejection is not simply apolitical, however, but reflects scepticism towards existing politics which provides the narrative problems that Lawrence explores. Sex becomes both a symptom of social disaffection and an existential orientation which disavows its political motivations. The codification of lived experience in the novel constitutes an ideological reconciliation of the conflict of the personal and the political. Sexual politics is, then, a disavowal of politics which is constitutive of the widespread social disaffection with collective political recognition. Lawrence's literary dissidence needs to be understood accordingly as an ideological mode of political disaffection.

To sustain such claims a detailed analysis of Lawrence's novels is needed, not least because his novels continually find new ways to represent and displace these problems as dynamics of recognition and misrecognition. Focusing on the tale rather than the teller, detailed analysis also needs to acknowledge impulses to represent experience which, even if realist, are not necessarily political. In broad terms, then, Lawrence's novels oscillate between the social and emotional recognitions made possible by literary realism and the displacement of realism by desires for sexual, personal or literary transcendence. This in part accounts for Lawrence's awkward status as a modernist writer torn between the realism of the nineteenth-century novel and attempts to find new formal articulations of experience. But the displacement of realism in Lawrence's novels is never complete, nor do his novels succeed in eradicating the contradictory political impulses which have gone into the desire for the novel to enable new kinds of recognition.

These tendencies can be illustrated by *St. Mawr*, one of Lawrence's most succinct and self-critical novels. The central female character, Lou Witt, is described as being 'at home anywhere and nowhere' (*SM*, 21). Her marriage is described as an inscrutable bond: 'A nervous attachment, rather than a sexual love. A curious tension of will, rather than a spontaneous passion' (24). Into this Platonic marriage, in which husband and wife become like brother and sister, is thrown Lou's fascination with the novel's central symbolic animal, a horse called St. Mawr. Animated by dark intimations of the almost god-like animal consciousness of this stallion, the novel develops this symbol almost as a parody of Lawrencean sexual symbolism, despite speeches by Lou to the effect that 'I don't know one single man who is a proud living animal' (61) which suggest the misogynist projection of an authorial ideology of phallic consciousness. The novel's sympathies with Lou and her mother also articulate a bitter rejection of the inadequacies of men after the catastrophe of the First World War. The novel implies a critique of male degeneration through war and industrialism which might be explained by Lawrence's pacifism, but can also be read as a more literal reflection of the shortage of men after the war. In short, the social conditions of the novel's sexual narratives are also historical.

In the terms of the novel, Lou experiences a more generalised vision of evil in individuals and society, rejecting socialism, bolshevism, fascism and production 'heaped upon production'. Lou is portrayed as thinking that 'The individual can but depart from the mass, and try to cleanse himself . . . Retreat to the desert, and fight. But in his soul adhere to that which is life itself, creatively destroying as it goes' (80). This celebration of existential isolation as the struggle of the will to power is nevertheless ascribed to a female character through the rejection of recognisable political coordinates. The novel suggests a possible resolution to such conflicts in a new kind of marriage between Lou's mother and the parodically Lawrence-like character Lewis, a relationship which could be seen as prefiguring the relationship between Connie and Mellors in *Lady Chatterley's Lover*. But in *St. Mawr*, the unreality of such reconciliations is highlighted by making the desire to retreat to the desert into a literal flight to the desert in New Mexico. The mysterious power of St. Mawr is written off as the horse becomes a slavish admirer of a 'long-legged black Texan mare' (132). The mooted relation between Lou and Phoenix – a suggestive name in Lawrence's writing – is also reduced to a kind of animal farce. Described as 'an American, son of a Mexican father and a Navajo Indian mother, from Arizona' and 'an odd piece of debris' from the war, we are told of Phoenix that: 'When you knew him well, you recognised the real half-breed' (24–25). The conditions of such recognition within any implied readership remain hard to specify.

In a complex passage later in the novel, however, Phoenix is described through free indirect projection of Lou's consciousness: 'the aboriginal phallic male in him simply couldn't recognise her as a woman at all' (135). The 'old, secretive, rat-like male' (136) in Phoenix also views Lou as an economic opportunity. But the primal narrative is abruptly rejected by a voice that seems to belong to both Lou and the narrator: 'When Phoenix presumed she was looking for some secretly sexual male such as himself, he was ridiculously mistaken. Even the illusion of the beautiful St. Mawr was gone. And Phoenix, roaming round like a sexual rat in promiscuous back yards! – *Merci, mon cher!*' (SM, 137). The narrative debunks characteristic Lawrencean tropes of sexuality. Similarly, Lou's deluded conception of herself as an eternal Vestal Virgin is mocked by the dirt-like inertia of the landscape. The concluding pages abandon the novel's characters for an extended lyrical description of the conscious but desperate struggle of a New England woman to humanise the wild animosity of nature. This becomes

Lou's rejection of men and cheap sex for what she describes as a kind of sexual relation with the wild spirit of the land. The novel's conclusion mischievously redescribes this as a cheap purchase of property.

St. Mawr oscillates between the realistic portrayal of the rejection of existing male society and explorations of the illusions of narrative transcendence. The displacement of realism takes place along two axes: spiritual and environmental. Despite the desire to find new reconciliations through escape from an exhausted European civilisation, the novel reveals the groundlessness of this desire. Lawrence himself had travelled the political distance from the rejection of England to recognition of the limits of the sexual, racial and natural utopia he explored. The end of *St. Mawr* leaves open the possible regeneration of civilisation through new sexual relations, but frames this within a pessimistic analysis of the groundlessness of such possibilities in existing society.

Against Millett's perception of a shift from love to power, it could be argued, then, that Lawrence's trajectory up to *Lady Chatterley's Lover* reveals not a persistent interest in the politics of sex, but dramatisations of the rejection of both politics and sexual relations as illusory resolutions of social conflict. This might in turn argue a more profound critique of the relation between possessive individualism in sexual relationships and the conflicts of private property and social being. Even if such arguments go against authorial intention, Lawrence's novels offer sustained representations of the contradictions inherent in attempts by individuals to reject existing society. There is, then, an underlying politics in the rejection of existing communities and the focus on individual relationships exemplified by a work such as *Women in Love*. This politics reflects both a sense of lost community and scepticism towards recipes for rebuilding community.

Perhaps the most explicit context for this sense of loss is provided by Lawrence's brief essay 'Return to Bestwood', written and published in 1926. The essay describes Lawrence's return to his home town during the long miners' strike after the General Strike. As well as remembering his family, the essay describes his response to the shadows of his former self along a trajectory not dissimilar to that ascribed to Lou Witt: 'One is driven back to search one's own soul, for a way out into a new destiny' (*PII*, 264). Yet Lawrence offers a sense of his own political agenda on what he sees as the 'brink of a class war': 'I know that we could, if we would, establish little by little a true democracy in England: we could nationalize the land and industries and means of transport, and make the whole thing work infinitely better than at present, *if we would*' (*PII*, 265).

Socialist impulses are only momentary in Lawrence's thinking, but appear elsewhere in his writings. In a letter of 1921, for example, he wrote: 'If I knew how to, I'd really join myself to the revolutionary socialists now . . . I don't care for politics. But I know that there *must* and *should* be a deadly revolution very soon' (iii. 649). In the epilogue for the second edition of *Movements in European History*, he wrote that 'Myself, personally, I believe that a good form of socialism, if it could be brought about, would be the best form of government. But let us come down to experience' (*MEH*, 262). He goes on to describe the failure of socialism in post-war Italy. Such moments are linked to a drift from political struggle towards a more politically indeterminate conception of 'life': 'You've got to smash money and this beastly *possessive* spirit. I get more revolutionary every minute, but for *life's* sake. The dead materialism of Marx socialism and soviets seems to me no better than what we've got. What we want is life, and *trust*' (vii. 98). These dynamics generate the intuitive politics underlying his mistrust of existing politics but this negativity also finds its way into the radical tone of his prose. This perhaps explains Wyndham Lewis's perception of 'natural' communism in Lawrence's writing.

Partly what motivates Lawrence's sense of crisis in 'Return to Bestwood', then, is the political correlation between his umbilical relation to Eastwood and his fictional descriptions of 'Bestwood'. Through this displaced fictional identity, Eastwood provides an important narrative context in *The White Peacock*, *Sons and Lovers*, *Women in Love*, *The Lost Girl*, *Aaron's Rod* and *Lady Chatterley's Lover*. The 'devouring nostalgia' and 'infinite repulsion' he feels for his old home and home-town reveal a sense of lost community, combined with the urge to escape, as the political motivation behind many of his novels. The displacement of the essay's realism takes the form of imagining proto-fascistic solutions: 'Hopeless life should be put to sleep, the idiots and the hopeless sick and the true criminal. And the birth-rate should be controlled' (*PII*, 265). Lawrence's difficulties in reconciling a critique of Eastwood with his sense of class solidarity are crystallised by his experience of the General Strike and this motivates the explicit return to such questions in the versions of *Lady Chatterley's Lover*.

Conclusion: sexual politics as the displacement of politics

Raymond Williams has suggested that Lawrence works out his emotional response to the General Strike in the writing of *Lady Chatterley's Lover*.[22] This provides a way of understanding the political subtexts motivating the shift from realism into sexual fantasy in the final version of *Lady Chatterley's Lover*. Graham Holderness has argued that: 'In the final version of the novel "class" is abolished. Such a denial of history is the necessary precondition for the relationship between Connie and Mellors;

history presents no obstacle to its fulfilment, its symbolic reconciliation of real contradictions.'[23] Similarly, Scott Sanders has argued that: 'As Lawrence mutes the social message in *Lady Chatterley's Lover*, he accents the sexual message . . . *Lady Chatterley's Lover* reads less like a political fable and more like a sexual tract.'[24] In *The First Lady Chatterley*, Parkin is secretary of the Communist League, whereas in the final version he becomes the gamekeeper Mellors. This is the opposite trajectory to that explored in *Aaron's Rod*, in which Aaron leaves his position as secretary to the Miners' Union to explore new possibilities of economic and sexual freedom.

It is tempting, then, to see Lawrence's revisions as a process in which the displacement of politics by sexual politics is an ideological retreat from class consciousness. But this underestimates the extent to which the novels are critical of sexual solutions to the political problems represented in the novel. Peter Scheckner has argued that 'even the least political version – the final one – suggests that a retreat from history or society into a mythic realm of sex or blood consciousness was an inadequate response to a political problem'.[25] Thus it is reductive to read Lawrence's sexual politics without reference to the political contradictions informing his novels:

> The themes of flawed sexuality, the failure of modern consciousness to effect change, the irrelevance of class struggle, and the regenerating potential of genital power can be found in the three *Chatterley* novels. So can a counter notion that social and economic relationships, as much as sexuality, determine our destinies. Lawrence was experimenting with disparate ideas.[26]

His experiments remain unstable. The tensions between class struggle, power and sexuality in Lawrence's writing need detailed analysis as processes of recognition and misrecognition rather than as schematic illustrations of a politically incorrect position.

If recognition of the desire for sexual solutions to political contradictions is highlighted, it becomes possible to read Lawrence's earlier novels in a fashion which combines the perspectives suggested by Raymond Williams and Kate Millett. There are a number of important political contexts informing Lawrence's novels, not least his critical relation to his 'home' and industrial society; his pacifist rejection of the World War; and his interest in radical political experiments. But if the most striking feature of his novels is their exploration of personal relations as political allegories, then the focus on sex cannot simply be determined as an expression of class politics. The more difficult role of sexual politics in Lawrence's writing and in his critical reception is as a representation of the role of individualist 'sexuality' in the displacement of politics. The immediacy and mediation of personal relations cannot be read as if sex does not matter, any more than politics can be understood without reference to the role of sexuality in the misrecognition of political interests. Perhaps the most striking ideological feature of Lawrence's representation of the relation between politics and sex is then the desire for immediacy and a sustained neglect of the political institutions of the state which mediate economics and personal relations. Lawrence's struggles to represent how the politics of eros might resolve class war remain unresolved. His representations can then be understood as explorations into the ideological displacement of politics and the widespread distrust of the state and the economy as decisive structures in struggles for recognition and human happiness.

In his 'Study of Thomas Hardy' Lawrence explained his conception of art: 'every work of art adheres to some system of morality. But if it be really a work of art, it must contain the essential criticism on the morality to which it adheres' (*Hardy*, 89). Lawrence set himself the self-critical task of using the novel to express his sense of the contradictions of life: 'Artistic form is a revelation of the two principles of Love and the Law in a state of conflict and yet reconciled' (*Hardy*, 90). But Lawrence also resists carrying this dialectical sense of conflict over from artistic form into political reform: 'I only ask that the law shall leave me alone as much as possible . . . What does the law matter? What does money, power, or public approval matter? All that matters is that each human being shall *be* in his own fulness' (*Hardy*, 14, 16). His resistance to legal structures of recognition extends to the core of his conception of the loss of male freedom in the actualisation of recognition through marriage. This specifies the aesthetics of his novels within the displaced politics of sexual politics.

Despite persistent confusions in Lawrence's reception, there is much in Lawrence's writing that illuminates differences between politics and sex, between power and love. In *Fantasia of the Unconscious* he argued that:

> Sex holds any *two* people together, but it tends to disintegrate society, unless it is subordinated to the great dominating male passion of collective *purpose* . . . It cuts both ways. Assert sex as the predominant fulfilment, and you get the collapse of living purpose in man. You get anarchy. Assert *purposiveness* as the one supreme and pure activity of life, and you drift into barren sterility, like our business life of today, and our political life.   (*F&P*, 110–11)

There is much to disagree with in Lawrence's writings, but the dialectical relation of sex and politics can be read as a representation of the way the politics of class consciousness are displaced by the ideology of sexuality. Lawrence allows us to see how the focus on sexual politics becomes one way for individuals to take refuge from political contradictions in narratives of personal conflict. Beyond mere disagreement, then, the politics of misrecognition in Lawrence's novels are representative of broader resistances to politics.

NOTES

1 Harry T. Moore, *The Priest of Love*, revd edn (London: Heinemann, 1974).
2 Mark Spilka, *The Love Ethic of D. H. Lawrence* (London: Dobson, 1958), p. 3.
3 Kate Millett, *Sexual Politics* (London: Rupert Hart-Davis, 1970), p. 238. All references hereafter included in the main text.
4 Michel Foucault, *The History of Sexuality: An Introduction*, trans. Robert Hurley (Harmondsworth: Penguin, 1979).
5 For a general discussion of Nietzsche's influence on Lawrence see Colin Milton, *Lawrence and Nietzsche* (Aberdeen: Aberdeen University Press, 1987), and Kingsley Widmer, *Defiant Desire: Some Dialectical Legacies of D. H. Lawrence* (Carbondale and Edwardsville: Southern Illinois University Press, 1992). A more definite model for Lawrence's thinking is provided by A. Schopenhauer, 'The Metaphysics of Sexual Love', in *The World as Will and Representation*, trans. E. F. J. Payne (New York: Dover, 1966), II 531–67.
6 Graham Hough, *The Dark Sun: A Study of D. H. Lawrence* (London: Duckworth, 1956), p. 151.
7 Anaïs Nin, *D. H. Lawrence: An Unprofessional Study*, with intro. by Harry T. Moore (London: Black Spring Press, 1985), p. 57. Compare Lydia Blanchard, 'Women Look at Lady Chatterley: Feminine Views of the Novel', *D. H. Lawrence Review*, 11, 3 (Fall 1978), 246–59. For a phallic defence of Lawrence, see Peter Balbert, *D. H. Lawrence and the Phallic Imagination: Essays on Sexual Identity and Feminist Misreading* (London: Macmillan, 1989).
8 For a theoretical discussion of the politics of recognition, see Axel Honneth, *The Struggle for Recognition: The Moral Grammar of Social Conflicts*, trans. Joel Anderson (Cambridge: Polity, 1995). See also Jessica Benjamin's books, *The Bonds of Love* (London: Virago, 1990); *Like Subjects, Like Objects: Essays on Recognition and Sexual Difference* (London: Yale University Press, 1995); and *Shadow of the Other* (London: Routledge, 1997).
9 For a discussion of Lawrence's response to contemporary feminist movements, see Hilary Simpson, *D. H. Lawrence and Feminism* (London: Croom Helm, 1982). For a range of essays on related themes, see *Lawrence and Women*, ed. Anne Smith (London: Vision Press, 1978).
10 Wyndham Lewis, *Enemy Salvoes: Selected Literary Criticism*, ed. C. J. Fox (London: Vision, 1975), p. 121.
11 Christopher Caudwell, *Studies in a Dying Culture* (London: Bodley Head, 1938), p. 58.
12 Terry Eagleton, *Criticism and Ideology: A Study in Marxist Literary Theory* (London: Verso, 1976), pp. 157–58.
13 T. S. Eliot, *After Strange Gods: A Primer in Modern Heresy* (New York: Harcourt, Brace & Co., 1934), pp. 63–64.
14 F. R. Leavis, *D. H. Lawrence: Novelist* (1955; Harmondsworth: Penguin, 1964), p. 101.
15 Ibid., p. 271.

16 Frank Kermode, *Lawrence* (London: Fontana, 1973), p. 136.

17 D. H. Lawrence, *Fantasia of the Unconscious* (Harmondsworth: Penguin, 1971), p. 17.

18 Raymond Williams, *Culture and Society: 1780–1950* (Harmondsworth: Penguin, 1961), p. 213.

19 Simone de Beauvoir, *The Second Sex*, trans. H. M. Parshley (Harmondsworth: Penguin, 1972), p. 280.

20 Jeff Weeks, 'The Development of Sexual Theory and Sexual Politics', in *Human Sexual Relations: A Reader*, ed. Mike Brake (Harmondsworth: Penguin, 1982), p. 293. See also Wilhelm Reich, *The Sexual Revolution*, trans. Theodore P. Wolfe (London: Vision, 1951), p. xxv.

21 For a critique of Millett, see Cora Kaplan, 'Radical Feminism and Literature: Rethinking Millett's *Sexual Politics*', *Red Letters: Communist Party Literature Journal*, 9 (n.d.), 4–16.

22 Raymond Williams, *The English Novel: From Dickens to Lawrence* (1970; London: Paladin, 1974).

23 Graham Holderness, *D. H. Lawrence: History, Ideology and Fiction* (Dublin: Gill and Macmillan, 1982), p. 226. For further discussions of the versions of *Lady Chatterley's Lover*, see Michael Squires, *The Creation of 'Lady Chatterley's Lover'* (Baltimore and London: Johns Hopkins Press, 1983); *D. H. Lawrence's 'Lady': A New Look at 'Lady Chatterley's Lover'*, ed. Michael Squires and Dennis Jackson (Athens, GA: University of Georgia Press, 1985); G. R. Strickland, 'The First *Lady Chatterley's Lover*', in *D. H. Lawrence: A Critical Study of the Major Novels and Other Writings*, ed. A. H. Gomme (Sussex: The Harvester Press, 1978), pp. 159–74; Richard Wasson, 'Class and the Vicissitudes of the Male Body in Works by D. H. Lawrence', *D. H. Lawrence Review*, 14, 3 (Fall, 1981), 289–305.

24 Scott Sanders, *D. H. Lawrence: The World of the Major Novels* (London: Vision Press, 1973), p. 181.

25 Peter Scheckner, *Class, Politics, and the Individual: A Study of the Major Works of D. H. Lawrence* (London and Toronto: Associated University Presses, 1985), p. 13.

26 Scheckner, *Class, Politics, and the Individual*, p. 169.

12

FIONA BECKET

Lawrence and psychoanalysis

Why is it important to think about the connections between D. H. Lawrence and psychoanalysis? Although he was acquainted with a number of psychoanalysts, and despite his interest in the instinctual life of men and women, Lawrence was never in analysis and quite early on developed a dislike of those whom he called 'the Freudians'.[1] Psychoanalysis was, in his lifetime, a relatively new science, and in his writings Lawrence demonstrates an awareness of and an interest in a range of contemporary scientific developments. It is no surprise, then, that he became familiar with, and wrote about, popular Freudianism, and was also aware of popular representations of Jung's work: this is evident from Lawrence's published *Letters*. The fact that Lawrence chose to refer negatively to Freud's theses or, more accurately, to his *own* versions of Freud's thought, is perhaps where critical interest begins. When his contemporaries began to interpret his novels (particularly *Sons and Lovers* in 1913) using Freud's hypotheses about the unconscious life of the writer, Lawrence began a period of strident resistance, most often in his letters, to this mode of reading. Such resistance, the stuff of psychoanalysis, is grist to his critics' mill, and many works of criticism since Lawrence's death have examined, and sought to demonstrate, the validity of psychoanalytic readings of his work. Less diagnostically, others have sought to evaluate the broader significance of his relation to the psychoanalytic and some have seen in his work a post-Freudian position.[2]

'[S]ix little essays on Freudian Unconscious'

By 1921 Lawrence's notoriety was well established (*The Rainbow* was suppressed in 1915, prosecuted under the Obscene Publications Act of 1857), alongside a reputation for significant literary achievement. In 1921 and 1922 he published two books notionally on the subject of psychoanalysis which, on the basis of their titles alone, must have suggested to his more timorous critics that, once again, Lawrence was about to violate the sanctuary of sex, so efficiently were psychoanalysis and the sexual linked in popular imagining. These volumes were *Psychoanalysis and the Unconscious* and *Fantasia of the Unconscious*, first published in New York. The critic John Middleton Murry, for a time a close friend of Lawrence, rated *Fantasia* more highly than *Psychoanalysis*. In language which is strikingly similar to Lawrence's own on the status of psychoanalysis in modern culture, Murry printed his opinion that, among his contemporaries, Lawrence was unusual in realising 'the scope, the *envergure*, of the problems of which psychoanalysis has touched the fringe'.[3] It is a statement that underlines Lawrence's value to the young intelligentsia of the day as a cultural critic, tuned in to the wider significance of the psychoanalytic as a mode of human understanding beyond the confined, private (and dearly purchased) clinical space. The tone of Lawrence's books from the beginning is, however, suspicious of Freud. To underline this fact commentators are fond of quoting anti-Freud statements from the books: at the opening of *Psychoanalysis* Freud is 'the psychiatric quack' (*F&P*, 201). He is disapprovingly represented as an adventurer (and trespasser) in search of human origins, origins that explain our behaviour and 'sicknesses': 'Suddenly he [Freud] stepped out of the conscious into the unconscious, out of the everywhere into the nowhere, like some supreme explorer.' What he finds in his 'cavern of dreams', suggests Lawrence, is 'Nothing but a huge slimy serpent of sex, and heaps of excrement, and a myriad repulsive little horrors spawned between sex and excrement' (203). In place of this 'sack of horrors', repressed material, Lawrence wishes to substitute what he calls the 'pristine unconscious', origin of non-deliberate physical and emotional impulses which underpin his own fictional representations of strong feelings like love and hate. So *Psychoanalysis* and *Fantasia* do not represent merely a complaint against psychoanalysis. More centrally, they form part of his long-running preoccupation with unconscious, or non-deliberate, aspects of human feeling which, crucially, pre-dated his introduction to 'Freudianism'. This preoccupation is evident in even his earliest discursive writing, the early non-fiction such as the Foreword to *Sons and Lovers* (written in 1913 and never intended for publication), 'Study of Thomas Hardy' (written in 1914 and published posthumously) and 'The Crown' (begun in 1915). These works offer preliminary sketches in which Lawrence articulates, often in a highly metaphorical language, his own preoccupation with the birth of the self, most frequently as the result of an encounter with an other.

These writings hint at some of the contexts for Lawrence's interest in non-deliberate functioning and feeling common to all human beings. He was interested in dreams and dreaming, for instance, but opposed Freud's *theorising* of dream as articulated in his major work *Die Traumdeutung* (*The Interpretation of Dreams*, 1900). He also rejected Freud's formulations of infant sexuality: early on he told his friends that in the writings that were to become *Psychoanalysis* and *Fantasia* he was writing on 'Child Consciousness' (*F&P*, 148, 160) which sounds like a revision of the main principles of psychoanalysis. He felt appalled that the first critics of *Sons and Lovers* should interpret its central relationship between mother and son as an Oedipal drama, and further seek by implication to identify Paul Morel with Lawrence himself. To his admirers Lawrence's work confirmed Freud's opinion that aesthetic representation often anticipated psychoanalytic observations.[4] At that time Lawrence, by his own admission, was not knowledgeable about Freud's writings. In the context of comments on Edwin August Björkman's preface to his play *The Widowing of Mrs. Holroyd* (1914), Lawrence states 'I never did read Freud, but I have heard about him since I was in Germany' (ii. 80). Frederick Hoffman in his book *Freudianism and the Literary Mind* suggests that by the twenties most young writers had some familiarity with Freud's language, even if the ideas had become distorted and over-simplified in the telling, but what is interesting is Lawrence's consistent resistance to Freud rather than any easy acquiescence with his ideas. In 1914, in the related contexts of his despair at war and his psychological need to define a personal life-affirming philosophy, he states, 'I am not Freudian and never was – Freudianism is only a branch of medical science, interesting' (ii. 218). By 1916, following prominent psychoanalytic assessments of *Sons and Lovers*, he felt less inclined to be measured in his comments: to his friend Barbara Low, an analyst, he wrote, 'I hated the Psychoanalysis [*sic*] Review of *Sons and Lovers*. You know I think "complexes" are vicious half-statements of the Freudians: sort of can't see wood for trees. When you've said Mutter-complex, you've said nothing . . . a complex is not simply a sex relation: far from it' (ii. 655).[5] Granted that among his acquaintances he could count prominent British psychoanalysts including David Eder and Barbara Low, it is nevertheless Frieda Weekley, a divorcée who married Lawrence in 1914, who is most often credited with introducing him to the basics of Freudian psychoanalysis. For a while part of a fashionable free-thinking clique in Munich, with Freud's writings available to her, she had, however, encountered his ideas in the course of an earlier relationship with 'renegade psychoanalyst and anarchist', Otto Gross.[6]

Among the books that Lawrence did not read, but which contributed to a general awareness of Freud, not least in the culture of the fashionable literati, many of whom were associated with Bloomsbury, must be counted *The Interpretation of Dreams*, available in English from 1913; David Eder's translation of *On Dreams* (1914); A. A. Brill's edition of *Psychopathology of Everyday Life* (1914); and Barbara Low's *Psycho-Analysis: A Brief Outline of Freudian Theory* (1920). Leonard and Virginia Woolf began to publish the International Psycho-Analytical Library in 1924 from their Hogarth Press, beginning the production in English of the Standard Edition of Freud's work, under the general editorship of James Strachey, in that year. Whether Lawrence liked it or not, Freud and his disciples were on the horizon.

The title of *Psychoanalysis and the Unconscious* echoes the English title of C. G. Jung's *Psychology of the Unconscious* (American edition, 1919) where, appropriately for Lawrence, Jung spells out his departure from Freud. Lawrence's sequel study, *Fantasia of the Unconscious*, continues the ironic tone of his attacks on the psychoanalytic enterprise. Although in *Fantasia* Lawrence counts Jung and Freud among those who have helped to kick-start his polemic, he can no more be properly called a Jungian than a Freudian. A spatial imagination is required if Lawrence's criticisms of psychoanalysis are to be thoroughly understood. Freud, with his metaphorisation of the concepts 'conscious'/ 'unconscious' as territories of the mind, located human identity and motivation 'in the head'. He established mental and sexual imperatives for human behaviour, and blurred the distinctions between them. At least this was Lawrence's perspective. The phrase 'in the head' was a pejorative verbal formula that Lawrence often employed: in *Fantasia* he repeatedly uses the phrase 'sex in the head' to describe a deliberate, if not prurient, concentration in his contemporaries on sex where regrettably 'sensual passion' has been displaced by a 'mental-conscious' fixation on genital pleasure (*F&P*, 84–85, 249). Misreaders of *Lady Chatterley's Lover* may be surprised by this distinction. One of Lawrence's principal aims in his writing of 'six little essays on Freudian Unconscious' (iii. 466) was to re-locate unconscious functioning, or feeling, in the *body*, challenging the psychoanalytic emphasis on *mind*. Critics who concentrate on Lawrence as anti-Cartesian are referring precisely to his attempts to close the mind/body division that conceptually orders his culture.[7] It is in part this anti-Cartesian stance that explains the predominance of the bizarre language of the body's centres of feeling in both *Psychoanalysis* and *Fantasia*; this is the language which refers pseudo-scientifically to the functions of the 'plexuses' and 'ganglia', nerve-centres located between the chest and base of the spine. In the sixth chapter of *Psychoanalysis* Lawrence is quite unequivocal about this: 'We can quite tangibly deal with the human unconscious. We trace its source and centres in the great ganglia and nodes of the nervous system. We establish the nature of the spontaneous consciousness at each of these centres; we determine the polarity and the direction of the polarized flow' (*F&P*, 243). In fact these centres are ambivalently present in the body as Lawrence closes the distinction between the literal and the metaphorical in pursuit of his philosophy of feeling. What is evident from this statement is Lawrence's refusal to *polarise* conscious and unconscious functioning. For Freud the two states are in opposition: that which is *un*conscious may become conscious. For this to happen a shift must take place; something must be transformed. Lawrence has an investment in bringing the two 'realms' much closer, hence in his writing the words 'conscious' and 'unconscious' are often interchangeable in ways they cannot be in psychoanalysis. This is to signal something central to an understanding of Lawrence's relationship to Freud: the fact that very often Lawrence's attention is on Freud's *language*, so that frequently his critique operates at the level of discourse prior to doctrine.

A new idiom

In the opening chapters of *Psychoanalysis*, Lawrence begins his attempt to destabilise what he understands by Freud's definition of 'the unconscious'. He does so without acknowledging that for Freud, too, it is a dynamic, a changing conception. For Lawrence, not surprisingly in a writer with such an idiosyncratic and highly personal vocabulary, the issue quickly becomes one of language. The unconscious, he suggests, is 'unanalysable, undefinable, inconceivable' (*F&P*, 214). Freud's problem is his insistence on analysis, on definition, on making the unconscious conscious. The new science of psychoanalysis is in bondage to a 'mental conception' (215) of that which patently, to Lawrence, defies being known. Indeed, that what is *un*conscious remains *un*knowable is very much the point. In the course of his argument he shifts between the validity of the idea of the unconscious as dynamic process, and the 'contents' of the unconscious as providing material for psychological investigation. Actions, behaviour, gesture, sickness: these are for Lawrence the indications of an unconscious or involuntary mode of existence common to all which, if nothing else, shows one that one is alive. Freud might broadly agree. Lawrence's objection is to the quantifying of the unconscious as part of a rational, positivistic exercise; the reduction, as he sees it, of infinite modes of response to a set of symptoms. He states his view at the beginning of *Psychoanalysis*, arguing that he has no use for a position which sets up the unconscious merely as the repository of negative responses, of that which is bad, anti-social, sick in individual experience. Occasionally he offers a definition to illuminate his own position – 'By the unconscious we also mean the soul'; 'the unconscious is the creative element' (215) – but more often than not the qualifier, for instance 'soul', is also subject to redefinition within the Lawrencean lexicon. So when Lawrence refers to 'unconscious' functioning he does not mean the same thing as Freud. This difference between them is crucial. Freud saw analysis as a way to normalise his patients – psychoanalysis is a clinical science – by defining and treating neuroses rationally. In his published case studies successful analysis results in the individual's integration or re-integration into society, family or an appropriate social unit. Lawrence, on the other hand, is focused on individuals' capacity to resist their socialisation, their social conditioning, where (as in 1914–18) society itself is 'sick'. To a significant degree, then, Lawrence writes his books on the unconscious as an iconoclast, a dissenter.

Unconscious feelings, at least in *Psychoanalysis* and *Fantasia*, are related most often to love and hate, and then to a range of human responses and relationships that can be defined within this opposition. Some examples from the fiction show how Lawrence was developing his ideas in literary contexts, often to the mystification of his readers. In *Aaron's Rod*, written between 1917 and 1921, he spells out his own despair at what the war signified in terms of the disintegration of individual selfhood and the development of a 'mass-consciousness' or 'will' which disrupted individual self-development. In a chapter called 'The War Again', Rawdon Lilly, the Lawrence-figure in the novel, describes his view of the disintegrative processes of modernity in the context of a world that has been at war:

> Damn all masses and groups, anyhow. All I want is to get *myself* out of their horrible heap: to get out of the swarm. The swarm to me is nightmare and nullity – horrible helpless writhing in a dream. I want to get myself awake, out of it all – all that mass-consciousness, all that mass-activity – it's the most horrible nightmare to me. No man is awake and himself.   (*AR*, 119)

What is stated clearly here is Lawrence's personal philosophy of individual value, where attacks on that value stimulated by modern 'mental-consciousness' (promoting the nation, for example, as more important than the individual) are felt *physically* in the sick, and sickened, body of the man. There is a reminder here of the 'nightmare of history' from which James Joyce's hero, Stephen Dedalus, is trying to awaken at the end of *A Portrait of the Artist as a Young Man*. That which Lilly aches for in this speech is the birth, or re-birth, of the individual, independent self that Lawrence describes in the metaphoric language of the body in *Psychoanalysis* and *Fantasia*.

Also in *Aaron's Rod* is a less well-integrated example of Lawrence's view that unconscious feeling resides in the body. In a chapter called 'A Punch in the Wind', Jim Bricknell describes to Rawdon Lilly his inability to feel love as he once could. A war veteran, he is one of the 'dead' in Lilly's 'swarm'. His description of emotional feeling residing in the body's nerve centres adopts the language of *Psychoanalysis* and *Fantasia*, both of which were committed to paper as the novel took its final form. Describing a capacity for love which has now been obstructed by his inevitable participation in the movement of history, Bricknell complains to Lilly, '"Why man, you don't know what it was like. I used to get the most grand feelings – like a great rush of force, or light – a great rush – right here, as I've said, at the solar plexus"' (*AR*, 80). This emphasis on the body's material centres of feeling somehow deadened by the drift of modernity is introduced in *Psychoanalysis* once Lawrence's repudiations of Freud are more or less out of the way after the first chapter. So it is that Lawrence, like Freud in this respect, shifts from a focus on the individual to the broadest movements of a culture.

A further, frequently cited, example of the significance of these material centres for Lawrence occurs in *Women in Love*. In the 'Excurse' chapter, as Birkin and Ursula begin to withdraw from the social and economic ties that bind them, an awareness of her love for Birkin is reached by Ursula through the touch of his body but not in a conventional coital context. In a long passage representing the kind of language that many of Lawrence's readers cannot stomach, Ursula 'unconsciously' traces with her fingers the back of Birkin's thighs, 'following some mysterious life-flow there . . . the strange mystery of his life-motion . . . down the flanks' (*WL*, 313). The description continues in this vein: 'She had established a rich new circuit, a new current of passional electric energy, between the two of them, released from the darkest poles of the body and established in perfect circuit' (*WL*, 314).

The language of flows, circuits and plexuses (the language of the body) that these examples represent are evidence of Lawrence at this time searching for a new and different idiom with which to define and identify unconscious, or more accurately, non-verbal, experience. It is one of the chief paradoxes of Lawrence's writing that he labours to cast the *non*-verbal into language: as a writer that is what he engages himself to do. Changes in his writing style which constitute the development of this new language can also be noticed in his literary criticism, particularly his studies of American writing. The early versions of these essays are collected in a volume posthumously entitled *The Symbolic Meaning*. The official volume, published by Thomas Seltzer in America in 1923, Lawrence entitled *Studies in Classic American Literature*. Although Lawrence would not have used the phrase, these essays are frequently viewed as examples of psychoanalytic criticism.[8] This is not because of any visible adherence to Freud, but because in his readings of the American writers Lawrence refers constantly to unconscious orders of self and cultural representation.

The first pages of an early version of the essay on Crèvecoeur, nominally about *Letters from an American Farmer*, employs the language of the body that is familiar from *Psychoanalysis* and *Fantasia*. Establishing Benjamin Franklin, the subject of the preceding essay, and Crèvecoeur in a dual relationship to each other (Franklin representative of abstraction and 'spirit', Crèvecoeur of 'emotion and sensation'), Lawrence idiosyncratically gives much of the narrative over to the developing infant, to the nerve centres of breast and bowel ('the cardiac plexus and the solar plexus'), to instinctive 'root-knowledge' versus 'mental consciousness' and to the development of what is obscurely referred to as the positive 'centripetal' self (*Symbolic*, 55–57). He sees the relevance of developing this language in a work of literary criticism because he is trying to describe the centres of feeling from which the literary artist, despite himself, responds to his world.[9] This form of expression is largely omitted from the later version of the essay on Crèvecoeur printed in *Studies in Classic American Literature*. Nevertheless the experiences of the American writer have been creatively apprehended by Lawrence in the terms set out in *Psychoanalysis* and *Fantasia*. In the early essay, Crèvecoeur, despite frequent lapses into 'mental-consciousness', becomes at times in his writing the type of the fulfilled artist, living and working at an unconscious level, ordered by the psycho-biology, variously termed 'the psychic body' (*Symbolic*, 189) and later 'the biological psyche' (*F&P*, 104), mapped by Lawrence. Always focused on artistic responsibility, in the last version of the essay Lawrence writes that 'An artist usually intellectualizes on top, and his dark under-consciousness goes on contradicting him beneath. This is almost laughably the case with most American artists. Crèveceour is the first example' (*SCAL*, 31). Lawrence's skill, typically, was to read his own obsessions into the works of his subjects, while yet bringing out something distinctive and lasting in his readings of the other.

The 'American' book has, perhaps uneasily, retained its critical value. An awareness of the radical nature of Lawrence's choice of American writing has perhaps diminished on reaching the end of a century in which aspects of popular American culture have become dominant, not least in European contexts. For Lawrence, however, disenchanted with his native culture, the American writing that he targeted could usefully be seen as 'Other'. Hence, Lawrence creatively and productively exploited what he perceived as cultural and *emotional* difference as part of his critique of an increasingly homogeneous and exhausted European civilisation. It is *European* 'mental-consciousness' that Lawrence, a discontent, rejects in his representation of Crèvecoeur's 'unconscious' harmony with his American surroundings. Crèvecoeur is 'renegade' as an *artist* when he returns to his European roots.

Mark Kinkead-Weekes, the most recent biographer of Lawrence's middle years, suggests that the value of the American essays is in part that they signal a change of direction in Lawrence's artistic and personal development which, crucially, had an impact on the writing he produced after *Women in Love*: 'these essays would form the basis for a new kind of *psychology* which would make him a different kind of novelist, and turn out to have educational and political implications' (*TE* 439, emphasis added). The question is, why would Lawrence need 'a new kind of psychology'? Part of the answer rests in a particular concentration in Lawrence's writing of this period on origins, which has a personal as well as a political inflection. The issue for Lawrence is bound up with his dissatisfaction and disenchantment with the spiritually bankrupt condition of Europe, the 'old world', as he sees it. His view might be summed up by Birkin's words to the gathered company at the end of the 'Continental' chapter of *Women in Love*: '"They say the lice crawl off a dying body", said Birkin, with a glare of bitterness. "So I leave England."' (*WL*, 396). Lawrence was emotionally, intellectually and literally doing the same.

In the 'new psychology' of the American essays and the books on the unconscious, Lawrence develops a language in which he metaphorises origin in non-historical contexts. He focuses on the developing foetus and the infant as he expounds and expands his psycho-biology. By doing so he establishes himself in possession of a discourse in which the birth of consciousness and the birth of self are continually addressed through metaphor. Aware of the elusiveness of his medium, language, metaphor becomes in Lawrence's writing an extremely personal mode of understanding. *Psychoanalysis* and *Fantasia* in particular are highly metaphorical pieces of writing, although 'discursive'. In the course of his examination the integrity of individual consciousness is persistently the bottom line. This is why we can say that despite his concentration in these books on the baby, Lawrence is in fact interested in the birth and re-birth of the *self*, not the birth of children. It is in the context of descriptions of developing individual selfhood that he develops a language of attraction and repulsion which he uses in several contexts to chart alternately the dependency on, and the repudiation of, one individual in relation to another. For example, in the chapter of *Fantasia* called 'Plexuses, Planes and so on', he describes the infant's pleasure in, and positive responsiveness to, the mother; the infant feels and displays a 'rapture' which 'surges from that first centre of the breast, the sun of the breast, the cardiac plexus' (*F&P*, 39). However, focused as he so often is on dualities, Lawrence also then describes the inevitable repudiation of this positive relationship as the infant necessarily differentiates itself from the mother: 'The mother is suddenly set apart, as an object of curiosity, coldly, sometimes dreamily, sometimes puzzled, sometimes mockingly observed.' This repudiation, Lawrence reports, has a physical basis, 'It is the reaction of the great voluntary plexus between the shoulders' (*F&P*, 40). The process so described is not posited as part of a direct progression, an ascendancy, into a state of greater physical and emotional maturity; it is rather a 'to and fro', a series of wordless negotiations between the infant and mother as the two individuals assert both their relation to each other *and* their independent selfhood. It is, after all, the integrity of the self which is at stake, and often the self in adulthood. It is in this context, recognising the metaphorical basis of Lawrence's thought about subjectivity, that we must revisit Lawrence's claim that *Fantasia*, at least, is an essay on 'Child Consciousness'.

Perhaps alone among his modernist contemporaries Lawrence made the genealogy of 'consciousness' his principal subject. With an emphasis different from his literary contemporaries, he writes about the birth and re-birth of the self without advocating self-consciousness. Uniquely, he locates the birth of consciousness not in thought or language but in the blood, and advocates the values of 'blood-consciousness' as a non-deliberate, non-cerebral feature of human being so that, in the books on the unconscious, the narrative returns to the sensual body. 'Blood-consciousness', 'the elemental consciousness of the blood' (183) is not the same thing as instinct which is a limited and circumscribed response to external stimuli; but it stands in for the wordless impulses from which human beings act. An over-developed 'mental-consciousness' might stamp it out for good, leaving the individual as little more than a cipher or automaton. 'Blood-consciousness' is one of Lawrence's most persistent metaphors; a hybrid construction in which the force of the word 'consciousness' is often overlooked by virtue of its proximity to 'blood'. By 'blood' Lawrence is not referring to racial criteria but to 'life-blood', a quality of the life force which has preoccupied him throughout.

Questions of self and body

The language of the body developed most extensively in *Fantasia* does more than correct the implausibilities of the mind/body opposition that Lawrence perceives in psychoanalysis (an opposition variously described by him as the difference between 'light' and 'dark' where 'dark' is positive). It represents the importance in Lawrence's personal philosophy of the 'lower body'. In the example quoted above from *Women in Love*, Ursula locates the source of Birkin's attractiveness for her in his loins and thighs. In *Lady Chatterley's Lover*, Connie Chatterley feels the transforming effects of sex with Mellors, herself deriving unsought pleasure from anal penetration where sensuality obliterates the learned responses of shame ('mental-consciousness') in relation to the sexual topography of anus and arse. What is evoked towards the conclusion of *Lady Chatterley's Lover* in a heterosexual context occurs much earlier (1918) in a version of Lawrence's essay on Whitman which could not be published at the time of composition because of its direct, positive expressions of male same-sex desire, expressions that are rarely so overt in Lawrence.[10] There Lawrence speaks of the importance of the base of the spine as a centre of positive feeling in the lower body, and the (changing) values he ascribes to the taboo entrances of the body, affirming, against the tenor of his more frequently voiced opinions, the possibility of satisfactory sexual relationships between men.[11]

It is in these broad contexts that Lawrence controversially essentialises women ('Woman is really polarized downwards, towards the centre of the earth . . . her deepest consciousness is in the loins and belly – *LCL*, 188), railing against self-consciousness (particularly in women), and opposing sex 'as an end in itself' to a 'sex relation' (186) achieved between 'unconscious' individuals. At this point it becomes necessary to underline a feature of the books on the unconscious, and particularly *Fantasia*, which, if not overlooked, is not often given critical priority even while so many commentators are interested in Lawrence's representations of gendered identities. Thorough analyses of representations of women in Lawrence's writing need to show cognisance of the determined and unequivocal misogyny of the bulk of *Fantasia*; and of the personal contexts underpinning what have to be among Lawrence's most negative statements on women occurring, significantly, alongside those on the psychoanalytic.

Chapters 7 and 8 of *Fantasia*, 'First Steps in Education' and 'Education and Sex in Man, Woman and Child', continue earlier themes in Lawrence's discursive writing although his position on education is never fixed. In the context of a work which is notionally about psychology and sex, his preoccupations with education become the basis for some stridently expressed opinions about the fundamental incompatibility of men and women in this over-conscious culture, and the subsequent need to treat their education differently. He rejects his earlier views on the co-existence in men *and* women of male *and* female elements: a sort of alchemy of sex he explores most thoroughly first in 'Study of Thomas Hardy'. In *Fantasia* his philosophy is one of partial segregation of the sexes and his language one of contamination and arrest; he emphasises the suffocation of masculine selfhood as a result of long-term proximity to the female. In 'First Steps in Education', in pursuit of keeping children at a level of unconditioned freedom, Lawrence advocates, however polemically, the segregation of the sexes in schools and, more radically, the denial of formal education until the age of ten. Boys are then to be schooled in physical activities and crafts and industrial skills; girls in a 'domestic workshop' and, briefly, some manual skill. The introduction of ideas to young minds is off the agenda; the arrival of ideas as the result of dynamic experience is allowed for. In a spectacularly undemocratic way (for Lawrence is not interested in democracy or equal rights), he denies a life of ideas to all but the few who can handle it; and never allows it to women. Women especially must be protected from ideas; girls must be kept busy perfecting the domestic arts: 'Anything to keep her busy, to prevent her reading and becoming self-conscious' (*F&P*, 87). Taken out of context this diatribe is ignorant and inexcusable; taken in context, even allowing for irony, it is hardly more acceptable, but the emphasis on 'self-consciousness' developed in the context of his writing on the psychosexual (where 'psychosexual' indicates the psychological dimensions of sexual identity) is the clue to a kind of reading. In the first place it is symptomatic of Lawrence's resistance to the cerebral, self-aware society around him. Although such resistance has sometimes been dealt with quite reductively by his commentators, it remains a feature of reading Lawrence. More specifically, as he perceives it, the anatomisation of sex and sexual difference, and the tendency to indulge in critiques of culture that are cynical and unresponsive to what he perceives to be a *natural* balance in human relationships, have resulted in a neurasthenic (neurotic), self-indulgent society of 'neuters' (87–88). Lest Lawrence's readers become too literal, the 'neuters' here signify a repudiation of the sexual self as the result of getting 'sex in the head', as Lawrence puts it elsewhere in *Fantasia of the Unconscious*. Consequently, as *Fantasia* proceeds, the debate turns defensively to 'manliness'. At adolescence boys are to be removed from their female relatives and given 'some real manly charge' (113). A symbolic and violent re-birth is imagined for boys to give them some respect for manliness. This imagined violence on the body, which spells out separateness, singleness, is a substitute for the breast-focused infant–mother physicality where the mothering of the infant is represented as potentially and dangerously all-consuming. At the beginning of 'Parent Love' (*Fantasia*, chapter 10) 'manly independence' (117) is the antidote to the repressive love of a mother for her son in her emotional substitution of him for the husband. The autobiographical drift of the argument is easy to see: in the first place Lawrence's emotional dependency on his biological mother, and a desire for her support and validation, are well documented. At the time of writing *Fantasia* a level of conflict in his married relationship also gave an edge to Lawrence's insistence on masculine independence; this is also represented in *Women in Love* and *Aaron's Rod*, novels which assert man's rejection of woman and of the *egoïsme à deux*. In the context of this repudiation of female society Lawrence re-establishes the traditional association of women with the physical life. Both his books on the unconscious privilege the psychosexual in the arguments they present on manliness.

Another level of anxiety is also associated with the body in *Fantasia*, more specifically the sick body. Lawrence was troubled for most of his life by diseases of the lungs and respiratory system. It would appear from his letters that he went into denial about his own afflictions when he could. Consequently, he was squeamish about tuberculosis when he had to confront it in others, most notably in his friend Katherine Mansfield. He pays some attention in his writings on the unconscious to the sicknesses of the physical body as psychosomatic symptoms. In the 'five senses' chapter of *Fantasia*, in a spirit perhaps of self-diagnosis, he bizarrely attributes illnesses of the lungs in children to their parenting: children who have been 'induced to love too much' (by their mothers) are susceptible to lung and heart ailments which are fatal in the long term: 'It means derangement and death at last' (59). Kidney failure, anaemia, diarrhoea and bad teeth are ascribed to excesses of feeling, forced, in the first instance, from the child by its demanding parents. No one can deny that Lawrence was familiar with physical suffering or that he knew about the capacity of the body to intrude on his own mental and physical activities. Possibly his re-drawing of the body in a positive light was to compensate for a weak constitution: breast, belly, hands, arms, elbows, wrists, thighs, knees, feet, face and buttocks are itemised in 'The Five Senses' as centres of positive feeling and communication, a mapping of the sensual body which finds representation in the fiction and which is in tune, post-Freud, with the holism of contemporary 'alternative' therapies. Consciously or not, these diagnostic episodes in *Fantasia* contradict the logic of Freud's case studies (Freud's published descriptions of his patients, their symptoms and their analysis under him). Such case studies represent now well-known instances of the disruptive and subversive unconscious in operation. Caught up in his own logic Lawrence asserts the conscious life of the body as the field that must be 'read' to a degree that 'mind' practically disappears from his books. To assert the primacy of the body over the opaque intangible structures of the mind; that is his position. It is a position which he knows to be iconoclastic.

There is another possibility aligned to the emphases in *Fantasia* on manliness: that Lawrence felt himself emasculated, feminised, by his illnesses in some fundamental way which might nourish his often strident assertions in that book about masculine singleness and masculine value. He may have seen himself in the increasingly sickly Katherine Mansfield to whom he wrote in 1918, '– on ne meurt pas: I almost want to let it be reflexive – on ne se meurt pas: *Point!*' (iii. 307). To his friend Beatrice Campbell, in the course of a prolonged bout of 'Flu' and its 'complications', he felt able to write, let us hope at least partly tongue in cheek: 'I . . . properly hate my condition, I can tell you. I suppose I'll get strong enough again one day to slap Frieda in the eye, in the proper marital fashion. At present I am reduced to vituperation' (iii. 335). So, in the books on the unconscious, women's association with the physical life is asserted, but a man's physical nature is underlined; the sick body is feminine, or feminised, while a healthy male body achieves a proud singleness; bodies male and female at best come temporarily into dynamic contact, and part; the body of the child develops appropriately only if the mind of the child is saved from self-consciousness, the 'mental-consciousness' of the age which results in unsexed 'neutered' beings.

It is at this point in his writing, at least in his revision of *Fantasia*, that Lawrence exhibits an increasing tendency to demonise the mother figure, in contrast to his earlier position. In the 'Parent Love' chapter, he inverts the Oedipal relationship described by Freud (in Lawrence's short-hand, the 'incest-motive'), making the mother into the prime mover. Figured as demanding degrees of love that are in excess of her lot, the mother who experiences a lack 'rabidly . . . turns to her son' (124). The adverb is telling. Confined to the family unit of man, woman and child that underpins his dissertation, Lawrence describes the feeling-frenzy into which woman falls if her husband, fulfilled in the marriage relation, is not yet man enough to withdraw into his own spiritual singleness, leaving her to mature quietly. If he fails to do this, and yet cannot satisfy his wife's hunger for excessive feeling, 'the unhappy woman beats about for her insatiable satisfaction, seeking whom she may *devour*. And usually, she turns to her child. *Here she provokes what she wants*' (125, emphasis added). What is destroyed in the child (and the principal focus is on *sons*) is his sexual self. His encounter with an ideal love has negated his capacity for physical love in his future relationships with women. So Lawrence reasons. It is a diagnosis that owes little to an understanding of Freud or psychoanalysis more broadly, and yet which owes much to anxieties about the psychoanalytic as a way of mapping family relations.

What are being described here are repudiations of Freud or what Lawrence took to be Freudian formulations, as starting places for his own genealogy of the unconscious. Aware of the importance of dream analysis in Freud's clinical practice, and concerned to reinforce his counter-views on involuntary physical responses to external conditions, Lawrence introduced a chapter on 'Sleep and Dreams' to *Fantasia*. This chapter begins as an extension of Lawrence's work on individuality as something that runs counter to a modern 'mass' culture. He builds on the content of the 'Cosmological' chapter which has little to do with psychoanalysis and everything to do with the establishment of a Lawrencean myth-system, a highly metaphorised narrative pressed into the service of a philosophy of harmony between the individual and the earth. It is into this schema that his representation of sleep and dream fits. Amplifying his emphasis on flows of energy through the body via the material centres of plexuses and ganglia, which many commentators have likened to chakras (although Lawrence typically reworks such concepts to accord with his own 'metaphysic' or personal philosophy), he develops the notion of an 'earth-current', a transforming medium which passes through the sleeping individual. As it does so it gives rise to random images. The mind is the neutral receptacle of these images which are generated from the *body's* centres of consciousness. 'Dream-images' they may be, but they are not to be ascribed personal psychological meanings unless, over-determined, they speak obviously to a conscious anxiety; otherwise, Lawrence insists, they are the result of somatic stimuli.

From this position, Lawrence manages obliquely to offer a criticism of the formal and narrative preoccupations of his contemporaries writing fiction. Speaking out against what he perceives to be a dominant narrative tendency in his modernist contemporaries, he argues that the disconnected fragments that characterise daily mental experience, 'swept' into the unconscious, lack significance as the basis of personal narratives: 'We should not think of taking all these papers, piecing them together, and making a marvellous book of them, prophetic of the future and pregnant with the past' (164). With this sideswipe at his contemporaries interested in what Virginia Woolf called 'the dark places of psychology',[12] Lawrence tries to disrupt the formal links between narratives of the unconscious and modernist writing. His description of sleep draws attention to the material body: the physical mechanism of sleep shifts the focus from uncanny parables of the self in dreaming to the physical centres, and thereby constitutes a rejection of psychoanalytical accounts of the subject, real or imagined. When Freud resurfaces in the chapter the context is once again a posited sex relation with the mother or dominant women within the family unit. What is emphasised is a rejection during sleep of the 'emotional image' of mother and sister (168); his resistance to the disturbance caused by this imagery is uppermost in the male dreamer. Familiarly now, this resistance is to the arrest in his individual development caused by the memory of the emotional tie: it spells fear, not desire (the two are polarised in Lawrence's philosophy). Without informed reference to Freud's notion of 'wish-fulfilment', what is represented is an idiosyncratic repudiation of a version of the contemporary wisdom on dreaming, underpinned by Lawrence's rejection of the language of psychoanalysis.

Lawrence did not write explicitly or extensively about the discipline of psychology or psychoanalysis after *Fantasia*. In 1927 he published 'A New

Theory of Neuroses: A Review of *The Social Basis of Consciousness* by Trigant Burrow', and references were made to the psyche and what is referred to as 'subjective–objective consciousness' in a discussion of individuality as he developed an essay on his contemporary, 'John Galsworthy' (final version, 1928). Nevertheless, after 1922, that watershed year for literary modernism, Lawrence was committed to writing discursively and developed themes and debates begun or extended in his books on the unconscious. Of particular interest are the writings on 'manliness' and gendered identities in many of the essays that were revised and collected in *Assorted Articles* (1930). 'Enslaved by Civilization' takes up the debate about the education of boys; 'Matriarchy' is where Lawrence refers to social responsibility in the hands of women and posits a social space for men freed up to bond in brotherhood; there is a raft of essays on 'modern' women including 'Insouciance', 'Give Her a Pattern', 'Do Women Change?' and 'Cocksure Women and Hensure Men'. In *Assorted Articles* and elsewhere, debates on masculinity developed in *Psychoanalysis* and *Fantasia* are combined with discussions of 'civilization', as in 'Is England Still a Man's Country?', 'Germans and English', 'The State of Funk' and 'On Coming Home'. 'On Being a Man' and 'On Human Destiny', written shortly after the publication of *Fantasia*, combine some of these themes with reference to states of 'human consciousness' explored in the books on the unconscious but on the whole the debates and, crucially, Lawrence's mode of expression, have moved on.[13]

That Lawrence was troubled by the popularity of psychoanalysis cannot be denied. That he was frequently scathing about its fundamental premises, as he understood them, is a matter of record. What is less frequently asserted, and what may usefully be borne in mind, is Lawrence's concern with the *language* of psychoanalysis, the given terms with which to articulate the complexity of the unconscious life.

NOTES

1 Sigmund Freud (1856–1939). Freud's associates included Carl Gustav Jung (1875–1961) and Alfred Adler (1870–1937), who departed from Freud's theories and developed their own schools of psychoanalytic thought.
2 For a range of approaches, see Frederick J. Hoffman, *Freudianism and the Literary Mind*, 2nd edn (Baton Rouge, LA: Louisiana State University Press, 1957); Daniel A. Weiss, *Oedipus in Nottingham: D. H. Lawrence* (Seattle: University of Washington Press, 1962); Murray M. Schwartz, 'D. H. Lawrence and Psychoanalysis: An Introduction', *D. H. Lawrence Review*, 10, 3 (Fall 1977); Gilles Deleuze and Félix Guattari, *Anti-Oedipus: Capitalism and Schizophrenia*, trans. Robert Hurley *et al.* (London: The Athlone Press, 1984; repr. 1990); R. A. Gekoski, 'Freud and English Literature 1900–30', in *The Context of English Literature 1900–1930*, ed. Michael Bell (London: Methuen, 1980), pp. 186–217;

Elizabeth Wright, *Psychoanalytic Criticism: Theory in Practice* (London and New York: Routledge, 1984; repr. 1989); Anne Fernihough, 'The Tyranny of the Text: Lawrence, Freud and the Modernist Aesthetic', in *Modernism and the European Unconscious*, ed. Peter Collier and Judy Davies (Cambridge: Polity Press; Oxford: Basil Blackwell, 1990), pp. 47–63; Linda Ruth Williams, *Sex in the Head: Visions of Femininity and Film in D. H. Lawrence* (Hemel Hempstead: Harvester Wheatsheaf, 1993); 'Lawrence and the Psychoanalytic', special issue of the *D. H. Lawrence Review*, ed. Howard Booth, Elizabeth Fox and Fiona Becket, 27, 2–3 (1997/1998).

3 John Middleton Murry in *Algemeen Handelsblad*, 31 March 1923. Reprinted in *D. H. Lawrence: The Critical Heritage*, ed. R. P. Draper (London: Routledge and Kegan Paul, 1970), pp. 184–87; p. 186.

4 See Sigmund Freud, *Art and Literature*, The Penguin Freud Library, 14 (Harmondsworth: Penguin, 1990).

5 See Alfred Booth Kuttner, untitled review of *Sons and Lovers*, *New Republic*, 2 (10 April 1915), pp. 255–57. Reprinted in *D. H. Lawrence: The Critical Heritage*, ed. Draper, pp. 76–80. See also Alfred Booth Kuttner, 'A Freudian Appreciation', *Psychoanalytic Review*, 3 (July 1916), pp. 295–317. Reprinted in *D. H. Lawrence: 'Sons and Lovers' Casebook*, ed. Gāmini Salgādo (London: Macmillan, 1969).

6 See Richard Noll, *The Jung Cult: Origins of a Charismatic Movement* (London: Fontana, 1996), p. 107. See also 'The Otto Gross – Frieda Weekley Correspondence', transcribed, translated and annotated by John Turner with Cornelia Rumpf-Worthen and Ruth Jenkins, special issue of the *D. H. Lawrence Review*, 22, 2 (Summer 1990).

7 René Descartes (1596–1650). French philosopher who expounded a theory of dualism.

8 Elizabeth Wright, *Psychoanalytic Criticism: Theory in Practice* (London and New York: Routledge, 1984; repr. 1989).

9 These material centres of feeling are also outlined at the end of 'The Two Principles', in *The Symbolic Meaning*, excluded from *Studies in Classic American Literature* (*Symbolic*, 188–89).

10 See the unpublished 'Prologue' chapter to *Women in Love*, printed in the Cambridge edition of the novel (1987), pp. 489–506. See also Hugh Stevens's chapter in this volume.

11 For a discussion of the unpublished essay on Whitman see *TE*, 453–57.

12 Virginia Woolf, 'Modern Fiction', in *The Essays of Virginia Woolf*, ed. Andrew McNeillie (London: The Hogarth Press, 1986–), iv (1994), 157–65 (p. 162).

13 Most of these essays are reprinted in *PII*. For both versions of 'John Galsworthy' see *Hardy*, 207–20, 247–52. In a recent discussion of some of these essays, Howard J. Booth examines the relation between Lawrence's thought on psychoanalysis, on race and on empire. See '"Give me *differences*": Lawrence, Psychoanalysis, and Race', *D. H. Lawrence Review*, 27, 2–3 (1997/1998), pp. 171–96.

13

SANDRA M. GILBERT

Apocalypse now (and then). Or, D. H. Lawrence and the swan in the electron

Look then
where the father of all things swims in a mist of atoms
electrons and energies, quantums and relativities
mists, wreathing mists,
like a wild swan or a goose . . .

And in the dark unscientific I feel the drum-winds of his wings
Lawrence, 'Give Us Gods'

Prophecy *versus* postmodernism: Lawrence at the millennium

Inevitably, so Lawrence might have said, death and rebirth, or at any rate *transformation* of some kind, have been both projects and subjects for the much anticipated and perhaps overhyped millennium, an event towards which he and his cohort of modernists seem to have been far more sensitively attuned than we ourselves. Rough beasts and second comings, chantings in orgy on summer morns, new styles of will, deaths of the old gang, strange lights in the sky, doves descending and swans arising: the apocalyptic ambitions of Lawrence's generation loom as grandly over ours as Stravinsky heaves high over MTV, Virginia Woolf over Fay Weldon.

To be sure, countless futurologists, numerologists, Pyramidologists, theosophists, astrologists, satanists, Cayce-ites, pentecostalists, and any number of other old-school and New Age prophets have pursued their visions among us. From Ruth Montgomery, an erstwhile journalist who asserted in her *Herald of the New Age* that in the summer of 1999 the Earth would '"flip" on to its side', with the result that the poles would 'shift to South America and the Pacific respectively' to the British esotericist Benjamin Creme, who claimed that the Himalayan master 'Lord Maitreya' had descended from his mountain fastness to inaugurate the Age of Aquarius predicted by Madame Blavatsky in the nineteenth century, acolytes of pop apocalypse arose in the 1990s to predict either the beginning of the end or the end of the beginning or both.[1] Extra-terrestrials would soon arrive to redeem us, said some, while others claimed that a host of quasi-angelic ETs would sweep the best of us off to the stars so that at least a few humans could survive the earthquakes and tidal waves generated by the wild careenings of the north and south poles across the earth's surface.

'Signs are taken for wonders', declared Eliot's Gerontion, that dull head among the windy spaces of the pre-'postmodern', or as Yeats so infamously put it, 'The best lack all conviction, while the worst, Are full of passionate intensity.'[2] 'Are we nothing, already, but the lapsing of a great dead past?' asked Lawrence in 'To Let Go or To Hold On –?', one of his late *Pansies*, commenting in another that the living dead in 'their seething minds / have phosphorescent teeming white words / of putrescent wisdom' (*Poems*, 429, 441). Even here the modernists would seem to have anticipated us and thus trumped us in their trumpetings of doom as well as of transformation. Surrounded by visionaries who are merely what the French call *médiatique* while struggling all too belatedly with the compelling fantasies of powerful precursors, it is perhaps no wonder that our potentially serious seers are contorted with just the sort of irony Lawrence so often deplored and so roundly repudiated. We 'have already passed [the Apocalypse] unawares', Jean Baudrillard has lamented, 'and now find ourselves in the situation of having overextended our own finalities, of having short circuited our own perspectives, and of already being in the hereafter, that is, without horizon and without hope'.[3] Whether or not Catherine Keller is right in arguing that precisely because we are 'paralysed by irony, deactivated, we collude with the cruder endtime scenarios of our period',[4] it is certain that trapped in trivia, muffled in the mechanised deadliness of a dailiness more virtual than vital, even (alas) more vitiated than vicious, most ambitious artists must wonder how we can produce texts of 'Apocalypse now' that are even remotely competitive with modernist imaginings of 'Apocalypse then'. And considering that we are such incorrigible sceptics, why *should* we?

Lawrence's comparatively straightforward imaginings of a personal as well as a cultural apocalypse marked by death and transfiguration may help explain why in the 1980s and 1990s he was deemed unfashionable in some academic quarters. Lawrence took his own and his society's life – and afterlife – so seriously that his reputation, in a sense his 'afterlife' as a writer, has probably suffered. Because he is perhaps the ultimate pre-'postmodernist' in his repudiation of the hopeless, horizonless aesthetic cultivated by disciples of, say, Baudrillard or Beckett or even Judith Butler, Lawrence offers us a vision many *au courant* intellectuals find embarrassing to espouse. For, paradoxically, at his best the author of *Sons and Lovers*, *Women in Love* and

Lady Chatterley's Lover is, *pace* Yeats, full of passionate intensity, while at our worst we ourselves lack all conviction, not to mention passion. Like a number of other writers of the modernist period, he has been labelled a proto-fascist reactionary, a racist, a misogynist, an elitist, and no doubt in a range of other formulations a paradigmatic, politically incorrect Bad Boy. Yet though with-it academics may find him distasteful or excessively intense, the appearance of four new biographical volumes in the last decade proves that he continues to enthrall readers and writers alike, despite his massive peccadilloes. Or perhaps, in fact, it is precisely Lawrence's intellectual as well as political incorrectness that haunts and intrigues so many of us; perhaps – as scholars of his life along with his art – we are bemused, even bewitched, by the ways *he doesn't* fit into our current systems of thought.

For not only is Lawrence the famously self-proclaimed poet of the present in what has become a kind of cultural afterwards, an era of postmodernity, he is also the prophet of what used to be called 'primitivism' in an age when the very concept 'primitive' has been castigated as Eurocentric and chauvinistic. He is the priest of spontaneity in an era of parody, the sage of sacred sex in *Playboy* country. He is the acolyte of intuition, of blood-wisdom, of mystical 'lapsings' from consciousness – the impassioned enemy of mechanised rationality – in a thought-tormented, computerised, hypertextual, theory-driven culture. Indeed, to evoke Keats, Lawrence is an unreconstructed Romantic who is 'certain of the holiness of the Heart's affections and the truth of Imagination'[5] in a virulently *anti-* as well as post-Romantic age. Thus too, and maybe most troublesome of all, Lawrence is the paradigm of authorial energy, the proponent of authorial *authority*, in a period when that mystical being once known as 'the author' has sickened, failed, faded, been pronounced dead, and buried with considerable deconstructive fanfare.

Wringing the neck of sophistication: Lawrence and modernism

Of course, Lawrence's thought was in notable ways a product of its time. Though many of his views now seem eccentric, he began his career as an exceptionally talented, neo-Romantic, vaguely Swinburnean, vaguely Hardyesque schoolteacher-poet-novelist but shortly after his first meeting with the free-thinking, free-love-loving Frieda von Richthofen Weekley he began to develop a set of what he later called 'pollyanalytics' that were profoundly influenced by avant-garde German thinkers (from Nietzsche to Freud to Otto Gross). And the apparently spontaneous and improvisational style of 'continual, slightly modified repetition' (*WL*, 486) in which he propounded his creed had affinities with German Expressionism too, as well as with the pulsing incantations of Walt Whitman's *vers libre* as mediated by (among many English Whitmanites) that other post-Swinburnean priest of love, Edward Carpenter. Nevertheless, though Lawrence's aesthetic style *and* intellectual substance were rooted in fertile ground that nurtured distinctively modern ways of seeing and modes of being, his was by and large the road not taken by English-language modernism, as we now understand that intellectual movement. In a sense, indeed, his life was a romance of *anti*-modernism, or at the least of an *other* modernism, a modernism that went underground in the Pound/Eliot era, as Michael Bell observes in chapter 10 of this volume.

Clearly the reception of Lawrence's distinctive modernism and to some extent the very nature of that modernism itself had origins in the social gulf that separated him not just from Eliot, Ford and even Pound but also from, among other contemporaries, the well-bred 'Bloomsberries' who wielded such cultural power. Compare, for instance, the tone of affectionate mockery in which Virginia Woolf wrote of 'Tom Great Tom' in his 'four-piece suit' with the faint upper-crust sneer that animates her dismissive remark that Lawrence's late *Pansies* and *Nettles* 'read like the sayings that small boys scribble upon stiles to make housemaids jump and titter'.[6] Or consider the even more scathing, High Church contempt with which, later still, Eliot himself formulated his posthumous attack on the provenance of Lawrence's 'strange gods': 'Nothing could be much drearier (so far as one can judge from his own account), than the vague hymn-singing pietism which seems to have consoled the miseries of Lawrence's mother, and which does not seem to have provided her with any firm principles by which to scrutinize the conduct of her sons.'[7]

What was fundamentally most damning, however, was what is still probably most problematic about Lawrence: his own profoundly anti-Wildean commitment to the importance of being earnest in what had already, with the ascendancy of Eliot, become an age of irony and parody, self-consciously stylish order and allusively ambiguous myth. For earnest is what Lawrence was, despite his famous gift for mimicry, his high spirits, his wry sense of the comic. His alternative modernism sought in all seriousness to engage the chaos and pathos of the present without a single concession to the knowing smile of the Bloomsbury drawing-room, the disaffected twitch of a Laforguian eyebrow. True, he knew how his work would be received and dismissed ('Oh leave off saying I want you to be savages') yet even so he insisted on reiterating a commitment to what he called 'the new', a *naïveté* 'sufficiently sophisticated to wring the neck of sophistication'[8]:

> Tell me, is the gentian savage, at the top of its coarse stem?
> Oh what in you can answer to this blueness?   (*Poems*, 684)

Perhaps most 'naïve' of all, Lawrence's was a modernism that bloomed into mystical and mysterious risks 'at the top of its [seemingly] coarse stem', a modernism – more specifically – that confronted, transcribed and sought (with varying degrees of success) to analyse the sexual anxieties, class tensions and racial conflicts most contemporaries burlesqued, repressed or suppressed. With seamless and often shocking candour, he addressed such issues, in novels, stories, poems, essays, letters. Driven literally as well as allegorically around the world by the energy of his need to excavate and analyse the lumpier secrets buried in the west's cultural unconscious, the man who wrote *Sons and Lovers*, *Women in Love* and *The Plumed Serpent* was often an all too embarrassingly sincere archaeologist of what have since become politically incorrect emotions. From his famously proto-Freudian analysis, in *Sons and Lovers*, of the fearsome milk of mother love, to his disturbing transcription, in *Women in Love*, of an openly extremist meditation on the apocalyptic 'dissolution' represented by an African statue of a woman in childbirth, Lawrence cultivated a potentially appalling spiritual honesty. Boasted the intrepid Frieda, 'he dares to come out in the open and plants his stuff down bald and naked'.[9] At the same time, he never minded changing his mind, any more than he minded changing his place. 'You don't catch me going back on my whiteness', he declared just after leaving Ceylon in 1922 (iv. 234), but two years later he praised Forster's *Passage to India* with the comment that 'the repudiation of our white bunk is genuine, sincere, and pretty thorough' (v. 143).

Given such fierce fidelity to what he experienced as the truth of his own imagination, it is perhaps no wonder that, along with Yeats, Lawrence was one of the twentieth century's most brilliant English-language 'apocalyptists', an oracular elegist of his own life as well as of 'our white bunk' whose visions of cultural as well as personal death-and-transfiguration were 'genuine, sincere, and pretty thorough'. Etymologically the very word 'apocalypse' is derived from the Greek *Apo-kalypso,* meaning 'to unveil; thus to reveal, to disclose', which as Catherine Keller observes 'Prebiblically . . . connotes the marital stripping of the veiled virgin'.[10] From our perspective, therefore, John of Patmos's powerfully authored Apocalypse or Book of Revelation is both sexually incorrect in its vehement vaunting of the empowered male gaze at the haplessly stripped female subject ('I John *saw*') and theoretically suspect in its egocentric and logocentric assumption that there can be *a* gaze, *a* Word, a singular and uniquely knowable subject. Yet such a rending of the veil between us and the naked truth of history – such a revelation or vision, that is, of the naked truth of generation (death) and regeneration (birth) – was a project that haunted Lawrence as it did Yeats, a project central in major prose texts the two produced almost simultaneously in the 1920s and in a number of late or (in the case of Yeats) relatively late poems associated with those texts.

In a sense, indeed, Yeats's *A Vision* and Lawrence's *Apocalypse* have the same title, but in any case they have very much the same goal: the stripping of veils from the primal scenes and secrets out of which time itself, as we humans experience it, is over and over again constituted. Of the two authors, Yeats was of course more famously a would-be mage or adept of the hermetic wisdom he called 'mummy truths', but Lawrence was also widely read in mystical lore. Indeed, both writers could no doubt teach a thing or two to the New Age 'popalyptists' among us. What to my mind most interestingly links these acolytes of an anti-ironic modernism, however (and in this respect Yeats was surely as anti-ironic as Lawrence), is their characteristic sexualisation of the apocalyptic moment, a visionary strategy that seems to be the literary consequence of a literalisation of the etymology of *apo-kalyptos*: the stripping of the nymph or virgin, the unveiling of the bride who is in a sense what Walter Benjamin very differently defined as the angel of history.[11]

The lady and the dragon: Lawrence and apocalypse

> And there appeared a great wonder in heaven; a woman clothed with the sun, and the moon under her feet, and upon her head a crown of twelve stars: and she being with child cried, travailing in birth, and pained to be delivered.
>
> And there appeared another wonder in heaven: and behold, a great red dragon . . . and the dragon stood before the woman . . . [and] she brought forth a man child . . . And there was war in heaven. (*A*, 119)

This 'pagan birth-myth is very brief', Lawrence explains in his late commentary on the Book of Revelation, yet though a mere 'fragment' it is 'really the pivot of the Apocalypse' (119). Indeed, he continues, 'this wonder-woman clothed in the sun and standing upon the crescent of the moon' is 'splendidly suggestive of the great goddess of the east, the great Mother' who looms so 'far, far back in history . . . in the days when matriarchy was still the natural order' that it was very likely 'a book of her "mystery" and initiation ritual which gave rise to the existing Apocalypse' (120–21). Or rather, he implies, John's Apocalypse was founded on 'a book of her "mystery"' coupled with the mystery of that 'other wonder', the 'Dragon'. And, clearly, if the mother goddess's mystery is that of the womb, the dragon's is that of the Lawrencean phallus, for coiling 'within us potent and waiting, like a serpent', the dragon 'is the symbol of the fluid, rapid, startling movement of life within us', a 'potency which can lie quite dormant . . . and yet be ready to leap out unexpectedly' (123). The Greeks, Lawrence adds, would have called this potency the 'god' in a man while 'modern philosophers may call it' by the all too 'thin' words 'Libido or *Elan Vital*', but in any case 'in his good aspect, the dragon is the great vivifier, the great enhancer of the whole universe' (123–24).

That the confrontation between wonder-woman and wonder-dragon is *au fond* a sort of primal scene is surprisingly enough a point Lawrence does not specifically explore, but it is clearly implicit in the structure of his own narrative as well as that of the episode from Revelation that he excerpts, in which the mystical mother travails while the 'great red dragon' 'stands' before her. And that this primal scene of generation, degeneration and ultimately regeneration moves history itself *is* a point the author makes quite explicit. 'The long green dragon with which we are so familiar on Chinese things is the dragon in his good aspect of life-bringer, life-giver, life-maker, *vivifier* [emphasis mine]' (124), Lawrence comments, while 'the red dragon is the great "potency" of the cosmos in its hostile and destructive activity'. Moreover, the green dragon

> becomes with time the red dragon. What was our joy and our salvation becomes with time, at the end of the time-era, our bane and our damnation. What was a creative god, Ouranos, Kronos, becomes at the end of the time-period a destroyer and a devourer. The god of the beginning of an era is the evil principle at the end of that era. For time still moves in cycles [and the] good potency of the beginning of the Christian era is now the evil potency of the end.
>
> (125)

It hardly seems necessary to note the Yeatsian parallels in this cyclical view of history, and in any case Phillip Marcus has examined them in some detail in an incisive analysis of 'Lawrence, Yeats and "the Resurrection of the Body"' that deals primarily with *The Escaped Cock*, while W. Y. Tindall long ago demonstrated Lawrence's use of occult sources on which Yeats also was heavily dependent.[12] Nor is it necessary to note the centrality in *A Vision* of the primal scene between Zeus and Leda that for the Irish writer constitutes at least one among a set of *primi mobili* of history, recurrent annunciations defined in the chapter entitled 'Dove or Swan?' Rather, I would like to focus not just on the remarkable similarity between the two writers' virtually voyeuristic acts of attention to the sexual couplings at the heart of time but also on Lawrence's varied and often, I think, quite richly detailed poetic efforts at the linguistic *enactment* of key aspects of such ritual events. For what gives Lawrence's last imaginings of personal as well as cultural death and transfiguration their special resonance, it seems to me, is his unselfconscious, perhaps indeed his desperate, willingness to move from wistful gazing to wishful *apo-kalypso* to wilfully empowered fantasies of participation in the sexual mysteries of metamorphosis. Thus I want to argue that after many episodes of what he had earlier called 'sore-hearted looking' at, for instance, the 'marriage of the living dark' consummated in one of the early drafts of 'Bavarian Gentians', the poet shamanistically becomes, first, a member of the wedding and then, both personally – as an isolate being passing through the great doors of death and rebirth – and publicly – as a representative of his culture-in-crisis – the new soul who is a product of that union.

It is in his own Leda poems, of course, as well as, more obviously, in his better-known and rather scandalously sexual late painting depicting just how bird meets girl that Lawrence most obviously (and soreheartedly, or at least wistfully) *looks* at the moment of annunciation which also so preoccupied Yeats. Beginning with 'Swan' and including 'Leda', 'Give Us Gods' and 'The Spiral Flame', this sequence – included in *Pansies* – evidently evolved out of the draft entitled 'Religion', a piece in which the poet frankly and truculently argued for the authoritative structures of patriarchal religion ('Life is nothing without religion / and religion nothing without the father of all things / stooping over his bride') and *against* the scientific world-view represented by the 'complicated little [atomic] knots' of modern physics, in which 'the electron behaves and misbehaves incomprehensibly . . . and [makes a] considerable mess that isn't even worth the name of universe any more' (*Poems*, 949–50). As Lawrence struggled to refute such notions, 'the father of all things' appears to have surfaced in his consciousness as 'a wild swan, or a goose' swimming (as he notes in a passage from which I have drawn my epigraph) 'in a mist of atoms/electrons and energies, quantums and relativities'. What quickly fired his imagination, however, as it had Yeats's before him, was the apocalyptic potential quite literally incarnated in the coupling of such a creature with a human female. In meditating on this coupling, both poets were working with an iconographic tradition that goes back at least as far as Correggio through, later, Boucher and Géricault, and that, as Bram Dijkstra has most recently shown, was particularly absorbing to artists during the nineteenth-century *fin de siècle*.[13] As Yeats and Lawrence indicated in various ways, however, both were fairly conscious of their swerves from that tradition, which by the time they embarked on their verses had become rather more prurient than reverent.

Reported Yeats, whose Leda poem had been solicited by the editor of a political review, 'I thought "After the individualist, demagogic movement, founded by Hobbes and popularised by the Encyclopedists and the French Revolution, we have a soil so exhausted that it cannot grow that crop again for centuries." Then I thought "Nothing is now possible but some movement, or birth, from above preceded by some violent annunciation."'[14] And Lawrence clearly had the same feeling. The way they had for Yeats too, however, 'bird and lady' quickly 'took possession of the scene' as the poet became enthralled by his own desirous gaze at a savagely sexual conflagration. Note that Lawrence's series begins with a relatively calm contemplation of the father-god-as-swan:

> Far-off
> at the core of space
> at the quick
> of time
> beats
> and goes still
> the great swan upon the waters of all endings,
> the swan within vast chaos, within the electron.

But even this first poem in the group, 'Swan', quickly moves towards voyeuristic marvellings along with some barely disguised Oedipal envy of the endlessly phallic 'father of all things' who 'stoops, now / in the dark / upon us', because

> he is treading our women
> and we men are put out
> as the vast white bird
> furrows our featherless women
> with unknown shocks
> and stamps his black marsh-feet on their white and marshy flesh.

(Poems, 435–36)

By the midpoint of the series – the long 'Give Us Gods' – moreover, the poet is quite explicit about the sexual responsiveness of 'our women', from whom he has now become estranged, admitting that they are 'our weird women' since they have been 'stamped' or imprinted with the mark of the swan, who 'treads' them 'with dreams and thrusts that make them cry in their sleep'. Still, estranged though he is (and even, as he punningly notes, more than a little 'put out'), this enthralled seer has nonetheless the power of his own prophetic insight: 'Where there is woman there is swan', he declares, adding tauntingly, 'Do you think, scientific man, you'll be father of your own babies? / Don't imagine it. / There'll be babies born that are cygnets, O my soul!' Nor are the weirdly – that is to say, *fatedly* – possessed women of his vision exactly downtrodden by the deific swan who 'treads' them and evokes their entranced, orgasmic utterances. Politically incorrect though it may seem, Lawrence's vision of 'bird and lady' is by and large produced from the voyeuristic perspective of a non-participant in the scene who can celebrate but never rival either the 'feathered glory' of the swan's phallus or the female generative potency with which that 'glory' intersects to (re)produce a new history.[15]

Indeed, as Lawrence's resignation to the weirdness of 'our women' implies, Leda and all those other virgin brides of the god are not necessarily passive vessels, innocent and inert. The poet's comment on the inseparability of woman and swan ('Where there is woman there is swan') leaves tantalisingly open the question of which came first, lady or bird, and in doing so privileges female desire just as Yeats himself had in a speech he gave to one of the characters in *The Herne's Egg*, who remarks that some women 'make / An image of god or bird or beast / To feed their sensuality', adding that such mythographers as Ovid never 'knew / What lonely lust dragged down the gold / That crept on Danae's lap, nor knew / What rose against the moony feathers / When Leda lay upon the grass'.[16] Freudian in its modernity, such a comment implies that it may indeed be female desire which propels the cycles of generation forward. Perhaps, Yeats suggests, Leda only *seems* to be a passive vessel, terrified of the white rush and the feathered glory; perhaps it was *her* will that called the god's will into being. Similarly, Lawrence asserts that the apocalyptic congress of human mother and divine father is at the very least an erotic encounter between figures whose equal share in the narrative of origins excludes merely human males.

Even while much of Lawrence's voyeuristic late poetry was written from the marginalised perspective of a non-participant in the primal scene, such exclusion from both power and pleasure elicited mixed feelings from this writer who had always wanted not only his readers but himself to be, as he once put it, 'in the thick of the scrimmage' (v. 201). By contrast with the Yeats of *Supernatural Songs*, who abjectly positioned himself as the hermit Ribh reading his 'holy book' in the light of the sexual conflagration generated by the ecstatic couplings of two ghostly lovers, Lawrence hoped for what we would now define as a piece of the action.[17] And interestingly, in 'Spiral Flame', the last poem of his Leda/swan series, he does imagine himself joining the party, through a move by which he not only assimilates the swan's potency into himself and all (human) men but also implies a linguistic connection between, on the one hand, the encounter of wonder-dragon and wonder-woman, and, on the other, that of (to reuse Yeats's formulation) bird and lady. Foregrounding a key word he uses in *Apocalypse* to characterise the potency of the (good) magic dragon – 'the life-bringer, life-giver, life-maker, *vivifier* [emphasis mine]' – he declares in this most overtly revolutionary of the poems in his sequence that the traditional Christian God is dead, along with His ancient Graeco-Roman precursors:

> Yet, O my young men, there is a vivifier.
> There is a swan-like flame that curls round the centre of space
> and flutters at the core of the atom,
> there is a spiral flame-tip that can lick our little atoms into fusion

so we roar up like bonfires of vitality
and fuse in a broad hard flame of many men in a oneness.

And lest there be any misunderstanding about who and what is here being
'vivified', the poet goes on to extol the 'ruddy god in our veins . . . fiery god
in our genitals!', adding that this now humanised swan-potency can, will and
must bring about a specifically sociocultural apocalypse:

And the same flame that fills us with life, it will dance and burn the house down,
all the fittings and elaborate furnishings
and all the people that go with the fittings and the furnishings,
the upholstered dead that sit in deep arm-chairs.

(Poems, 439–40)

Bird, flame and the enactment of renewal: Lawrence has here begun to
imagine himself as a phallic member of a wedding into whose plot he had
also ambivalently inscribed himself as both the voyeuristic but paralysed
non-participant Clifford Chatterley and the revisionary father-cum-nurturer
of baby birds whose name, 'Mellors', dramatically revises the name of that
primordial father 'Morel'. By the time he produces 'Phoenix', moreover, his
most triumphantly emblematic vision of death-and-rebirth, lady and bird
and flame together with the very object of resurrection have become one, as
the poet asserts that

The phoenix renews *her* youth
only when she is burnt, burnt alive, burnt down
to hot and flocculent ash.
Then the small stirring of a new small bub in the nest.

(Poems, 728, emphases mine)

'Are you willing to be sponged out . . .?': Lawrencean death and rebirth

'Phoenix' begins with oblivion ('Are you willing to be sponged out, erased,
cancelled . . . dipped into oblivion?'), a poignant but quite understandable
preoccupation of Lawrence's in those exhausted, pain-stricken last months
he spent, dying, in the south of France – and a preoccupation that would
seem to have little immediate relevance to the primal scene at which he so
desirously gazed in both *Apocalypse* and the Leda sequence. I want finally
to argue, however, that in the greatest of Lawrence's *Last Poems* the act of
looking and a homage to oblivion paradoxically merge, as the writer's gaze
at an episode of apocalyptic (re)generation becomes a looking at a (or *the*?)
primal scene inexorably enacted in and through oblivion. Most obviously,
this poet guides himself with the 'blue, forked torch' of a Bavarian gentian,
that oxymoronic 'torch-flower of the blue-smoking darkness', into the

voluptuary 'halls of Dis' where the death-god enfolds as his bride the wonder-woman here named Persephone (though she might as well be called Leda). Then, in one draft of 'Bavarian Gentians', Lawrence finds himself transfixed by the transfiguring illumination that 'torches of darkness' shed on the primal scene while in another he imagines himself more intimately implicated in the episode – 'wedding guest/at the marriage of the living dark' – and truly, therefore, a member of the wedding.

Where, literally, is this marriage performed if not in the bulb or, to draw a word from 'Phoenix', the 'bub' of the gentian that is the core or heart of its new life, out of which fresh roots must descend in the underground awakening and a fresh stem be born in a renewed journey towards light and sight? In a first, pencilled version of the poem, entitled 'Glory of Darkness', Lawrence wrote 'it is dark / and the door is open / to the depths', adding

> and all the dead
> and all the dark great ones of the underworld
> down there, down there
> down the blue depths of mountain gentian flowers
> cold, cold
> are gathering to a wedding in the [winter] dark
> down the dark blue path
>
> (*Poems*, 959 – brackets Lawrence's)

And isn't this botanically accurate journey 'down there, down there' into the cold and the oblivion of the underworld precisely the journey that he himself will take in his superbly daring 'Ship of Death'? 'What is it?' asked Lawrence in 'Medlars and Sorb-Apples',

> What is it, in the grape turning raisin,
> In the medlar, in the sorb-apple,
> Wineskins of brown morbidity,
> Autumnal excrementa;
> What is it that reminds us of white gods?
>
> Gods nude as blanched nut-kernels,
> Strangely, half-sinisterly flesh-fragrant
> As if with sweat,
> And drenched with mystery.   (*Poems*, 280)

As early as this poem from *Birds, Beasts and Flowers*, the poet had begun a visionary identification with the godly soul of the seed or bulb (a god 'nude as [a] blanched nutkerne[l]') who must each Fall undertake a lonely journey down 'the winding, leaf-clogged, silent lanes of hell'. But by the time he wrote his more necessitous *Last Poems* he was ready to claim that for souls, as for seeds, the way up and the way down are one and the same.

Certainly Lawrence made his increasingly urgent sense of the parallels among flowers/bulbs/seeds and the (human) dead quite clear in another of his most important late texts, *Sketches of Etruscan Places*, observing in 'Cerveteri' that 'the etruscan cities vanished as completely as flowers [but] the tombs, like *bulbs*, were underground' (*SEP*, 13; emphasis mine), and commenting in 'Tarquinia' that under the hill of the necropolis 'the dead lie buried and quick, as *seeds*, in their painted houses underground' (33–34; emphasis mine), for to 'the peoples of the great natural religions the afterlife was a continuing of the wonder-journey of life' (130). And 'The Ship of Death' is of course explicitly a record of the 'longest' voyage in that 'wonder-journey': 'the dark flight down oblivion'. Here, however, Lawrence makes his most radical, even breathtaking move from a voyeuristic vision of the primal scene to a ritually imagined participation in the mystery of its secret generativity, as he follows his vegetation god 'nude as [a] blanched nut-kerne[l]' into the very centre of the underworld.

The poem begins with 'apples falling like great drops of dew / to bruise themselves an exit from themselves', reminding the poet that 'it is time to go, to bid farewell / to one's own self, and find an exit / from the fallen self'. As the seed exits from the apple, this conceit implies, so the quick soul that is the seed of the new self must exit from the dying body. Again the poet utters his warning, more insistently: the 'grim frost is at hand, when the apples will fall / thick, almost thundrous, on the hardened earth' (*Poems*, 716–17), and again his preacherly extended metaphor implicitly figures the 'frightened soul' as the apple's seed, 'shrinking, wincing from the cold / that blows upon it through the orifices' of Eden's rotting fruit. But now, as the soul/seed passes through the 'cruel bruise' that is analogous to what the poet elsewhere calls one of the 'dark doors where souls pass silently / holding their breath, naked and darkly alone / entering into the other communion' (*Poems*, 711), it must take refuge in its little self-made ship of death, a vessel of transfiguration humbly equipped with a 'store of food and little cooking pans' just as the bulb, seed or egg – all germinal vehicles of regeneration that haunted Lawrence – come *toute ensemble* with nutrients for new life.

That the ship very likely *is* at least the husk of the seed is once more suggested by metaphoric and metonymic juxtapositions in *Sketches of Etruscan Places*, this time juxtapositions of tombs-as-bulbs and the dead-as-seeds with, on the one hand, 'the little bronze ship of death that should bear [the dead one] over to the other world' and, on the other hand, 'the Ark, the *arx*, the womb . . . of all the world, that brought forth all the creatures' and that is at the same time the '*arx*, where life retreats in the last refuge . . . the ark of the covenant, in which lies the mystery of eternal life, the manna and the mysteries' (*SEP*, 20). Entering the Ark or ship of death that is the husk of the seed or germ of new life, the poet-seer ceremonially embarks on the 'deepening black darkening still' of oblivion, the death sea of 'the end' across which he must journey towards those waters of the beginning that swell the *arx* or womb of time. (And here the poem itself enacts, without spelling out, the pun on 'Ark' and '*arx*' as well as the connection made in *Sketches of Etruscan Places* between Noah's Ark and the Ark of the Covenant.)

But where now is the primal scene of sexual coupling enacted by bird and lady or by wonder-dragon and wonder-woman (or for that matter by gamekeeper and lady)? It is, I would claim, a scene now unseen because the poet has longingly and rather daringly positioned himself at its very heart, in the place of the newborn soul entering what Freud called the 'oceanic bliss' of oneness or atonement with the 'pink flood' of maternal amniotic waters.[18] It is into and through these waters, surely, that Lawrence's fantasised soul journeys in the vessel of the seed that is the ship of death – journeys, 'faltering and lapsing', towards rebirth. The metaphors shaping the poet's narrative of its passage are, to be sure, implicitly drawn from animal as well as plant life – offering at worst a confusion and at best an excess of tropes for regeneration – but in any case, whether through confusion or excess, the poem ends with a beginning as, at the crack of dawn signalling delivery from husk or womb, ark or *arx*, the 'frail soul steps out, into her house again' (*Poems*, 720). And that this soul's new home is ambiguously described as '*her* house' is also quite suggestive, since the soul itself is figured as masculine in all the other verses and variants that make up a 'Ship of Death' sequence analogous to the Leda series. (In 'After All Saints' Day', for instance, 'the little, slender soul sits swiftly down, and takes the oars' while love from the living breathes 'on *his* small frail sail . . . helping *him* on' (*Poems*, 723).) '*Her* house' therefore connotes a new residence *in* or *with* the 'wonder-woman clothed in the sun and standing upon the crescent of the moon . . . the great Mother' who looms so far back in time that 'a book of her "mystery" and initiation ritual [probably] gave rise to the existing Apocalypse'. Perhaps, indeed, through (his) travel and ('her') travail the poet has imagined himself finally achieving a rebirth into a renovated history.

Dark matters: beyond the millennium

Such a birth of the new was of course an apocalyptic event that preoccupied more than a few of the modernists. Yeats's Magi brooded over the 'uncontrollable mystery on the bestial floor' and Eliot's very different Magi were transformed by their 'cold coming' towards a 'Birth' that signified their own death; Wallace Stevens dreamt of how 'our blood, commingling, virginal, / With heaven' might bring 'requital to desire', and H.D. fantasised the birth of an at least semi-divine child to those mythic 'New Mortals' Achilles, son of the 'sea-mother' Thetis, and Helen, daughter of Leda and the swan.[19] Several generations later, however, ourselves at sea on the horizonless waters of postmodernity, we seem far closer to that bleak pre-modernist Thomas Hardy, who entered the twentieth century gazing at a grim landscape that seemed 'the Century's corpse outleant', a field in which the 'ancient pulse of germ and birth / Was shrunken hard and dry'. Noting sardonically the 'happy good-night air' of an aged, frail and 'darkling' thrush, Hardy wondered if there 'trembled' through that song some 'blessed Hope, whereof he knew / And I was unaware'.[20] If we change the rhetoric a little here – make it rather more comic, more parodic, more aware of the quotidian banality shaping what Hardy elsewhere called 'life's little ironies' – how easily such estrangement from 'blessed Hope' might speak for an age in which the Madonna who was once a mother goddess has become a media queen named 'Madonna'-in-quotation-marks, while Leda-and-the-swan have devolved into parts of a very expensive costume once worn to a Hollywood party by yet another still quite *médiatique* media queen, Marlene Dietrich.[21]

'Only two topics can be of the least interest to a serious and studious mind – sex and the dead', Yeats wrote to Olivia Shakespear in 1927, and Lawrence wouldn't have altogether disagreed, though he would probably have formulated the point rather differently.[22] At the end of the twentieth century, however, a hundred years after Yeats joined the Golden Dawn and some seventy-five years after Lawrence embarked on his passionate pilgrimage towards Rananim, most English-speaking poets seem unable or unwilling to take the risks of apocalyptic vision, perhaps because the dangers of such vision when it is crudely and cruelly realised were manifested in the totalitarian holocausts of recent history, but perhaps for other reasons we are not yet ready to understand. In any case, for such descendants of the modernists as Sylvia Plath and James Merrill, members of what Helen Sword has defined as 'a literary generation caught between modernism's mythopoetic nostalgia and postmodernism's self-conscious romance with commodity culture', the game-playing spiritualism of the Ouija board has replaced the prophetic *gnosis* of Revelation.[23] And when Plath's Sibyl and Leroy toy with vision in her 'Dialogue over a Ouija Board', the only vaguely apocalyptic apparatus they encounter is 'plumage of raw worms', while, as Sword observes, Merrill's epic *The Changing Light at Sandover* suits contemporary sensibilities precisely because it is 'packaged in self-conscious camp and deflective candor'.[24] As for Plath's and Merrill's countless non-spiritualist contemporaries, most offer readers merely a bare minimum of (lower-case) revelation delineated through the quotidian particulars of personal confessions.

It remains for us, then, to wonder what vision Lawrence might have achieved had he too been positioned, as we are, in the horizonless afterlife of a century's corpse 'outleant'. The author of 'The Ship of Death', wrote Aldous Huxley, 'had eyes that could see, beyond the walls of light, far into the darkness, [into] the environing mystery'.[25] And despite (or perhaps because of) his famous distaste for rational science, what Lawrence saw as he looked into what he sardonically called 'the dark unscientific' may have predicted what some of our scientists are only just now beginning to discern themselves. Wilfully weird or naïve though some of his metaphors may seem, for instance, the swan in the electron and the soul in the bulb point towards still unsolved mysteries whose enigmatic force might dissolve the walls of irony that imprison so many post-postmodern intellectuals. 'During the past twenty years,' writes the physicist Timothy Ferris:

> theory and observation alike have indicated that at least ninety percent, and perhaps as much as ninety-nine percent, of the mass of the universe is dark. It is invisible not because it is far away . . . but because it neither emits nor absorbs light. At least some of the dark matter is made of familiar stuff, but most of it may be of an exotic nature as yet unknown.[26]

Though Lawrence could not have known about this newly identified 'dark matter', dark matters had always been in some sense his business, if only because, as Huxley also commented, for this poet of death and rebirth 'existence was one continuous convalescence; it was as though he were newly reborn from a mortal illness every day of his life'.[27] His personal history, then, as well as his cultural moment especially equipped him for the kind of apocalyptic testimony that has made his visions of the afterlife and the afterlife of his visions both problematic and powerful. Whatever our own, ironic disbeliefs, however, we cannot doubt his oracular certainty nor can we, finally, scoff at the sincerity with which he speaks to us from beyond the grave. As early as 1917, after all, in a poem entitled 'Resurrection', he predicted the contour of the narrative that would shape his late, apocalyptic imaginings:

> Now, like a strange light breaking from the ground,
> I venture from the halls of shadowy death
> A frail white gleam of resurrection . . .
>
> If they would listen, I could tell them now
> The secret of the noiseless, utter grave,
> The secret in the blind mouth of the worm . . .
>
> Now like a cyclamen, a crocus flower
> In putrid autumn issuing through the fall
> Of lives, I speak to all who cannot hear.   (*Poems*, 744–45)

NOTES

1 'Prophesies', 66, in Ruth Montgomery with Joanne Garland, *Herald of the New Age* (London: Grafton, 1987); Benjamin Creme, *Maitreya's Mission*, 3 vols. (Amsterdam and London: Share International Foundation, 1993–97).

2 'Gerontion', in T. S. Eliot, *The Complete Poems and Plays* (London: Faber and Faber, 1969), p. 37; W. B. Yeats, 'The Second Coming', in *Collected Poems*, 2nd edn (London: Macmillan, 1950), p. 211.

3 Included in *Looking Back on the End of the World*, trans. David Antal, ed. Dietmar Kamper and Christoph Wulf (New York: Semiotext(e), 1989), p. 54, quoted in Catherine Keller, *Apocalypse Now and Then* (Boston: Beacon Press, 1996), p. 13.

4 Keller, *Apocalypse Now*, p. 14.

5 *Letters of John Keats: A Selection,* ed. Robert Gittings (Oxford: Oxford University Press), pp. 36–37.

6 Clive Bell, *Old Friends* (1956; London: Cassell, 1988), p. 120; Virginia Woolf, 'Notes on D. H. Lawrence', in *The Moment and Other Essays* (London: The Hogarth Press, 1947), pp. 79–82, p. 79.

7 *After Strange Gods* (New York: Harcourt, Brace, 1934), p. 42.

8 Preface to *Chariot of the Sun*, by Harry Crosby, in *P*, 262.

9 Frieda Lawrence, *Memoirs and Correspondence*, ed. E. W. Tedlock (London: Heinemann, 1961), pp. 185–86.

10 Keller, *Apocalypse Now*, p. 1.

11 Walter Benjamin, section ix, 'Theses on the Philosophy of History', in *Illuminations*, trans. Harry Zohn, ed. Hannah Arendt (London: Fontana, 1973), pp. 245–55, p. 249.

12 Marcus cites Tindall and others who noted Lawrence's reading of 'Madame Blavatsky's *The Secret Doctrine*, Frazer's *The Golden Bough*, Burnet's *Early Greek Philosophy*, the *Upanishads* [and] even such less well known texts as Balzac's "occult" novel *Seraphita*' (Marcus, 'Lawrence, Yeats and "the Resurrection of the Body"', in *D. H. Lawrence: A Centenary Consideration*, ed. Peter Balbert and Phillip Marcus (Ithaca: Cornell University Press, 1985), p. 217). Nevertheless, although he does discuss *Apocalypse* in some detail, Marcus's primary focus is on *The Escaped Cock*.

13 Bram Dijkstra, *Idols of Perversity: Fantasies of Feminine Evil in Fin-de-Siècle Culture* (Oxford: Oxford University Press, 1986), pp. 314–18.

14 Introduction to *The Cat and the Moon and Certain Poems* (1924), cited in A. N. Jeffaries, *A Commentary on the Collected Poems of W. B. Yeats* (London: Macmillan, 1968), p. 296.

15 For a very different reading of Lawrence's Leda poems (along with those by Yeats and Rilke), see Helen Sword, 'Leda and the Modernists', *PMLA* (March 1992), 305–18.

16 *The Herne's Egg*, in *Collected Plays*, 2nd edn (London: Macmillan, 1952), pp. 643–78, p. 649.

17 'Ribh at the Tomb of Baile and Aillinn', in *Collected Poems*, pp. 327–28.

18 Sigmund Freud, *Civilization and its Discontents*, trans. James Strachey, with a biographical introduction by Peter Gay (New York: W. W. Norton & Co., 1961), pp. 11, 15.

19 Yeats, 'The Magi', in *Collected Poems*, p. 141; T. S. Eliot, 'The Journey of the Magi', in *Complete Poems and Plays*, p. 103; Wallace Stevens, 'Sunday Morning', in *The Collected Poems of Wallace Stevens* (London: Faber and Faber, 1955), p. 68; H.D., *Helen in Egypt* (New York: New Directions, 1961), pp. 288–89.

20 'The Darkling Thrush', in *Collected Poems* (London: Macmillan, 1952), p. 137.

21 For an account of this event – a party thrown by Basil Rathbone and his wife, to which guests were invited to 'Come as the one you most admire' – see Maria Riva, *Marlene Dietrich: By Her Daughter* (New York: Knopf, 1993), pp. 350–51, 366. Notes Riva: 'No film costume was ever worked on and perfected more than the one for Leda and her swan. When Dietrich was finally sewn into that costume, what an incredible sight! Clustered short "greek statue" curls framed her face, leaving her neck bare for her swan to curl his neck gently around it and pillow his head on one swelling breast. Her body sheathed in sculpted white chiffon, she stood within his all-enveloping passionate embrace. They were truly "one". There might have been some who did not know the story of Leda and her swan, but no one could misunderstand the emotion my mother represented' (351). In the meantime, as if to elaborate the theme of narcissism, the young actress Elizabeth Allan, Dietrich's 'escort' for the evening, was dressed in top hat and trousers as 'Marlene Dietrich'. (I am grateful to Joan Schenkar for pointing me towards this episode.)

22 *The Letters of W. B. Yeats* (London: Rupert Hart-Davis, 1954), p. 730.

23 Helen Sword, 'James Merrill, Sylvia Plath, and the Poetics of Ouija', *American Literature*, 66, 3 (September 1994), 553–72, p. 556.

24 Sylvia Plath, 'Dialogue over a Ouija Board', in *Collected Poems*, ed. Ted Hughes (London: Faber and Faber, 1981), pp. 276–86, p. 279; Helen Sword, 'James Merrill, Sylvia Plath, and the Poetics of Ouija', p. 567.

25 Introduction to *The Letters of D. H. Lawrence* (London: Heinemann, 1932), p. xiv.

26 *The Whole Shebang: A State-of-the-Universe(s) Report* (New York: Touchstone Books, 1997), p. 121.

27 Huxley, Introduction to the *Letters*, p. xxx.

14

CHRIS BALDICK

Post-mortem: Lawrence's critical and cultural legacy

The risen phoenix

The risen phoenix became Lawrence's adopted emblem when, in December 1914, he found a picture of the mythical bird in a book that he was reading on Christian symbolism, and sketched a copy of it for his friends. Variations upon this phoenix design have adorned the dust-jackets and title pages of the many reprints of his books, including Heinemann's Phoenix Edition of the 1950s; and *Phoenix* was the title chosen by E. D. McDonald in 1936 for his edition of Lawrence's uncollected articles. A plaster phoenix still stands above the concrete slab encasing Lawrence's ashes in the shrine erected by his widow at Taos, New Mexico. The emblem commemorates his preoccupation with bodily resurrection, along with his recurrent literary theme of the shedding of old skins and selves for new. Lawrence's true afterlife has of course been in the Word, not in the Flesh, but its fitful cycles of immolation and revival seem still to rehearse the fate of the fabulous bird: in a posthumous career quite unlike that of any writer of his time, the risen Lawrence has undergone periodic ritual incineration, only to re-emerge in strange new plumage, ensuring that the 'Lawrence' we have made of his remains has never been at rest.

The continuing presence of D. H. Lawrence in modern culture since his death in 1930 relies to an unusual degree not only upon the flaring up of intense controversies about his standing as a prophet and as a writer, but also upon the resurrection of previously uncollected or lost writings. 'Our' Lawrence is the author of a large body of posthumous works: shortly after his death there appeared the verse collection *Nettles* and the *Assorted Articles*, and in the same year were published *The Virgin and the Gipsy*, *A Propos of 'Lady Chatterley's Lover'* and *Love Among the Haystacks*; the following ten years brought *Apocalypse* (1931), *Sketches of Etruscan Places* (1932), *Last Poems* (1932), *A Collier's Friday Night* (1934), *A Modern Lover* (1934), *Phoenix* (1936) and, most importantly, Aldous Huxley's edition of

The Letters (1932). After a gap of twenty-five years, another corpus was brought into the public domain in the sixties: not just the unexpurgated *Lady Chatterley's Lover* (1959/60), but Harry T. Moore's edition of *The Collected Letters* (1962), the early versions of Lawrence's American literature essays collected as *The Symbolic Meaning* (1962), *The Complete Poems* (1964), *The Complete Plays* (1965) and a second volume of miscellaneous prose works published as *Phoenix II* (1968). Along with these came five more volumes of Lawrence's letters to particular correspondents, and *John Thomas and Lady Jane* (1972). Further rediscoveries followed: Lawrence's 'lost' novel *Mr Noon* finally appeared in 1984, some important suppressed passages of *Sons and Lovers* were restored in Helen and Carl Baron's edition of 1992, and yet more correspondence surfaced in the seven-volume Cambridge edition of *The Letters* (1979–93). The Cambridge edition of the *Works*, still in progress, promises further Lawrenceana, notably 'Paul Morel'.

Through this continually unfolding canon of posthumously published writings, some of which are especially significant in the revaluing of his life's work, Lawrence makes his own contribution to the shaping of his critical reputation. Here it is worth making special mention of a single letter, dated 5 June 1914, to his publisher's reader Edward Garnett, concerning an early draft ('The Wedding Ring') of what became *The Rainbow* and *Women in Love*. This is the letter in which Lawrence declares in defence of his new methods: 'You mustn't look in my novel for the old stable ego of the character.' This document came before the public in the 1932 edition of *The Letters*, in the introduction to which Huxley highlights it as an especially valuable exhibit, and interprets it as a central clue to both Lawrence's artistic purposes and the difficulties readers face in his writings. Since that time, the Garnett letter has enjoyed a privileged place in the explication of Lawrence's fiction, so much so that examination candidates are commonly expected to learn some of its formulations by rote. Some other self-justificatory writings belong in the same class: the unpublished essays 'Why the Novel Matters' and 'Study of Thomas Hardy' appeared for the first time in 1936 in *Phoenix*, while two other important essays that had appeared in fairly obscure journals in the twenties were reprinted along with them: 'Morality and the Novel' and 'Surgery for the Novel – or a Bomb'. These works, like the Garnett letter, have come to be read as indispensable aids to the understanding of Lawrence's fiction. The effect, then, was that characteristics of Lawrence's work that may have appeared in his lifetime as the involuntary foibles of an untutored barbarian could be re-interpreted after his death as the deliberate innovations of a critically self-conscious pioneer. The Lawrence of 1936 could thus re-illuminate and perhaps redeem the Lawrence of 1915 or 1920.

With this important qualification, the after-Lawrence or posthumous Lawrence consists of course in what others have made and remade of him and of his works. In today's critical wisdom it goes without saying that this Lawrence is, in the leaden Franglais of the scholastics, a 'site of contestation'; or, in English, disputed ground. This chapter will restrict itself to the evolution of the principal disputes and the principal refashionings of Lawrence since his death, in what has become an enormous library of literary-critical writings about him. In doing so, it will as far as possible skirt around the more strictly biographical literature that Paul Eggert has reviewed in chapter 9 above. Later in the chapter, a wider prospect will appear, of Lawrence's presiding cultural influence in the wake of the celebrated 'Lady Chatterley' trial of 1960, beyond the pages of literary-critical books and articles. In conclusion, I offer some observations on the current state of Lawrence criticism, and on its possible future directions.

Posthumous controversies: the 1930s

The months following Lawrence's death on 2 March 1930 were marked by a flurry of obituaries, tributes, reminiscences, elegies, post-mortem reflections, and reviews of his immediately posthumous works, some of these provoking responses and further exchanges in the letters pages of literary journals. Memoirs and reminiscences of a largely personal kind by Lawrence's relatives, disciples and associates continued to appear for the next five years; but alongside these there unfolded a debate cast in more formally literary-critical terms about the stature of his writings. The disciples complained that Lawrence was being widely dismissed in the press as a sex-crank, but in fact there were some fulsome public declarations of Lawrence's high literary standing, notably from E. M. Forster, who called him the greatest novelist of his generation, and from critics who had never met Lawrence at all, such as the ageing Arnold Bennett and the young F. R. Leavis. Bennett's tribute, made in his weekly column in the *Evening Standard*, carried with it the authority of the country's highest-paid and most influential book-reviewer. In what amounted to an instruction to buy up every available Lawrencean text, Bennett offered a speculator's 'tip' that in future years first editions of Lawrence's books would fetch higher prices than those of any other modern author. As for critical judgement on these works, he hesitated just short of Forster's verdict, finding many of the writings too undisciplined, but still declared that 'no finer work has been done in our time than Lawrence's finest'.[1]

From the younger generation, the most interesting early tribute was that of the 34-year-old F. R. Leavis, a temporary lecturer in the English Faculty of the University of Cambridge. Writing in the June 1930 number of the *Cambridge Review*, Leavis compares Lawrence's genius with that of William Blake, but finds troubling kinds of monotony, fanaticism and mechanical iteration in the modern author's novels; the short stories he commends more unreservedly, along with the 'masterpiece', *Lady Chatterley's Lover*. His article, later expanded into a pamphlet, closes by questioning the assumption that *Lady Chatterley's Lover* really 'represents greater health and vitality' than such a book as Forster's *A Passage to India*: a wholehearted acceptance of the former would mean abandoning the civilised values of the latter.[2] Leavis would later become the foremost defender of Lawrence's literary work, and of its 'health and vitality', but in this first verdict (later rescinded with wincing self-reproach) he is guarded, showing no great enthusiasm for *The Rainbow* or for *Women in Love*, nor for the narrowness of the 'prophetic' stance. The critical caution here owes much to T. S. Eliot's essay on Blake in *The Sacred Wood* (1920): admiring the heretic's honesty, but regretting his monotonous insistence. For at this stage Leavis was Eliot's true disciple. What changed his mind, and carried him over to the Lawrence camp, was in the first place the disturbing spectacle of the American poet–critic ganging up with Lawrence's sometime friend and ally John Middleton Murry in the character-assassination of the dead prophet, and in the second place the appearance in 1932 of *The Letters*.

Eliot and Murry were the two critics best placed to influence Leavis's generation. Each edited a distinctive literary journal projecting his position in criticism and cultural politics: Eliot's *Criterion* and Murry's *Adelphi* represented opposed poles of 'classical' and 'Romantic' principle, and had been sparring with each other for several years about cultural and religious tradition, with Eliot deploring the undisciplined 'inner voice' of the Romantic and Protestant mentality, and Murry upholding its supreme value for modern culture. Murry's *Adelphi* had been launched in 1923 partly as a vehicle for the Lawrencean gospel, although Lawrence himself quickly became disappointed with the directions in which Murry was steering the journal. By 1930, though, Murry was placed among Lawrence's friends and followers in the role of Judas Iscariot opposite Lawrence's Jesus, having 'betrayed' his master on more than one occasion. There had been an extremely harsh review of *Women in Love* in 1921, whispers that he had tried to seduce Lawrence's wife Frieda in 1923, and the 'Last Supper' at the Café Royal, at which Murry had bestowed upon the Eastwood messiah the traitor's kiss. The last and greatest betrayal was the publication in 1931 of Murry's *Son of Woman: The Story of D. H. Lawrence*.

Murry's purpose in writing his psychobiography of Lawrence was not literary-critical evaluation but analysis of Lawrence the man and prophet: his sexual incapacity, his loathing for women, and his failure to become a second Jesus Christ. The fictional works are treated as almost direct commentaries upon the various stages of his struggle to subdue a sexually unsatisfied Frieda. In defence of this approach, he claims that Lawrence was not attempting to create Art but to do something more important – to utter the adventures of his soul. The novels are therefore appraised not as artistic successes or failures but according to the degree of self-knowledge they display. On this criterion, *Sons and Lovers* is an evasion of the author's true problems, *Women in Love* and *St. Mawr* are dismissed as self-deceiving fantasies, whilst *Aaron's Rod* is nominated the greatest of the novels because it reveals a rare moment of harmonious self-knowledge. Catherine Carswell's riposte to Murry in her memoir *The Savage Pilgrimage* (1932) is even less concerned with literary quality and more with the vindication of Lawrence's sexual prowess and secular sainthood; but in a rare moment of aesthetic digression she names *The Plumed Serpent* as her hero's greatest novel, the one in which he displays to the full 'the blazing virtue of potency'.[3] This was not an eccentric opinion: E. M. Forster had singled out the same novel as Lawrence's finest in a radio broadcast two years earlier. The relative values of Lawrence's works were still very far from being settled at this stage. J. C. Squire's obituary notice in the *Observer* had preferred Lawrence's travel books to all his novels, and, as we have seen, F. R. Leavis favoured the short stories.

Eliot clearly relished the sight of his chief critical adversary turning so cruelly upon his own former hero in *Son of Woman* and pronouncing him a false prophet. In his review for the *Criterion* in July 1931, he pronounced Murry's book 'brilliant' and 'definitive'. 'The victim and the sacrificial knife', he added with bloodthirsty glee, 'are perfectly adapted to each other.'[4] He sums up Lawrence's life as a story of spiritual pride, emotional sickness, self-deception, and a kind of ignorance that would not have been remedied by an Oxbridge grooming. Indeed, if Lawrence had become a Cambridge don, Eliot speculates, his kind of ignorance 'might have had frightful consequences for himself and for the world'.[5] These words were read with outrage by Leavis and his wife Queenie (also a literary historian and critic), who convinced herself that Eliot was referring unmistakably to her husband.[6] F. R. Leavis himself, without abandoning the Eliotic view of literary history that inspires his *New Bearings in English Poetry* (1932), began to reconsider the limits of Eliot's authority. Apart from the disquieting signs of dogmatism in Eliot's appeals to religious 'orthodoxy', there had been a sinister remark in his 1930 essay on Baudelaire, in which he had suggested that it would be less 'boring' to regard sex as evil than to view it cheerfully as life-enhancing. Compared with this, Lawrence's attitude to sex seemed to be saner, and his religious view of life more affirmative, than Eliot's.

At the end of 1931, meetings were held in Cambridge at which students sympathetic to the Leavises proposed the launch of a journal. At least two of them wanted an openly Lawrencean magazine, to be called the *Phoenix*; but the result was a broader literary review, *Scrutiny* (1932), in which F. R. Leavis launched a much more vigorous defence of Lawrence, in a series of reviews that signalled his displeasure at Eliot's failures. The first, 'Reminiscences of D. H. Lawrence' (September 1932), values Lawrence's writings principally as evidence of his personal qualities:

> If we find him great, the supreme importance of his books is perhaps that they assure us he existed. Those of them which are most successful as art are in some ways saddening and depressing. The fact of personal existence of which they assure us is perhaps the most cheering and enlivening fact the modern world provides. Here was a man with the clairvoyance and honesty of genius whose whole living was an assertion of what the modern world has lost.[7]

Leavis then wrote two reviews of *The Letters*, one for the *Listener*, the other for *Scrutiny*. The first resists Eliot's picture of Lawrence as an eccentric Rousseauist egotist, and claims to the contrary that he was incapable of egotism or self-deception. *The Letters* are greeted as one of the most important books of the age, but again as testimony to the supremely important fact that Lawrence actually walked upon this earth. The review for *Scrutiny* (December 1932), though, is the most barbed in its revenge upon Eliot. After reaffirming that 'Lawrence was greater than his writings', Leavis here rebuts Eliot's diagnosis of Lawrence as a 'sick' soul by calling the letters as evidence that he was 'normal, central and sane to the point of genius, exquisitely but surely poised'. Furthermore, Lawrence was nothing less than 'the finest literary critic of his time' (which could only mean that Eliot had been dethroned from that eminence), who offered a serious kind of 'classicism' distinct from Eliot's own 'classiosity'. Turning to Eliot's own remarks on sex in the Baudelaire article, Leavis congratulates Lawrence because 'he did not turn against life, or find it necessary to run to damnation to escape ennui' – as Eliot, it is implied, had done. It is Lawrence, more than anyone of his time, Eliot included, who offers hope for the future of humanity, because 'he may be said to represent, concretely in his living person, the essential human tradition'.[8]

The remarkable feature of Leavis's defection to the Lawrencean cause is the extent to which it appeals to the letters rather than to the fiction, and more generally to the 'living person' rather than to the art. No substantial case having been made for any of his novels, it is the personal quality of spiritual sanity alone that now places Lawrence above the life-denying Eliot. Leavis's enthusiasm for *The Letters* may be explained partly by the model they offered of the critic as fearless outsider, a role that Leavis himself, still without a secure academic post, was feeling his way into. This kind of attraction, though, does not account for the messianic qualities attributed to Lawrence by *Scrutiny*. It seems that some unacknowledged religious hunger, of a kind to which Murry was also susceptible, had asserted itself. Murry's search for a saviour had led him to become Lawrence's Judas, whereas Leavis had now assumed the role of St Paul.

Lawrence's reputation in the thirties clearly suffered from the destructive work of Murry and Eliot, the latter continuing his campaign against the Lawrencean 'heresy' in *After Strange Gods* (1934). Ever watchful against the conspiracies of the fashionable intelligentsia, F. R. Leavis began his review of *Phoenix* in *Scrutiny* (December 1937) with a sarcastic summary of what appeared to him to be the prevailing critical wisdom on Lawrence: that he was *passé*, a humourless fanatic of no relevance to today's problems. It has become accepted since then in Lawrencean lore that the *Marxisant* intellectuals of the thirties blithely dismissed Lawrence in these terms, or as a dangerous precursor of Hitler. On the contrary, the leading Leftist poets in England, W. H. Auden and Stephen Spender, both admired Lawrence greatly, while disagreeing with his doctrines, and Spender's review of *Phoenix* in *Left Review* (January 1937) made very clear distinctions between Lawrence and Nazism, applauding Lawrence indeed as a great, original revolutionary.[9] The left-leaning critic Cyril Connolly in his *Enemies of Promise* (1938) includes a commendation of Lawrence's writings as 'always vigorous, thoughtful and alive, the enemy of elaboration and artifice, of moral hypocrisy and verbal falseness'.[10] Certainly there was much less public discussion of Lawrence in the late thirties and throughout the forties than there had been in the five years following his death. This can be attributed quite reasonably to a general redirection of intellectual energies in this period away from sexual psychology and towards pressing economic and political problems.

Reviving Lawrence: the 1950s

Serious interest in Lawrence's works revived significantly in the fifties, providing some foundation for the more generalised Lawrenceanisms of the sixties. This Lawrence revival is sometimes seen as having been brought about almost single-handedly by the critical efforts of F. R. Leavis in his *Scrutiny* articles of the early fifties, expanded into a book, *D. H. Lawrence, Novelist*, in 1955. In fact there were several other contributory labours, including biographies by Richard Aldington (1950) and Harry T. Moore (1951), and such critical studies as Mark Spilka's *The Love Ethic of D. H. Lawrence* (1955) and Graham Hough's *The Dark Sun* (1956). Penguin

Books had also reprinted a large selection of Lawrence's works, with introductions by Aldington, in 1950. Leavis's work had the major impact, however, partly because it carried the prestige of a critic who had by now become something of a charismatic prophet in his own right, followed by a loyal corps of devoted ex-students.

It is in *D. H. Lawrence, Novelist* that Leavis at last offers a semblance of literary-critical justification for his high valuation of Lawrence, although much of it consists of quotations pointed to as self-evident signs of genius. Leavis is still fighting old battles here, against Murry and above all against Eliot, the disputed ground again being that of Lawrence's alleged humourless rage or his lack of education, cultural tradition and intelligence. Leavis's response to these charges is to place Lawrence in a genuine cultural tradition of provincial English nonconformism, along with George Eliot. In a forthright chapter on 'Lawrence and Art', he contrasts Lawrence's healthy instinct for life with the revulsion from life shown in Eliot's 'Flaubertian' tradition; this instinct itself is seen as a higher form of 'intelligence' than Eliot's. There is much commentary in *D. H. Lawrence, Novelist* on Lawrence's sure handling of his fictional materials, but the assertion of Lawrence's value comes back again to personal qualities. Still gainsaying Eliot's claims that Lawrence was 'sick', Leavis declares flatly that there is 'no profound emotional disorder in Lawrence, no obdurate major disharmony; intelligence . . . is not thwarted or disabled by inner contradictions in him, whether we have him as artist, critic, or expositor'.[11] It is a major weakness of Leavis's account that it can find no way of dealing with the contradictions of Lawrence other than denying their very existence. Leavis conceives of Lawrence's vision of the world as a stable, normative and incomparably 'diagnostic' guide to the crisis of modern civilisation. Lawrence's work is 'an immense body of living creation in which a supreme vital intelligence is the creative spirit – a spirit informed by an almost infallible sense for health and sanity'.[12] As this impassioned defence of Lawrence's genius reaches its conclusion, Leavis finally declares the novelist to be infallible, and Eliot unfit to pass judgement upon him:

> I repeat with, if possible, even greater conviction what I have said before: he has an unfailingly sure sense of the difference between that which makes for life and that which makes against it; of the difference between health and that which tends away from health. It is this that makes him a so much better critic than Eliot, whose major value-judgements, when he risks them (especially in the contemporary field), have nearly always been bad – often disastrously bad.[13]

The language of sickness and health in which Lawrence's reputation had for so long been entangled is here turned against his accusers: far from embodying a sickness, Lawrence is both the diagnostician and the cure.

D. H. Lawrence, Novelist imposed a stabilisation of the Lawrencean canon. Its placing of *Women in Love* at its pinnacle, just above *The Rainbow*, along with its dismissal of *The Plumed Serpent*, was accepted by most of the critics who came after Leavis, such as Eliseo Vivas in *D. H. Lawrence: The Failure and the Triumph of Art* (1960) and Julian Moynahan in *The Deed of Life* (1963), and has since settled into a consensus that looks surprisingly solid when compared with the differing preferences of the early thirties. Critics writing on Lawrence in Leavis's wake tended to concentrate upon the novels and related writings of the middle period, with *Sons and Lovers* and *Lady Chatterley's Lover* taking up honourable subsidiary positions. Scholarly investigation into the evolution of Lawrence's beliefs, in such works as H. M. Daleski's *The Forked Flame* (1965) and Mark Kinkead-Weekes's 'The Marble and the Statue' (1968), was devoted to explicating the wartime essays as the genesis of symbolic polarities in *Women in Love*. Lawrence's poems, travel writings and prophetic tracts were at the bottom of the critical agenda.

The 'Lady Chatterley' trial

Meanwhile, the extensive reprinting of Lawrence's works in the 1950s by Heinemann and by Penguin reached a point of no return when Penguin's director, Sir Allen Lane, decided in 1959 to go ahead with an unexpurgated *Lady Chatterley's Lover*. The same novel had recently been acquitted of indecency in American courts, on hitherto inadmissible grounds of literary merit; and a similar 'public interest' defence was now to be allowed in English law, under the amended Obscene Publications Act of 1959. The famous 'Lady Chatterley' trial (1960), which became a landmark in public attitudes, was a test case of the new legislation, and in many ways a staged charade: the book was 'published' by handing copies to the police, and Sir Allen was not placed in the dock of the Old Bailey. The prosecution, and later the judge in his summing-up, digressed from the issue of obscenity into that of adultery, while the defence introduced a number of doubtful 'experts'. Both sides fell into inconsistencies on the important legal (and literary-critical) question whether an author's intention in writing a book should be taken into account. It later emerged that the jury was predisposed, by a majority of nine to three, to acquittal, the other three being sufficiently swayed by the eminent defence witnesses to withstand a flagrantly biased summing-up.

The testimony of the numerous defence witnesses (there were none for the prosecution) provides a useful indication of the height at which Lawrence's reputation stood at the end of the fifties. Graham Hough testified that he was 'generally recognized to be one of the most important novelists of this century and one of the greatest novelists in any century'; Joan Bennett, another Cambridge literary critic, valued him as the greatest writer of fiction since Hardy and Conrad; and the Cambridge historian Noel Annan declared Lawrence to be 'the greatest imaginative writer in this century in English literature'.[14] Additional testimonials to Lawrence's genius and moral seriousness were given on oath by Rebecca West, E. M. Forster and C. Day-Lewis, along with some younger literary critics and teachers including Richard Hoggart and Raymond Williams.

Conspicuous by his absence from the trial was F. R. Leavis, who had by now decided that *Lady Chatterley's Lover* was an artistically and morally false work, and that he would not collaborate with a new liberal orthodoxy in overvaluing it. Nevertheless, the powerful terms in which he had defined Lawrence's value still asserted themselves at the trial. For it was as a *normal, healthy* writer that the author of *Lady Chatterley's Lover* was defended and vindicated at the Old Bailey. Opening the case for the defence, George Gardiner insisted that Lawrence was a puritan moralist who abhorred casual sex but regarded sex between a man and a woman in a permanent relationship as 'healthy, wholesome, normal, and to be encouraged'.[15] He later called to the witness-box an educational psychologist, James Hemming, who testified that 'the content of *Lady Chatterley's Lover* is an antidote, a positive antidote to the shallow, superficial values of sex which are widely current today and which are now corrupting the attitude of young people towards sex'.[16] Far from being a corrupter of the young, then, Lawrence offered a 'reverential' attitude to sex that could safeguard vulnerable teenagers against the lures of commercialised titillation. Gardiner reassured the jury that they had before them 'a book in which there is no kind of perversion at all', a claim to which the prosecution's response was oddly muted: feeling unable to spell out the meaning of a passage obscurely referring to anal penetration, the prosecuting counsel merely read it aloud, and raised the faint suggestion of something unspeakable – an innuendo that 'visibly shocked some members of the Jury'.[17] Lawrence's reputation for sincere cleanliness survived the trial, as Penguin's acquittal amounted to a certificate of health for a writer once widely regarded as 'sick'. Penguin's edition of the novel, now legal and of course a runaway bestseller, carried an introduction by Richard Hoggart which declared emphatically that '*Lady Chatterley's Lover* is *not* a dirty book. It is clean and serious and beautiful.'[18] Millions of people read, not always in a clean and serious frame of mind, this and the other, sometimes opportunistically reprinted, works of 'the author of Lady Chatterley's Lover'. In a decade of volatile cultural dissent, Lawrence now appeared to represent the modern ideals of solitary literary integrity pitted against a hypocritical social system, and of innocuous openness in releasing the discussion of sex from a culture of shame. In such a glowing light he became one of the patron saints of 'The Sixties'.

Canonisation and demonisation: 1960–1970

As the sole working-class hero of modern English literature, Lawrence was already established as an inescapable exemplar for the post-1945 'angry' generation of provincial and working-class novelists, and for some other literary intellectuals from proletarian backgrounds, such as Raymond Williams and Richard Hoggart. Williams, interviewed in 1977, recalled that 'If there was one person everybody wanted to be after the war, to the point of caricature, it was Lawrence.'[19] It is worth noting here that Lawrence was for that generation somebody to *be*, not just a writer to imitate or to be 'influenced' by. As for literary influence, there were few so reckless as to incorporate the Lawrencean manner into their prose styles.[20] Lawrence's commanding presence in the fifties and sixties was rather a matter of his perceived personal authenticity and integrity, enhanced by awareness of his working-class heritage and his hostility to a bourgeois 'establishment'. Lawrence was generally valued less as a literary artist than as a guide to genuine living and to personal resistance against a soulless civilisation.

One way of deciphering the new configuration of the sixties in Britain is to note the significant incursion of men from the provinces, often of working-class origins too, into some of the traditional cultural centres (national newspapers, the expanding universities), and their more visible presence in newly influential cultural forms such as television, features journalism, photography and popular music. The influx of these new men, some of them bluntly self-assertive and bearded like Lawrence, was felt to embody a democratic reinvigoration of an effete or neutered national life. Its imaginary significance was, then, congruent with the romance structure of *Lady Chatterley's Lover* itself, in which the more authentic potency of the man of the people awakens the dormant princess who is imprisoned within an impotent patrician elite. According to this ancient but rediscovered myth, an ossified social system and its class barriers could be overcome by the force of male sexual charisma. Lawrence's own life-story (coalminer's son elopes with daughter of the aristocracy) appeared to underwrite the fairytale sexual politics of the age. In this rather nebulous sense, Lawrence was a presiding spirit of sixties libertarianism, although progressive opinion at the time tended to overlook his desperate authoritarian fantasies, his horror of masturbation, his belief that children should be thrashed regularly for the good of their lumbar ganglia and, most blindly, the misogyny of much of his work.

It is a commonplace that Lawrence the puritan would have been horrified by the sexual 'permissiveness', as it was called, of the sixties. And in some measure his authority was called upon at the time precisely in order to resist it. The energetic Leavisite educationalist David Holbrook, for instance, wrote a sequence of highly regarded books in the sixties – *English for Maturity* (1961), *The Secret Places* (1964) and *The Exploring Word* (1967) – in which Lawrence's works are repeatedly invoked as sources of an emotional 'wholeness' urgently required by children and their teachers in a dangerous modern world of commercialised insincerity. Although Holbrook follows the new Leavisite line in regretting *Lady Chatterley's Lover* as a 'false' work, he promotes Lawrence not only as 'the century's greatest imaginative writer',[21] but as a healthy antidote to the mechanical and selfish models of sexuality offered to young people by comic-strips, Hollywood movies and skiffle bands. For the growing number of teachers in the sixties who saw the role of literature as one of fostering imaginative resistance to a utilitarian culture, Lawrence became in this sense a touchstone of human values. *Sons and Lovers* was accepted into the school syllabus, and was followed inevitably by *Brodie's Notes on 'Sons and Lovers'* (1966). At the higher levels of academic life, meanwhile, critical discussion of Lawrence's writings expanded into an 'industry', complete with its own journal, the *D. H. Lawrence Review* (from 1968). The *Review*'s founding editor, James C. Cowan, later compiled a bibliography listing no fewer than 1,400 books and articles about Lawrence published in the sixties. By the end of that decade, university departments of English commonly presented Lawrence to their students as a 'central' figure of modern literature and of moral wisdom.

The reverential acceptance of Lawrence as a figure of authority was dispelled by Kate Millett's bold work of feminist iconoclasm in *Sexual Politics* (1970). Drawing upon some brief remarks made by Simone de Beauvoir in *Le Deuxième sexe* (1949), Millett's chapter on Lawrence undertakes a full-scale assault upon Lawrence's male-supremacist attitudes. It begins by doubting the credentials of *Lady Chatterley's Lover*, which had become accepted as a woman-friendly vision of mutual tenderness, but which appears upon closer inspection to be a one-sided glorification of phallic dominance. Reviewing Lawrence's other major novels, Millett reads these as projections of Lawrence's personal 'campaign against the modern woman',[22] culminating in the demented misogynist sadism of 'The Woman Who Rode Away'. Millett does acknowledge the artistic merits of *Sons and Lovers* and *The Rainbow*, but otherwise her account of the fiction is relentless in presenting Lawrence as the pontiff of a murderous phallic cult. Her interpretation of *Women in Love* is especially crude in simply equating Birkin with Lawrence and in overlooking Ursula's sceptical resistance: '*Women in Love* presents us with the new man arrived in time to give Ursula her comeuppance and demote her back to wifely subjection.'[23] In the context of Lawrence's exalted reputation in the sixties, Millett's critique was a refreshing corrective, but it tended only to stand the idol on his head, merely inverting Leavis's uniformly life-affirming genius and turning him into a uniformly death-dealing maniac. Millett seems unaware of the existence of a fuller analysis of Lawrence's misogyny in Murry's *Son of Woman*, and fails to benefit from its stronger grasp of the writer's inner divisions and contradictions. What is most disablingly lacking in both Leavis's and Millett's approaches, indeed, is any developed sense of Lawrence's works as self-contradictory. Criticism of Lawrence came of age only when it rediscovered this principle.

Sexual conundrums

The re-emergence of the 'contradictory' Lawrence can be traced in the more perceptive studies published in the sixties, in which the wholesomely affirmative writer of Leavis's portrait is challenged or balanced by emphases on his perverse, destructive side: Eliseo Vivas's *D. H. Lawrence* presented a more 'savage' Lawrence, Kingsley Widmer's *The Art of Perversity* (1962) offered a 'demonic' Lawrence, and Colin Clarke's *River of Dissolution* (1969) countered Leavis directly with a 'satanic' Lawrence. Clarke's book in particular insisted that what appear to be differentiated as positive and negative terms in Lawrence are often interchangeable, and that disintegration, dissolution and corruption are welcomed as necessary phases of growth. Amply illustrated from *Women in Love* and other texts, this argument helped to dispose of the healthily 'normal' Lawrence of the Leavisites. Clarke, like Spilka before him, also encouraged readers to view Lawrence's writings not as embodiments of a fixed doctrine but as explorations of varying possible positions, all subject to revision and sudden reverse. This less doctrinal, more exploratory and agonistic Lawrence became established in the public mind with Ken Russell's surprisingly faithful film version of *Women in Love* (1969), in which the most memorable scene is that in which Alan Bates (Birkin) and Oliver Reed (Gerald) wrestle naked by firelight; the film successfully rendered the self-questioning and potentially homoerotic dimensions of Lawrence that had been submerged in the Lady Chatterley brouhaha. In the wake of these successive challenges to Leavisian wholesomeness, Gãmini Salgãdo's 1976 essay, 'Taking a Nail for a Walk', insists even more upon the self-cancelling, paradoxical, Janus-faced nature of *Women in Love*, in which each argument is shadowed by an endorsement of its incompatible opposite. In the following years, the critical forces of deconstruction and psychoanalysis more generally emphasised the indeterminacy and ambivalence of literary texts, including Lawrence's. This tradition culminates in Linda Ruth Williams's lively book *Sex in the Head* (1993), which pursues Lawrencean self-contradiction through the lens of film theory, showing how a variety of Lawrence's texts disavow what they most desire and desire what they most disavow.

Williams's *Sex in the Head* describes itself as a feminist 'dehabilitation' of Lawrence rather than a rehabilitation. For the most part, however, the rediscovered contradiction, doubleness and paradox in his writings has opened the way to strategies of critical redemption by which Lawrence can be salvaged from the accusations levelled by Millett. If all is not as it seems in Lawrence, but quite the opposite at the same time, then the ostensible phallicist may even turn out to be a misunderstood feminist sympathiser, or even a woman in disguise. Norman Mailer, who was placed in the dock with Lawrence in *Sexual Politics*, responded in his *The Prisoner of Sex* (1971) that Lawrence, despite his temporary deviation into the cult of phallic mastery, was a true worshipper of women, and indeed understood them as no other writer had done before, partly because he was spiritually female himself. A similar view of Lawrence as a kind of woman writer hidden under a masculine appearance is offered in Carol Dix's *D. H. Lawrence and Women* (1980). Much more cautiously, the feminist critic Philippa Tristram in 'Eros and Death' (1978) found Lawrence capable of genuine imaginative identification with women, especially in *The Rainbow*, until he lost his way by polarising Eros and Death as male and female. On the other hand, Angela Carter's irreverent article 'Lorenzo as Closet-Queen' (1975) claims that Lawrence has no real understanding of women's hearts because he is too interested in their clothes: his mode of female impersonation reveals him to be an abject stocking-fetishist.[24] In feminist criticism after the seventies, and in the broader domain of gender studies that includes gay literary research, these puzzles and paradoxes of Lawrence's sexual identity have to some extent kept critical discussion of his work alive when it seemed most doomed. Lawrence thus lives on, no longer as a hero but as a symptomatic case-study in the psychoanalysis of fetishism or sado-masochism. Williams's *Sex in the Head* shows how Lawrence's kind of fantasy places him in dominant and submissive positions at the same time. Likewise, Jonathan Dollimore's *Sexual Dissidence* (1991) claims that Lawrence the misogynist also fantasises sex from the woman's position, contaminating heterosexuality with his own repressed homoeroticism.

Future directions

In academic literary studies since the 1980s, the assumption is more and more often found that a writer's work is of interest and of value only to the extent that it may be shown to 'transgress', 'subvert' or otherwise to cast in doubt what are held to be conventional models of gender, sexuality and race. Lawrence's visibility in academic criticism, much diminished since the zenith of the sixties, has been preserved by this trend, under the special parole appropriate to a 'prisoner of sex': as a fascinating case of unwitting self-sodomy illustrating the tortured illogic of misogynist and homophobic repressions. It is unclear where the study of Lawrencean sexualities will go from here, though one possible line of enquiry is signalled by Hugh Stevens's chapter elsewhere in this volume. Its exploration of the imbrication of sex and nationhood in Lawrence's writing after the outbreak of the First World War marks a step in the direction of a more fully historicised Lawrence. But Lawrence the shocking sex-prophet is finished, having been humiliated by Millett and domesticated by the adaptation, not just of *The Rainbow* but of *Lady Chatterley's Lover*, into run-of-the mill television costume drama. In this new phase of Lawrence's public reception, marked by his assimilation into televisual 'heritage' exhibits scarcely distinguishable from the James–Hardy–Doyle–Forster pageants, it falls to the serious student of literature to direct more attention, first, to Lawrence the *writer* (there are still few substantial analyses of his alarmingly uneven prose style), and second, to the true historical complexities of his engagement with the socio-economic and cultural transformations of his age. Useful work on this 'historical' Lawrence has been done in the Marxist tradition, notably by Graham Holderness in *D. H. Lawrence: History, Ideology and Fiction* (1982), although most of it has concentrated on the 'rooted' Lawrence of the Nottinghamshire coalfields, and not enough on the exiled Lawrence of the post-war pilgrimage. In historicist approaches, exile and international travel are still too often regarded merely as an exit from 'real' history; more recent attention to the importance of migration in the culture of the twentieth century may yet refresh our sense of Lawrence in his time.

A further domestication from which Lawrence will require some careful dislodging consists in his doubtful recruitment, in academic discourse, into the movement of 'modernism' – a homogenising term that now tends to engross all attention to literature in the first half of the twentieth century, to the exclusion of all other currents. Some critics have assumed that Lawrence is so obviously a modernist that the point needs no substantiation; others that he stands equally obviously outside the Eliot–Joyce–Woolf circuit. Michael Bell's chapter in this volume has already indicated the importance of looking beyond those alternatives. Of recent attempts to solve this conundrum, the most original is Tony Pinkney's *D. H. Lawrence* (1990; published in the USA as *D. H. Lawrence and Modernism*), which sees the author of *The Rainbow* as the inventor of a northern or 'Gothic' modernism as remote from the the classicism of Eliot and the Imagists as it is from Edwardian realism. Pinkney's thesis rests precariously upon some hair-raisingly schematic equations, for example between the aridity of classicism and the dryness of the anus; but his account of the ways in which *Women in Love* and *The Plumed Serpent* struggle against mainstream modernism is always valuably provocative, suggesting many new lines of investigation.

It is more than usually hazardous to predict the shape of Lawrence's cultural presence in its next phase. From one angle it may appear that his reputation has sustained such wounding blows from friend and foe alike that it could subside at any moment into near-oblivion, leaving (let us guess almost at random) only *Sons and Lovers* and the *Studies in Classic American Literature* in living currency. From another, the example of the sixties shows that whenever there is a general resurgence of youthful 'Romanticism' – and in advanced capitalist societies there frequently will be – then it will seek out its 'prophetic' precursors. The development both of 'postmodern' hostility to scientific reason and of 'New Age' cultural phenomena (astrological paganism, ecological primitivism, animal liberationism) indicates just such a context, in which an unrecognisably revised Lawrence canon, perhaps headed by *St. Mawr*, *Birds, Beasts and Flowers* and *Mornings in Mexico*, might emerge. In such a context, the study of Lawrence's life and works will have its value both for the postmodern 'heretics' to take their own bearings, and for guardians of orthodoxy to comprehend the roots and the dynamics of Romanticism in the twenty-first century. The same context will demand, too, an enlarged and more exact understanding of the Protestant matrix from which Lawrence and his successors develop their notions of personal and religious conscience. Finally, it may lead us back to the extraordinary physiological speculations of *Fantasia of the Unconscious*, in search of some clue to the widespread abandonment of empirically proven remedies in favour of 'alternative' medicine and 'holistic' discourses of the body. If so, it would resurrect those commanding metaphors of Lawrence criticism that were discarded in the reaction against Leavis without having been fully unravelled: sickness and health.

NOTES

1 *D. H. Lawrence: A Critical Anthology*, ed. H. Coombes (Harmondsworth: Penguin, 1973), p. 222.
2 F. R. Leavis, *Valuation in Criticism and Other Essays*, ed. G. Singh (Cambridge: Cambridge University Press, 1986), p. 22.
3 Catherine Carswell, *The Savage Pilgrimage: A Narrative of D. H. Lawrence*, 2nd edn (London: Secker, 1932), p. 192.
4 *D. H. Lawrence: The Critical Heritage*, ed. R. P. Draper (London: Routledge, 1970), p. 359.
5 Ibid., p. 361.

6 See Ian McKillop, *F. R. Leavis: A Life in Criticism* (London: Allen Lane, 1995), pp. 191–92.

7 Coombes (ed.), *D. H. Lawrence*, pp. 252–53.

8 Ibid., pp. 276–80.

9 Stephen Spender, *The Thirties and After: Poetry, Politics, People* (London: Macmillan, 1978), pp. 41–45.

10 Cyril Connolly, *Enemies of Promise* (Harmondsworth: Penguin 1961), p. 71.

11 F. R. Leavis, *D. H. Lawrence, Novelist* (Harmondsworth: Penguin, 1964), p. 29.

12 Ibid., p. 81.

13 Ibid., p. 377.

14 *The Trial of Lady Chatterley: Regina v. Penguin Books Limited*, ed. C. H. Rolph (Harmondsworth: Penguin, 1961), pp. 42, 61–62, 158.

15 Ibid., p. 30.

16 Ibid., p. 118.

17 Ibid., p. 221. In what has become a voluminous literature on Lawrencean anality, a legend has grown up that the anal sex episode (pp. 258–59 of the Penguin edition) was entirely overlooked at the trial, by a legal establishment risibly ignorant of all unorthodox pleasures. In fact this passage was quoted in part by Raymond Williams, and later recited in full in the prosecution's closing speech. Far from ignoring the passage, the prosecutors chose to tread carefully in mentioning it, for fear of antagonising the jury.

18 D. H. Lawrence, *Lady Chatterley's Lover*, 2nd edn (Harmondsworth: Penguin, 1961), p. v.

19 Raymond Williams, *Politics and Letters: Interviews with New Left Review* (London: Verso, 1979), p. 126.

20 Some interesting exceptions to this rule may be found in the early works of Doris Lessing. Compare, for example, the opening pages of her 1963 short story 'To Room Nineteen' with the similarly sarcastic depiction of an 'ideal' couple in the title story of Lawrence's *England, My England* (1922).

21 David Holbrook, *The Exploring Word: Creative Disciplines in the Education of Teachers of English* (Cambridge: Cambridge University Press, 1967), p. 210.

22 Kate Millett, *Sexual Politics* (London: Rupert Hart-Davis, 1971), p. 263.

23 Ibid., p. 262.

24 Philippa Tristram, 'Eros and Death (Lawrence, Freud and Women)', in *Lawrence and Women*, ed. Anne Smith (London: Vision, 1978), pp. 136–55. Angela Carter, *Nothing Sacred: Selected Writings* (London: Virago, 1982), pp. 161–68.

PAUL POPLAWSKI

Guide to further reading

The works of D. H. Lawrence

The following list provides details, where available, both of the standard scholarly edition of Lawrence's works, published by Cambridge University Press, and of its partner paperback edition published in Penguin's Twentieth-Century Classics series. The Cambridge edition, under the general editorship of James T. Boulton and Warren Roberts, began publication in 1979 and several volumes are currently still in preparation; the Penguin Lawrence Edition, with John Worthen as Advisory Editor, began publication in 1994. The Penguin edition prints the same texts as Cambridge and therefore the editors of individual volumes are the same for both editions. The Penguin edition, however, carries new introductions and explanatory notes, and it occasionally supplies corrections to the original Cambridge texts. Alternative publication details are given for works not yet available in the Cambridge edition.

All Cambridge volumes are published by Cambridge University Press at Cambridge and this information is abbreviated throughout to 'Cambridge'. All Penguin editions are published at Harmondsworth, Middlesex. The few pre-1994 Penguin editions cited here *do not* make use of the texts established by the Cambridge edition. After the initial publication date, the most recent date of reprinting is given for such editions. Where relevant, the date of original publication of each work is given in brackets immediately after the title.

NOVELS

Aaron's Rod (1922), ed. Mara Kalnins. Cambridge, 1988. Penguin, intro. Steven Vine, 1995.
The Boy in the Bush [co-authored by M. L. Skinner] (1924), ed. Paul Eggert. Cambridge, 1990. Penguin, intro. Paul Eggert, 1996.
The First Lady Chatterley (1944). Penguin, 1973.

John Thomas and Lady Jane (in Italian, 1954; in English, 1972). Penguin 1973.

Kangaroo (1923), ed. Bruce Steele. Cambridge, 1994. Penguin, intro. Macdonald Daly, 1997.

Lady Chatterley's Lover (1928), ed. Michael Squires. Cambridge, 1993. Penguin, intro. Michael Squires, 1994. See also *The First and Second Lady Chatterley Novels*, ed. Dieter Mehl and Christa Jansohn. Cambridge, 1999.

The Lost Girl (1920), ed. John Worthen. Cambridge, 1981. Penguin, intro. Carol Siegel, 1995.

Mr Noon, ed. Lindeth Vasey. Cambridge, 1984. (Part 1 1934; the unfinished Part 11 published here for the first time.) Penguin, intro. Lindeth Vasey and Peter Preston, 1996.

The Plumed Serpent (Quetzalcoatl) (1926), ed. L. D. Clark. Cambridge, 1987. Penguin, intro. L. D. Clark and Virginia Crosswhite Hyde, 1995. See also *Quetzalcoatl: The Early Version of 'The Plumed Serpent'*, ed. Louis L. Martz. Redding Ridge, CT: Black Swan Books, 1995.

The Rainbow (1915), ed. Mark Kinkead-Weekes. Cambridge, 1989. Penguin, intro. Anne Fernihough, 1995.

Sons and Lovers (1913), ed. Helen Baron and Carl Baron. Cambridge, 1992. Penguin, intro. Helen Baron and Carl Baron, 1994. See also *D. H. Lawrence: 'Sons and Lovers': A Facsimile of the Manuscript*, ed. Mark Schorer. Berkeley: University of California Press, 1977.

The Trespasser (1912), ed. Elizabeth Mansfield. Cambridge, 1981. Penguin, intro. John Turner, 1994.

The White Peacock (1911), ed. Andrew Robertson. Cambridge, 1983. Penguin, intro. Michael Black, 1995.

Women in Love (1920), ed. David Farmer, Lindeth Vasey and John Worthen. Cambridge, 1987. Penguin, intro. Mark Kinkead-Weekes, 1995. See also *The First 'Women in Love'*, ed. Lindeth Vasey and John Worthen. Cambridge, 1998.

SHORT FICTION

The Complete Short Novels, ed. Keith Sagar and Melissa Partridge. Penguin, 1982; reprinted, 1990. A convenient anthology of seven short novels, including *The Virgin and the Gipsy* and *The Escaped Cock*, which are not yet available in the Cambridge edition. See also *The Escaped Cock*, ed. Gerald M. Lacy. Los Angeles: Black Sparrow Press, 1973.

England, My England and Other Stories (1922), ed. Bruce Steele. Cambridge, 1990. Penguin, intro. Michael Bell, 1995.

The Fox, The Captain's Doll, The Ladybird (1923), ed. Dieter Mehl. Cambridge, 1992. Penguin, intro. David Ellis, 1994. ('The Fox' first published in 1920; the collection first published under the main title *The Ladybird*.)

Love Among the Haystacks and Other Stories, ed. John Worthen. Cambridge, 1987. Penguin, intro. Keith Cushman, 1996.

The Princess and Other Stories, ed. Keith Sagar. Penguin, 1971; reprinted, 1981. Contains stories not yet available in the Cambridge edition.

The Prussian Officer and Other Stories (1914), ed. John Worthen. Cambridge, 1983. Penguin, intro. Brian Finney, 1995.

Selected Short Stories, ed. Brian Finney. Penguin, 1982; reprinted, 1989. A comprehensive selection with an incisive introduction and detailed notes.

St. Mawr [1925] *and Other Stories*, ed. Brian Finney. Cambridge, 1983. Penguin, intro. Charles Rossman, 1997.

The Virgin and the Gipsy (1930). Penguin, 1970; reprinted, 1990.

The Woman Who Rode Away and Other Stories (1928), ed. Dieter Mehl and Christa Jansohn. Cambridge, 1995. Penguin, intro. N. H. Reeve, 1996.

POETRY

Lawrence compiled eleven complete volumes of poetry in his lifetime (two published posthumously), as follows: *Love Poems and Others* (1913), *Amores* (1916), *Look! We Have Come Through!* (1917), *New Poems* (1918), *Bay* (1919), *Tortoises* (1921), *Birds, Beasts and Flowers* (1923), *The Collected Poems of D. H. Lawrence*, 2 volumes (1928), *Pansies* (1929), *Nettles* (1930), *Last Poems* (1932). Current editions are as follows.

The Collected Poems (1928) are available under the misleading title *The Works of D. H. Lawrence*. Hertfordshire: Wordsworth Editions, 1994.

The Complete Poems of D. H. Lawrence, ed. Vivian de Sola Pinto and Warren Roberts. Penguin, 1977; reprinted, 1994. The Cambridge edition of Lawrence's poetry is still in preparation, and this, therefore, is the most comprehensive collection currently available.

D. H. Lawrence: Selected Poems, ed. Mara Kalnins. London: Dent (Everyman's Library), 1992.

D. H. Lawrence: Selected Poems, ed. Keith Sagar. Penguin, 1972; revised as *D. H. Lawrence: Poems*, 1986.

PLAYS

The Complete Plays of D. H. Lawrence. London: Heinemann, 1965. Until recently, the only collection containing all ten of Lawrence's plays (eight complete and two unfinished); but now superseded by the Cambridge *Plays* (see following item).

The Plays, ed. Hans Schwarze and John Worthen. Cambridge, 1999.

Three Plays by D. H. Lawrence: A Collier's Friday Night, The Daughter-in-Law, The Widowing of Mrs. Holroyd, ed. Raymond Williams. Penguin, 1969. Contains an excellent introduction by Williams.

The Widowing of Mrs. Holroyd and The Daughter-in-Law, ed. Michael Marland. London: Heinemann Educational, 1968; reprinted, 1988.

NON-FICTION

Apocalypse [1931] *and the Writings on Revelation*, ed. Mara Kalnins. Cambridge, 1980. Penguin, intro. Mara Kalnins, 1995.

D. H. Lawrence: Selected Critical Writings, ed. Michael Herbert. Oxford and New York: Oxford University Press, 1998.

Fantasia of the Unconscious [1922] and *Psychoanalysis and the Unconscious* [1921]. Penguin, 1971; reprinted 1986.

Mornings in Mexico (1927). Penguin Travel Library, 1986. See also the text edited by Ross Parmenter. Salt Lake City: Gibbs M. Smith, 1982.

Movements in European History (1921), ed. Philip Crumpton. Cambridge, 1989.

The Paintings of D. H. Lawrence. London: Mandrake Press, 1929. A rare book of reproductions published to coincide with an exhibition of Lawrence's paintings in London in 1929. See also: *Paintings of D. H. Lawrence*, ed. Mervyn Levy. London: Cory, Adams and Mackay, 1964 (includes critical essays on Lawrence's art); and *D. H. Lawrence: Ten Paintings*. Redding Ridge, CT: Black Swan, 1982.

Phoenix: The Posthumous Papers of D. H. Lawrence, ed. Edward D. McDonald. London: Heinemann, 1936. With the following item, a comprehensive collection of Lawrence's essays. (See also *D. H. Lawrence: A Selection from Phoenix*, ed. A. A. H. Inglis. Penguin, 1971; reprinted, 1979.)

Phoenix II: Uncollected, Unpublished and Other Prose Works by D. H. Lawrence, ed. Warren Roberts and Harry T. Moore. London: Heinemann, 1968.

Reflections on the Death of a Porcupine and Other Essays (1925), ed. Michael Herbert. Cambridge, 1988.

Sea and Sardinia (1921), ed. Mara Kalnins. Cambridge, 1997. Penguin, intro. Jill Franks, 1999.

Sketches of Etruscan Places [1932] *and Other Italian Essays*, ed. Simonetta de Filippis. Cambridge, 1992. Penguin, intro. Simonetta de Filippis, 1999.

Studies in Classic American Literature (1924). Penguin, 1971; reprinted, 1990. See also *The Symbolic Meaning: The Uncollected Versions of Studies in Classic American Literature*, ed. Armin Arnold. London: T. J. Winterson, 1962.

Study of Thomas Hardy [1936] *and Other Essays*, ed. Bruce Steele. Cambridge, 1985.

Twilight in Italy [1916] *and Other Essays*, ed. Paul Eggert. Cambridge, 1994. Penguin, intro. Stefania Michelucci, 1997.

LETTERS

The Letters of D. H. Lawrence. 7 volumes. General Editor, James T. Boulton. Cambridge, 1979–93. *Volume VIII: Index*, ed. James T. Boulton. Cambridge, forthcoming. For a selection from these volumes, see *The Selected Letters of D. H. Lawrence*, ed. James T. Boulton. Cambridge, 1997 (paperback edn, 2000)

Criticism and scholarship

There are over 650 books or pamphlets on Lawrence and literally thousands of essays. The following list, therefore, is necessarily highly selective. I have been guided in making my choices by several – not always mutually compatible – criteria. (i) I have obviously tried to choose works which are accessible, reliable and accurate, and which offer a high standard of critical scholarship. (ii) I have tried to maintain a reasonable balance in covering different aspects of Lawrence's life and works, while at the same time being mindful of those aspects likely to be of most interest to students and the general reader (rather than to the scholar or specialist). (iii) I have generally given priority to works published in the last fifteen years or so, though I have also included a substantial number of older works, both for the purposes of historical perspective and because, by common critical consent, certain works have come to be seen as 'classics' in the field with a continuing importance for criticism today. (iv) I have, to some extent, also tried to reflect the overall balance of interests represented within the other chapters in this book, although my main priority has been to produce an *internally* coherent and balanced bibliography. (v) Finally, and regrettably, as a negative criterion, I have not been able to include works in other languages, nor many works produced in other countries that are not readily available in Britain: this *is* regrettable, as critical interest in Lawrence is nothing if not international, and as there has been such a lot of useful work produced (both English-language and other) in non-Anglo-American contexts (particularly in Europe, India and Asia).

As in the first section, publication details for works published by Cambridge University Press and Penguin are abbreviated to Cambridge and Penguin respectively.

(A) BIBLIOGRAPHICAL SOURCES

Cowan, James C. *D. H. Lawrence: An Annotated Bibliography of Writings About Him*. 2 volumes. De Kalb, IL: Northern Illinois University Press, 1982, 1985. A comprehensive chronological listing of books, articles and reviews, with brief summaries and comments. Volume I, covering 1909–60, has 2,061 entries; volume II, covering 1961–75, has 2,566 entries.

D. H. Lawrence Review. Currently edited by William M. Harrison at the State University of New York, Geneseo. An important forum for contemporary debate on Lawrence and an invaluable source of bibliographical information. See, in particular, the journal's annual checklists of criticism.

Poplawski, Paul. *D. H. Lawrence: A Reference Companion*. Westport and London: Greenwood Press, 1996. A comprehensive guide to criticism and scholarship. Contains ninety-eight separate bibliographies, with individual sections on each of Lawrence's works, and a guide to criticism differentiated according to critical approach (feminist, psychoanalytical, etc.). Also contains a biography by John Worthen, and two important chapters on 'Lawrence and Film' by Nigel Morris (with a filmography and bibliography of related criticism).

The Works of D. H. Lawrence: A Chronological Checklist. Nottingham: D. H. Lawrence Society, 1995. Booklet summarising dates of composition and publication of Lawrence's works. See also Preston's *Chronology* and Sagar's *Calendar*, cited below, and the appendices to the three Cambridge biographies listed under section (B).

Preston, Peter. *A D. H. Lawrence Chronology*. London: Macmillan, 1994. A full chronological record of Lawrence's life and writing career.

Rice, Thomas Jackson. *D. H. Lawrence: A Guide to Research*. New York and London: Garland, 1983. A well-structured and reliable annotated bibliography of primary and secondary sources. Contains 2,123 entries with a terminal date of 1 January 1983.

Roberts, Warren. *A Bibliography of D. H. Lawrence.* 2nd edn. Cambridge, 1982. Revised 3rd edn. forthcoming. Definitive primary bibliography of Lawrence's works, also incorporating an important secondary bibliography. Organised into the following sections: (A) Books and pamphlets; (B) Contributions to books; (C) Contributions to periodicals; (D) Translations; (E) Manuscripts (compiled by Lindeth Vasey); (F) Books and pamphlets about D. H. Lawrence (243 works listed to 1981; the 3rd edition will list in excess of 700 works).

Sagar, Keith. *D. H. Lawrence: A Calendar of His Works.* Manchester: Manchester University Press, 1979.

(ed.) *A D. H. Lawrence Handbook.* Manchester: Manchester University Press, 1982. Contains a wealth of varied information and two invaluable bibliographies: Dennis Jackson's 'A Select Bibliography, 1907–79 [of writings by and about Lawrence]', pp. 1–58; and Rose Marie Burwell's 'A Checklist of Lawrence's Reading', pp. 59–125.

(B) BIOGRAPHIES

See under Ellis, Kinkead-Weekes and Worthen for the scholarly three-volume Cambridge biography of Lawrence – now the most up-to-date and authoritative work in the field.

Ellis, David. *D. H. Lawrence, Volume III: Dying Game, 1922–1930.* Cambridge, 1998.

Kinkead-Weekes, Mark. *D. H. Lawrence, Volume II: Triumph to Exile, 1912–1922.* Cambridge, 1996.

Sagar, Keith. *The Life of D. H. Lawrence: An Illustrated Biography.* London: Eyre Methuen, 1980; paperback edn. 1982.

D. H. Lawrence: Life into Art. Harmondsworth: Penguin, 1985.

Worthen, John. *D. H. Lawrence: A Literary Life.* London: Macmillan, 1989. Concentrates on Lawrence's career as a professional writer.

D. H. Lawrence [Volume I]: The Early Years 1885–1912. Cambridge, 1991.

'A Biography'. In Poplawski, *Reference Companion*, cited in (A) above, pp. 3–93.

(C) ANTHOLOGIES AND ESSAY COLLECTIONS

Given the vast amount of critical work on Lawrence, the quickest way to gain one's bearings within the field is by consulting some of the many available compilations of criticism. I list below a selection of these, with a particular emphasis on recent publications.

Balbert, Peter, and Phillip L. Marcus (eds.) *D. H. Lawrence: A Centenary Consideration.* Ithaca and London: Cornell University Press, 1985.

Beynon, Richard (ed.) *D. H. Lawrence: 'The Rainbow'/'Women in Love'.* Duxford, Cambridge: Icon Books, 1997 (distributed by Penguin). Ranges beyond the two novels in the title to survey general critical attitudes towards Lawrence throughout the century.

Bloom, Harold (ed.) *D. H. Lawrence: Modern Critical Views*. New York: Chelsea House, 1986.

Brown, Keith (ed.) *Rethinking Lawrence*. Milton Keynes: Open University Press, 1990.

Donaldson, George, and Mara Kalnins (eds.) *D. H. Lawrence in Italy and England*. London: Macmillan, 1999.

Draper, R. P. (ed.) *D. H. Lawrence: The Critical Heritage*. London: Routledge, 1970; reprinted, 1997. Traces Lawrence's critical reception from the very beginning of his career and collects valuable reference materials (contemporary reviews, etc.) that would otherwise be inaccessible.

Eggert, Paul, and John Worthen (eds.) *D. H. Lawrence and Comedy*. Cambridge, 1996.

Ellis, David, and Ornella De Zordo (eds.) *D. H. Lawrence: Critical Assessments*. 4 volumes. East Sussex: Helm Information Ltd, 1992. An indispensable anthology of nearly 200 essays and reviews covering the whole history of Lawrence's critical reception.

Heywood, Christopher (ed.) *D. H. Lawrence: New Studies*. London: Macmillan, 1987.

Iida, Takeo (ed.) *The Reception of D. H. Lawrence Around the World*. Fukuoka, Japan: Kyushu University Press, 1999. Fourteen authoritative essays surveying Lawrence's critical reception around the world, including a comprehensive survey of 'Lawrence in Britain 1930–1998' by Peter Preston.

Jackson, Dennis, and Fleda Brown Jackson (eds.) *Critical Essays on D. H. Lawrence*. Boston: G. K. Hall and Co., 1988. See especially the excellent introduction: 'D. H. Lawrence's Critical Reception: An Overview', pp. 1–46.

Meyers, Jeffrey (ed.) *D. H. Lawrence and Tradition*. London: Athlone, 1985.

Poplawski, Paul (ed.) *Writing the Body in D. H. Lawrence: Essays on Language, Representation and Sexuality*. Westport, CT: Greenwood, forthcoming.

Preston, Peter, and Peter Hoare (eds.) *D. H. Lawrence in the Modern World*. London: Macmillan, 1989.

Ross, Charles L., and Dennis Jackson (eds.) *Editing D. H. Lawrence: New Versions of a Modern Author*. Ann Arbor: University of Michigan Press, 1996.

Salgādo, Gāmini (ed.) *D. H. Lawrence: 'Sons and Lovers': A Selection of Critical Essays*, Casebook series. London: Macmillan, 1969.

Salgādo, Gāmini, and G. K. Das (eds.) *The Spirit of D. H. Lawrence: Centenary Studies*. London: Macmillan, 1988.

Smith, Anne (ed.) *Lawrence and Women*. London: Vision, 1978.

Spender, Stephen (ed.) *D. H. Lawrence: Novelist, Poet, Prophet*. London: Weidenfeld and Nicolson, 1973.

Squires, Michael, and Keith Cushman (eds.) *The Challenge of D. H. Lawrence*. Madison: University of Wisconsin Press, 1990.

Widdowson, Peter (ed.) *D. H. Lawrence*. London and New York: Longman, 1992. See especially Widdowson's introduction on 'Post-modernising D. H. Lawrence', pp. 1–27.

(D) GENERAL STUDIES

Most of the works listed here discuss a range of Lawrence's works from a fairly general perspective, although several of them narrow that perspective somewhat according to a particular special interest, usually clearly signalled in the title.

Bell, Michael. *D. H. Lawrence: Language and Being*. Cambridge, 1992.

Bonds, Diane S. *Language and the Self in D. H. Lawrence*. Ann Arbor, MI: UMI Research Press, 1987.

Clarke, Colin. *River of Dissolution: D. H. Lawrence and English Romanticism*. London: Routledge and Kegan Paul, 1969.

Cowan, James C. *D. H. Lawrence's American Journey: A Study in Literature and Myth*. Cleveland, OH, and London: The Press of the Case Western Reserve University, 1970.

 D. H. Lawrence and the Trembling Balance. Pennsylvania: Pennsylvania State University Press, 1990.

Daleski, H. M. *The Forked Flame: A Study of D. H. Lawrence*. London: Faber, 1965. 2nd edn, Madison: University of Wisconsin Press, 1987.

Doherty, Gerald. *Theorizing Lawrence: Nine Meditations on Tropological Themes*. New York: Peter Lang, 1999.

Fernihough, Anne. *D. H. Lawrence: Aesthetics and Ideology*. Oxford: Oxford University Press, 1993.

Ford, George H. *Double Measure: A Study of the Novels and Stories of D. H. Lawrence*. New York: Holt, Rinehart & Winston, 1965.

Franks, Jill. *Revisionist Resurrection Mythologies: A Study of D. H. Lawrence's Italian Works*. New York: Peter Lang, 1994.

Goodheart, Eugene. *The Utopian Vision of D. H. Lawrence*. Chicago, IL, and London: University of Chicago Press, 1963.

Hamalian, Leo. *D. H. Lawrence and Nine Women Writers*. London: Associated University Presses, 1996.

Holderness, Graham. *D. H. Lawrence: History, Ideology and Fiction*. Dublin: Gill and Macmillan, 1982.

Hough, Graham. *The Dark Sun: A Study of D. H. Lawrence*. London: Duckworth, 1956.

Hyde, G. M. *D. H. Lawrence*. London: Macmillan, 1990.

Hyde, Virginia. *The Risen Adam: D. H. Lawrence's Revisionist Typology*. Pennsylvania: The Pennsylvania State University Press, 1992.

Jarrett-Kerr, Martin. *D. H. Lawrence and Human Existence*. London: Rockliffe, 1951 (under pseudonym of Father William Tiverton). Revised, London: SCM Press, 1961.

Kermode, Frank. *Lawrence*. London: Fontana, 1973.

La Chapelle, Dolores. *D. H. Lawrence: Future Primitive*. Denton, TX: University of North Texas Press, 1996.

Leavis, F. R. *D. H. Lawrence: Novelist*. London: Chatto and Windus, 1955.

Lewiecki-Wilson, Cynthia. *Writing Against the Family: Gender in Lawrence and Joyce*. Carbondale: Southern Illinois University Press, 1994.

Millett, Kate. *Sexual Politics*. London: Rupert Hart-Davis, 1971.

Moynahan, Julian. *The Deed of Life: The Novels and Tales of D. H. Lawrence*. Princeton: Princeton University Press, 1963.

Pinkney, Tony. *D. H. Lawrence*. Hemel Hempstead: Harvester Wheatsheaf, 1990.

Poplawski, Paul. *Promptings of Desire: Creativity and the Religious Impulse in the Works of D. H. Lawrence.* London and Westport, CT: Greenwood Press, 1993.

Sagar, Keith. *The Art of D. H. Lawrence.* Cambridge, 1966.

Scheckner, Peter. *Class, Politics, and the Individual: A Study of the Major Works of D. H. Lawrence.* London: Associated University Presses, 1985.

Siegel, Carol. *Lawrence Among the Women: Wavering Boundaries in Women's Literary Traditions.* Charlottesville and London: University Press of Virginia, 1991.

Simpson, Hilary. *D. H. Lawrence and Feminism.* London and Canberra: Croom Helm, 1982.

Sklenicka, Carol. *D. H. Lawrence and the Child.* Columbia and London: University of Missouri Press, 1991.

Spilka, Mark. *The Love Ethic of D. H. Lawrence.* Bloomington: Indiana University Press, 1955.

   Renewing the Normative D. H. Lawrence: A Personal Progress. Columbia: University of Missouri Press, 1992.

Stewart, Jack, *The Vital Art of D. H. Lawrence: Vision and Expression.* Carbondale: Southern Illinois University Press, 1999.

Vivas, Eliseo. *D. H. Lawrence: The Failure and the Triumph of Art.* London: George Allen and Unwin, 1960.

Weiss, Daniel. *Oedipus in Nottingham: D. H. Lawrence.* Seattle: University of Washington Press, 1962.

Wexler, Joyce Piell. *Who Paid for Modernism? Art, Money, and the Fiction of Conrad, Joyce, and Lawrence.* Fayetteville: University of Arkansas Press, 1997.

Widmer, Kingsley. *Defiant Desire: Some Dialectical Legacies of D. H. Lawrence.* Carbondale: Southern Illinois University Press, 1992.

Williams, Linda Ruth. *Sex in the Head: Visions of Femininity and Film in D. H. Lawrence.* Hemel Hempstead: Harvester Wheatsheaf, 1993.

   D. H. Lawrence. Plymouth: Northcote House, 1997.

Worthen, John. *D. H. Lawrence and the Idea of the Novel.* London: Macmillan, 1979.

   D. H. Lawrence, Modern Fiction Series. London: Edward Arnold, 1991.

(E) INDIVIDUAL NOVELS

Baker, Paul G. *A Reassessment of D. H. Lawrence's 'Aaron's Rod'.* Ann Arbor, MI: UMI Research Press, 1983.

Balbert, Peter. *D. H. Lawrence and the Psychology of Rhythm: The Meaning of Form in 'The Rainbow'.* The Hague: Mouton, 1974.

Björkén, Cecilia. *Into the Isle of Self: Nietzschean Patterns and Contrasts in D. H. Lawrence's 'The Trespasser'.* Lund, Sweden: Lund University Press; Bromley: Chartwell-Bratt, 1996.

Black, Michael. *D. H. Lawrence: Sons and Lovers.* Cambridge, 1992.

Britton, Derek. *'Lady Chatterley's Lover': The Making of the Novel.* London: Unwin Hyman, 1988.

Clark, L. D. *Dark Night of the Body: D. H. Lawrence's 'The Plumed Serpent'.* Austin: University of Texas Press, 1964.

Clarke, Colin (ed.) *D. H. Lawrence: 'The Rainbow' and 'Women in Love': A Casebook*. London: Macmillan, 1969.

Draper, R. P. *'Sons and Lovers' by D. H. Lawrence*, Macmillan Master Guides series. London: Macmillan, 1986.

Edwards, Duane. *'The Rainbow': A Search for New Life*. Boston: Twayne, 1990.

Finney, Brian. *D. H. Lawrence: 'Sons and Lovers'*, Penguin Critical Studies series. Penguin, 1990.

Harvey, Geoffrey. *Sons and Lovers*, The Critics Debate series. London: Macmillan, 1987.

Holderness, Graham. *Women in Love*, Open Guides to Literature Series. Milton Keynes and Philadelphia: Open University Press, 1986.

Jackson, Dennis, and Lydia Blanchard (eds.) *D. H. Lawrence Review* 20 (Summer 1988): Special Issue on *Mr Noon*.

Miko, Stephen J. *Toward 'Women in Love': The Emergence of a Lawrentian Aesthetic*. New Haven and London: Yale University Press, 1971.

Murfin, Ross C. *'Sons and Lovers': A Novel of Division and Desire*. Boston: Twayne, 1987.

Ross, Charles L. *'Women in Love': A Novel of Mythic Realism*. Boston: Twayne, 1991.

Rylance, Rick (ed.) *'Sons and Lovers': Contemporary Critical Essays*, New Casebook Series. London: Macmillan, 1996.

Squires, Michael. *The Creation of 'Lady Chatterley's Lover'*. Baltimore: Johns Hopkins University Press, 1983.

Squires, Michael, and Dennis Jackson (eds.) *D. H. Lawrence's 'Lady': A New Look at 'Lady Chatterley's Lover'*. Athens, GA: University of Georgia Press, 1985.

Whelan, P. T. *D. H. Lawrence: Myth and Metaphysic in 'The Rainbow' and 'Women in Love'*. Ann Arbor, MI, and London: UMI Research Press, 1988.

(F) SHORT FICTION

Blanchard, Lydia. 'D. H. Lawrence'. In *Critical Survey of Short Fiction*. Vol. v, ed. Frank N. Magill. Englewood Cliffs, NJ: Salem Press, 1981, pp. 1788–94.

Cushman, Keith. *D. H. Lawrence at Work: The Emergence of the 'Prussian Officer' Stories*. Sussex: Harvester, 1978.

Harris, Janice Hubbard. *The Short Fiction of D. H. Lawrence*. New Brunswick, NJ: Rutgers University Press, 1984.

Kearney, Martin F. *The Major Short Stories of D. H. Lawrence: A Handbook*. New York: Garland, 1997.

Mackenzie, Kenneth. *The Fox*. Milton Keynes: The Open University Press, 1973.

Poplawski, Paul. *Language, Art and Reality in D. H. Lawrence's 'St. Mawr': A Stylistic Study*. Lewiston, Queenston, Lampeter: The Edwin Mellen Press, 1996.

Thornton, Weldon. *D. H. Lawrence: A Study of the Short Fiction*. New York: Twayne, 1993.

Widmer, Kingsley. *The Art of Perversity: D. H. Lawrence's Shorter Fictions*. Seattle: University of Washington Press, 1962.

(G) POETRY

Banerjee, Amitava. *D. H. Lawrence's Poetry: Demon Liberated: A Collection of Primary and Secondary Source Material.* London: Macmillan, 1990.

Blackmur, R. P. 'D. H. Lawrence and Expressive Form'. In *The Double Agent.* New York: Arrow, 1935, pp. 103–20. Reprinted in his *Language as Gesture.* New York: Harcourt, Brace, 1952, pp. 286–300. A seminal essay, much debated.

Davey, Charles. *D. H. Lawrence: A Living Poet.* London: Brentham Press, 1985.

De Vries-Mason, Jillian. *Perception in the Poetry of D. H. Lawrence.* Berne: Peter Lang, 1982.

Gilbert, Sandra M. *Acts of Attention: The Poems of D. H. Lawrence.* Ithaca and London: Cornell University Press, 1972. 2nd edn., Carbondale: Southern Illinois University Press, 1990.

Laird, Holly A. *Self and Sequence: The Poetry of D. H. Lawrence.* Charlottesville: University Press of Virginia, 1988.

Lockwood, M. J. *A Study of the Poems of D. H. Lawrence: Thinking in Poetry.* London: Macmillan, 1987.

Mackey, Douglas A. *D. H. Lawrence: The Poet Who Was Not Wrong.* San Bernardino, CA: Burgo Press, 1986.

Mandell, Gail Porter. *The Phoenix Paradox: A Study of Renewal Through Change in the 'Collected Poems' and 'Last Poems' of D. H. Lawrence.* Carbondale and Edwardsville: Southern Illinois University Press, 1984.

Marshall, Tom. *The Psychic Mariner: A Reading of the Poems of D. H. Lawrence.* New York: Viking, 1970.

Murfin, Ross C. *The Poetry of D. H. Lawrence: Texts and Contexts.* Lincoln: University of Nebraska Press, 1983.

Oates, Joyce Carol. *The Hostile Sun: The Poetry of D. H. Lawrence.* Los Angeles: Black Sparrow Press, 1973. Reprinted in her *New Heaven, New Earth.* London: Gollancz, 1976, pp. 37–81.

Saldanha, Rita. *World Anew: Themes and Modes in the Poetry of D. H. Lawrence.* India: Creative, 1997.

(H) PLAYS

Malani, Hiran. *D. H. Lawrence: A Study of His Plays.* New Delhi, India: Arnold-Heinemann; Atlantic Highlands, NJ: Humanities Press, 1982.

Nath, Suresh. *D. H. Lawrence: The Dramatist.* Ghaziabad, India: Vimal Prakashan, 1979.

Sagar, Keith, and Sylvia Sklar. 'Major Productions of Lawrence's Plays'. In Sagar's *Handbook,* cited under (A), pp. 283–328. Details of 13 major productions, with photographs and extracts from reviews.

Sklar, Sylvia. *The Plays of D. H. Lawrence: A Biographical and Critical Study.* London: Vision, 1975. To date, still the most comprehensive and scholarly study.

(I) NON-FICTION

Becket, Fiona. *D. H. Lawrence: The Thinker as Poet*. London and New York: Macmillan, 1997.

Black, Michael. *D. H. Lawrence: The Early Philosophical Works: A Commentary*. London: Macmillan, 1991.

Ellis, David, and Howard Mills. *D. H. Lawrence's Non-Fiction: Art, Thought and Genre*. Cambridge, 1988.

Gordon, David J. *D. H. Lawrence as a Literary Critic*. New Haven and London: Yale University Press, 1966.

Hostettler, Maya. *D. H. Lawrence: Travel Books and Fiction*. Berne: Peter Lang, 1985.

Janik, Del Ivan. *The Curve of Return: D. H. Lawrence's Travel Books*. Victoria, BC: University of Victoria Press, 1981.

Montgomery, Robert E. *The Visionary D. H. Lawrence: Beyond Philosophy and Art*. Cambridge, 1994.

Tracy, Billy T., Jr *D. H. Lawrence and the Literature of Travel*. Ann Arbor, MI: UMI Research Press, 1983.

(J) SELECTED ESSAYS

Davies, Alistair. 'Contexts of Reading: The Reception of D. H. Lawrence's *The Rainbow* and *Women in Love*'. In *The Theory of Reading*, ed. Frank Gloversmith. Sussex: Harvester, 1984, pp. 199–222.

Doherty, Gerald. 'White Mythologies: D. H. Lawrence and the Deconstructive Turn'. *Criticism* 29 (Fall 1987): 477–96.

Dollimore, Jonathan. 'The Challenge of Sexuality'. In *Society and Literature 1945–1970*, ed. Alan Sinfield. London: Methuen, 1983, pp. 51–85.

Gilbert, Sandra. 'Feminism and D. H. Lawrence'. *Anaïs* 9 (1991): 92–100.

Gordon, David J. 'Sex and Language in D. H. Lawrence'. *Twentieth Century Literature* 27 (1981): 362–75.

Haegert, John W. 'D. H. Lawrence and the Aesthetics of Transgression'. *Modern Philology* 88 (1990): 2–25.

Hamalian, Leo. 'D. H. Lawrence and Black Writers'. *Journal of Modern Literature* 16 (Spring 1990): 579–96.

Ingersoll, Earl. 'Staging the Gaze in D. H. Lawrence's *Women in Love*'. *Studies in the Novel* 26, 2 (Fall 1994): 268–80.

Kiberd, Declan. 'D. H. Lawrence: The New Man as Prophet'. In his *Men and Feminism in Modern Literature*. New York: St Martin's Press, 1985, pp. 136–67.

Kinkead-Weekes, Mark. 'The Marble and the Statue: The Exploratory Imagination of D. H. Lawrence'. In *Imagined Worlds: Essays on Some English Novels and Novelists in Honour of John Butt*, ed. Maynard Mack and Ian Gregor. London: Methuen, 1968, pp. 371–418.

Lodge, David. 'Lawrence, Dostoevsky, Bakhtin: D. H. Lawrence and Dialogic Fiction'. *Renaissance and Modern Studies* 29 (1985): 16–32.

Martin, Graham. '"History" and "Myth" in D. H. Lawrence's Chatterley Novels'. In *The British Working-Class Novel in the Twentieth Century*, ed. Jeremy Hawthorn. London: Edward Arnold, 1984, pp. 63–76.

Ragussis, Michael. 'D. H. Lawrence: The New Vocabulary of *Women in Love*: Speech and Art Speech'. In his *The Subterfuge of Art: Language and the Romantic Tradition*. Baltimore and London: Johns Hopkins University Press, 1978, pp. 172–225.

Salgādo, Gāmini. 'Taking a Nail for a Walk: On Reading *Women in Love*'. In *The Modern English Novel: The Reader, The Writer, and The Work*, ed. Gabriel Josipovici. London: Open Books, 1976, pp. 95–112.

Shaw, Marion. 'Lawrence and Feminism'. *Critical Quarterly* 25 (Autumn 1983): 23–27.

Spilka, Mark. 'Lawrence Up-Tight, or the Anal Phase Once Over'. *Novel: A Forum on Fiction* 4 (Spring 1971): 252–67. See also ensuing discussion in volume 5 of the same journal.

Squires, Michael. 'D. H. Lawrence's Narrators, Sources of Knowledge and the Problem of Coherence'. *Criticism* 37 (Summer 1995): 469–91.

Stewart, Garrett. 'Lawrence, "Being", and the Allotropic Style'. *Novel* 9 (Spring 1976): 217–42.

Wallace, Jeff. 'Language, Nature and the Politics of Materialism: Raymond Williams and D. H. Lawrence'. In *Raymond Williams: Politics, Education, Letters*, ed. W. John Morgan and Peter Preston. London: Macmillan, 1993, pp. 105–28.

INDEX

Achebe, Chinua, 71
Aldington, Richard, 120, 131, 158, 165,
  259, 260
Annan, Noel, 262
anthropology, 2, 46, 113–14, 181
apocalyptic thought, 10, 34, 58–59, 61,
  77–78, 235–52
  see also 'New Age' cultural phenomena
Appignanesi, Lisa, 187
Asquith, Cynthia, 113, 114, 168
Auden, W. H., 128, 259

Bachofen, J. J., 45
Bakhtin, Mikhail, 33, 113, 190
Balbert, Peter, 34, 214n.7
Barthes, Roland, 158–59, 164
Bataille, Georges, 113–14
Bates, Alan, 265
bathos, 1, 115–17
Baudelaire, Charles, 257, 258
Baudrillard, Jean, 236
Bayley, John, 113
Baynes, Rosalind, 35, 47n.6, 177n.23
Beauvoir, Simone de, 124, 204, 264
Beckett, Samuel, 236
Bell, Michael, 2, 5, 10, 29n.7, 30n.18, 173,
  238, 267
Benjamin, Walter, 240
Bennett, Arnold, 138, 152n.6, 189, 255
Bennett, Joan, 262
Bergson, Henri, 182
Biblical language and metaphor 5, 11, 44,
  62, 78, 127, 147–48, 166, 189, 209,
  239–50, 253, 256–57, 258, 259
  see also apocalyptic thought; Christianity;
  Paul, St
biography, 8, 9, 30n.12, 36–37, 47n.6, 123,
  157–77, 197, 224–25, 237, 255,
  256–57, 259

see also Cambridge Biography of D. H.
  Lawrence
Björckman, Edwin August, 219
Blackmur, R. P., 121
Blake, William, 120, 256
Blavatsky, Madame, 235
blood consciousness, *see* physical
  consciousness
Bloomsbury, 53, 58–59, 166, 219, 238
Brett, Dorothy, 73, 79
Brill, A. A., 220
Brooke, Rupert, 165
Brooks, Cleanth, 4
Bunyan, John, 116
Burgess, Anthony, 50
Burnet, John, 129, 167, 180
Burrow, Trigant, 170, 231–32
Burrows, Louie, 138, 160, 162
Burton, Sir Richard, 52–53, 63
Butler, Judith, 236

Cambridge Biography of D. H. Lawrence, 9,
  30n.12, 159, 160–70, 224–25
Cambridge Edition of the Works of D. H.
  Lawrence, 6–7, 28, 111–12, 163–64,
  176n.15, 254, 271
Cannan, Gilbert, 165
capitalism, 16, 90–92, 96–97, 101, 198,
  201, 204–6, 210, 268
  see also industrialism
Carpenter, Edward, 238
Carswell, Catherine, 157, 165, 257
Carter, Angela, 266
Carter, Frederick, 78
Cather, Willa, 172
Caudwell, Christopher, 203
Chambers, Jessie, 2, 17, 18, 19, 20, 54, 119,
  138, 139, 160, 161, 162, 170
Chambers, Jonathan David, 54

Index

Index